ANALYTIC PHILOSOPHY IN AMERICA

ANALYTIC PHILOSOPHY IN AMERICA

And Other Historical and Contemporary Essays

SCOTT SOAMES

PRINCETON UNIVERSITY PRESS
PRINCETON AND OXFORD

Published by Princeton University Press, 41 William Street, Princeton,
New Jersey 08540
In the United Kingdom: Princeton University Press, 6 Oxford Street,
Woodstock, Oxfordshire OX20 1TW
press.princeton.edu

Library of Congress Cataloging-in-Publication Data
Soames, Scott.
Analytic philosophy in America : and other historical and
contemporary essays / Scott Soames.
        pages cm
Includes bibliographical references and index.
ISBN 978-0-691-16072-6 (hardcover : alk. paper) 1. Analysis
(Philosophy)—United States—History—20th century. 2. Philosophy,
American—20th century. I. Title.
B808.5.S625 2015
146'.40973—dc23   2013023267

British Library Cataloging-in-Publication Data is available

This book has been composed in Charis SIL
Printed on acid-free paper. ∞
Printed in the United States of America
10 9 8 7 6 5 4 3 2 1

TO

MARTHA, GREG, AND BRIAN

Contents

PART THREE
CURRENT TOPICS

Introduction

The fifteen essays collected in this volume include three (essays 3, 4, and 8) that have not previously been published, two (2, 6) that are forthcoming, six (5, 7, 11, 13, 14, 15) that were published between 2011 and 2014, and four (1, 9, 10, 12) that were published between 2007 and 2010. The essays are divided thematically into three sections. The first, which contains the essay from which the title of the volume is taken, consists of seven broad overviews of important movements, advances, and pivotal individual figures in the analytic tradition. The second section continues with three essays on historical issues and controversies in analytic philosophy. The final section is devoted to current questions, including one chapter on different kinds of Millian responses to Frege's puzzle, one on the proper understanding of natural kinds and natural kind terms within a broadly Kripkean account of the necessary a posteriori, and three new essays bringing philosophy of language to bear on the philosophy of law.

PART ONE: MILESTONES

Essay 1, *Analytic Philosophy in America*, traces the development of analytic philosophy in the United States, starting with the pragmatism of Charles Sanders Peirce, William James, and (later) Clarence Irving Lewis, and continuing through the great immigration of philosophers of science, philosophical logicians, and logical positivists from the turn of the twentieth century to the outbreak of World War II. With the absorption of this stream of philosophical talent, centers of philosophical logic and analytic philosophy grew at the City College of New York, the University of Chicago, Berkeley, UCLA, and elsewhere. By the early 1950s, the first great analytic department in America had emerged at Harvard under the leadership of WillardVan Orman Quine, and by the mid-1960s the analytic tradition had become the dominant philosophical force in America. Other significant developments chronicled in the essay include the troubled history of philosophy at Yale; the inspiring success of the program at Wayne State; the rise of powerful departments at Michigan, Pittsburgh, and MIT; and the emergence of the great Princeton department led by Carl Hempel, Gregory Vlastos, Saul Kripke, and David Lewis.

In addition to covering these institutional matters, the essay provides broad-brush overviews of some of the most important philosophical debates that occupied American analytic philosophers during the last half of the twentieth century—the Quine/Carnap debate about meaning and analyticity, the struggle over modality, the rise of philosophical logic and its application to the study of natural language, the Davidsonian program, Saul Kripke and the end of the linguistic turn, John Rawls and the resuscitation of normative theory, and a smattering of other, more specialized topics.

Essay 2 discusses the methodology that guided logico-linguistic analysis from Gottlob Frege's 1879 *Begriffsschrift* to Rudolf Carnap's 1934 *The Logical Syntax of Language*. In the first four decades of this period, culminating with Bertrand Russell's 1918–19 lectures on *The Philosophy of Logical Atomism*, analysis was viewed as an increasingly powerful tool employed in the service of solving traditional philosophical problems. The logicist reduction of arithmetic to what was taken to be logic was the driving force, providing the exemplar of philosophical analysis and the model for extending it beyond the philosophy of mathematics. The methodology is indicated by the role played by A2 in answering Frege's guiding philosophical questions Q1 and Q2:

Q1. What are natural numbers?
Q2. What is the source of arithmetical (and other mathematical) knowledge?
A1. Zero is the set of concepts true of nothing, 1 is the set of concepts true of something and only that thing, 2 is the set of concepts true of some distinct x and y, and only those things, and so on.
A2. Numbers are whatever they have to be in order to explain and justify our pretheoretic arithmetical knowledge.

Despite the brilliance of Frege's logicist achievement, it couldn't withstand the shock of Russell's paradox. Although by 1910 Russell was able to revive a version of the reduction, the technical picture—which had become more complicated—would support neither the reduction's initial ambitious epistemic goals nor Russell's then-current metaphysical aims, which were marred by his infamous "no-class" fantasy. Despite these shortcomings, Russell continued to view logical and linguistic analysis as the key to philosophical progress and attempted, in *Our Knowledge of the External World* (1914) and *The Philosophy of Logical Atomism* (1918–19), to explain empirical knowledge by "analyzing" the constituents of the world into momentary sense data, of which everything else, including their perceivers, was a "logical construction." The result was "analysis" in the service of vast, epistemically driven, metaphysical system building.

Although Ludwig Wittgenstein's *Tractatus* (1922) is also presented as a form of logical atomism, complete with metaphysical simples designated by logically proper names of an imagined logically perfect language, his "analysis" is not epistemic. Whereas Russell's aim was to find a metaphysical foundation for explaining ordinary and scientific knowledge (which he assumed must conform to his largely empiricist conception), Wittgenstein's aim was to articulate a parallel between language and reality that would fit his conception of the collapse of metaphysical and epistemic modalities into logical modalities. The key ideas were as follows:

(i) All necessity is linguistic necessity, in that it is the result of our system of representing the world, rather than the world itself. There are sentences that are necessarily true, but there are no necessary facts corresponding to them. These sentences tell us nothing about the world; their necessity is due to the meanings of words (and therefore is knowable a piori).

(ii) All linguistic necessity is logical necessity.

(iii) Logical necessity is determinable by form alone.

With these doctrines in place, it was a short step to the tractarian test for intelligibility. According to the *Tractatus*, every meaningful statement S falls into one of two categories: either (i) S is contingent (true in some possible worlds and false in others), in which case S is both a truth function of atomic sentences and something that can be known to be true or false only by empirical investigation, or (ii) S is a tautology or contradiction that can be known to be such by formal calculations. Since these doctrines leave no room for meaningful philosophical claims, the young Wittgenstein saw his achievement as effectively ending philosophy.

Of course it didn't, though it did play a large role in influencing the next stage(s) of analytic philosophy. Essay 2 closes with a brief discussion of Carnap's blending of the empiricism of Russell with Wittgenstein's linguistic turn in philosophy, leading to Carnap's 1934 manifesto: "Philosophy is to be replaced by the logic of science—that is to say by the logical analysis of concepts and sentences of the sciences."[1]

---

[1] Page 292 of *The Logical Syntax of Language* (London: Kegan Paul), which is an English translation of Carnap (1934).

Essay 3 is a case study of the process by which the attempt to solve philosophical problems sometimes leads (often in unanticipated ways) to the birth of new domains of scientific inquiry. My discussion traces how advances in logic and the philosophy of mathematics, starting with Frege and Russell, provided the foundations for what became a rigorous and scientific study of language, meaning, and information. After sketching the early stages of the story, I explain the importance of modal logic and "possible worlds semantics" in providing the foundation for the last half century of work in linguistic semantics and the philosophy of language. In the second half of the essay, I argue that this foundation is insufficient to support the most urgently needed further advances. The central problem is that the entities used in contemporary theories to play the role of information associated with sentences are not genuinely representational, and so they cannot explain how sentences "expressing them" manage to represent anything as being one way or another. Since these entities are also too coarse-grained even to serve as models of the needed information, a more realistic conception is required. To this end, I propose a new conception of truth-evaluable information as inherently representational cognitive acts of certain kinds. The essay closes by explaining how this conception of propositions can be used to illuminate the notion of truth; vindicate the connection between truth and meaning; and fulfill a central, but so far unkept, promise of possible worlds semantics.

Essay 4 picks up where Essay 3 leaves off, chronicling the troubled history of propositions in the thought of Russell, Wittgenstein, Peter Strawson, and John Langshaw "J. L." Austin. After noting the central role of propositions and propositional functions in Russell's philosophical logic, I explain how and why his early Platonistic conception of propositions was defeated by the so-called problem of "the unity of the proposition." I then show how, by reversing one of his key explanatory priorities, the cognitive conception of propositions sketched in Essay 3 can be used to solve the unity problem and to reinstate a conception of propositions capable of playing the role required of them in his philosophical logic. The tragedy for Russell is that although he correctly realized that his prior conception of propositions would never do—and advanced an alternative view incorporating the insight that the mind, rather than a realm of Platonic entities is the true source of intentionality—he wasn't able to put his insight into a workable form. Instead of constructing a true cognitive theory of propositions, he tried to eliminate propositions entirely using his notorious "multiple relation theory of judgment." After explaining how this theory arose, and pinpointing its fatal defects, I argue that it contained a kernel of truth from which a proper cognitive theory of propositions can be constructed—which Russell unfortunately missed. I then point out the consequences of this failure for *Principia Mathematica* (1910) and for one of the central arguments for his theory of descriptions in "On Denoting" (1905).

Next, the discussion moves to Wittgenstein's *Tractatus* (1922), in which propositions are thought of as interpreted sentences in an ideal language underlying natural languages like English. I argue that this view has two main virtues. First, it takes the intentionality of "propositions" to be derived from the cognitive activity of agents who use its names to designate certain stipulated objects while using the structural relation uniting the names in the mental sentence to predicate a stipulated relation of those objects. This analysis explains how "elementary propositions" represent, and so have, truth conditions. Second, since these "propositions" are themselves interpreted sentences, understanding such a sentence does not involve knowing, of any Platonic entity, that the sentence expresses it. This was an advance.

Nevertheless, I argue that the tractarian theory of propositions suffers from three difficulties common to today's "language of thought" theories of cognition: (i) the arithmetic of genuine propositions differs from that of sentences in a mental language, (ii) there is no reason for thinking that all possible believers of a given proposition share a single system of mental representation, and (iii), most fundamentally, the explanation of an agent's mastery of any system of representation tacitly presupposes the antecedent existence of genuine cognitive propositions. The key point to grasp is that cognitive acts and operations—and dispositional mental states defined in terms of them—can be inherently and systematically representational without, in all cases, involving a symbolic representational medium. For want of a cognitive theory of propositions incorporating this insight, many philosophers have been pushed into prematurely postulating a linguistic basis of all propositional attitudes. Though the *Tractatus* did not offer a full-blown system of this sort, it was a precursor of such theories that were to appear a half century later.

Essay 4 concludes with a discussion of the rejection of propositions by ordinary- language philosophers, who repudiated the idea that understanding expressions is, at bottom, knowing certain semantic facts about them—e.g., that name n refers to object o, that predicate F stands for property P, and that sentence S expresses proposition p. Instead, they argued, understanding a word, phrase, or sentence consists in *knowing how to use it.* Insofar as this abandonment repudiated traditional Platonic conceptions of propositions, it was a positive step. What these philosophers had no way of seeing was that the then-unknown cognitive theory of propositions could accommodate their idea that understanding a sentence is knowing how to use it—the accommodation being that to understand S is to be disposed to use it to perform the cognitive act that *is* the proposition S expresses. Unfortunately, their failure to see this was accompanied by a failure to appreciate that some conception of propositions is needed to accomplish theoretical goals to which they were committed. In the essay, I illustrate this by showing how the theory of presupposition growing out of Strawson's fertile insights in "On Referring" (1950) and *Introduction to Logical Theory* (1952) was crippled, and thus blocked from reaching its full potential, for lack of an adequate conception of propositions. I close by further indicating how both sides of the Austin/Strawson truth debate failed for want of proper bearers of truth.

Essay 5 discusses the achievements of W.V.O. Quine and his place in analytic philosophy. The essay begins with Carnap's logical empiricism, which set the context for Quine's first major article in philosophy, "Truth by Convention" (1935). After devoting a section to Quine's penetrating critique of the linguistic theory of the a priori, I turn to his long battle against quantified modal logic. At this stage he was willing (for the sake of argument) to accept the notion of necessity as *analyticity* (defined as a sentence that either is a logical truth or can be turned into one by substituting synonyms for synonyms). What he was not willing to accept was the idea that sense can be made of attaching an analyticity operator to an open formula (relative to an assignment of objects to variables). Since analyticity, which was the ruling conception of necessity by those then developing quantified modal logic, is a linguistic notion defined only for closed sentences, this was a genuine problem that Quine was correct in raising. From here, he developed two lines of attack. The first was that, the interpretation of necessity aside, quantified modal logic violates certain fundamental logical and semantic principles. In this he was wrong. The second was that if necessity is analyticity, then there are insuperable problems preventing the development of a theoretically interesting system of quantified modal logic. In this Quine was largely right, even though he failed, along with others, to foresee that an acceptable metaphysical interpretation of necessity would not be long in coming (in Kripke's *Naming and Necessity*).

The discussion in Essay 5 next turns to "Two Dogmas of Empiricism" (1951). I explain both Quine's largely effective critique of analyticity, as it was then understood, and the problems that plagued his combination of holistic verificationism with an underdetermination thesis that paired each consistent empirical theory T with alternative theories logically incompatible with, but empirically equivalent to, T. Then, I take up the connection between his logical, semantic, and ontological views in "On What There Is" (1948), explaining how that article initiated his famous dispute with Carnap over analyticity and ontology. A discussion follows of the impetus for Quine's movement from his critique of analyticity to his later doctrines of the Indeterminacy of Translation and the Inscrutability of Reference. The essay closes with an explication of these radical doctrines, the role played by Quine's physicalism, and his ineluctable march to what I argue to be a radical and self-undermining semantic eliminativism.

Essay 6 is devoted to one of the most fascinating figures of the twentieth century, David Lewis. The key to understanding this author of so many works in so many areas of philosophy is, I think, to see how his views are related to those of his colleague Kripke as well as to those of his teacher Quine. Like Kripke, but unlike Quine, Lewis embraced the modalities (necessity and a priority) that Quine rejected. Also like Kripke, Lewis had no sympathy for Quine's early verificationism or his flights from intension and intention, and he was straightforwardly a realist about science in general. However, despite these similarities with Kripke, Lewis's analysis of necessity could not be more different from Kripke's. Whereas Kripke made no attempt to provide a reductive analysis of modal notions, Lewis was committed to a thesis, called *modal realism*, according to which "possible worlds" are neither properties nor sets of propositions but concrete universes as real as our own, spatially and temporally disconnected from ours, made up of many things, some of which are "counterparts" of ourselves and familiar things in our environment. These, Lewis thought, are what we are really talking about when we make claims about what *could* or *would* have been otherwise with us and our surroundings (under certain conditions).

Many found this view to be incredible. For most Kripkeans, world-states are either sets of propositions that could have been true, or properties that the universe could have had. Just as we recognize properties ordinary objects don't have but could have had, so, in the latter view, we recognize (maximal) properties—metaphysically possible world-states—the universe doesn't have but could have had. For any such property W, the universe *could* have had W, and if did, certain propositions *would have* been true. Note the use of modal notions—*what could have been* and *what would have been true if such and such had been so-and-so*. There is no attempt to define possible world-states in nonmodal terms or to reduce the modal to the nonmodal.

For Lewis, modal reductionism was required by his ambitious philosophical naturalism, and so was not an option. His grand philosophical goal was to reduce the mental to the physical, causation to counter-factuals, counterfactuals to possible worlds, and possibility and necessity to quantification over ordinary (though very large and remote) objects. The desired destination was a metaphysically homogeneous reality constituted by momentary point-sized objects (given in physics) instantiating purely qualitative universals—natural properties and relations (also given in physics)—related by similarity, difference, and spatiotemporal relations across multiple universes, but *not* related by "occult," empirically unexplainable forces or connections. It is here, I argue, that we see the enduring influence of Quine's naturalism and extensionalism. The underlying philosophical purpose of Lewis's modal realism and counterpart theory was to reduce an intensional object-language to a purely extensional semantic metalanguage, in the service of an antecedently desired conception of reality. Whereas Quine taught that vindicating naturalism and extensionalism required eliminating intensional facts and rejecting intensional constructions, his student David Lewis tried to show that intensional facts are just a species of extensional facts, and that intensional constructions in language are no threat to the integrity of an austere, naturalistic vision of reality.

This is my perspective on Lewis, from which Essay 6 assesses the different aspects of his grand project. But that isn't all. Since a number of Lewis's views and achievements—particularly in philosophical logic and the philosophy of language—can be assessed independently of his grand metaphysical reduction, these, too, are addressed in the essay.

In Essay 7, which was originally written in 2005 but not published until 2011, I discuss what I take to be one of the outstanding philosophical achievements of the twentieth century—Saul Kripke's treatment of the necessary a posteriori and concomitant distinction between epistemic and metaphysical possibility. In the essay, I extract the enduring lessons of his treatment of these matters and disentangle them from errors and confusions that mar some of his most important discussions. I argue that there are, in fact, two Kripkean routes to the necessary a posteriori—one correct and philosophically far-reaching, the other incorrect, philosophically misleading, and the source of damaging errors that persist to this day. In addition, the last two sections of the essay connect two false principles involved in the second, unsuccessful, route to the necessary a posteriori with the plausible and potentially correct idea that believing a singular proposition that o is F always involves also believing a richer more descriptively informative proposition in which some further property plays a role in the agent's thoughts about o. After explaining why this idea won't save the failed second route to the necessary a posteriori, I suggest that it may help reconcile Kripke's insights with the lessons of Frege's puzzle.

PART TWO: HISTORICAL PROBLEMS AND CONTROVERSIES

Essay 8 develops a puzzle for the Frege-Russell analysis of quantification, widely seen as a fundamental advance in semantics and philosophical logic. The key idea is that quantifiers express higher-level properties that are predicated of lower-level properties. In this analysis, (1a) expresses a proposition that consists of the property *being true of everything* and the property *being F*, the first of which is predicated of the second.

    1a. ∀x Fx / Everything is F

Thus, the proposition expressed by (1a) is the proposition expressed by (1b); call it 'Proposition 1'.

    1b. The property *being F* is true of everything.

However, since (1b) itself contains the universal quantifier being analyzed, it would seem that the analysis may apply again. The two-place predicate 'is true of' that occurs in (1b) expresses a relation holding between properties and objects. Since 'everything' stands in the second argument-place of this predicate, (1b) is a universally quantified sentence that expresses the same proposition as (2a).

    2a. Everything is such that *the property being F* is true of it.

According to the Frege-Russell analysis, (2a) expresses a proposition that consists of the property *being true of everything* and the property *being an object of which the property F is true*, the first of which is predicated of the second. Call this proposition, which is expressed by (2a) and (2b), 'Proposition 2'.

    2b. The property being an object of which the property being F
        is true is true of everything.

Since (1a) expresses the same proposition as (2a), while both express only one proposition, Proposition 1 = Proposition 2. The cycle can be repeated, producing a hierarchy of propositions each of which is identified with all the others:

    Proposition 1: The proposition that *being F* is true of everything.
    Proposition 2: The proposition that *being an object of which being
        F is true* is true of everything.
    Proposition 3: The proposition that *being an object of which (being
        an object of which being F is true) is true* is true of everything.

However these propositions do not appear to be identical. On the contrary, they must be distinct if (i) propositions are structured combinations of their constituents (as Frege, Russell, and many others take them to be), and (ii) the constituents *being F, being an object of which that property—being F—is true*, and so on, are themselves structurally distinct (despite being true of the same objects). Since I accept the Frege-Russell analysis of quantification, along with both (i) and (ii), I need to block the argument at some early stage. Essay 8 explores options for doing so and identifies the one I take to be most promising.

Essay 9 explores a historical issue mentioned in Essay 2—Russell's "no class theory," originally expressed by his contextual definition of classes in *Principia Mathematica*. The aim of the essay—which was written in response to a published objection to one of my earlier works— was to argue, against the objector, that Russell's supposed elimination achieves no genuine ontological economy. The point at issue involves how the quantification in the contextual definition is to be understood. My thesis in the paper is that if the quantification is objectual, then no significant ontological reduction of classes to anything else is achieved, no matter what the range of the variables is taken to be. What I didn't consider, because my critic did not raise the issue, is that Russell's quantification might be substitutional, in a sense that is now reasonably well understood. In recent years, some Russell scholars have trumpeted the virtues of such an interpretation, among which is the sense it makes of the "no-class theory."

Such an interpretation does make some sense of Russell's philosophical remarks about that theory, about the significance of his logicist reduction, and about the ability of the reduction to serve as a model for similar reductions outside the philosophy of mathematics. However this substitutional interpretation is not sufficient, since it is inconsistent with important aspects of Russell's philosophical logic and is technically inadequate to support his logicist reduction. In short, if substitutional quantification is the source of the "no class theory," then the theory is not vindicated, but refuted. The foregoing is argued at length in chapter 10 of *The Analytic Tradition*, volume 1, forthcoming from Princeton University Press—which fulfills the promise made for expanded discussion made in the last paragraph of Essay 9.

Essay 10 examines the dispute between Quine and Carnap about how to understand ontological commitment and what ontology to adopt. The central dispute is over Carnap's acceptance of abstract objects, including numbers, properties, and propositions, which Quine characterizes in "On What There Is" (1948) as a form of Platonism. Carnap vigorously disagrees, responding in "Empiricism, Semantics, and Ontology" (1950, 1956). For him, commitments to these things are unproblematic consequences of accepting an optimal theoretical framework for doing science. Philosophers haven't seen this because, he believes, they have approached ontology in an unscientific way. The key to rectifying the problem, he argues, is to distinguish (i) internal ontological questions that arise within a framework for describing the world, and so can be decided by evidence (making the questions empirical rather than metaphysical), from both (ii) external ontological pseudoquestions that purport to be about the world even though they can't be settled by evidence (and so are objectionably metaphysical) and (iii) purely practical questions about which frameworks are most fruitful for scientific investigation.

Carnap's "frameworks" are linguistic—interpreted languages the meanings/empirical contents of the sentences of which are the sense experiences that would confirm them. Since analytic sentences are, he believes, accepted independent of any empirical confirmation, he takes them to be empty of empirical content and hence to make no claim whatsoever about the world. In accepting the "framework" of natural numbers, we simply lay down what amount to meaning postulates that determine the arithmetical truths. Although these truths include claims to the effect that there are numbers satisfying various conditions—*and hence that there are numbers*—such claims are empty of "cognitive content" and hence not to be regarded as making genuine existence claims about the world. The same, Carnap thinks, can be said for claims about properties and propositions.

So expressed, Carnap's position depends on a strong logical empiricist doctrine of analyticity, which was subject to Quine's critique in "Two Dogmas." Although Carnap offered an intriguing a response to it in 1955, I argue that it is not enough to save his ambitious conception of analyticity. However, his position in the ontological dispute with Quine remained strong. At the time, both he and Quine were verificationists about the cognitive contents of empirical theories, despite disagreeing over whether the individual sentences used to express a theory could be assigned their own contents, reflecting their particular contributions to the content of the whole. Rejecting Carnapian analyticity and embracing a form of meaning/verification holism, Quine plausibly argued that such parceling out of verificatory content was not possible. However, in the end, this point was not dispositive. In the presence of their shared verificationism, the essence of Carnap's ontological position survived the loss of analyticity, and Quine's victory on the subsidiary point was, I argue, pyrrhic. Nevertheless, for those of us who aren't verificationists, this can't be the end of the story. If verificationism about the contents of theories is dropped, the ontological import of Quine's critique of analyticity is reinstated, leaving Carnap's attractive ontology in need of some other source of support.

PART THREE: CURRENT TOPICS

Essay 11 offers a systematic assessment of Kit Fine's *Semantic Relationism* (2007), in which he presents a "relational" version of Millianism (about names and related expressions). The essay compares this version of Millianism with the standard nonrelational version. The essay focuses on their different responses to two aspects of Frege's puzzle—one involving the cognitive, assertive, and conversational contents of uses of nonhyperintensional sentences, the other involving the propositions expressed by attitude ascriptions. Regarding the first aspect of the puzzle, I argue that the two versions of Millianism give comparable and largely correct results. Regarding the second, I show that relational Millianism faces counterexamples that are easily handled by nonrelational Millianism, when both are combined with a reasonable semantics for attitude verbs.

Although particular counterexamples can be handled by following Fine in positing (to my mind unmotivated) systematic ambiguities in the attitude verbs, I show that doing so allows one to re-create all the difficulties raised for non-relational Millianism *within relational Millianism itself*. At this point, the position of the two theories is not symmetric. Whereas nonrelational Millianism has identified and articulated various extra semantic factors—including guises, ways of entertaining a proposition, pragmatic enrichment, the distinction between semantic and assertive content, the multiple assertion theory, and the least common denominator conception of meaning—to deal with this aspect of Frege's puzzle, nonrelational Millianism arises from the conviction that these factors won't solve the problem. The relationist faces a dilemma. If the nonrelational story won't work, as the relationist maintains, then he or she has no way of dealing with the re-created problems, which include all those that motivated relationism in the first place. So, either nonrelational Millianism is roughly correct, or capable of being made so (perhaps, in part, by adding some elements of relationism), in which case (full-strength) relational Millianism won't be needed, or nonrelational Millianism is incorrect (and irredeemable), in which case relational Millianism is, too.[2]

Essay 12 takes simple natural kind terms—like 'green', 'gold', 'water', 'tiger', and 'light'—to be Millian terms that rigidly designate

---

[2] The last section of essay 11 (prior to the appendix) has been slightly revised to eliminate earlier misunderstandings and to include new footnotes. These reflect the view I adopt in *Rethinking Language, Mind, and Meaning*, which accommodates some elements of Fine's relationism in a cognitive account of propositions in which Fine's coordinated propositions may serve as contents of some speech acts, though not as the semantic contents of sentences used to perform them.

properties typically determined by a reference-fixing stipulation to the effect that the general term is to designate whatever property provides the explanation of why, at actual world-state, all, or nearly all, the samples of items associated with the term by speakers who introduce it have the observational properties they do. It makes sense to introduce a term in this way when (i) the objects to which we wish to apply the term are similar in some respects, which guides our application of it, and allows us, fallibly but reliably, to apply it to new cases; (ii) these similarities have, and are believed by us to have, a single unifying explanation, which, although we typically don't know it, we rightly believe to involve counterfactual-supporting generalizations relating unspecified features of (nearly) all the similar-appearing objects to the respects in which they are similar; and (iii) we wish to use the term in law-like generalizations and explanations—and so don't want to identify its semantic content with the cluster of observed similarities.

If G is a simple general term introduced in this way, p is the (unique) property satisfying the reference-fixing description for G (and so is the Millian semantic content of G), ⌜is G⌝ is a predicate, and P is a complex common noun phrase (like 'substance molecules of which are composed of two hydrogen atoms and one oxygen atom') the extension of which at any world-state is the set of instances of p at that world-state, then ⌜∀x (x is G iff x is P)⌝ will be a necessary truth.[3] For it to be an instance of the necessary a posteriori, it must express a proposition that is knowable *only* a posteriori, which will be so only if one can know the singular proposition that predicates of p the property expressed by ⌜all and only instances of it are G⌝. This singular proposition can, of course, be known a posteriori. The trick is to explain why it can only be so known. It is easy to see that we will be defeated if we identify, for example, the property *being water*—which, we may suppose, is both the referent and the content (meaning) of 'water' —with the property *being a substance molecules of which are composed of two hydrogen atoms and one oxygen atom*, which is the content (meaning) of the common noun phrase 'substance molecules of which are composed of two hydrogen atoms and one oxygen atom'. But now we have a puzzle, since it seems all but inevitable to suppose that this latter property is identical with the property *being water*. Essay 12 is devoted to solving this puzzle.

Essay 13 combines recent work on vagueness in the philosophy of language with recent work in the philosophy of law on the value of vagueness in certain legal situations. The question at issue is whether leading philosophical theories of what vagueness is can account for the positive utility of certain kinds of legal vagueness. The two theories

---

[3] Note, this may be so whether or not ⌜∀x □ (x is t iff x is P)⌝ is true.

put to the test are (i) epistemicism, according to which vagueness is a matter of irremediable ignorance of the sharp borderlines separating cases in which (totally defined) vague predicates apply from those in which their negations do, and (ii) the theory according to which vague predicates are (a) only partially defined, leaving a range of borderline cases in which there is no fact of the matter regarding the application or nonapplication of the predicates, and (b) context sensitive, which results in constantly shifting lines separating the defined from the un-defined cases. After distinguishing several kinds of legal vagueness, I test these theories against one subtype of legal vagueness—in which the content of a law is vague because lawmakers employ a vague term in adopting an authoritative legal text. Since the test involves the con-straints the two theories place on later authoritative interpretations of such a vague text, the test incorporates a plausible, but potentially con-troversial, assumption (for which I argue elsewhere) about the central legal norm governing such interpretation.

Against this background it is shown, first, that there is a range of cases in which both theories provide reasonable rationales for correct resolutions of legal vagueness, but, second, that there is a further range of legal cases in which only the partial-definition/context-sensitivity theory of vagueness gives the right results. So, although both theories can rightly accord a degree of utility to some kinds of legal vagueness, the partial-definition/context-sensitive theory does a better job overall, while the epistemicist theory faces severe challenges in certain kinds of cases. Unless this shortcoming can be traced to defects in empirical assumptions about the legal actors in such cases, a mischaracterization of the proper norm governing legal interpretation, or outright mistakes about which legal results are correct or desirable, epistemicism must be seen as failing to fully account for the value of vagueness in the law.

Essay 14 is concerned with the content of legal norms governing the interpretation of legal texts by legally authoritative actors in a legal system. As such, a theory of legal interpretation, in the sense I intend, is a theory of the content of the law, codified or uncodified, governing legally authorized interpreters. Thought of in this way, it is a non-normative empirical theory related to, but distinct from, (a) empirical theories about what the mass of judges in a particular legal system actually do in the cases before them, (b) moral theories about what they morally should do in particular cases, and (c) politically norma-tive theories about what the role of the judiciary should be in an ideal system. The most important question to be answered by such a theory is,What precisely is required of legally authoritative interpreters, how much and what kind of latitude are they allowed, and what factors are they to take into account in their interpretations? After formulating my own broad, rather traditional, answer to this question, I provide illustrative details concerning both real and hypothetical legal cases in the United States, including matters of statutory and constitutional interpretation.[4] I close by raising a substantial question about whether the interpretative practices of the Supreme Court of the United States— which themselves play an important role in determining the content of existing legal norms of interpretation—fit my traditional conception of interpretation or whether, on the contrary, they establish a new, more expansive conception.

Essay 15 takes the project a step further. It begins by articulating the principles underlying the two key dimensions of a new, deferentialist, theory of legal interpretation—the identification of original asserted or stipulated content, and the nature of the deference required when new circumstances demand that judges make new law. These principles are then applied to the interpretation of the due process clauses of the Fifth and Fourteenth Amendments to the Constitution of the United States. Relying on extensive historical research by Nathan Chapman and Michael McConnell of Stanford University Law School, I summarize the evolution of due process thinking from the *Magna Carta*, through the 1628 Petition of Right in the British Parliament, to Parliamentary disputes in the 1770s, and ending in American reactions to the Coercive Acts of (1774), which helped shape the founders' understanding of the "due process" language of the Fifth Amendment.[5] This background is used to specify the original content of the stipulation expressed by the framers and ratifiers of the clause "*[No] person shall . . . be deprived of life, liberty, or property, without due process of law.*"

From there the story turns to the interpretation of the clause up to and beyond the Civil War and its incorporation in the Fourteenth Amendment. The first significant expansion in the interpretation of the clause, leading to a doctrine of "substantive due process," occurred in the infamous *Lochner* line of cases at the turn of the twentieth century. Although this doctrine was correctly repudiated during the New Deal, I show how it remerged in new form in a modern line of cases including *Griswold v. Connecticut, Roe v. Wade, Planned Parenthood v. Casey,* and *Lawrence v. Texas,* which, I argue, cannot withstand deferentialist scrutiny. Since the Supreme Court has provided no other coherent *judicial* justifications for these decisions, I suggest that the cases must be

---

[4] One of my hypothetical cases, involving the Plainsboro town council, is a slightly modified version of the one that appeared in the original article in the *NYU Journal of Law and Liberty.*

[5] Nathan S. Chapman and Michael W. McConnell, "Due Process as Separation of Powers," *Yale Law Journal* 116 (2012): 1672–1807.

understood as implicitly premised on a nondeferentialist conception of judicial responsibility.

Unfortunately, this nondeferentialist conception—which encompasses a retreat from the traditional separation of powers doctrine in favor of a more expansive conception of the legislative authority of the Supreme Court—has not been made sufficiently explicit. To this end I sketch one avowedly nondeferentialist conception of judicial responsibility, one straightforwardly deferentialist conception, and one conception that is a hybrid of the two. Taken as competing accounts of the existing norms governing legal interpretation by legally authorized actors (typically the judiciary), the real dispute, is, I argue, between the deferentialist and the hybrid view.

In adjudicating this dispute, it is crucial to distinguish descriptive questions from their normative counterparts. Given the two competing conceptions, one can ask which most closely approximates the legal norms that presently exist in the United States, or one can ask which set of norms is morally or politically preferable. Although I don't purport to resolve these questions, I cite what I take to be powerful normative advantages of the deferentialist conception, along with corresponding descriptive factors that suggest it enjoys considerable support from the educated populace plus the army of relevant legal actors in the United States. Although, the hybrid conception has grown stronger and become a contender for defining the legal norms governing judicial action, I argue that it faces stubborn conceptual limitations that have prevented it from displacing the more traditional deferentialist conception. I end with a suggestion of how the deferentialist might approach the daunting challenge of gradually rectifying the results of many past nondeferentialist decisions.

Origins of These Essays

Essay 1: "Analytic Philosophy in America," in *The Oxford Handbook of American Philosophy*, Cheryl Misak, ed., Oxford: Oxford University Press, 2008, 449–81. Reprinted by permission of Oxford University Press.

Essay 2: "Methodology in Late 19th and Early 20th Century Analytic Philosophy," in *The Oxford Handbook of Philosophical Methodology*, H. Cappelen, T. Gendler, and J. Hawthorne, eds., Oxford: Oxford University Press, 2013. Reprinted by permission of Oxford University Press.

Essay 3: "Language, Meaning, and Information: A Case Study on the Path from Philosophy to Science," is based on a lecture delivered to the College of Arts and Sciences of Lehigh University, March 13, 2012.

Essay 4: "For Want of Cognitively Defined Propositions: A History of Insights and Lost Philosophical Opportunities." New for this volume.

Essay 5: "The Place of W.V.O. Quine in Analytic Philosophy," in *A Companion to W.V.O. Quine*, E. Lepore and G. Harman, eds., John Wiley and Sons, 2013. Reprinted with permission of John Wiley and Sons.

Essay 6: "David Lewis's Place in Analytic Philosophy," in *Companion to David Lewis*, Barry Lower and Jonathan Schaffer, eds., Blackwell, forthcoming. Reprinted with permission of Blackwell Publishing.

Essay 7: "Kripke on Epistemic and Metaphysical Possibility," in *Saul Kripke*, Alan Berger, ed., Cambridge: Cambridge University Press, 2011, 78–99. Reprinted with permission of Cambridge University Press.

Essay 8: "What is the Frege/Russell Analysis of Quantification?" is based on a lecture given at the Richard Cartwright Memorial Conference, MIT Department of Linguistics and Philosophy, October 1, 2011.

Essay 9: "No Class: Russell on the Contextual Definition and Elimination of Sets," *Philosophical Studies*, 139, 2008, 213–18. Reprinted with the permission of Springer Publishing.

Essay 10: "Ontology, Analyticity, and Meaning: The Quine-Carnap Dispute," in *Metametaphysics*, David Chalmers, David Manley, and Ryan Wasserman, eds., Oxford: Oxford University Press, 2009, 424–43. Reprinted with the permission of Oxford University Press.

Essay 11: "Two Versions of Millianism," in *Reference and Referring*, William Kabascenche, Michael O'Rourke, and Mathew Slater, eds., Cambridge, MA, MIT Press, 2012, 83–118. Reprinted with the permission of MIT Press.

Essay 12: "What are Natural Kinds?" *Philosophical Topics* 35 (2007): 329–42. Reprinted with the permission of the Arkansas University Press.

Essay 13: "Vagueness and the Law," in *The Routledge Companion to the Philosophy of Law*, Andrei Marmor, ed., New York and London: Routledge, 2012. Reprinted with the permission of Routledge Publishers.

Essay 14: "Toward a Theory of Legal Interpretation," *NYU Journal of Law and Liberty* 6 (2011): 231–59. Reprinted with the permission of the NYU School of Law.

Essay 15: "Deferentialism: A Post-Originalist Theory of Legal Interpretation," *Fordham Law Review* 82 (2013, 101–122). Reprinted with the permission of the Fordham Law Review.

PART ONE

Milestones

1

Analytic Philosophy in America

The leading preanalytic philosopher in America, and one of its giants of all time, was Charles Sanders Peirce (1839–1914). Having received a scientific education (including a Harvard BS in chemistry in 1863), he lectured on logic and philosophy of science at Harvard (1864–65, 1869–71) and Johns Hopkins (1879–84), after which he moved to Milford, Pennsylvania, where he continued to write prodigiously. His greatest contributions were in logic, including a syntax for quantification theory (1870) and (1883), and a truth-functionally complete system based on what later came to be called "the Sheffer stroke." Though his contributions were, in many respects, parallel to those of Gottlob Frege, the two logicians worked independently, with the writing of Frege, through its influence on Bertrand Russell, becoming the more widely known. Still, Alfred North Whitehead was an admirer whose knowledge of quantification theory was said to have come substantially from Peirce, while Hilary Putnam (1982) observed that much that is "quite familiar in modern logic actually became known to the logical world through the efforts of Peirce and his students." In 1985, W.V.O. Quine identified Peirce as sharing credit with Frege for the development of modern quantification theory, and cited his influence on Ernst Schröder and Giuseppe Peano.

Outside of logic, Peirce's philosophy of pragmatism—or, as he called it, "pragmaticism"—was widely admired. In epistemology, he was an antifoundationalist, resisting the idea of a privileged starting point of maximally certain statements (e.g., of private sensation) and adopting, as a guiding hypothesis, the idea that the application of scientific method to intersubjectively verifiable claims would, through a process of self-correction, lead different investigators to converge on a common result, no matter what their starting points. While not definitively identifying truth with that which would be confirmed in the limit of ideal (scientific) inquiry, Peirce did think that the practical consequences of true beliefs provided grounds for expecting them to be confirmed by continuing investigation. Correspondingly, he took the meaning of a theoretical claim to be its experiential "cash value"—the collection of possible empirical observations that would verify it. He had little patience with metaphysical speculation about "things in themselves" underlying observed phenomena, or grand metaphysical systems. In all these ways, Peirce exerted a strong influence on those who would follow. Peircean reverence for logic, respect for science, suspicion of apriori metaphysics, and emphasis on the practical consequences of theoretical differences found fertile soil and took root in America, creating a hospitable environment for the later growth, and distinctive shape, of analytic philosophy there.

The other great American pragmatist was William James (1842–1910). Like Peirce, James had a scientific education in chemistry, anatomy, and medicine at Harvard, where he received an MD in 1869. He taught physiology in 1872, and in 1875 he set up the first laboratory for experimental psychology in America. Between 1885 and 1907 he was professor of psychology and philosophy at Harvard, during which period he gave *The Varieties of Religious Experience* (1902) as the Gifford Lectures at Edinburgh, and published *Pragmatism* in 1907. Though influenced by Peirce, James's outlook was less scientific, and his audience broader. Whereas for Peirce truth and meaning rested on the intellectual foundation of possible observation, for James they rested on what it is beneficial to believe. To the extent that religious beliefs help us live better lives, they pass the Jamesian pragmatic test for truth, just as scientific beliefs do.

Third in the trio of preanalytic pragmatists was John Dewey (1859–1952), who earned his PhD in philosophy from Johns Hopkins in 1884, where he encountered Peirce. Between 1884 and 1930, Dewey taught at the Universities of Michigan, Minnesota, Chicago, and (for the last twenty-four years) at Columbia. Like Peirce, he was an antifoundationalist and believer in the self-correcting nature of empirical investigation in a community of inquirers. Like Quine, who was to follow, he held that there are no absolute first principles that are either known with certainty or beyond rational revision in light of new experience. Truth, for Dewey, was warranted assertability. Though less influential than Peirce in the later development of analytic philosophy, Dewey's views on education, and other social issues, had a large and controversial impact.

Along with pragmatism, realism and naturalism characterized much American philosophy between Peirce and Quine. Peirce wrote in 1896, "Nothing can be more completely false than that we can experience only our own ideas. That is indeed without exaggeration the very epitome of *all* falsity" (Peirce, CP 6.95). The independence of the perceived from the perceiver, and the known from the knower, was emphasized in *The New Realism* (1912) by philosophers such as Edwin Bissell Holt and Ralph Barton Perry. As John Passmore (1957) noted, their conception of perception was similar to that given in George Edward Moore's "The Refutation of Idealism" (1903), while their rejection of "internal relations" paralleled a similar rejection, central to the rebellion of Moore and Russell against absolute idealism. (The importance of the rejection for New Realists was in their observation that when a knows b, the relational properties of knowing b, and of being known by a, are not essential to a and b, respectively.) By 1920, another brand of realism, Critical Realism, was on the scene. Advocated by Arthur Oncken Lovejoy, George Santayana, and Roy Wood Sellars, among others, it struggled to reconcile the objective physical world, revealed in perception, with an irreducible Kantian residue added by the perceiver to the content of experience. Although disputes between these varieties of realism have now lost much of their force, it is striking how congenial the broad themes of naturalism, respect for science and common sense, and suspicion of idealism and other apriori speculation were to the growth of analytic philosophy in America.

THE TRANSITION TO ANALYTIC PHILOSOPHY

The American transition to analytic philosophy was mediated by several pivotal figures, institutions, and events. One such figure was Morris Cohen (1880–1947). Born in Russia, educated at City College of New York, with a 1906 Harvard PhD, he taught at City from 1912 to 1938, and at the University of Chicago from 1938 to 1941. Known for his interest in logic and the philosophy of science, he was a committed naturalist who recognized no nonscientific methods capable of attaining knowledge in philosophy. One of his students was the Czechoslovakian born Ernest Nagel (1901–85), who, after earning his BA at City, got his PhD in 1931 (under Dewey) from Columbia, where (with the exception of a year at Rockefeller University in the 1960s) he spent his career teaching and writing about the philosophy of science, and explaining the centrality of logic to philosophy. His little book, *Gödel's Proof* (1958) coauthored with James R. Newman, introduced the incompleteness theorems to many students, while his main work, *The Structure of Science* (1961), summed up the results of decades of teaching and research on the nature of explanation, and the logical structure of scientific knowledge.

Of all the transitional figures, the greatest was C. I. Lewis (1883–1964). While earning his BA (1905) and PhD (1910) from Harvard he worked with, and was influenced by, William James, Josiah Royce, and Ralph Barton Perry. After teaching at Berkeley for nine years, he returned to take a position at Harvard in 1920, from which he retired thirty-three years later, having taught many who would become leading analytic figures—including Quine, Roderick Chisholm, Roderick Firth, William Frankena, Nelson Goodman, and Norman Malcolm. He finished his career at Stanford University in 1960. An eclectic thinker and system-builder, Lewis combined an element of perceptual realism, filtered through Perry; a Kantian element, filtered through Josiah Royce; and a pragmatic element, filtered through Peirce (whose work he encountered when given the job of cataloging the latter's vast unpublished writings). Like Perry, Lewis believed that perception and knowledge require an independent reality given in experience. Like Royce he was convinced that experience is the result of structuring and interpreting the given in terms of "apriori" concepts added by the mind. Like Peirce, Lewis held that (i) our concepts—even the "apriori" ones—are not fixed by the nature of the mind but are revisable in light of experience, and (ii) the meanings of concepts, thoughts, and experience lie in their pragmatic success in anticipating and predicting new experience and grounding successful action. These ideas were worked out in his two major works, *Mind and the World Order* (1929) and *An Analysis of Knowledge and Valuation* (1946), which were among the most widely read of their day—the former being the subject of a memorable seminar at Oxford led by J. L. Austin and Isaiah Berlin in the 1936–37 academic year.

Lewis's relation to the logical positivists was ambiguous. He shared their scientific naturalism, their emphasis on logical analysis, and their view of testable consequences as the basis of empirical significance, but he vigorously opposed their noncognitivism about value, their physicalism, and their embrace of "the linguistic turn." For him, the primary bearers of meaning and truth were mental: thoughts, concepts, and experiences. Of most importance for analytic philosophy was his pioneering work in modal logic, included in his widely read *Symbolic Logic* (1932), coauthored with Cooper Harold Langford. Lewis's main contribution was in formulating a series of increasingly strong axiomatic systems (the S-systems) of the modal propositional calculus (with operators for necessity and possibility)—which provided the basis for (i) later axiomatic extensions to the predicate calculus by Ruth Marcus (1946) and Rudolf Carnap (1946), (ii) the fledgling semantic treatment in Carnap (1947), and (iii) the revealing model-theoretic interpretations of the S-systems in Saul Kripke (1959) and (1963). For Lewis, the philosophical moral drawn from the competing axiomatic systems was that logical first principles are not decidable apriori but must be judged by their pragmatic success—a conclusion that, no matter what its ultimate merits, was premature in light of later work. Finally, the distinction in Lewis (1946) between the different "modes of meaning of a term"—(i) its extension, consisting of things to which it refers or applies; (ii) its "comprehension" (now called its "intension"), consisting of a mapping of possible world-states to extensions; and (iii) its "signification," consisting of a concept or property determining (ii)—was an important forerunner of later developments in analytic philosophy of language.

In understanding the transition to the analytic period in America, it is important to remember that analytic philosophy is not a fixed body of substantive doctrine, a precise methodology, or a radical break with most traditional philosophy of the past—save for varieties of romanticism, theism, and absolute idealism. Instead, it is a discrete historical tradition stemming from Frege, Moore, Russell, Wittgenstein, and the logical positivists, characterized by respect for science and common sense, belief in the relevance of logic and language for philosophy, emphasis on precision and clarity of argumentation, suspicion of apriori metaphysics, and elevation of the goals of truth and knowledge over inspiration, moral uplift, and spiritual comfort—plus a dose of professional specialization. All these tendencies were already present in America—preeminently at Harvard, but also at Columbia, City College of New York, the University of Michigan, and other environs. They were reinforced by repeated visits to America to teach and lecture by Moore (1940–44) and Russell (1896, 1914, 1924, 1927, 1929, 1931, 1938, 1939, 1940–42), and the addition to the Harvard philosophy faculty in 1924 of the coauthor of *Principia Mathematica*, Alfred North Whitehead. Each had a noticeable impact on the locals. For example, Quine—whose first great paper, "Truth by Convention" (1936), appeared in a collection in honor of Whitehead—described his 1931 encounter with Russell as his "most dazzling exposure to greatness," while his later Harvard colleague, Morton White, said that his experience of Moore at Columbia in the early 1940s was "one of the most refreshing episodes in [his] philosophical education." By then, all that was needed for America to enter the stream of analytic philosophy was for the works of its philosophers to regularly, and in large numbers, enter the torrent flowing from its British and European sources.

THE BEGINNINGS OF ANALYTIC PHILOSOPHY

The emergence of analytic philosophy in America was marked by three events above all others—(i) the arrival from Europe of leading logicians, philosophers of science, logical positivists, and other analytic philosophers; (ii) the transformation of the Harvard department led by Quine in the 1950s and 1960s; and (iii) the vast postwar expansion in higher education in America, which came to encompass a substantial drain in philosophical talent from Britain to the United States—including (for varying lengths of time) such figures as Paul Grice, Stuart Hampshire, J. O. Urmson, and Philippa Foot.

The first, and most dramatic, of these events was the arrival of an enormously gifted and distinguished group of émigrés from Europe. Among them were Herbert Feigl (1902–88), arriving from Vienna in 1931; Rudolf Carnap (1891–1970), arriving from Prague in 1935; Carl Hempel (1905–97), arriving from Germany in 1937; Hans Reichenbach (1891–1953), arriving from Germany by way of Turkey in 1938; Gustav Bergman (1906–87), coming from Vienna in 1938; Alfred Tarski (1901–83), from Poland in 1939; and Kurt Gödel (1906–78), arriving from Vienna in 1940.

Feigl, who studied philosophy of science and probability under Moritz Schlick, and was a member of the Vienna Circle, first taught at the University of Iowa from 1931 to 1940, and then at the University of Minnesota from 1940 to 1973. He is best known for his partnership with Wilfrid Sellars in (i) coediting the collection *Readings in Philosophical Analysis* (1949), which was for decades a staple in the classrooms of analytic philosophers, and (ii) cofounding the journal *Philosophical Studies* in 1950 as a forum for the new school of "analytic philosophy."

Carnap, the world's premiere logical positivist, taught at the University of Chicago from 1936 to 1952, with a year's visit at Harvard in 1941–42. From 1952 to 1954 he was at the Institute for Advanced Study in Princeton, after which he held a chair in philosophy at UCLA from 1954 to 1962. Carnap had studied logic with Frege, and Carnap's own students included such notable American philosophers as Richard Jeffrey (subjective probability) and David Kaplan (the logic of demonstratives). Among Carnap's major works published during his years in America were "Testability and Meaning" (1936–37), *Introduction to Semantics* (1942), *Meaning and Necessity* (1947, 1956b), *The Logical Foundations of Probability* (1950a), and "Empiricism, Semantics, and Ontology" (1950b, 1956b).

Reichenbach, another leading positivist and preeminent philosopher of science, studied civil engineering, physics, mathematics, and philosophy—working under, or attending the lectures of, David Hilbert, Max Planck, and Albert Einstein. In the 1920s, he published several books interpreting relativity theory, and in 1930, together with Carnap, he took over editorship of *Erkenntnis*, the leading journal of logical positivism. In 1935, while in Turkey, he published *The Theory of Probability*. After moving to the United States, Reichenbach accepted a position at UCLA, where he remained until his death in 1953. Among his students there was Hilary Putnam, who was to become a leading philosopher at Princeton, MIT, and Harvard. Reichenbach's major American works included *Experience and Prediction* (1938), *Philosophic Foundations of Quantum Mechanics* (1944), *Elements of Symbolic Logic* (1947), and *The Rise of Scientific Philosophy* (1951).

In his first year in America, Hempel, who had been a well-known contributor to logical positivism in Europe, held a position as a research associate at the University of Chicago, arranged by Carnap. From 1939 to 1948, Hempel taught in New York, at City College and Queens, after which he went to Yale, where he stayed until 1955. In that year he joined the Princeton department, where he became—with the renowned classical philosopher Gregory Vlastos—the nucleus of what was to become one of the world's great centers of analytic philosophy. Hempel remained at Princeton until his retirement in 1973, after which he spent another decade teaching at the University of Pittsburgh. Upon retiring from there, Hempel returned to Princeton (which had kept his house and office for him), where he spent the rest of his life. His major American works include "Studies in the Logic of Confirmation" (1945); "A Definition of Degree of Confirmation," with Paul Oppenheim (1945); "Studies in the Logic of Explanation," with Oppenheim (1948); "The Empiricist Criterion of Meaning" (1950); *Aspects of Scientific Explanation* (1965), and *Philosophy of Natural Science* (1966).

Bergmann, who had been associated with the Vienna Circle, taught at the University of Iowa from 1939 to 1974 and was president of the Western Division of the American Philosophical Association in 1967–68. His students went on to teach in many philosophy departments throughout the country.

Alfred Tarski had already done his path-breaking work on truth and logical consequence when he set off from Poland in August 1939 (on what turned out to be the last boat before the Nazi-Soviet invasion) to lecture at the Congress for Unified Science at Harvard University. Finding that he had no country to return to, Tarski remained in the United States. Though initially unable to secure a regular faculty position, he held a two-year post as research associate at Harvard, arranged by Quine, and taught two courses in logic at the City College of New York. After spending 1941–42 (with Gödel) at the Institute for Advanced Study in Princeton, Tarski moved to the mathematics department at Berkeley, where he remained. Acknowledged as one of the greatest logicians of all time, he was also a dedicated and influential teacher. As leader of the PhD program in Logic and the Methodology of Science at Berkeley, Tarski both exercised a strong influence on his younger colleagues, like Dana Scott, and supervised twenty-four dissertations, including those of Richard Montague and Solomon Feferman. These three in turn substantially influenced the course of analytic philosophy, as well as the programs of their respective institutions (Scott at Princeton, Montague at UCLA, and Feferman at Stanford). The trio of Tarski, Gödel (at the Institute for Advanced Study in Princeton from 1940 to his death in 1978), and Alonzo Church (Princeton from 1929 to 1967, and UCLA from 1967 to 1990—whose students included Anthony Anderson, Leon Henkin, Stephen Kleene, Hartley Rogers, J. B. Rosser, Dana Scott, and Alan Turing) not only transformed the mathematical study of symbolic logic but also exerted a powerful force on the study of philosophical aspects of logic by analytic philosophers.

The second factor leading to the triumph of analytic philosophy in America was the transformation of the Harvard department, led by Quine (1908–2000)—the one man more responsible than any other for the decisive analytic turn in America. In 1932, he finished his PhD dissertation at Harvard on Russell's *Principia Mathematica*. During the next year, Quine held a fellowship that allowed him to travel to Europe, where he met, or attended seminars given by, Carnap, Tarski, Lesniewski, Lukasiewicz, Schlick, Hahn, Reichenbach, Gödel, and Ayer. (He had already met Feigl in 1930.) The relationship with Carnap was the deepest. Back at the Harvard Society of Fellows for three years, Quine gave lectures expounding Carnap and published his well-known paper "Truth by Convention" (1936), which grew out of them. There, Quine attacked the linguistic theory of the apriori, then popular among the positivists. In opposition to the view that all apriori knowledge, including knowledge of logic, is knowledge of linguistic convention, he pointed out that the potentially infinite scope of logical knowledge would require it to be derived from a manageable set of allegedly conventional axioms. But since knowledge of logic is presupposed by such derivations, it cannot be explained by them. The objection, which to this day remains powerful, illustrates a characteristic feature of Quine's thought. Starting with the problems posed by his positivist mentors, he isolated a central tenet about meaning in their proposed solution, and exposed an inherent problem. Quine's reaction was not, of course, to give a nonlinguistic account of the apriori, but to purify empiricism by giving up the apriori altogether.

The same dynamic is illustrated in his discussion of ontological commitment in "On What There Is" (1948) and of analyticity in "Two Dogmas of Empiricism" (1951)—where his skepticism about analyticity and his holism about empirical content are on display. With Carnap and other positivists, Quince agreed that (i) the empirical content of our claims is to be found in the observations that will confirm them, and (ii) necessity is to be identified with analyticity, if it exists at all. Unlike them, he rejected any account of empirical content, or meaning, that portions it out to sentences one by one, and, in so doing, he ended up discarding analyticity, apriority, and necessity in the bargain. The end result was a version of empiricism of the same sort as that of the logical positivists, only more radical, in which meaning plays no privileged epistemic role. Thus it was that philosophy in America entered the mainstream of analytic philosophy, altering its course.

By 1951 Quine was a world-renowned figure. However, despite having been a senior professor at Harvard for ten years (interrupted by a stint of military service in World War II), he was still in the minority there—as illustrated by the department's rejection of his 1948 proposal to offer a position to Carnap. In those years, his chief allies were first, Henry Aiken, who joined the department in 1946, and later, Morton White, whose appointment in 1948 was instigated by Aiken and Quine. With these appointments, and the retirement of C. I. Lewis in 1953, the department was ready for change. In the 1950s and 1960s, largely under the philosophical leadership of Quine and the chairmanship of White, Harvard added Roderick Firth, Burton Dreben, Israel Scheffler, Rogers Albritton, Stanley Cavell, John Rawls, Nelson Goodman, Hilary Putnam, and Robert Nozick. By the end of that period they had gathered as fine a collection of philosophers as could be found anywhere.

The 1950s and 1960s also saw a lively interaction grow up between the philosophers at Harvard and those at Oxford. Having met Isaiah Berlin in 1949, White spent a year at Oxford and came away deeply impressed not only by Berlin but also by Gilbert Ryle, John Austin, H.L.A. Hart, and Paul Grice. Shortly thereafter, Austin, Hart, and Grice were lecturing at Harvard. First, Austin spent the spring of 1955 at Harvard giving *How to Do Things with Words* (later published in 1962) as the William James Lectures. Then, Hart spent the 1956–57 academic year teaching philosophy and law, to be followed by Grice, who lectured at Harvard in the late 1950s before giving "Logic and Conversation," as the William James Lectures of 1967 (eventually published in Grice [1989]).

This interaction between the Quine-led descendants of Carnap and the Ryle-Austin-Grice-led descendants of Wittgenstein encompassed the most important strands of the analytic philosophy of the day. Both sides were well represented at Harvard, and nowhere in the philosophical world was the intellectual ferment more lively. What was true of Harvard was also increasingly true of America as a whole—as visits by, and longer-term professorships for, leading British philosophers, including Elizabeth Anscombe, Philippa Foot, Stuart Hampshire, David Pears, and J. O. Urmson, brought important nonpositivist perspectives to the rapidly advancing ranks of analytic philosophers in America. Although in the end the Quinean-Peircean logical and scientific strand of analytic philosophy proved to be the strongest, both at Harvard and across America, the tradition was enlarged, implicitly refuting Quine's infamous echo, "philosophy of science is philosophy enough," of Carnap's original call to arms (from *The Logical Syntax of Language* (1934, 1937)), "Philosophy is to be replaced by the logic of science—that is to say, by the logical analysis of the concepts and sentences of the sciences."

By the early 1970s analytic philosophy was dominant in America. Fueled by the enormous postwar expansion in higher education, the number of faculty positions in philosophy—to be filled overwhelmingly by analytic philosophers—expanded rapidly. Membership in the American Philosophical Association rose from 747 in 1940 to 1,248 in 1950; 1,984 in 1960; 2,725 in 1970; and 5,125 in 1980. These numbers reflected the growth of several powerful analytic departments. Chief of these was Princeton's, which—with Paul Benacerraf, John Burgess, Michael Frede, Gilbert Harman, Richard Jeffrey, Saul Kripke, David Lewis, Thomas Nagel, Thomas Scanlon, and Margaret Wilson, among others—was, by the end of the 1970s, widely regarded as the top of the heap. Close behind, specializing in the philosophy of science, was Pittsburgh's, which had come into its own as a great department when Wilfrid Sellars arrived from Yale in 1963, bringing with him a group of that institution's best young philosophers. Throughout the period, Michigan's department retained its reputation for preeminence in ethics and metaethics, a position it had held since the arrival of the famous emotivist Charles Stevenson in 1946 (from Yale). Two other programs, those at UCLA and at Cornell, also deserve special notice. Having welcomed Reichenbach and Carnap, acquired Montague and Church, and hired its own brilliant PhD David Kaplan, UCLA's department was almost without peer in the study of philosophical logic. With the addition of Tony Martin, Tyler Burge, Rogers Albritton, and Philippa Foot, it became a powerhouse in the arsenal of analytic philosophy. Meanwhile, Cornell had become the home of Wittgensteinianism in America—under the influence of Norman Malcolm, who studied with Wittgenstein at Oxford, and Max Black, who wrote an important work on the *Tractatus*. When Sydney Shoemaker, Keith Donnellan, and (later) Robert Stalnaker were added, Cornell's program attained a prominent position of continuing strength. Other leading departments between 1940 and 1980 included those at Berkeley, Stanford, MIT, and Brown.

The staggering growth in the quality and quantity of analytic philosophy in that period, and the extent of its dominance throughout the country, is illustrated by a dramatic contrast between two departments at very different institutions. The first was the philosophy department at Wayne State University, located in downtown Detroit, which served a predominantly lower middle-class and working-class student population. Such was the abundance of available talent, and the enthusiasm of young philosophers entering the profession, that between 1955 and 1970 the philosophy department at Wayne acquired a reputation for precision, passion, and fierce analytical argumentation that had few rivals anywhere. Among the prominent philosophers who spent substantial portions of their careers at Wayne were Richard Cartwright, Hector-Neri Castaneda, Edmund Gettier, Keith Lehrer, Michael McKinsey, George Nakhnikian, Alvin Plantinga, and Robert Sleigh. In 1967, the leading journal, *Nous*, was started at Wayne by Castaneda (a student of Sellars'). By contrast, philosophy at Yale, one of America's great, elite universities, suffered. Setting itself in the 1940s and 1950s resolutely against the rising tide of analytic philosophy, and fancying itself the defender of a less scientific, more humanistic and metaphysical tradition, the department denied tenure to Stevenson in 1946, refused to promote Hempel in 1955, lost Sellars in 1963, and declined to renew Stalnaker's contract in the early 1970s. By the late 1980s, with only three senior professors, it was stripped of its power over appointments, and placed in receivership. At the dawn of the new century, it was only beginning to recover. Such was the contrast between embracing (Wayne) and dismissing (Yale) analytic philosophy in America.

With the background set, and the institutional terrain surveyed, it is time to turn to leading philosophical themes and figures in American analytic philosophy.

THE QUINE/CARNAP DEBATE ABOUT MEANING, REFERENCE, AND ANALYTICITY

The logical empiricist Carnap divided meaningful sentences into two classes—the analytic and the synthetic—with the content of synthetic sentences explicated in terms of observations that would verify them. Quine in part agreed and in part disagreed. While happy to identify the meanings of comprehensive theories with the observations that would confirm them, he attacked Carnap's distinction between sentences as based on the false presupposition that a scientifically defensible conception of meaning could sensibly be applied to individual sentences, taken one by one. This meant rejecting the idea that sentences, or other expressions, could be synonymous, as well as the idea that they could be true in virtue of meaning. Carnap replied that the intensional notions of meaning and synonymy could not be rejected without also rejecting the extensional notions of truth and reference. Regarding that course as too radical, he developed an account of the integrated connections between extensional and intensional notions, as well as an explanation of how empirical evidence bears on assignments of semantic values to expressions.

An early follower of Tarski, Carnap correctly distinguished Tarski's notion of truth from epistemic notions like certainty and confirmation, with which truth had often been confused— "Truth and Confirmation" (1949). Rightly noting that these confusions had prevented truth from playing a central role in earlier positivist accounts of meaning, Carnap made it the basis for his own subsequent semantic theories— "Intellectual Autobiography" (1963). (Unfortunately, like other early theorists, he wrongly took the notion of truth needed for this task to be Tarski's own formal notion. Fortunately, his semantic theories do not depend on this error.) In *Introduction to Semantics* (1942) Carnap laid out his truth-conditional conception of meaning, extending it to modal languages in *Meaning and Necessity* (1947), where necessary truth was identified with analyticity. Later, in "Meaning and Synonymy in Natural Languages" (1956a), he tried to show how the meaning of a term, over and above its reference, can play an important role in empirical theorizing about language users. He argued that although there are empirical uncertainties in establishing the meaning and reference of a given term, there are sound empirical methods for bringing evidence to bear on both questions. As a result, he concluded, meaning and reference are in the same boat. Thus, Carnap thought, Quine was wrong to dismiss intensional notions like meaning and synonymy while apparently retaining extensional notions like reference (and truth). Contrary to Quine, Carnap maintained that the intensional and the extensional are scientifically on a par—both required, and both respectable.

Quine's response was to agree that meaning and reference are on a par, but to up the ante by rejecting both. This, in the end, was the legacy of his doctrine of the indeterminacy of translation and the inscrutability of reference—presented in *Word and Object* (1960), "Reply to Chomsky" (1969), "Ontological Relativity" (1969), and "On the Reasons for the Indeterminacy of Translation" (1970). The problem, as he saw it, was that neither theories assigning sameness of meaning to sentences, nor those assigning reference to subsentential expressions, are determined by possible (behavioral) data bearing on their confirmation. Moreover, Quine claimed, the addition of all truths statable in the language of physical science would not resolve the indeterminacy. Since he held (roughly) that all genuine truths are determined by the physical truths, he concluded that statements attributing sameness of meaning to sentences, or reference to subsentential expressions, do not qualify as objective truths.

Though spectacularly provocative, this view did not command lasting assent. The argument for it suffers from implicit ambiguities involving the determination relation—no resolution of which seems capable of simultaneously vindicating all Quinean premises (Soames 2003b, chap. 10). In addition, the indeterminacy theses appear to be self-undermining. Taken together, they amount to radical eliminitivism about the ordinary notions of meaning, reference, and truth—coupled with a proposal to replace them with scientifically respectable notions of stimulus meaning, disquotational Tarski reference, and Tarski truth. The difficulty is that without the notions Quine proposed to eliminate, the crucial theses on which his doctrines depend appear to be unstatable (Soames 2003b, chap. 11). Thus, it is not clear that his position is sustainable.

THE STRUGGLE OVER MODALITY AND THE RISE OF PHILOSOPHICAL LOGIC

As noted, in 1946 Marcus and Carnap independently extended Lewis's axiomatic treatment of the modal propositional calculus to the predicate calculus (with quantification). In 1947, Carnap coupled this treatment with a primitive possible-worlds semantics. However, this extension of logic to include quantification into modal constructions provoked vigorous Quinean objections (Quine 1943, 1947, 1953) which, unfortunately, were not carefully distinguished from one another for decades. Quine's strongest, and most justifiable, point was—as Burgess (1998) explained—that there was a mismatch between the formal innovation of quantifying into modal constructions, and the informal, philosophical explanations given by modal logicians of the content of the necessity operator they employed. When the question was asked: *What notion is it the logic of which is formally captured by systems containing this operator?* the answer commonly given was that *necessity* was *logical truth* or *analyticity*. Quine, of course, had problems with analyticity. However, what exercised him about quantified modal logic was that since analyticity is supposed to be a property of sentences, quantifying into a construction governed by the necessity operator amounts to attributing *truth in virtue of meaning*—not to a sentence, but to a pair consisting of a formula containing a free occurrence of a variable and an object serving as value of the variable. The idea that such a pair could be true in virtue of meaning, Quine thought, made no sense. Whether or not sense could, in principle, be made of it, modal logicians at the time were not doing so. Thus, he understandably concluded, quantified modal logic rests on a mistake.

More generally, Quine concluded it is unintelligible to (objectually) quantify into any construction for which substitution of coreferential singular terms sometimes fails to preserve truth. This was a definite error, though one not clearly recognized for many years—Kaplan (1986), Kazmi (1987), Richard (1987), and Soames (1995). Distracted by this error, defenders of modal logic—Smullyan (1947, 1948), Fitch (1949), Marcus (1960, 1961), and Follesdal (1961)—focused on what they took to be the need for logical languages to contain name-like terms (pure tags) that resisted failure of substitutivity (under coreference) everywhere. However, the definitive response to Quinean objections to quantified modal logic was not to invent a special class of terms but to stop viewing necessity as analyticity, to start thinking of it as truth at all counterfactually possible world-states, and to explain what it is for a statement that a given object has, or lacks, a specified property at such a state to be true. These moves, hinted at in the formal Kripke semantics for modal logic, were made explicit in Kripke's 1970 lectures that became *Naming and Necessity* (1980), and reinforced by David Kaplan's 1971 manuscript, which became "Demonstratives" (1989).

After the development of the Kripke semantics, progress in philosophical logic exploded. Similar treatments of tense logic, building on Arthur Prior's *Time and Modality* (1957), and intuitionist logic, soon followed. The most comprehensive program was spelled out in a series of papers by Richard Montague, published in the 1960s and early 1970s and collected in his *Formal Philosophy* (1974). There, Montague articulated a highly generalized system of intensional logic that served as a framework for analyzing the syntax, semantics, and pragmatics of large fragments of natural language. This work not only influenced the philosophical logicians who were to follow but also provided the basis for an approach to semantics in theoretical linguistics that has lasted into the new century. Formal, truth-conditional semantics of the languages of modern symbolic logic began with Tarski in the 1930s. Then, with the philosophical logic of Marcus, Carnap, Prior, Kripke, Montague and others, the range of linguistic constructions amenable to these techniques was expanded to include those expressing time and tense, necessity and possibility, and many others. David Kaplan's "Demonstratives" extended this program to include another essential feature of natural language—context-sensitive sentences containing indexicals like *I, we, you, she, that, now, today,* and *actually.* By the end of the century, it had become possible to imagine the day in which natural languages would be treatable in something close to their entirety by descendants of the logical techniques initiated by Tarski.

One of the most important philosophical applications of the new logic was the development of the Stalnaker-Lewis treatment of counterfactual conditionals (Stalnaker 1968, 1975, 1978; D. Lewis 1973a). The problem, which had long been of interest to analytic philosophers, had been illuminated but not solved by Nelson Goodman in "The Problem of Counterfactual Conditionals" (1947), and *Fact, Fiction, and Forecast* (1954). On the Stalnaker-Lewis approach—widely credited as a significant advance—*If it had been the case that A, then it would have been the case that B* is true iff among the world-states at which A is true, those in which B is also true are more similar to the actual world-state than those in which B is false (with the relevant similarity relation depending on aspects of the context of utterance). In addition to providing solutions to logical and semantic problems, this analysis had the effect of legitimizing and clarifying the role of counterfactuals in illuminating a variety of philosophically important concepts. See, for example, Lewis (1973b, 1986b) on causation, Stalnaker (1984) on mental content, and Lewis (1997) on dispositions.

THE DAVIDSONIAN PROGRAM

Similar in aim to modal semantics, but different in execution, the program of Donald Davidson (1917–2003) attempted to provide a philosophically revealing truth-conditional theory of meaning for natural language, based on the work of Tarski. However, whereas philosophical logicians in the Carnap-Kripke-Montague-Kaplan tradition employed complex systems of intensional logic—in which the truth of sentences is relativized to possible world-states, plus, in many cases, times or contexts—Davidson worked within the simple extensional framework that Tarski had used. His aim—as indicated in Davidson (1965, 1967a, 1970, 1973a, 1973b)—was to construct finitely axiomatizable theories of truth for natural languages L that allow one to derive—from axioms specifying the referential properties of its words and phrases—a true T-sentence, ⌜"S" is a true sentence of L if and only if p⌝, for each sentence S of L. Since such a theory would give the truth conditions of every sentence on the basis of its semantically significant structure, it would, Davidson thought, count as a theory of meaning for L. He envisioned such a theory being empirically tested by comparing the conditions in which speakers hold particular sentences to be true with the truth conditions the theory assigns to those sentences. In Davidson's view, the correct theory of meaning is, roughly, the theory T_M according to which the conditions in which speakers hold sentences to be true most closely match the conditions in which T_M, plus our theory of the world, predicts the sentences to be true. Roughly put, Davidson takes the correct theory to be the one according to which speakers of L turn out to be truth tellers—*modulo* instances of explicable error—more frequently than on any other interpretation of L.

This bold idea generated responses of two sorts. The first attempted to implement the program by giving analyses of natural-language constructions in Davidsonian terms. Leading examples dealt with (i) event nominals and adverbial modification, Davidson (1967b) and Higginbotham (1983); (ii) propositional attitude ascriptions, Davidson (1968) and Larson and Ludlow (1993); (iii) metaphor, Davidson (1978); and (iv) pronouns, Evans (1977) and Higginbotham (1980). The second sort of response to Davidson's program questioned his grounds for taking a theory of truth to be a theory of meaning. Emphasizing that theories of truth do not assign any entities to sentences to serve as their meanings, and also do not issue in theorems about what individual sentences mean, Davidson initially rested his claim that they, nevertheless, qualify as theories of meaning on the contention that one who knew that which they stated would thereby grasp the intricate system of connections relating the truth conditions of every sentence in the language to those of every other. It was the systematicity of this knowledge that convinced him that knowledge of an appropriate truth theory T_M for L would be sufficient for understanding its sentences. However, this was a mistake—as was shown in Foster (1976), which demonstrated that one could know that which was stated by T_M while systematically misunderstanding the sentences of L to which it assigned truth conditions. Although Davidson's "Reply to Foster" (1976) modified the original justification for taking his theories of truth to be theories of meaning, the new justification was shown to fail in Soames (1992). Since then other attempted justifications have been offered—(e.g., Higginbotham 1991, 2006; Larson and Segal (1995)—but the issue remains controversial.

Today, the Davidsonian program continues as one approach among many to the semantics of natural language. As a historical matter, its larger place in the analytic tradition in America came from the role it played in connecting different strands of the tradition. Its concern with the application of logical techniques to the task of understanding natural language connected it to the technically more sophisticated work of the philosophical logicians. Its emphasis on explaining semantic competence in terms of a complex mapping between the surface structure of sentences and their underlying logical forms connected it to the ideas of linguistically minded philosophers, intent on making common cause with Chomskian generative grammarians. Davidson's avoidance of the intensional—and his determination to explicate both the meanings of sentences and the contents of the beliefs they are used to express in terms of the extensional notions of truth and reference, plus the slender attitude of an agent's holding a sentence to be true—connected him to Quine's naturalism and "flight from intension." Finally, Davidson's systematic, but logically quite simple, approach to the theory of meaning connected his work to those philosophers—particularly, but not exclusively, in Britain—who continued to believe that meaning had a central role to play in philosophy and who were frustrated by the failure of earlier, ordinary-language philosophers to provide a fruitful way of studying it.

KRIPKE AND THE END OF THE LINGUISTIC TURN

The most important development in the last thirty years of the twentieth century was the challenge posed to theses (i)–(iv) growing out of the work of Saul Kripke (1980), Hilary Putnam (1970, 1975a), and David Kaplan (1989).

   (i) The meaning of a term is not its referent but a descriptive sense that encodes conditions necessary and sufficient for determining reference.
  (ii) Since the meaning of a word is the descriptive sense that a speaker associates with it, meaning is transparent. If two words mean the same, then anyone who understands both should be able to figure that out by checking the sense that he or she associates with them. Word meanings and mental contents are determined by factors internal to agents.
 (iii) Apriori and necessary truth amount to the same thing. Both are grounded in meaning.
  (iv) Metaphysical claims about objects having or lacking properties essentially—independently of how they are described—make no sense. Even if a term t designates an object o and ⌜Necessarily t is F (if t exists)⌝ is true, there will always be another term t* designating o for which ⌜Necessarily t* is F (if t* exists)⌝ is false. Since it would be arbitrary to give either sentence priority in determining the essential properties of o, the idea that objects have, or lack, such properties must be relativized to how they are described.

Prior to the Kripke-inspired attack on these doctrines, analytic philosophers typically regarded all possibility to be linguistic possibility, and the necessary, the apriori, and the analytic to be one. Even Quine, who rejected modality, took *necessity, apriority,* and *analyticity* to be different names of the same discredited notion. Those who rejected such austerity typically lumped the three notions together and continued to view the job of philosophy as the discovery of illuminating conceptual—i.e., analytic-apriori-necessary—truths through the analysis of meaning.

All that changed with Kripke's introduction of rigid designation, direct reference, and nondescriptionality. His argument that names and natural kind terms are rigid designators, and so not equivalent to descriptions associated with them by speakers, was the entering wedge. He next used rigid designation to rebut Quine's famous objection to essentialism, enshrined in (iv). A rigid designator t of an object o is one that picks out o in all possible circumstances in which o exists. Thus, when t is rigid, the question of whether o has the property expressed by F essentially is equivalent to the question of whether the sentence ⌜Necessarily t is F (if t exists)⌝ is true. The truth values of other sentences, containing nonrigid designators, are irrelevant. Once this was seen, the objection to the intelligibility of essentialism collapsed (Soames 2003b, chap. 14).

With both a nondescriptive semantics and a rehabilitated conception of essentialism in place, Kripke next showed how to generate instances of the necessary aposteriori. If n is a name or indexical that rigidly designates an existing object o, F expresses an essential property of o, and knowledge that o has this property requires empirical evidence, then the proposition expressed by ⌜If n exists, then n is F⌝ is both necessary and knowable only aposteriori (see Soames 2006). Suddenly, the necessary and the apriori were no longer the same, and the idea that one, or both, might arise from something beyond the linguistic became credible.

With this essentialist route to the necessary aposteriori came a distinction between conceivability and genuine possibility—between ways things could conceivably be versus ways things could really be (or have been). The distinction is typically drawn in terms of possible worlds or, better, possible world-states. For the Kripkean, possible states of the world are not alternative concrete universes but abstract objects (see Stalnaker 1976, 1984). Metaphysically possible world-states are maximally complete ways the real concrete universe could have been—maximally complete properties the universe could have instantiated. Epistemically possible world-states are maximally complete ways the universe can coherently be conceived to be—maximally complete properties that the universe can be conceived of as instantiating and that one cannot know apriori that it doesn't, or couldn't, instantiate (see Salmon 1989; Soames 2003b, 2005, 2007.) These two sets of properties are different. Just as there are properties that ordinary objects could have had and other properties they couldn't have had, so there are certain maximally complete properties the universe could have had—metaphysically possible world-states—and other maximally complete properties the universe couldn't have had—metaphysically impossible world-states. Just as some of the properties that objects couldn't have had are properties that one can conceive them as having, and that one cannot know apriori that they don't, or couldn't, have, so some maximally complete properties that the universe couldn't have had are properties that one can conceive it as having, and that one cannot know apriori that it doesn't, or couldn't, have. These states of the world are epistemically, but not metaphysically, possible. In this picture, the reason empirical evidence is required for knowledge of necessary truths that are knowable only aposteriori is to rule out metaphysically impossible, but epistemically possible, world-states in which they are false.

This was the heart of the philosophical revolution led by Kripke and his allies. By the time it was over, (i)–(iv) had been called into question, and rejected by many. Most important, the decoupling of necessity, apriority, and analyticity enlarged the scope of philosophical inquiry—including metaphysical inquiry about essence—beyond that which could be grounded in the analysis of meaning. The linguistic turn, it appeared, had met its match.

RAWLS AND THE RESUSCITATION OF NORMATIVE THEORY

A similar transformation occurred at about the same time in ethics, political philosophy, and the philosophy of law. The period from the mid-1930s to the early 1960s was the heyday of emotivism and evaluative noncognitivism. For many years, one of America's most well known analytic writers in ethics was Charles Stevenson, whose 1937 "The Emotive Meaning of Ethical Terms," and 1944 *Ethics and Language*, had become classics. In these works, he argued that the function of evaluative terms—like *good, bad, right,* and *wrong*—was not to describe the world, or courses of action, but to express one's emotional attitude toward them. Sentences containing such terms were not, he maintained, used to make statements that could be true or false, but to express feelings and guide action. As a result, normative theories about the right and the good could not be objects of knowledge, or even rationally justified belief, and so were excluded from the proper domain of philosophy. As Stevenson put it at the end of his famous article (1937), since "*x is good* is essentially a vehicle for suggestion, it is scarcely a statement which philosophers, any more than other men, are called upon to make. To the extent that ethics predicates the ethical terms of anything, rather than explains their meaning, it ceases to be a reflective study." Accordingly, he thought, the only job for the moral philosopher was to explain how evaluative language works. Ethics had been swallowed by metaethics.

This view, which had grown more sophisticated in the 1950s, was, at the end of that decade, subjected to a powerful objection known as *the Frege-Geach point*, forcefully advanced not only by the British philosopher Peter Geach, in Geach (1960), but also by an American, John Searle, in Searle (1962). The objection is based on the observation that when evaluative sentences like *that is good* occur as clauses in larger, descriptive sentences, their meanings make systematic contributions to the truth conditions of statements made by utterances of the larger sentences. Since evaluative sentences have the same meanings when used on their own as when they occur as clauses of larger sentences, their meanings cannot be identified with any set of emotional responses accompanying their use, or any action—like commending or guiding choices—that may be performed by uttering them on their own. Thus, the idea that evaluative sentences have descriptive content, or something like it, was revived, facilitating a renaissance in normative theory that was already under way.

One sees this renaissance in the writings of theorists like Joel Fineberg, Richard Brandt, Kurt Baier, and Thomas Nagel from the late 1950s through the early 1970s. But above all, one sees it in the work of John Rawls (1921–2002)—particularly, "Justice as Fairness" (1958), "The Sense of Justice" (1963), and his classic *A Theory of Justice* (1971). It is hard to exaggerate the impact of this book on the moral and political philosophy of the time. Fully informed by the relevant social science, guided by a plausible and self-conscious methodology, and deeply learned about the conceptual and historical underpinnings of utilitarianism, deontology, contractarianism, equalitarianism, and libertarianism, *A Theory of Justice* brought to analytic philosophy the most compelling and systematic study of fundamental normative questions it had ever seen.

The central idea is that a just society is one the basic structure of which would be freely and unanimously chosen by rational, self-interested agents in a fair bargaining procedure for determining the fundamental rules governing their social interaction. The procedure involves the selection of principles under constraints defined by what Rawls calls *the original position*—a hypothetical situation in which one possesses all relevant knowledge of general facts about human nature and society while being deprived of any knowledge of one's own abilities, desires, or place in the social order that could lead one to favor principles benefiting oneself. Given these constraints, Rawls argues that two general principles emerge as the basis for a just society—one guaranteeing to each citizen the most extensive set of basic liberties compatible with similar liberties for all, and the other (the so-called difference principle) stipulating that social and economic inequalities (attached to positions open to everyone under conditions of equality of opportunity) are to be tolerated only to the extent that the least well off individuals in the system are better off than the least well off would be under any alternative system. The elaboration of these principles involves balancing liberty, equality, and utility while making room for rights, and rejecting classical utilitarianism. Rawls's argument also can be read as justifying a liberal-left (but not too far left) redistributionist version of modern democratic capitalism—a fact that prompted criticisms from both the socialist left and the libertarian right.

The most well known of these was the libertarian classic *Anarchy, State, and Utopia* (1974), written by Rawls's Harvard colleague Robert Nozick (1938–2002). In part a negative critique of Rawls and in part a positive alternative, its central idea is that liberty is the dominant political value. For Nozick, the distribution of goods is governed by principles of historical entitlement, which, in contrast with Rawls's end-result principles, are entirely procedural. According to the entitlement theory, any distribution of goods that arises by a series of just steps—including the voluntary exchange of assets by parties entitled to them ("capitalist acts between consenting adults")—is itself just. Since any pattern of distribution can be disrupted by such voluntary exchanges, this means that no such pattern—strict equality, the difference principle, total utility, maximum average utility, or any other— can be constitutive of a just society. This was Nozick's most provocative conclusion.

Rawls and Nozick brought political philosophy in particular—and ambitious moral theory in general—squarely into the mainstream of the analytic tradition, both of which continue to be important foci of attention, as illustrated by Thomas Scanlon's contractarian approach to obligation in *What We Owe to Each Other* (1998). A similar revival, led (in America) by Ronald Dworkin's (1931–2013) *Taking Rights Seriously* (1977) and *Law's Empire* (1986), took place in the philosophy of law. In 1969, Dworkin, who had earned BAs from Harvard in 1953 and Oxford in 1955, and an LLB from Harvard Law in 1957, succeeded the great legal positivist H.L.A. Hart in the Chair of Jurisprudence at Oxford. There, he soon became known as the chief critic of Hart's positivism—a view according to which legal validity is a matter of fidelity to the institutional sources of positive law and, except at the margins, is independent of substantive moral considerations. As opposed to this view, Dworkin argued for a theory of "constructive interpretation" in which neither the contents of laws, nor their applications to particular cases, are, in principle, entirely determined by the routine application of conventional, legal rules—independent of any moral assessment of the consequences of particular applications, and any judgment about how those consequences bear on the social purposes of the laws and the intentions of those who enacted them. For Dworkin, all adjudication requires the judge to weigh substantive moral concerns with existing legal history so as to arrive at the most just and morally desirable principles for achieving the legitimate ends of the law while accommodating, so far as is reasonably possible, the results of past decisions and existing legal practices. Although this process may seem to allow extraordinary judicial discretion in determining both the results reached in particular cases and the contents of the laws involved in those cases—to the delight or consternation of partisans of different stripes—Dworkin doesn't view it that way. Insisting that the mix of normative and factual considerations required by his theory determines unique results even in "hard cases," he denies that judges have the authority to create new law (or to arrive at results outside the law), and he charges them with what he admits to be the difficult and complicated task of discovering the unarticulated law that he believes already to be there. In all of this, he provides a sophisticated, though controversial, philosophical rationale for the prevailing liberal-left practice of jurisprudence of the past half century—in much the same the way that Rawls provided a rationale for liberal-left understandings of modern democratic welfare-states, with free-market economies. Though the debate over Dworkin's views, led by such figures as Joseph Raz, has been vigorous, it does not seem to have been politically freighted in quite the way that the Rawls-Nozick debate was. Nevertheless, there was no shortage of spirited controversy involving Dworkin, who started at New York University Law School in 1975 and was Frank Henry Sommer Professor of Law, with an appointment in philosophy, from 1994 to 2011.

A COLLECTION OF SPECIALTIES

By the end of the twentieth century, analytic philosophy in America, and elsewhere, had broadened to include active research programs on nearly all topics of traditional philosophical concern. In metaphysics, physicalism, the nature of time and space, and problems of material constitution were hotly debated, and at least one full-blown metaphysical system—that of David Lewis (1941–2001)—commanded center stage. In epistemology, the Gettier problem—Gettier (1963)—generated a vast literature on what, beyond true, justified belief, constitutes knowledge. One central idea—espoused in such works as Goldman (1967) and Dretske (1981)—is that knowledge is true belief that is caused in the right way. Another innovation was contextualism—pioneered in Cohen

(1986, 1988, 1998) and DeRose (1992, 1995, 2002), and adopted in Lewis (1996). According to this view, standards of justification incorporated in the predicate *know* are sensitive to variations in the context of utterance, with important consequences for a variety of epistemological problems, including those posed by skepticism.

In the philosophy of mind, lively and intense discussion centered around a cluster of related topics: functionalism about mental states (e.g., Putnam [1967a,1967b]; Fodor [1968]; and Lewis [1980]); the computational theory of mind (e.g., Fodor [1975, 1979,1983] and Searle [1980, 1984]); scientifically acceptable notions of mental content (e.g., Burge [1979] and Fodor [1987, 1990]); intentionalism (the view that all there is to the content of any mental state is its representational content) (e.g., Harman [1990]; Tye [1995]; Dretske [1995]; and Byrne [2002]); the controversy over phenomenal qualities (so called *qualia*) (e.g., Nagel [1974]; Shoemaker [1982, 1994]; and Thau [2002]); and the nature of consciousness (e.g., Lycan [1996]). Ethics saw vigorous debates over utilitarianism (e.g., Scheffler [1982] and Kagan [1989], as well as the development of sophisticated metaethical theories (e.g., Harman [1977] and Gibbard [1990, 2003]). In the philosophy of science, nothing attracted as much attention as Thomas Kuhn's *The Structure of Scientific Revolutions* (1962). However, the true sequel to the general conception of science espoused by the logical empiricists was probably the marriage of semantic realism with pragmatic verificationism found in the constructive empiricism of Bas van Fraassen's *The Scientific Image* (1980). Since then, overall characterizations of the scientific enterprise have largely been replaced by more specialized, and highly focused, studies of particular problems of individual sciences.

This is only a small sample of the immense range and variety of topics under active investigation by analytic philosophers in America. With a few exceptions—most notably religion, and perhaps also aesthetics—it is doubtful that any philosophical topics have ever received as much scrutiny as they do now. Even in religion and aesthetics, the situation has improved with the work of such distinguished analytic philosophers as Alvin Plantinga, William Alston, and Peter van Inwagen in the philosophy of religion;Kendall Walton, Arthur Danto, Stanley Cavell, and Paul Ziff in aesthetics; and George Wilson in the aesthetics of film. If there is a systemic problem with analytic philosophy today, it does not lie in a neglect of subject areas or in a paucity of approaches for dealing with different problems but in the difficulty, in an age of unprecedented abundance, of formulating unifying synthetic overviews of the sort for which philosophers have traditionally been known.

QUALITY, QUANTITY, AND IDENTITY

At the beginning of the twentieth century, American philosophy was, with the exception of a solitary genius (Peirce) working alone in Milford, Pennsylvania, essentially the philosophy of the Harvard department—then dominated by the pragmatist William James, the absolute idealist Josiah Royce, and the realist Ralph Barton Perry. Analytic philosophy did not yet exist in America, but its precursor, pragmatism, was at its zenith. A half century later, in the early 1950s, the last of the great preanalytic pragmatists—C. I. Lewis—retired from Harvard, leaving the department in the capable hands of Quine—the first, world-class, analytic philosopher in America. Although Harvard was still the center of things, and would remain so for another two decades, arrivals from Europe, supplemented by a growing number of home-grown products, had established firm analytic footholds at UCLA, Berkeley, Chicago, Columbia, Michigan, Cornell, Brown, the University of Pennsylvania, and elsewhere. Twenty years later, in the mid-1970s, philosophy in America was analytic philosophy, and the baton of leadership had been passed to the Princeton department of Saul Kripke and David Lewis.

By then, the vast expansion in higher education had produced a surge in the number of professional philosophers, and the rise of many competing centers of philosophical excellence—including the powerful department at Pittsburgh and the small, but increasingly influential, department at MIT. These trends continued through the turn of the new century, when two new departments—those at NYU and Rutgers—rose to the top, and the number of philosophers continued to grow. By then, the number of strong departments with highly effective graduate programs had risen to about twenty, with a great deal of impressive philosophical talent spread far beyond them. Philosophers were now thoroughly professionalized, and their work—the primary audience for which was other professional philosophers—was much more specialized.

Although the appearance of philosophical genius is unpredictable, and can hardly be quantified, the overall quality of philosophy done throughout the country appears to be higher than ever before. What is truly staggering, however, is the increase in quantity. As noted earlier, the membership reported by the American Philosophical Association rose from 747 in 1940 to 5,125 in 1980. In 1990 it was 8,336; in 2000 it was 10,474; and in 2006 it reached more than 11,200. Members are not simply teachers. A large number are active in research, and publish regularly. Thus, it is not surprising that the number of outlets for publication in philosophy has also grown to accommodate them. For example, the *Directory of American Philosophers 2004–2005* reported 267 journals publishing philosophy in the United States, and 168 philosophical societies.

Even these numbers are misleadingly low. To focus only on the United States is to falsely presuppose that there is today a distinctively American philosophical community, producing its own recognizable type of philosophy. There isn't. Philosophy in America today is, overwhelmingly, philosophy in the analytic tradition. However, there is no longer an American strain of the tradition that is substantially different from what is found in Britain, Australia, New Zealand, Canada, or even in the increasingly large and numerous enclaves found in non-English-speaking countries to which analytic philosophy has spread. The size and influence of philosophy done in America is, to be sure, considerably greater than that done elsewhere. But this philosophy is by no means done only by Americans. More and more, there is a single, integrated community of analytic philosophers from different countries, within which individuals move back and forth. America is the center of the community, but it doesn't define it.

REFERENCES

Austin, J. L. 1962. *How to Do Things with Words. Cambridge:* Harvard University Press.
Ayer, Alfred Jules, ed. 1959. *Logical Positivism.* New York: Free Press.
Byrne, Alex. 2002. "Intentionalism Defended." *Philosophical Review* 110: 199–240.
Burgess, John. 1998. "Quinus ab Omni Naevo Vindicatus," in Ali Kazmi, ed., *Meaning and Reference.* Calgary: University of Calgary Press.
Burge, Tyler. 1979. "Individualism and the Mental," in Peter French, Theodore Uehling Jr., and Howard Wettstein, eds., *Midwest Studies in Philosophy*, vol. 4. Minneapolis: University of Minnesota Press.
Carnap, Rudolf. 1936–37. "Testability and Meaning." *Philosophy of Science* 3:419–71 and 4:1–40.
———. (1934) 1937. *Logische Syntax der Sprache.* Translated as *The Logical Syntax of Language.* London: Kegan Paul.
———. 1942. *Introduction to Semantics.* Cambridge: Harvard University Press.
———. 1946. "Modalities and Quantification." *Journal of Symbolic Logic* 11: 33–64.
———. 1947. *Meaning and Necessity.* Chicago: University of Chicago Press.
———. 1949. "Truth and Confirmation," in Feigl and Sellars 1949.
———. 1950a. *The Logical Foundations of Probability.* Chicago: University of Chicago Press.
———. 1950b. "Empiricism, Semantics, and Ontology." *Revue International de Philosophie* 4:20–40; reprinted and revised in Carnap 1956b.

———. 1956a. "Meaning and Synonymy in Natural Languages." *Philosophical Studies* 7:33–47; reprinted in Carnap 1956b.

———. 1956b. *Meaning and Necessity*, 2nd exp. ed. Chicago: University of Chicago Press.

———. 1963. "Intellectual Autobiography," in P. A. Schilpp, ed., *The Philosophy of Rudolf Carnap*. La Salle, IL: Open Court.

Cohen, Stewart. 1986. "Knowledge and Context." *Journal of Philosophy* 83: 574–83.

———. 1988. "How to Be a Falliblist." *Philosophical Perspectives* 2:581–605.

———. 1998. "Contextualist Solutions to Epistemological Problems: Scepticism, Gettier, and the Lottery." *Australasian Journal of Philosophy* 76: 289–306.

Davidson, Donald. 1965. "Theories of Meaning and Learnable Languages," in *Yehoshua Bar-Hillel, ed., Logic, Methodology and Philosophy of Science: Proceedings of the 1964 International Congress*. Amsterdam: North-Holland Publishing Company; reprinted in Davidson 2001a.

———. 1967a. "Truth and Meaning." *Synthese* 17:304–23; reprinted in Davidson 2001a.

———. 1967b. "The Logical Form of Action Sentences," in N. Rescher, ed., *The Logic of Decision and Action*. Pittsburgh: University of Pittsburgh Press; reprinted in Davidson 2001b.

———. 1968. "On Saying That." *Synthese* 19:130–46; reprinted in Davidson 2001a.

———. 1970. "Semantics for Natural Languages," in B. Visentini, ed., *Linguaggi nella Societa e nella Tecnica*. Milan: Edizioni di Comunita; reprinted in Davidson 2001a.

———. 1973a. "In Defense of Convention T," in Hughes Leblanc, ed., *Truth, Syntax, and Modality*. Amsterdam: North-Holland Publishing Company; reprinted in Davidson 2001a.

———. 1973b. "Radical Interpretation." *Dialectica* 27:313–28; reprinted in Davidson 2001a.

———. 1976. "Reply to Foster," in Gareth Evans and John McDowell, eds., *Truth and Meaning: Essays in Semantics*. Oxford: Clarendon Press; reprinted in Davidson 2001a.

———. 1978. "What Metaphors Mean." *Critical Inquiry* 5:31–47; reprinted in Davidson 2001a.

———. 2001a. *Inquiries into Truth and Interpretation*. Oxford: Clarendon Press.

———. 2001b. *Essays on Actions and Events*. Oxford: Clarendon Press.

DeRose, Keith. 1992. "Contextualism and Knowledge Attributions." *Philosophy and Phenomenological Research* 52:913–29.

———. 1995. "Solving the Sceptical Problem." *Philosophical Review* 104:1–52.

———. 2002. "Assertion, Knowledge and Context." *Philosophical Review* 111:167–203.

Dretske, Fred. 1981. *Knowledge and the Flow of Information*. Cambridge, MA: MIT Press.

———. 1995. *Naturalizing the Mind*. Cambridge, MA: MIT Press.

Dworkin, Ronald. 1977. *Taking Rights Seriously*. Cambridge, MA: Harvard University Press.

———. 1986. *Law's Empire*. Cambridge, MA: Harvard University Press.

Evans, Gareth. 1977. "Pronouns, Quantifiers and Relative Clauses.". *Canadian Journal of Philosophy* 7:467–536.

Feigl, Herbert, and Wilfrid Sellars. 1949. *Readings in Philosophical Analysis*. New York: Appleton.

Fitch, Frederic B. 1949. "The Problem of the Morning Star and the Evening star." *Philosophy of Science* 16:137–41.

Fodor, J. A. 1968. *Psychological Explanation*. New York: Random House.

———. 1975. *The Language of Thought*. New York: Crowell.

———. 1979. *Representations*. Cambridge, MA: MIT Press.

———. 1983. *The Modularity of Mind*. Cambridge, MA: MIT Press.

———. 1987. *Psychosemantics: The Problem of Meaning in the Philosophy of Mind*. Cambridge, MA: MIT Press.

———. 1990. *A Theory of Content and Other Essays*. Cambridge, MA: MIT Press.

Follesdal, Dagfinn. 1961. *Referential Opacity and Modal Logic*. PhD diss., Harvard University.

Foster, J. A. 1976. "Meaning and Truth Theory," in G. Evans and J. McDowell, eds., *Truth and Meaning*. Oxford: Clarendon Press.

Geach, Peter. 1960. "Ascriptivism." *Philosophical Review* 69:221–25.

Gettier, Edmund. 1963. "Is Justified True Belief Knowledge?" *Analysis* 23: 121–23.

Gibbard, Alan. 1990. *Wise Choices, Apt Feelings: A Theory of Normative Judgment*. Cambridge: Harvard University Press.

———. 2003. *Thinking How to Live*. Cambridge: Harvard University Press.

Goldman, Alvin. 1967. "A Causal Theory of Knowing." *Journal of Philosophy* 64:335–72.

Goodman, Nelson. 1947. "The Problem of Counterfactual Conditionals." *Journal of Philosophy* 44:113–28.

———. 1954. *Fact, Fiction, and Forecast*. Cambridge: Harvard University Press.

Grice, Paul. 1989. *Studies in the Way of Words*. Cambridge: Harvard University Press.

Harman, Gilbert. 1977. *The Nature of Morality*. New York: Oxford University Press.

———. 1990. "The Intrinsic Quality of Experience." *Philosophical Perspectives* 4:31–52.

Hempel, Carl. 1945. "Studies in the logic of confirmation." *Mind* 54:1–16, 97–121.

———. 1950. "The Empiricist Criterion of Meaning." *Revue Internationale de Philosophie* 4:41–63; reprinted in Ayer 1959.

———. 1965. *Aspects of Scientific Explanation*. New York: Free Press.

———. 1966. *Philosophy of Natural Science*. Englewood Cliffs, NJ: Prentice-Hall.

Hempel, Carl, and Paul Oppenheim. 1945. "A Definition of Degree of Confirmation." *Philosophy of Science* 12:98–115.

———. 1948. "Studies in the Logic of Explanation." *Philosophy of Science* 15: 135–75.

Higginbotham, James. 1980. "Pronouns and Bound Variables." *Linguistic Inquiry* 11:679–708.

———. 1983. "The Logic of Perceptual Reports: An Extensional Alternative to Situation Semantics." *Journal of Philosophy* 80: 100–27.

———. 1991. "Truth and Understanding." *Iyyun* 40: 271–88.

———. (2006). "Truth and Reference as the Basis of Meaning," in Michael Devitt and Richard Hanley, eds., *Blackwell Guide to the Philosophy of Language*. Oxford: Blackwell.

Holt, Edwin; Marvin, Walter Taylor; Montague, W. P.; Perry, Ralph Barton; Pitkin, Walter; Spaulding, Edward. 1912. *The New Realism*. New York: Macmillan.

Houser, Nathan, Don Roberts, and James Van Evra, eds. 1997. *Studies in the Logic of Charles Sanders Peirce*. Bloomington: Indiana University Press.

Jackson, Frank, ed. 1991.*Conditionals*. Oxford: Oxford University Press.

James, William. 1902. *The Varieties of Religious Experience*. New York: Longmans, Green.

———. 1907. *Pragmatism: A New Name for Some Old Ways of Thinking*. New York: Longmans, Green.

Kagan, Shelly. 1989. *The Limits of Morality*. New York: Oxford University Press.

Kaplan, David. 1986. "Opacity," in Lewis E. Hahn and Paul A. Schilpp, eds., *The Philosophy of W.V. Quine*. La Salle, IL: Open Court.

———. 1989. "Demonstratives," in Joseph Almog, John Perry, and Howard Wettstein, eds., *Themes from Kaplan*. Oxford: Oxford University Press.

Kazmi, Ali. 1987. "Quantification and Opacity." *Linguistics and Philosophy* 10: 77–100.

Kripke, Saul. 1959. "A Completeness Theorem in Modal Logic." *Journal of Symbolic Logic* 24: 1–13.

———. 1963. "Semantical Analysis of Modal Logic I. Normal Modal Propositional Calculi." *Zeitschrift für Matematische Logik und Grundlagen der Mathematik* 9:67–96.

———. 1980. *Naming and Necessity*. Cambridge, MA: Harvard University Press.

Kuhn, Thomas. 1962. *The Structure of Scientific Revolutions*. Chicago: University of Chicago Press.

Kuklick, Bruce. 1977. *The Rise of American Philosophy*. New Haven, CT: Yale University Press.

———. 2001. *A History of Philosophy in America*. Oxford: Oxford University Press.

Larson, Richard, and Peter Ludlow. 1993. "Interpreted Logical Forms." *Synthese* 95:305–56; reprinted in Ludlow 1997.

Larson, Richard, and Gabriel Segal.1995. *Knowledge of Meaning*. Cambridge, MA: MIT Press.

Lewis, C. I. 1929. *Mind and the World Order*. New York: Charles Scribner's Sons.

———. 1946. *An Analysis of Knowledge and Valuation*. La Salle, IL: Open Court.

Lewis, C. I., and C. H. Langford. 1932. *Symbolic Logic*. New York: Appleton-Century.

Lewis, David. 1973a. *Counterfactuals*. Cambridge, MA: Harvard University Press.

———. 1973b. "Causation." *Journal of Philosophy* 70:556–67; reprinted in Lewis 1986a.

———. 1980. "Mad Pain and Martian Pain," in Ned Block, ed., *Readings in the Philosophy of Psychology*, vol. 1. Cambridge, MA: Harvard University Press; reprinted in Lewis 1983.

———. 1983. *Philosophical Papers*, vol. 1. New York: Oxford University Press.

———. 1986a.*Philosophical Papers*, vol. 2. New York: Oxford University Press.

———. 1986b. "Causal Explanation," in Lewis 1986a.

———. 1996. "Elusive Knowledge." *Australasian Journal of Philosophy* 74:549–67; reprinted in Lewis 1999.

———. 1997. "Finkish Dispositions." *Philosophical Quarterly* 47:143–58; reprinted in Lewis 1999.

———. 1999. *Papers in Metaphysics and Epistemology*. Cambridge: Cambridge University Press.

Ludlow, Peter, ed. 1997. *Readings in the Philosophy of Language*. Cambridge, MA: MIT Press.

Lycan, William. 1996. *Consciousness and Experience*. Cambridge, MA: MIT Press.

Marcus, Ruth. 1946. "A Functional Calculus of First Order Based on Strict Implication." *Journal of Symbolic Logic* 11:115–18.

———. 1960. "Extensionality." *Mind* 69:55–62.

———. 1961. "Modalities and Intensional Languages." *Synthese* 13:303–22.

Misak, Cheryl, ed. 2004. *The Cambridge Companion to Peirce*. Cambridge: Cambridge University Press.

Montague, Richard. 1974. *Formal Philosophy: Selected Papers of Richard Montague*. New Haven, CT: Yale University Press.

Moore, G. E. 1903. "The Refutation of Idealism." *Mind* 12:433–53.

Nagel, Ernest. 1961. *The Structure of Science*. London: Routledge and Kegan Paul.

Nagel, Ernest, and J. R. Newman. 1958. *Gödel's Proof*. New York: New York University Press.

Nagel, Thomas. 1974. "What Is It Like to Be a Bat?" *Philosophical Review* 83:435–50.

Nozick, Robert. 1974. *Anarchy, State, and Utopia*. New York: Basic Books.

Passmore, John. 1968 *A Hundred Years of Philosophy*, Baltimore: Penguin Books

Peirce, Charles Sanders. 1870. "Description for a Notation of the Logic of Relatives." *Memoirs of the American Academy of Arts and Sciences* 9:317–78.

———. 1883. "Note B: The Logic of Relatives," in C. S. Peirce, ed., *Studies in Logic by Members of the Johns Hopkins University*, 187–203. Boston: Little, Brown.

———. 1931–58. *Collected Papers of Charles Sanders Peirce*. Cambridge, MA: Belknap Press, i–vi, C. Hartshorne and P. Weiss, eds. (1931–35); vii and viii, A. Burks, ed. (1958).

Prior, Arthur. 1957. *Time and Modality*. Oxford: Clarendon Press.

Putnam, Hilary. 1967a. "The Mental life of Some Machines," in H. Castaneda, ed., *Intentionality, Minds, and Perception*. Detroit: Wayne State University Press; reprinted in Putnam 1975b.

―――. 1967b. "The Nature of Mental States," in W. H. Capitan and D. D. Merrill, eds., *Art, Mind, and Religion*. Pittsburgh: University of Pittsburgh Press; reprinted in Putnam 1975b.

―――. 1970. "Is Semantics Possible?" in H. Kiefer and M. Munitz, eds., *Language, Belief and Metaphysics*. Albany, NY: State University of New York Press; reprinted in Putnam 1975b.

―――. 1975a. "The Meaning of 'Meaning'," in K. Gunderson, ed., *Language, Mind and Knowledge*. Minneapolis: University of Minnesota Press; reprinted in Putnam 1975b.

―――. 1975b. *Collected Papers*, vol. 2. Cambridge: Cambridge University Press.

―――. 1982. "Peirce as Logician." *Historia Mathematica* 9:290–301.

Quine, W.V. 1936. "Truth by Convention," in O. H. Lee, ed., *Philosophical Essays for A. N. Whitehead*. New York: Longmans; reprinted in Quine 1966.

―――. 1943. "Notes on Existence and Necessity." *Journal of Philosophy* 40: 113–27.

―――. 1947. "The Problem of Interpreting Modal Logic." *Journal of Symbolic Logic* 12:43–48.

―――. 1948. "On What There Is." *Review of Metaphysics* 2:21–38; reprinted in Quine 1980.

―――. 1951. "Two Dogmas of Empiricism." *Philosophical Review* 60; reprinted and revised in Quine 1980.

―――. 1953. "Reference and Modality," in *From a Logical Point of View*. Cambridge, MA: Harvard University Press.

―――. 1960. *Word and Object*. Cambridge, MA: MIT Press.

―――. 1966. *The Ways of Paradox*. New York: Random House.

―――. 1969. "Reply to Chomsky," in Donald Davidson and Jaakko Hintikka, eds., *Words and Objections*. Dordrecht: Reidel.

―――. 1969. "Ontological Relativity," in *Ontological Relativity and Other Essays*. New York: Columbia University.

―――. 1970. "On the Reasons for the Indeterminacy of Translation." *Journal of Philosophy* 67:178–83.

―――. 1980. *From a Logical Point of View*, rev. 2nd ed. Cambridge: Harvard University Press.

―――. 1985. "In the Logical Vestibule." *Times Literary Supplement*, July 12; reprinted as "MacHale on Boole" in *Selected Logic Papers* (enlarged ed.). Cambridge, MA: Harvard University Press, 1995.

Rawls, John. 1958. "Justice as Fairness." *Philosophical Review* 67:164–94.

―――. 1963. "The Sense of Justice." *Philosophical Review* 72:281–305.

―――. 1971. *A Theory of Justice*. Cambridge, MA: Harvard University Press.

Reichenbach, Hans. 1935. *Wahrscheinlichkeitslehre: Eine Untersuchung über die logischen und mathematischen Grundlagen der Wahrscheinlichkeitsrechnung*. Leiden: Sijthoff. Translated as *The Theory of Probability: An Inquiry into the Logical and Mathematical Foundations of the Calculus of Probability*. Berkeley: University of California Press, 1948.

―――. 1938. *Experience and Prediction: An Analysis of the Foundations and the Structure of Knowledge*. Chicago: University of Chicago Press.

———. 1944. *Philosophic Foundations of Quantum Mechanics*. Berkeley: University of California Press.

———. 1947. *Elements of Symbolic Logic*. New York: Macmillan.

———. 1951. *The Rise of Scientific Philosophy*. Berkeley: University of California Press.

Rescher, Nicholas. 1994. *American Philosophy Today*. Maryland: Rowman & Littlefield.

Richard, Mark. 1987. "Quantification and Leibniz's Law." *Linguistics and Philosophy* 10:77–100.

Russell, Bertrand, and Alfred North Whitehead. 1910. *Principia Mathematica*. Cambridge: Cambridge University Press.

Salmon, Nathan. 1989. "On the Logic of What Might Have Been." *Philosophical Review* 98:3–34.

Scanlon, Thomas. 1998. *What We Owe to Each Other*. Cambridge: Harvard University Press.

Searle, John. 1962. "Meaning and Speech Acts." *Philosophical Review* 71:423–32.

———. 1980. "Minds, Brains, and Programs." *Behavioral and Brain Sciences* 3:417–24.

———. 1984. *Minds, Brains, and Science*. Cambridge: Harvard University Press.

Scheffler, Samuel. 1982. *The Rejection of Consequentialism*. Oxford: Clarendon Press.

Shoemaker, Sydney. 1982. "The Inverted Spectrum." *Journal of Philosophy* 79:357–81.

———. 1994. "Phenomenal Character." *Nous* 28:21–38.

Smullyan, A. F. 1947. "Review of Quine's 'The Problem of Interpreting Modal Logic'." *Journal of Symbolic Logic* 12:139–41.

———. 1948. "Modality and Description." *Journal of Symbolic Logic* 13:31–37.

Soames, Scott. 1992. "Truth, Meaning, and Understanding." *Philosophical Studies* 65:17–35.

———. 1995. "Revisionism about Reference." *Synthese* 104:191–216.

———. 2003a. *Philosophical Analysis in the Twentieth Century*, vol. 1. Princeton, NJ: Princeton University Press.

———. 2003b. *Philosophical Analysis in the Twentieth Century*, vol. 2. Princeton, NJ: Princeton University Press.

———. 2005. *Reference and Description*. Princeton, NJ: Princeton University Press.

———. 2006. "The Philosophical Significance of the Kripkean Necessary Aposteriori," in Ernest Sosa and Enrique Villanueva (eds.). *Philosophical Issues* 16:288–309.

———. 2007. "Actually." *Proceedings of the Aristotelian Society, Suppl. Vol.* 81:251–77.

———. 2008. "Truth and Meaning: In Perspective," in Peter French and Howard Wettstein, eds. *Midwest Studies in Philosophy* 32:1–19.

Stalnaker, Robert. 1968. "A Theory of Conditionals," in *Studies in Logical Theory, American Philosophical Quarterly Monograph Series*, no. 2. Oxford: Blackwell; reprinted in Jackson 1991.

———. 1975. "Indicative Conditionals." *Philosophia* 5:269–86; reprinted in Jackson 1991.

————. 1976. "Possible Worlds." *Nous* 10: 1976, 65–75; revised and reprinted as chapter 3 of Stalnaker 1984.

————. 1978. "Assertion," in Peter Cole, ed., *Syntax and Semantics 9: Pragmatics*. New York: Academic Press; reprinted in Stalnaker 1999.

————. 1984. *Inquiry*. Cambridge, MA: MIT Press.

————. 1999. *Context and Content*, Oxford: Oxford University Press.

Stevenson, Charles. 1937. "The Emotive Meaning of Ethical Terms." *Mind* 46:14–31.

————. 1944. *Ethics and Language*. New Haven, CT: Yale University Press.

Thau, Michael. 2002. *Consciousness and Cognition*. Oxford: Oxford University Press.

Tye, Michael. 1995. *Ten Problems of Consciousness*. Cambridge, MA: MIT Press.

Van Fraassen, Bas. 1980. *The Scientific Image*. Oxford: Oxford University Press.

White, Morton. 1999. *A Philosopher's Story*. University Park: Pennsylvania State University Press.

2

Methodology in Late Nineteenth- and
Early Twentieth-Century Analytic Philosophy

In the fall of 1910 and the winter of 1911, G. E. Moore gave a series of 20 lectures which were published 42 years later (in substantially their original form) as *Some Main Problems of Philosophy.*[1] The first lecture, "What is Philosophy?" is a useful indicator of the state of analytic philosophy in its early years. In it Moore discusses what he takes to be philosophy's most important questions, outlines competing answers, and points to what later lectures would make clear to be his own position on many of these questions. Looking back a century later, the contemporary reader can't help being struck by the thoroughly traditional conception of the aims of philosophy embraced by a founding father of a tradition that has often been seen as a revolutionary departure in the subject.

For Moore, the most important task of philosophy is to give a general description of the whole universe—by which he means an accounting of the kinds of things we know to be in it (material objects, human minds, etc.); the kinds of things which, though not known to be in it, may very well be (e.g., a divine mind or minds, human minds after death); and the relations holding among the different kinds of things (e.g., minds *attached* to bodies). Related to this metaphysical quest is the epistemological task of explaining how we are justified in knowing most of the things we ordinarily take ourselves to know. Finally, Moore thinks, there are questions of value—the rightness or wrongness of actions, the goodness or badness of states of affairs, and even the value of the universe as a whole. In short, metaphysics, epistemology, and ethics (traditionally conceived) make up the core of his conception of philosophy.

Were we to supplement this sketch with the contemporaneous views of the two other major analytic figures of the day—Frege and Russell—logic, language, and mathematics would be added to Moore's chief philosophical concerns. But the overall conception of philosophy

[1] Moore (1910–1911).

wouldn't change much. In these early days of the analytic tradition some previously neglected philosophical topics were given new prominence, but they didn't replace traditional concerns, which continued to be addressed in new ways.

The chief change was the rise of logical and linguistic analysis as the means to achieve essentially traditional ends. The great engine of innovation was logicism, which was motivated initially by two questions: What are numbers? and What is the basis of mathematical knowledge? It was Frege who led the way in answering these questions.[2] Convinced that the highest certainty belongs to elementary, self-evident principles of logic—without which thought itself might prove impossible—he believed that the sublime certainty of arithmetic and higher mathematics (save geometry), must be deductively based on logic itself.[3] It was to demonstrate this that he developed modern symbolic logic in his *Begriffsschrift*.[4] The key step after that was to derive arithmetic from logic by (i) specifying a small set of logical truths of the highest certainty to serve as axioms, (ii) defining all arithmetical concepts in terms of purely logical ones, and (iii) producing formal proofs of all arithmetical axioms from these definitions plus the axioms of logic.

The audacity of that program was partially mitigated by his muscular conception of logic. For Frege, logic carried its own ontology. An infinitely ascending hierarchy of predicates was matched by an infinitely ascending hierarchy of concepts they denoted. First-level concepts were functions from objects to truth values, second-level concepts were functions from first-level concepts to truth values, and so on. In addition, every concept had an extension (itself taken to be a kind of object), which we may regard as the set of entities (possibly empty) to which the concept assigned the value truth. Frege's "logical axioms" guaranteed the existence of multiple entities of this sort. Today many would say that his logic looks a lot like set theory, which is now widely regarded not as logic per se but as a fundamental mathematical theory in its own right.

But this is hindsight. The genius of Frege's philosophy of mathematics was his methodology for using his logico-set-theoretic foundation to address his deep philosophical questions about mathematics. Although prior to philosophical analysis we all know many arithmetical truths, we have no idea what numbers are and little understanding of how it is possible for us to achieve certain knowledge of them. *Frege's basic idea is that natural numbers are whatever they have to be in order to explain*

---

[2] See Frege (1884).
[3] See Frege (1893, sec. 14, and preface, sec. xvii).
[4] Frege (1879).

our knowledge of them. Thus the way to discover what they are and how statements about them are justified is to frame definitions of each number, as well as the notion *natural number*, that allow us to logically deduce what we pretheoretically know from the definitions and other unproblematic knowledge.[5] How, for example, should 2, 3, 5, and addition be defined so that facts like those in the following items 2a and 2b can be deduced from the definitions, plus our knowledge of logic plus empirical facts like those in item 1?

1. $\exists x \, \exists y$ (x is a black book on my desk & y is a black book on my desk & $x \neq y$ & $\forall z$ (z is a black book on my desk $\rightarrow z = x$ or $z = y$)) & $\exists u \, \exists v \, \exists w$ (u is a blue book on my desk & v is a blue book on my desk & w is a blue book on my desk & $u \neq v$ & $u \neq w$ & $v \neq w$ & $\forall z$ (z is a blue book on my desk $\rightarrow z = u$ or $z = v$ or $z = w$)) & $\forall x \forall y$ ((x is a black book & y is a blue book) $\rightarrow x \neq y$)

2a. The number of black books on my desk = 2 and the number of blue books on my desk = 3. (There are 2 black books on my desk and 3 blue books on my desk.)

2b. The number of books on my desk = 5. (There are 5 books on my desk.)

More generally, how might a proper understanding of what natural numbers and arithmetical operations are be used, first to derive our purely arithmetical knowledge from the laws of logic and then to derive empirical applications of that knowledge by appealing to relevant empirical facts? This, for Frege, is the most important question that a philosophical theory of number must answer.

The fact that no other philosophy of mathematics of his day could answer this question was the primary basis for his devastating critiques of Millian naturalism, psychologism, and crude formalism (as well as for his dismissal of Kant's conception of arithmetic as founded upon our experience of time). His most fundamental objections to Mill and others were (i) that they often don't even attempt to answer his fundamental question and (ii) that what they do say only gets in the way of a proper answer. Thus, he thought they offered no real theory of number at all. By contrast, his compelling conception of individual natural numbers as sets of equinumerous concepts (the extensions of which can be mapped 1–1 onto each other), his characterization of *the successor of n* (as the class of concepts G such that for some object x in the extension of G the concept *being a G that is not identical to x* is a member of n), and his definition of the natural numbers as consisting of zero plus its

---

[5] See Frege (1884, secs. 46, 56, 60, and 64–66).

ancestors under successor provided what appeared to be the basis for a powerful and elegant explanation of the knowledge to be explained.

Not one to rest with appearances, Frege painstakingly performed the needed derivations, in Frege (1903) which, unfortunately, could not stand the shock of Russell's paradox. Though Frege cobbled together a temporary fix—which wasn't proved to be inadequate until many years later—he knew that the game, as he had conceived it, was up. The inconsistency of his logico-set-theoretic system plus the daunting task of repairing it without loss of requisite power carried an obvious lesson. Logico-set-theoretic axioms that had seemed to provide a bedrock of certainty sufficient to ground arithmetic and all of mathematics had been proved to be faulty. Although they could be, and eventually were, satisfactorily revised in various ways, the price of such revision was a loss of either expressive power or perceived self-evidence, or both. Either way, Frege's ambitious conception of the goals of the logicist project could not be satisfied. In the end, the task of *justifying* arithmetical and other mathematical knowledge in terms of self-evident logical principles for which no similar problem of justification could arise had to be given up. Simply put, the arithmetical axioms to be proved were, if anything, more secure and less in need of justification than the "logical axioms" posited to prove them. Hence, the classical version of the logicist project foundered.

When it came time for Russell's version, both the logic and the philosophy had changed. Whereas Frege's higher-order logic involved ascending levels of quantification over concepts of progressively higher levels, Russell's is most naturally read as involving quantification over ascending orders of classes—individuals, classes of individuals, classes of classes of individuals, and so on. Whereas extensions of concepts— classes—are all available at the lowest level of Frege's system, in Russell's they come presorted, with all classes of elements of level n coming at the next level up. By dubiously treating the type restrictions regulating class availability as if they were constraints on the ability to speak meaningfully about classes at all, Russell was able to render his paradox unstatable, and so to preserve his system from contradiction. However, since the natural numbers had to be located at some specific level—they are classes the elements of which are classes of individuals—he needed his infamous Axiom of Infinity, which posits infinitely many *individuals* (nonclasses), to guarantee that he won't run out of numbers.

Hence, the philosophy underlying Russell's version of logicism had to change. *Logicism,* as classically understood, is the view that arithmetic and much of higher mathematics is derivable from pure logic and so is properly a branch of logic itself. However, in *Principia Mathematica*

(Russell and Whitehead 1910) and later work, Russell recognizes that the Axiom of Infinity is at best an empirical, rather than a logical, truth—as well as being one he does *not* know to be true. In light of this, Boolos (1994) makes a good case that Russell's considered view was a weaker form of logicism according to which *mathematical concepts* are reducible to *purely logical concepts*, even though the proofs of many mathematical truths require nonlogical existence claims about how many individuals there are.

This retreat, though significant, is not so bad—in part because it is extremely doubtful that the original, classical version of logicism is achievable and in part because the weaker version contributes to goals different from the original aim of *justifying* mathematics. By 1907 Russell had come to appreciate the central difficulty with doing that. *We are more certain of the axioms of arithmetic, and less in the dark about how we can know them to be true, than we are of the axioms of any purported system of logic or set theory to which they might be reduced.* As Russell realized, his own theory of types plus axioms of comprehension and infinity raise more questions, and are subject to greater rational doubt, than the arithmetical system he derives from it. Hence the former can't be used to justify the latter.

By this time he had come to view justification as going in the other direction—from the reduced theory to the reducing theory, rather than the other way. In Russell (1907) he argued that sometimes previously unknown, and unobvious, logical or mathematic truths can be justified by the fact that they provide *explanations* of the known and obvious truths that follow from them. The suggestion is that his unobvious logico-set-theoretic system is justified, at least in part, by the fact that the intrinsically obvious and antecedently justified theory of arithmetic follows from it.

As a principle of metaphysical methodology to be employed in developing philosophical foundations for mathematics the principle is not unattractive. Some logical and metamathematical claims may be more foundational and explanatory than others, even though the latter may be more epistemically obvious than the former. When looking for the fundamental structure of a subject, one should, according to the view suggested, use the latter to justify the former. But what exactly does this come to in Russell's case? In Russell (1907), he lays down three ways in which the derivation of arithmetic from his underlying system helps justify the latter. First, he says, in showing that the arithmetical axioms, and through them the theorems of classical mathematics, are derivable from his system, we see how our overall system of mathematical knowledge is (or can be?) organized, and how different parts of that system are related to one another. Second, he notes, the reduction can lead to useful extensions and unifications of mathematical knowledge, such as the extension of our ordinary notion of number to include transfinite numbers. Third, he claims that by illuminating the logical nature of mathematics we can throw light on the philosophical question of what mathematical knowledge amounts to and how it is achieved (Russell 1907, 282–83).

Although there may be merit in Russell's first two points, the third is more doubtful. Since his reduction relies on the Axiom of Infinity, which we don't antecedently know to be true, no appeal to it can explain how we achieved our antecedent knowledge of arithmetic and mathematics in general (supposing we have known these all along). Nor do we learn the Axiom of Infinity to be true by noting its role in Russell's reduction; he himself certainly didn't. So, it is hard to see how his particular reduction succeeds in explaining anything about our knowledge of arithmetic. These issues could, of course, be sidestepped by carrying out the reduction in another way—e.g., by deriving arithmetic from Zermelo-Fraenkel (ZF) set theory. But what would this accomplish? Is there some epistemic problem about arithmetic, and our knowledge of it, that is not equally a problem with ZF, and our knowledge of it? If so, I am not sure what it is.

That, of course, isn't how Russell saw things—in part because ZF was still on the horizon in 1910 and in part because he thought he had eliminated classes (sets) from his ontology. Although he allows himself to use the language of "sets/classes" he explicitly disavows commitment to them as entities. His general position is sketched in section 2 of chapter 3 of the introduction to Russell and Whitehead (1910).

> The symbols for classes, like those for descriptions, are, in our system, incomplete symbols: their uses are defined, but they themselves are not assumed to mean anything at all. That is to say, the uses of such symbols are so defined that when the *definiens* is substituted for the *definiendum*, there no longer remains any symbol supposed to represent a class. *Thus classes, so far as we introduce them, are merely symbolic or linguistic conveniences, not genuine objects as their members are if they are individuals.* (pp. 71–72; my emphasis)

The contextual definition of the usual class notation is given at *20.01.[6]

$$F (\{x: Gx\}) =_{df} \exists H [\forall y (Hy \leftrightarrow Gy) \& F(H)]$$

According to this definition, a formula that seems to say that F is true of the class of individuals satisfying G is really an abbreviation for a

---

[6] Russell and Whitehead (2010, 190).

more complex formula that says that F is true of something that is true of all and only the individuals that satisfy G. According to Russell, this something is "a propositional function." If propositional functions were still functions from individuals to old-fashioned Russellian propositions, then to say that such a function is true of an object would be to say that it assigns the object a true proposition, and to say that propositional functions are *extensionally equivalent* would be to say they are true of the same things. (Similarly for two properties or for a property and a propositional function.) So, whenever G and G* stand for extensionally equivalent properties or propositional functions, ⌜F ({x: Gx})⌝ and ⌜F ({x: G*x})⌝ will, according to the definition, agree in truth value—as they should.

Next, consider a propositional function that takes a property or propositional function as argument. Call it *extensional* iff whenever it is true of its argument A, it is true of all arguments extensionally equivalent to A. As Russell notes at *Principia *20*, not all propositional functions are extensional in this sense.

> [the propositional function designated by] 'I believe $\forall x\ \phi x$' is an *intensional* function [and so not extensional] because even if $\forall x$ $(\phi x \leftrightarrow \phi x)$, it by no means follows that I believe $\forall x\ \psi x$ provided that I believe $\forall x\ \phi x$. (p. 187)

Suppose that $p_{\phi x}$ and $p_{\psi x}$ are different but extensionally equivalent propositional functions, the former mapping an arbitrary individual a onto the proposition *that if a is a human, then a is a human* and the latter mapping a onto the proposition *that if a is a featherless biped, then a is a human*. Now let ϕ be a first-level predicate variable. Then, the propositional function designated by ⌜I believe $\forall x\ \phi x$⌝—which maps propositional functions onto propositions expressed by the corresponding belief ascriptions—may assign $p_{\phi x}$ a true proposition about what I believe while assigning $p_{\psi x}$ a false proposition. Thus, the propositional function designated by the belief ascription is *intensional*, rather than extensional. However, since, as Russell plausibly holds, *only* extensional propositional functions are relevant to mathematics, the system in Russell and Whitehead (1910) can be restricted to them. When one does this, the only thing about the proposition assigned by a propositional function to a given argument that matters to the construction is its truth value. This being so, we can reinterpret the entire construction in terms of functions from arguments to truth values (rather than propositions)—*without losing anything essential to the reduction.*[7]

---

[7] See Burgess (2005, 39–40).

Although the result is pleasing, Russell would not have liked it. A function from arguments to truth values is *the characteristic function of the set* of things to which it assigns truth. There is no mathematically significant difference between working with sets and working with their characteristic functions; anything done with one can be done with the other. Nor does there seem to be any important ontological or philosophical difference between the two. But then, Russell's treatment of classes as "logical fictions" would have been empty and pointless— which is how most of the mathematicians, logicians, and philosophers who followed Russell saw it.

By contrast, Russell took the elimination of classes seriously. By the time Russell and Whitehead (1910) was published his view of propositional functions had become a radically deflationary version of his earlier "realist" view of them as nonlinguistic entities. The result was a thoroughly deontologized interpretation of his technical reduction. In this work he speaks of propositions and propositional functions in various, not always consistent, ways. But most of the time he seems to take propositions to be sentences, and propositional functions to be formulas one gets from them by replacing an occurrence of an expression with a free occurrence of a variable. Thus, looking back in Russell (1940), he says "In the language of the second-order variables denote symbols, not what is symbolized" (p. 192), while in Russell (1959) he says "Whitehead and I thought of a propositional function as an expression" (p. 92). If this is so, it would seem that a sentence of the form '∀P . . . P . . . ' must mean that every value of the formula ' . . . P . . . ' is true.

Russell and Whitehead (1910) is replete with language like this. For example, in section 3 of chapter 3 of the introduction, Russell sketches the idea of a hierarchy of notions of truth that apply to the different levels of his type construction. Assuming that truth has already been defined for quantifier-free sentences at the lowest level, he explains first-order quantification as follows:

> Consider now the proposition ⌜∀x ϕx⌝. If this has truth of the sort appropriate to it, that will mean that every value of ϕx has "first truth" [the lowest level of truth]. Thus if we call the sort of truth that is appropriate to ⌜∀x ϕx⌝ "second truth," *we may define* ⌜∀x ϕ x⌝ *as meaning* ⌜*every value for* ' ϕ x' *has first truth* ⌝. . . . Similarly . . . *we may define* ⌜∃x ϕ x⌝ *as meaning* ⌜*some value for* ' ϕ x' *has first truth* ⌝.[8] (p. 42; my emphasis)

---

[8] I have here changed Russell's notation in inessential ways and used corner quotes to clear up some of the use/mention sloppiness.

Here, in addition to assuming that a similar explanation can be given for higher-order quantification, we are to assume that "first-truth" conditions and meanings have been given for quantifier-free sentences at the lowest level.

Although it might appear from the preceding that Russell took quantificational statements to express metalinguistic facts about language (even though their instances make entirely non-metalinguistic claims), this surely cannot be right. There is, however, another interpretation that could be given to his remarks.[9] In this interpretation, the quantifiers in Russell's reduction are what are now called "substitutional." So understood, they don't range over objects of any kind—linguistic or nonlinguistic—but rather are associated with substitution classes of expressions. Although their *truth conditions* are stated metalinguistically, *their content* is supposed to be nonlinguistic. Using objectual quantifiers over expressions, we can give substitutional *truth conditions* of quantified sentences in the normal way—as Russell does. $\ulcorner \forall x\, \phi x \urcorner$ and $\ulcorner \exists x\, \phi x \urcorner$ are true, respectively, iff all, or some, of their substitution instances are true, where the latter are obtained from replacing free occurrences of 'x' in ϕx by an expression in the relevant substitution class. This explanation will work, provided that the truth values of the sentences on which the quantified sentences depend are already determined before reaching the quantified sentences and so do not themselves depend on the truth or falsity of any higher-level, substitutionally quantified sentences.

There are three important points to note. First, if one combines the hierarchical restriction inherent in substitutional quantification with Russell's system of higher levels of quantification, the type restrictions he needs for his logicist reduction will fall out from the restrictions on substitutional quantification, without any need for further justification. Second, on the substitutional interpretation, there is no need for what look like higher-level "existential" generalizations—i.e., $\ulcorner \exists P\, \phi(P) \urcorner$, $\ulcorner \exists P_2\, \phi(P_2) \urcorner$, etc.,—to carry any ontological commitment. They won't—as long as the relevant substitution instances can be true even when the constant replacing of the bound variable doesn't designate anything. Third, for this reason, it is tempting to think that no quantificational statements in the hierarchy carry any ontological commitments not already carried by quantifier-free sentences at the lowest level. Since Russell took accepting the latter to commit one only to individuals and simple properties and relations, it would be natural for him to characterize classes, numbers, and nonlinguistic propositions and propositional

[9] This interpretation is defended in Landini (1998) and in Klement (2004).

functions as "logical fictions," while nevertheless appealing to them when "speaking with the vulgar," as he does in Russell (1919).

The virtue of the substitutional interpretation of quantification is that it makes some sense of Russell's ill-advised enthusiasm for his no-class theory. Its vice is that it is technically insufficient to support the reduction in *Principia* while undermining his other important achievements in philosophical logic. Although there are many arguments to be made along these lines, some rather complex, I will here briefly mention just one main point.[10] Russell's type theory involves quantification at each of its infinitely many levels. The first level includes what is now called "first-order quantification" over individuals. Though this can be simulated by first-order substitutional quantification, the price to be paid (required by Russell's Axiom of Infinity) includes positing infinitely many logically proper names of individuals. Though this is bad enough, a more far-reaching difficulty occurs with higher-order substitutional quantification.

At the next level we get second-order quantification. The associated predicates include all simple predicates used to construct atomic sentences, plus complex predicates. For any first-level sentence in which simple predicates occur, we need a complex predicate for each of the ways of abstracting one or more of the predicates via lambda abstraction—as illustrated by expressions like $\ulcorner \lambda F \lambda G[\phi (\ldots F \ldots G)] \urcorner$. All these predicates, simple and compound, are associated with the predicate variables. So, in the substitutional interpretation, $\ulcorner \forall X_1\ \phi(X_1) \urcorner$ is true iff every sentence is true that results from erasing the quantifier and substituting an occurrence of a predicate, simple or complex, associated with 'X_1' for each occurrence of 'X_1' in $\phi(X_1)$; similarly, the same holds for second-order existential quantification.

Looking at this argument from the outside (where we continue to allow ourselves to speak of classes), this means that our substitutional construal of second-order quantification parallels ordinary objectual second-order quantification over *those classes that are extensions of first-level predicates of individuals* (including complex predicates). This process is repeated for third-order quantification, except that here complex predicates are the only ones in the substitution class. This level mimics objectual quantification over *those classes that are extensions of second-level predicates, members of which are classes of individuals that are extensions of first-level predicates*. (This is the level at which Russellian natural numbers appear as classes of equinumerous classes.) The hierarchy continues uniformly from there on.

---

[10] For a much more thorough discussion see section 5 of chapter 10 of Soames (2014).

It is important to notice the diminished expressive power of the substitutional versions of higher-order quantifiers. Whereas the objectual quantifiers range over *all classes at a given level* —both those that are extensions of predicates at that level (of the Russellian logical language) and those that are not—the substitutional quantifier mimics only quantification over the former. If, as is standardly assumed, every sentence and every predicate is a *finite* sequence of the logical and non-logical vocabulary, the domain of all classes at a given level will far outstrip the domain of all classes that are the extensions of predicates at that level.[11] As a result, the expressive power of the underlying "logical" theory to which arithmetic is to be reduced is sharply diminished by treating its quantifiers substitutionally. Worse, this diminishment affects Russell's definition of *natural number* and his use of that definition to prove the crucial arithmetical axiom of mathematical induction (which, informally, says that if zero has a property, and if whenever a natural number has a property, its successor does too, then every natural number has the property). As a result, we lose the simple Fregean way of understanding and proving the induction axiom.[12]

Now that we recognize the power of *objectual* second-order quantification, and its relevance for arithmetic (e.g., second-order arithmetic is complete, whereas first-order arithmetic is not), the idea of depriving the higher-order system of *Principia Mathematica* of that power should be a nonstarter. We certainly shouldn't do so in order to avoid ontological commitment to classes. Though Russell wasn't in a position to know this in 1910, classes have proved so useful for all sorts of theories—not least of which model theories for logic and semantics—that giving them up seems virtually out of the question. It is not even clear that we would know how to investigate the differences between first- and second-order logic, and first- and second-order arithmetic, without classes.[13] To read *Principia Mathematica* in a way that distances Russell

---

[11] This can be avoided by allowing individual formulas to be infinitely long, and interpreting higher-order substitutional quantifications in terms of substitution instances that are infinitely long. This strategy is meticulously developed in Hodes (2012), which shows it to be needed by a substitutional interpretation of higher-order quantifiers in *Principia Mathematica* leading to a ramified theory of types, without classes or nonlinguistic propositions and propositional functions. As Hodes notes, the price of this approach is high, since it renders Russell's logical language incapable of being understood by agents whose cognitive powers are finite. See Gödel (1944) for related discussion.

[12] See section 5 of chapter 10 of Soames (2014) for details. For fruitful related discussion see Gödel (1944, 145–46).

[13] Although there are new interpretations of second-order systems that use the notion of plural quantification, and although these interpretations have important uses, it is doubtful that they should be seen as replacing or eliminating set-theoretic interpretations of second-order systems.

from the progress made in the tradition he helped create would be to let tenuous philosophical thoughts about the elimination of classes—which were at best underdeveloped—obscure his positive contribution. That said, it must be admitted that some thoughts of a substitutional sort seem to have played a (confused) role in stoking Russell's enthusiasm for his conception of logico-linguistic analysis as a method of ontological reduction in the philosophy of mathematics and beyond.

His next significant steps were taken in Russell (1914, 1918–1919), in which two broad tendencies are discernible. The first is an ambitious analytic reductionism, by which he sought to avoid ontological commitment to entities thought to be problematic. Just as he took his theory of descriptions and his analysis of ordinary names as disguised descriptions to provide the treatment of negative existentials needed to finally put to rest his earlier broadly Meinongian ontology,[14] so he took his multiple-relation analysis of judgment to eliminate propositions,[15] and his reduction of natural numbers to classes to dispense with an independent category of abstract objects. But that was only the beginning. His more radical view of classes themselves as "logical fictions" advanced a strikingly minimalist metaphysical agenda, present from Russell and Whitehead (1910) onward. In Russell (1914), he took a further ontological step in the service of epistemological concerns. It was there that he renounced commitment to physical objects as independently existing substances, characterizing them instead as "logical constructions" out of the objects of immediate sense perception. By this time his view of reality had been stripped of all abstract objects except "universals"—simple properties and relations—and all particulars except for individual selves (themselves to be eliminated in Russell 1918–19) and the fleeting, private objects of their immediate perception.

In all these works, we see the second broadly methodological tendency that linked his evolving metaphysical minimalism with an ambitious search for secure epistemological foundations. At this point, Russell's epistemological practice consisted of two distinguishable subtasks. The first was to isolate a domain of putative pretheoretic knowledge, which though revisable at the margins was taken to be, on the whole, beyond serious doubt. In the case of logicism this domain was our knowledge of arithmetic and other branches of mathematics; in the case of the external world it was our knowledge of physical science, and of the truth of most ordinary judgments about "physical objects." The second subtask was to identify a minimal set of underlying notions to be used to identify analytically primitive judgments or axioms, plus

[14] In Russell (1905) and (1919, chap. 16).
[15] In Russell (1912).

definitions from which the overwhelming majority of the pretheoretic claims taken as data could be analyzed/derived. Russell did not require the underlying axioms or definitions to be self-evidently obvious. It was enough that they could be used to explain how the pretheoretic claims under analysis could be known to be true while avoiding puzzles and paradoxes generated by the gratuitous postulation of entities the nature and existence of which we have no way of knowing.

Russell makes his methodology explicit in lecture 1 of Russell (1918–19). His aim was to outline the structure of a world we are capable of knowing, based on the ideas that (i) most of what we are given by the empirical and deductive sciences, and by the most fundamental judgments of common sense, is true and capable of being known; (ii) although we are justifiably confident of this, we do not know the real content of these truths; and (iii) the job of analysis is to elucidate this content, thereby explaining how we do, or at least could come to, know it. He warns that we can't anticipate the end result of analysis in advance and admonishes us not to dismiss what may seem to be highly revisionary characterizations of the knowable content of pretheoretic claims. At this point one wonders, is the task to explain what justifies the vast pretheoretic knowledge we already have, or is it to articulate what our evidence really justifies, and hence *what we could come to know if we adopted a frankly revisionary view of the world*. Although Russell often speaks as if he adheres to the first conception, the results he reaches suggest the second.

Applying his method to physics, he says:

> You find, if you read the words of physicists, that they reduce matter down to . . . very tiny bits of matter that are still just like matter in the fact that they persist through time, and that they travel through space. . . . Things of that sort, I say, are not the ultimate constituents of matter in any metaphysical sense. . . . *Those things are all of them . . . logical fictions. . . . It is possible that there may be all these things that the physicist talks about in actual reality, but it is impossible that we should have any reason whatsoever for supposing that there are.* (1918–19, 143–44; my emphasis)

Although this sounds startling—*Nothing really persists through time or moves through space?*—it is simply a recapitulation of the view for which Russell argues in *Our Knowledge of the External World*. There he maintains that the only *knowledge* we use material-object sentences (from physics or everyday life) to express is *knowledge of our own private sense data plus the private sense data of others*. The task he envisions (but only vaguely sketches) is that of translating all material-object sentences into other statements (logical forms of the originals) in which only agents and their sense data are explicitly mentioned. It is only in this way, he thinks, that one can capture what science really teaches, along with what we *justifiably* report when we talk about things like tables, chairs, desks, or human bodies. Although he takes it to be possible to imagine epistemically inaccessible entities beyond our sense data, he takes it to be *impossible* to provide any empirical justification for such speculative claims, which are unknowable.

The new element in Russell (1918–919) is his treatment of all sentient agents as *logical fictions*. Previously, he had regarded other minds as theoretical posits the justification of which was that they were needed in the logical construction of material objects. Since, in the presence of his implicit epistemology, this move had all the virtues of an appeal to the unknowable axiom of infinity to "explain" our knowledge of arithmetic, he needed to eliminate minds in his mature atomism. In the view outlined in lecture 8 of Russell (1918–19), each agent is a series of experiences that bear a similarity relation dubbed "*being experiences of the same person.*" Of course, series, along with classes, are *logical fictions* for Russell, so no persons or other agents *really* exist. The only genuinely existing particulars are momentary, private sense data. Some of these—call them "M-experiences"—are "mine," and others—call them "J-experiences"—are "Jones's." All M-experiences bear the relation *being experiences-of-one-person* to one another, and to nothing else, while all J-experiences bear that relation to one another, and to nothing else (including the M-experiences). So, when I say that *I exist* all I am really saying is that certain experiences are M-related. The same goes for Jones; when he says that *he exists* all he is saying is that other experiences are J-related.

The end result is a conception of reality in which all particulars are momentary sense data bearing certain relations to other sense data. Allowing ourselves some useful "logical fictions," we can describe these particulars as arranged into two different cross-cutting systems of "classes"—those that constitute "agents" and those that constitute the things—like tables, chairs, human bodies, etc. —which we pretheoretically (but ultimately misleadingly) describe "agents" as "perceiving." To be sure, Russell doesn't claim to know this fantastic conception of the universe to be correct. Still, it is his last pre-Tractarian stab at the truth. Who would have thought that supposedly hard-headed logical and linguistic analysis would lead to a metaphysical system as thoroughly revisionary of our ordinary conception of ourselves and the world presented to us in science or in ordinary life? More revisionary than Berkeley's system, Russell's analytic revisionism may surpass the dreamlike conception of Reality proposed by McTaggart (1921, 1927) as an eternal, unchanging community of human souls. If one thought that the new tradition in analytic philosophy had left such extravagant metaphysical speculation behind, Russell's example should convince one otherwise.

How did "logical analysis" lead to such a stupefying metaphysical vision? It did so because for Russell it was merely a tool in the service of a highly restrictive antecedent conception of what is required for empirical knowledge.[16] For the most part, he simply took it for granted without extended examination that perceptual evidence can't justify claims about genuine three-dimensional objects persisting through time which continue to exist whether they or not they are perceived. In addition to this implicit presupposition about what knowledge must be, he was committed to an unusual sort of fidelity to most of our ordinary knowledge claims about ourselves, material objects, and the deliverances of science. Taking the pretheoretic content of these to be utterly opaque to us—much as Frege, more understandably, took our pretheoretic conception of number to be essentially blank—Russell required that *the sentences* used to express what we pretheoretically take to be empirically known be capable of being systematically assigned contents that can be seen to be both true and justified by the restrictive body of sense experience he took to be available to us as evidence. In brief, a narrow and largely unreflective conception of what knowledge and justification consisted in, coupled with a commitment to speak with the vulgar, set the parameters for what counted as correct logic-linguistic analyses. "Analysis" yielded the results that it did, because, at this stage, it was merely a tool in the service of Russell's independent philosophical ends.

In assessing Russell's methodology concerning our knowledge of the empirical world it is instructive to compare his approach with that of Moore, as expressed in Moore (1909; lectures 5 and 6 of 1910–11; 1925; and 1939). When Moore took it to be evident that he knew that there were human hands, pencils, and what not, on the basis of perception, he did *not* mean merely that the *sentences* he used to report this knowledge could be assigned *some content or other* that would make them come out true and knowable. On the contrary, in Moore (1910–11, 1925) he rules out phemonenalistic "analyses" of the sort advocated by Russell as *not* capturing the content of what he pretheoretically knows. The great failure of Moore's epistemology was, of course, that he was never able to make clear just how it is that perceptual evidence justifies

---

[16] What conception is that? As a rule of thumb, it is the following: What the logical positivists were later to declare to be meaningless, because unverifiable, Russell at this stage merely labeled as in principle unknowable, and unjustifiable. This conception is discussed in chapter 11 of Soames (2014).

what he rightly took himself to know.[17] However, this does not negate the crucial Moorean lesson: *Broad philosophical theories about knowledge are answerable to our firmest pretheoretic convictions involving particular things that we know, which cannot be arbitrarily reconstrued, or overturned wholesale, when they conflict with philosophical theory.*

It is also instructive to contrast Frege's and Russell's transparent conceptions of meaning with their practice of assigning contents to sentences subject to philosophical analysis. When Frege presented his strategy for the logicist reduction he contended that "the content" of sentences about numbers was, in effect, given by his ingenious set-theoretical translations of them. However, it was not clear in 1884 what his notion of "content" was supposed to come to, since this was well before his distinction between sense and reference in Frege (1892). Moreover, it is clear that Fregean translations of ordinary sentences of arithmetic do not share the Fregean senses expressed by the arithmetical originals—since an agent who understands both may sincerely assent to one without assenting to the other. A similar point holds for Russell's version of logicism. Given the usual criteria employed by both philosophers for determining when two expressions, or sentences, mean the same thing (think of Russell on logically proper names), the pretheoretically given sentences undergoing logicist analysis do *not* mean the same thing as the sentences that provide the analyses. This is all the more evident for Russell's phenomenalist reduction of statements about the external world to statements about sense data. Thus there appears to be a sharp conflict between introspectivist accounts that take meaning to be highly transparent, seemingly favored by Frege and Russell, with some of their more ambitions philosophical claims about the fruits of logico-linguistic analysis. One way of dealing with this tension would be to take the results of "analysis" to replace, rather than explicate, the claims being analyzed. It is significant, however, that neither philosopher adopted this strategy forthrightly and consistently.

Up to now, I haven't said anything about modality. Since the distinction between necessary and contingent truth is mostly irrelevant when it comes to mathematics, it is not surprising that Frege and Russell were not concerned with it when developing their logicist views. However, when the focus of loco-linguistic "analysis" shifts to the external world, the distinction between what could and could not be, as well as between what would, as versus what wouldn't, be if various conditions were fulfilled, becomes relevant. Although Russell paid very little

---

[17] For attempts to improve on Moore, see Pryor (2000, 2004).

attention to these issues, he did not ignore them entirely, as illustrated by the following passage from Russell (1918–19):

> Particulars have this peculiarity, among the sort of objects that you have to take account of in an inventory of the world, *that each of them stands entirely alone and is completely self-subsistent.* It has the sort of self-subsistence that used to belong to substance, except that it usually only persists through a very short time. That is to say, *each particular that there is in the world does not in any way logically depend upon any other particular. Each one might happen to be the whole universe; it is merely an empirical fact that this is not the case.* There is no reason why you should not have a universe consisting of one particular and nothing else. That is a peculiarity of a particular. In the same way, in order to understand a name for a particular, the one thing necessary is to be acquainted with that particular. When you are acquainted with that particular, you have a full, adequate, and complete understanding of the name, and no further information is required. (p. 63; my emphasis)

In speaking of "particulars" Russell means his ultimate metaphysical simples—the momentary sense data named by logically proper names in the logically perfect language he imagines emerging at the end of analysis. Once this stage is reached, our description of the world will include names for all such particulars plus claims (quantified and otherwise) to the effect that they have various simple (unanalyzable) properties and stand in various such relations to one another. The point to notice about the passage is the way in which the *logical* independence of metaphysical simples is linked with their *modal or metaphysical* independence. Does Russell think that each simple concrete particular is *logically* independent of all others because each *could* exist in splendid isolation from all others, or is it the other way around? Although he may not have clearly distinguished the two, it is the latter that is most noteworthy here. What reason is there to think that each such particular could exist all by itself? Let n be a logically proper name of a concrete particular o. Since $\ulcorner \sim \forall x \; x = n \urcorner$ isn't a logical truth, it is *logically possible* for o to be the only existing concrete particular. The implicit (unargued) suggestion is that all logical possibility is modal or metaphysical possibility—in which case it will follow that it is *metaphysically possible* for o to be the only existing concrete particular. Since the converse inference is likely to seem even more plausible, I suspect that Russell implicitly takes modal necessity/possibility and logical necessity/possibility to coincide (despite the evident implausibility of supposing that a single sense datum, e.g., a single tactile sensation of hardness, could have existed by itself in the universe.)[18]

Next, notice his implicit assertion that for any concrete particular o, the claim that o isn't the only existing thing is "empirical," and hence *can be known only aposteriori*. Why would that be? Well, if all apriori truths are logically necessary, then the fact that the claim expressed by ⌜∼ ∀x x = n⌝ (where n names o) isn't logically necessary shows that it can't be known apriori. For one who shares Russell's grand vision of analysis, this reduction of epistemic modality to logical modality is well-nigh irresistible. It is a central aim of logical atomism to replace unanalyzed terms, predicates, and sentences/propositions—which may stand in conceptual relations to one another—with logically proper names, simple unanalyzable predicates, and fully analyzed sentences/ propositions. When this aim is achieved, the conceptual properties of, and relations holding among, unanalyzed expressions and sentences/ propositions are traced to genuinely logical properties of, and relations holding among, fully analyzed sentences/propositions of one's logically perfect underlying language. To take a simple example, it is knowable apriori that all squares are rectangles because the unanalyzed sentence *all squares are rectangles* is reduced, on analysis, to the fully analyzed logical form *all rectangles with equal sides are rectangles*, which is *logically necessary*—and hence knowable apriori. The idea that analyses with similar results can be carried through whenever we encounter conceptual dependencies in unanalyzed language is a driving force behind logical atomism. In this way, Russell is led down a path that makes a reduction of epistemic and metaphysical modalities to logical ones seem plausible.

When one moves to *The Tractatus*—Wittgenstein (1922)—one finds a superficially similar system of logical atomism that is put to a remarkably different purpose. Like Russell, Wittgenstein posits a multiplicity of metaphysical simples denoted by logically proper names of an imagined logically perfect language. However, his conception of the aim of analysis was not epistemic. Whereas Russell's aim was to find the right substratum for explaining all ordinary and scientific knowledge, Wittgenstein's was to articulate a parallel between language and reality that would make sense of his thesis that metaphysical necessity

---

[18] Not that he explicitly says so. On the contrary, his use of normally modal terms like "possible" and "necessary" is decidedly idiosyncratic. However, it is hard for anyone to get along without sometimes implicitly invoking metaphysically modal notions—as he does in using counterfactual conditionals in his informal discussion of the reduction in Russell (1914), and as he does in Russell (1918–19) in discussing possible states that the universe could be, or have been, in.

and epistemological apriority are logical necessity and nothing more.[19] In his picture, metaphysical simples are eternal, unchanging bare particulars with no intrinsic "material" properties of their own but with the possibility of combining with other simples to form atomic facts.[20] For every possible atomic fact, there is an atomic sentence of the ideal language that would be made true were the fact actually to exist.[21] Just as every atomic sentence (which specifies various simples as standing in one or another relation) is logically independent of every other such sentence, so every possible atomic fact is metaphysically independent of any other. Just as every assignment of truth values to atomic sentences is logically possible, so every corresponding combination of possible atomic facts is a (complete) genuinely possible way the world could have been. In keeping with this, Wittgenstein held that all meaningful sentences are truth functions of atomic sentences, which is itself quite remarkable despite the fact the he had a rather rich conception of truth functionality.[22] Thus, a specification of the atomic facts making up a possible world-state determines the truth value of every meaningful sentence at that world-state.[23] The "tautologies," which are made true by every assignment of truth values to atomic sentences, are true at every possible world-state; the logical contradictions, which are not made true by any assignment, are true at no possible world-states; and all other meaningful sentences are true at some world-states, but not others.[24] To understand a sentence is to know the possible world-states at which it is true.

Since all possible facts are atomic facts, there are no necessary facts for "tautologies" to state. Since they are true at all possible world-states, understanding them and knowing them to be true doesn't give one any information about the actual world-state—the way things actually are—that distinguishes it from any other merely possible ways things might be. This leads Wittgenstein to claim that "tautologies" are empty; they don't *say* anything.[25] They are simply the result of having a symbol system that includes truth-functional operators. So, Wittgenstein thought, whether something is a tautology should be determined

---

[19] Chapter 1 of Fogelin (1987) presents a clear and insightful sketch of the essential elements of tractarian metaphysics.

[20] *Tractatus* 2.01–2.033.

[21] *Tractatus* 3.2, 3.203, 3.21, 4.06, 4.1, 4.2, 4.21, 4.22, 4.211.

[22] *Tractatus* 3.31–3.315, 5, 5.2521, 5.2522, 5.254–5.32, 5.501, 5.552–5.523, 5.54, 6, 6.01. For detailed discussion of the account of truth function operations in the *Tractatus,* see Soames (2003, chap. 11).

[23] *Tractatus* 2.04, 4.26.

[24] *Tractatus* 4.06, 4.062, 4.46.

[25] Tractatus 4.46.

(and in principle be discoverable) by (examining) its form alone.[26] Thus we have (i)–(iii):[27]

(i) All necessity is linguistic necessity, in that it is the result of our system of representing the world, rather than the world itself. There are sentences that are necessarily true, but there are no necessary facts that correspond to them. These sentences tell us nothing about the world; rather, their necessity is due to the meanings of words (and therefore is knowable apriori).

(ii) All linguistic necessity is logical necessity.

(iii) Logical necessity is determinable by form alone.

With these doctrines in place, it was a short step to the Tractarian test for intelligibility. According to the *Tractatus*, every meaningful statement S falls into one of two categories: either (i) S is contingent (true at some possible world-states and false at others), in which case S is both a truth function of atomic propositions and something that can be known to be true or false only by empirical investigation; or (ii) S is a tautology or contradiction that can be known to be such by purely formal calculations. The paradigmatic cases of meaningful sentences are those in the first category. The sentences in the second category are included as meaningful because they are the inevitable product of the rules governing the logical vocabulary used in constructing sentences of the first category. For Wittgenstein, tautologies and contradictions don't state anything, or give any information about the world. But their truth or falsity can be calculated, and understanding them reveals something about our symbol system. Thus, they can be regarded as meaningful in an extended sense.

It was this doctrine about the limits of meaning/intelligibility, more than anything else, that captured the attention of analytic philosophers like Carnap in the 1920s and 1930s. Wittgenstein's route to the doctrine— via an utterly fantastic metaphysics and a completely unrealistic conception of an ideal, logically perfect language, somehow underlying our ordinary thought and talk—were, by and large, treated as baggage that could be dispensed with, so long as the emerging view of philosophy as nothing more than the logical analysis of language—scientific, mathematical, and/or ordinary—could be preserved and extended.

Indeed, it was this uncompromising view of philosophy that emerged from the *Tractatus* which had the strongest, the most immediate, and the most lasting impact. Just as, according to Wittgenstein, the most

---

[26] *Tractatus* 5.551, 6.126.
[27] *Tractatus* 6.1, 6.31, 6.37, 6.3751.

fundamental ethical claims are neither tautologies nor contingent statements about empirically knowable facts, so philosophical claims are, in general, neither tautological nor contingent statements about empirical facts. Like ethical sentences, they are non-sense. Hence, there are no meaningful philosophical sentences; there are no genuine philosophical questions; and there are no philosophical problems for philosophers to solve. It is not that philosophical problems are so difficult that we can never be sure we have discovered the truth about them. There is no such thing as the truth about them, because there are no philosophical problems.[28]

This view, dramatically expressed in the *Tractatus*, was taken over in less flamboyant form by Carnap and other logical positivists by the early 1930s.[29] The key *Tractarian* inheritance was the distinction between analytic and synthetic sentences, the former being empty of empirical content and knowable apriori on the basis of understanding their meanings alone, and the latter being contingent, knowable only aposteriori, and subject to one or another version of the verifiability criterion of meaning. There was, of course, also a substantial remnant of Russell in the appeal to sense experience as the touchstone of empirical meaning, which in turn led to a resurgence of phenomenalism in some quarters.[30] Despite the official exclusion of metaphysics, ethics, and other forms of traditional philosophical speculation, there was, of course, plenty of work for Carnap and his band of scientifically minded philosophers to do in attempting to work out precise and detailed formulations of what was to prove to be a very difficult view to sustain. It was at this stage that logical and linguistic analysis was officially proclaimed to be the essence of philosophy, rather than merely a powerful tool to be employed in the service of more or less traditional philosophical ends. Thus it is in Carnap (1934) that we find the bold philosophical manifesto "Philosophy is to be replaced by the logic of science—that is to say by the logical analysis of concepts and sentences of the sciences" (p. 292 of the English translation).

Looking back at the first 55 years of analytic philosophy, from Frege's *Begriffsschrift* to Carnap's *The Logical Structure of Language*, one finds enormous philosophical progress, especially in philosophical logic, the philosophy of mathematics, and the philosophy of language, but few enduring positive lessons about philosophical methodology and the role of analysis in philosophy. Despite the enormous advance of logicist

---

[28] *Tractatus* 4.11, 4.111, 4.112, 6.42, 6.423, 6.5-6.521, 6.53, 6.54, 7.

[29] For illuminating early statements of the positivist view, and its debt to Wittgenstein, see Schlick (1930–31), Carnap (1932), and the introduction to Ayer (1959).

[30] See, for example, Carnap (1928), Ayer (1936), Ayer (1940), and Schlick(1934).

philosophy of mathematics over what had preceded it, attempts to use the logicist conception of analysis as an excuse to rewrite the content of what is pretheoretically known in other areas to fit largely unexamined preconceptions about knowledge did not meet with very much success. Nor did the linguistic turn in philosophy—based as it was on an unfortunate conflation of the logical, linguistic, epistemic, and metaphysical modalities—provide a solid and broad-based foundation for linguistic and logical analysis. By contrast, Moore's reminder that ordinary pretheoretic convictions have a useful (though limited and fallible) role to play in evaluating philosophical theories was, though modest (when properly understood), of lasting value.

Other than that, my favorite statement of philosophical methodology from the period was an almost throw-away comment by Russell in lecture 8 of Russell (1918–19).

> I believe the only difference between science and philosophy is that science is what you more or less know and philosophy is what you do not know. Philosophy is that part of science which at present people choose to have opinions about, but which they have no knowledge about. Therefore every advance in knowledge robs philosophy of some problems which formerly it had, and if there is any truth, if there is any value in the kind of procedure of mathematical logic, it will follow that a number of problems which had belonged to philosophy will have ceased to belong to philosophy and will belong to science. (p. 154)

The point, as I would summarize it, is that philosophy is the way we approach problems that are presently too elusive to be investigated scientifically. The goal is to frame questions, explore possible solutions, and forge conceptual tools needed to advance to a more definitive stage of investigation. If one looks back at the philosophers in the first 60 years of the analytic tradition, it is impossible not to be impressed with their seminal contributions to the development of modern symbolic logic in all its present richness, the mathematical theory of computation, as well as to later advances in cognitive science and computational theories of mind, including the formulation of productive frameworks for investigating the semantics of natural human languages (to which the contributions of Frege and Russell can hardly be overestimated). These are, of course, only a few of the most obvious achievements of many ongoing lines of philosophical investigation initiated during the founding period of analytic philosophy. To my mind, they are far more important than the manifest philosophical failures that seem all too obvious when we focus narrowly on the shortcomings of individual philosophical projects and systems.

REFERENCES

Ayer, A. J. 1936. *Language, Truth, and Logic*. London: Gollancz; 2nd ed., 1946.
———. 1940. *The Foundations of Empirical Knowledge*. London: Macmillan.
———. 1959. ed. *Logical Positivism*. New York: Free Press.
Beaney, Michael, ed. 1997.*The Frege Reader*. Oxford: Blackwell.
Boolos, George. 1994. "The Advantages of Honest Toil over Theft," in Alexander George, ed., *Mathematics and Mind*. Oxford: Oxford University Press; reprinted in Boolos 1998.
———. 1988. *Logic, Logic, Logic*. Cambridge, MA: Harvard University Press.
Burgess, John. 2005. *Fixing Frege*. Princeton, NJ: Princeton University Press.
Carnap, Rudolf. 1928. *Der logische Aufbau der Welt*. Berlin-Schlachtensee: Weltkreis-Verlag; translated and reprinted as *The Logical Structure of the World*. Berkeley and Los Angeles: University of California Press, 1969.
———. 1932. "Überwindung der Metaphysik durch logische Analyse der Sprache," *Erkenntnis*, II; translated and reprinted as "The Elimination of Metaphysics through the Analysis of Language" in Ayer 1959.
———. 1934. *Logische Syntax der Sprache*, Schriften zur wissenschaftlichen Weltauffassung, hrsg. von Philipp Frank und Moritz Schlick, Band 8. Vienna: Verlag von Julius Springer. Translated as *The Logical Syntax of Language*. London: Kegan Paul, 1937.
Frege, Gottlob. 1879. *Begriffsschrift*, Halle, a. S., secs. 1–82; selections translated by Michael Beaney, ed., in *The Frege Reader*, 47–78. Oxford: Blackwell, 1997.
———. 1884. *Die Grundlagen der Arithmetik*. Breslau: Verlag von Wilhelm Koebner. Translated by J. L. Austin as *The Foundations of Arithmetic*. Oxford: Blackwell, 1950.
———. 1892. "Über Sinn und Bedeutung." *Zeitschrift fur Philosophie und philosophische Kritik*. Translated as "On Sense and Reference" by Max Black, in Peter Geach and Max Black, eds., *Translations from the Philosophical Writings of Gottlob Frege*. Oxford: Blackwell, 1970.
———. 1893. *Grundgesetze der Arithmetik*, vol. 1. Jena: H. Pole. Translated and edited as *The Basic Laws of Arithmetic*, vol. 1, by M. Furth. Berkeley and Los Angeles: University of California Press, 1964. Selections translated by Michael Beaney in Beaney 1997, 194–223.
———. 1903. *Grundgesetze der Arithmetik*, vol. 2. Jena: H. Pole. Translated and edited as *The Basic Laws of Arithmetic*, vol. 2, by M. Furth. Berkeley and Los Angeles: University of California Press, 1964. Selections translated by Michael Beaney in Beaney 1997, 258–89.
Fogelin, Robert. 1987. *Wittgenstein*. London and New York: Routledge.
Gödel, Kurt. 1944. "Russell's Mathematical Logic." in Schilpp, P. A., ed. 1944. *The Philosophy of Bertrand Russell*. Library of the Living Philosophers. La Salle, IL: Open Court.
Hodes, Harold. 2012. "Why Ramify?" Unpublished manuscript.
Klement, Kevin. 2004. "Putting Form before Function: Logical Grammar in Frege, Russell, and Wittgenstein." *Philosophers Imprint* 4 (no. 2): 1–47.

Landini, Greg. 1998. *Russell's Hidden Substitutional Theory*. Oxford: Oxford University Press.

McTaggart, J.M.E. 1921, 1927. *The Nature of Existence*, 2 vols. Cambridge: Cambridge University Press.

Moore, G. E. 1909. "Hume's Philosophy." *New Quarterly* (November); reprinted in Moore 1922.

———. 1910–11; 1985. *Some Main Problems of Philosophy*. London: George Allen and Unwin.

———. 1922. *Philosophical Studies*. London: Routledge and Kegan Paul.

———. 1925. "A Defense of Common Sense," in J. H. Muirhead, ed., *Contemporary British Philosophy*, 2nd ser. New York: Macmillan; reprinted in Moore 1958.

———. 1939. "Proof of an External World." *Proceedings of the British Academy* 25:273–300; reprinted in Moore 1958.

———. 1958. *Philosophical Papers*. London: George Allen and Unwin.

Pryor, James. 2000. "The Skeptic and the Dogmatist." *Nous* 34:517–49.

———. 2004. "What's Wrong with Moore's Argument?" *Philosophical Issues* 14:349–77.

Russell, Bertrand. 1905. "On Denoting." *Mind* 14:479–93.

———. 1907. "The Regressive Method of Discovering the Premises of Mathematics." Published posthumously in Douglas Lackey, ed., *Essays in Analysis*. New York: George Braziller, 1973.

———. 1912. *The Problems of Philosophy*. London: Williams and Norgate: New York: Henry Holt; reprinted. New York and Oxford: Oxford University Press, 1997.

———. 1914. *Our Knowledge of the External World*. Chicago and London: Open Court.

———. 1918–19. "The Philosophy of Logical Atomism." *Monist* 5 (no. 28): 495–527; continued in *Monist* 5 (no. 29): 32–63, 190–222, 345–80; reprinted in *The Philosophy of Logical Atomism*, with an introduction by David Pears. Peru, IL: Open Court , 1985; text citations are to the 1985 reprint.

———. 1919. *Introduction to Mathematical Philosophy*. London: George Allen and Unwin; reprinted, New York: Dover, 1993.

———. 1940. *An Inquiry into Meaning and Truth*. London: Unwin.

———. 1959. *My Philosophical Development*. London: Routledge.

Russell, Bertrand, and Alfred North Whitehead. 1910. *Principia Mathematica*, vol. 1. Cambridge: Cambridge University Press. Page numbers of citations in the text are to a later edition, *Principia Mathematica to *56*. Cambridge: Cambridge University Press, 1973.

Schlick, Moritz. 1930–31. "Die Wende der Philosophie." *Erkenntnis* 1; translated and reprinted as "The Turning Point in Philosophy," in Ayer 1959.

———. 1934. "Über das Fundament der Erkenntnis." *Erkenntnis* 4; translated and reprinted as "The Foundation of Knowledge," in Ayer 1959.

Soames, Scott. 2003. *Philosophical Analysis in the Twentieth Century*, vol. 1. Princeton, NJ, and Oxford: Princeton University Press.

———. 2014. *The Analytic Tradition in Philosophy*, vol. 1. Princeton, NJ, and Oxford: Princeton University Press.

Wittgenstein, Ludwig. 1922. *Tractatus Logico-Philosophicus*. English translation by C. K. Ogden, London: Routledge.

3

Language, Meaning, and Information

A CASE STUDY ON THE PATH FROM
PHILOSOPHY TO SCIENCE

Near the beginning of the final lecture of *The Philosophy of Logical Atomism*, in 1918, Bertrand Russell articulates a view of the relationship between philosophy and science for which there is much to be said. He says:

> I believe the only difference between science and philosophy is that science is what you more or less know and philosophy is what you do not know. Philosophy is that part of science which at present people choose to have opinions about, but which they have no knowledge about. Therefore every advance in knowledge robs philosophy of some problems which formerly it had . . . [and] a number of problems which had belonged to philosophy will have ceased to belong to philosophy and will belong to science. (p. 154)

In short, philosophy is the way we approach problems that are presently too elusive to be investigated scientifically. The goal is to frame questions, explore possible solutions, and forge conceptual tools needed to advance to a more definitive stage of investigation. My topic is the case study of this form of philosophical progress provided by the study of language, meaning, and information in the past 132 years.

The story begins with the development of modern symbolic logic instigated by Gottlob Frege and Bertrand Russell at the end of the nineteenth and beginning of the twentieth centuries. Initially, their goal was to answer two questions in the philosophy of mathematics: *What is the source of mathematical knowledge?* and *What are numbers?* They answered that *logic* is the source of mathematical knowledge, that *zero* is the set of concepts true of nothing, that *one* is the set of concepts that are true of something, and of only that thing, that *two* is the set of concepts true of some distinct x and y, and nothing else—and so on. Since the concept *being non-self-identical is true of nothing*, it is a member of the number zero; since the concept *being this year's Selfridge lecturer* is true of me and only me, it is a member of the number one; since the concept *being my child* is true of Greg and Brian Soames, and only them, it is a member of the number two. Other integers follow in train. Since numbers are sets of concepts, the successor of a number n is the set of concepts F such that for some object x of which F is true, the concept *being an F which is not identical to x* is a member of the number n. With zero and successor under our belts, we define the class of natural numbers as the smallest class that contains zero and that, whenever it contains something, always contains the successor of that thing. With this background in place, multiplication is defined as repeated addition, addition is defined in terms of counting, and counting is seen as repeated moving from a number to its successor. In this way all arithmetic was derived from what Frege and Russell took to be pure logic. When, in similar fashion, classical results of higher mathematics were derived from arithmetic, it was thought that all classical mathematics could be so generated. *In short, logic was seen the foundation of all mathematical knowledge.*

That was Frege and Russell's breathtaking dream. The reality was more complex. The first step in the project was the development of the modern *predicate calculus,* which combined traditional truth-functional logic—familiar from the Stoics onward—with a powerful new account of quantification (expressed by the words 'all' and 'some') supplanting the more limited syllogistic logic dating to Aristotle. The key move was to trade-in the subject/predicate distinction of syllogistic logic for an expanded version of the function/argument distinction from mathematics. Applied to quantification, this meant treating the claims expressed by ⌜Something is F⌝ and ⌜Everything is G⌝ as predicating *being instantiated* of the concept expressed by F and *being universally instantiated* of the concept expressed by G. The result was an enormous increase in expressive power.

Although Frege's first-order version of this system was sound and complete—in the sense of proving all and only genuine logical truths—the concepts needed to precisely state and prove this meta-metalogical result were still 50 years away. In itself, this didn't interfere with the reduction of mathematics to logic. More serious was the fact that at this early stage modern logic was intertwined with what is now called "naïve set theory"—according to which for every well-formed condition on objects statable in one's language there is a set—perhaps empty, perhaps not—of all and only the things satisfying that condition. To think of this as a principle of logic is to think that *talk* about an individual's *being so-and-so* is interchangeable with talk about it being in the set, or class, of things that are so-and-so.

When Russell's paradox demonstrated the contradiction at the heart of naïve set theory, the consequences for the project of reducing mathematics to logic were profound. It immediately became clear that the principles required to generate sets without falling into contradiction are less obvious, and subject to more genuine doubt, than the arithmetical principles that Frege and Russell hoped to derive from them. This undercut the strong initial epistemological motivation for reducing mathematics to logic. Partly for this reason, the ultimate demarcation between logic and set theory that worked itself out over the next few decades was one in which set theory came to be viewed by most as itself a kind of elementary mathematical theory, rather than a part of logic. Although reductions of arithmetic and classical mathematics to set theory could still be done, with illuminating results for the foundations of mathematics, the philosophical payoff was not as great as Frege and Russell first imagined. The philosophy of mathematics had made real progress, but its fundamental problems had not been solved.

This *philosophical* shortcoming was compensated for by the birth of new *scientific* investigations. Powerful systems of logic had been developed, together with new deductive disciplines—proof theory and model theory—to study them. A system of logic in the modern sense consists of a formally defined language, plus a proof procedure, often in the form of a set of axioms and rules of inference. A proof is a finite sequence of lines each of which is an axiom or a formula obtainable from earlier lines by inference rules. Whether something counts as a proof is decidable merely by inspecting the formula on each line and determining whether it is an axiom, and if it isn't, whether it bears the structural relation to earlier lines required by the rules. Since these are trivially decidable questions, it can always be decided whether something counts as a proof, thus forestalling the need to prove that something is a proof.

In a purely logical system, the aim is to prove all and only the *logical truths* as theorems and to be able to derive from any statement all and only its *logical consequences*. *Logical truth* and *logical consequence* are defined semantically. To think of these as semantic notions is, of course, to think of them as having something to do with *meaning*. Although this wasn't exactly how the founder of model theory, Alfred Tarski, initially conceived them, it is how his work was interpreted by Rudolf Carnap and many who followed. The key idea, in this interpretation, is that *we can study the meaning of sentences by studying what would make them true*. This is done by constructing abstract models of the world and checking to see which sentences are true in which models. When a sentence is true in all models it is a logical truth; when the truth of one sentence in a model always guarantees the truth of another, the second is a *logical consequence* of the first; when two sentences are always true together or false together they are *logically equivalent*, which is the logician's model for having the same meaning.

By the end of World War II the model and proof theories of the Frege-Russell predicate calculi were well understood, and philosophers were already building new projects on this foundation. The first new aim was to construct logical systems in which an operator—variously interpreted as *it is logically true that, it is analytically true that,* or *it is necessarily true that*—is added to the predicate calculus so that prefixing it to a standard logical truth produces a truth. Since the operator can be iterated, and so applied to its own output, the resulting logic is more complex than that. But apart from problems answering the question, *What is the logical, semantic, or metaphysical notion to be captured?* the technical ideas were pretty clear. Since these modal operators express operations defined in terms of truth at *model-like* elements, *logical models* for modal languages must contain such elements, often dubbed *possible world-states*. These are the items—thought of as *ways the world could have been (i.e., properties the world could have had)*—relative to which terms have referents and sentences are true or false.

Let S be a sentence that is interpreted by a model M. To say that *sentence S is true at world-state w of model M* is to claim that *what S says, when interpreted by M, would be true if the world were in state w*. In other words, S is true at w iff the way that S represents the world as being is a way the world would be if the world were in state w. With this understanding of what it is for S to be true *at a world-state*, one may (i) take the claim ⌜It is necessary that S⌝ to be true iff S is true at every world-state, (ii) take the claim ⌜It could have been true that S⌝ to be true iff S is true at some world-state, and (iii) take the claim ⌜If it had been the case that S, then it would have been the case that R⌝ to be true at w iff among the world-states at which S is true, some states at which R is true are more similar to w than are any world-states at which R is false.

As before, *logical truth* and *logical consequence* are defined in terms of truth in a model; this time the basic notion is truth at *a world* in a model. Logical equivalence is then sameness of truth value at all worlds of all models, which remains the logician's approximation of sameness of meaning. Proof and model theory for modal systems—to which Saul Kripke made famous contributions in the 1950s—are complicated versions of similar theories for propositional and predicate calculi. Although it remains controversial which axiomatic systems of modal logic are correct, this is owing in part to the fact that there are different modal notions to be formalized.

This new logical project brought with it a new philosophical focus. Frege's and Russell's interest in logic had been rooted in its role in answering their questions about mathematics. Since there are no distinctions between necessary and contingent truths of mathematics, the new interest in logics of necessity and possibility came from different sources. One source was the ubiquity of modal reasoning in philosophy itself, as well as its potential use in empirical science. Another, more important, source came from the Fregean conception of language that informed the development of logic from the start. In that conception, *for S to be meaningful is for it to represent the world as being a certain way, which is to impose conditions the world must satisfy if it is to be the way S represents it.* Since these are the truth conditions of S, being meaningful involves having truth conditions. Hence, it was thought, the systematic study of meaning requires a framework for specifying the truth conditions of sentences on the basis of their grammatical structure and the representational contents of their parts. This had already been achieved, to a limited extent, by the model theory of the predicate calculus. With modal logic, the truth conditions of sentences provided by an intended model plus the theory of truth at a world of a model were, *for the first time*, strong enough to be realistic approximations of the *meanings* of sentences. To learn *what the world would have to be like* to conform to the way a sentence represents it to be *is* to learn something approximating its meaning.

The significance of this development for the study of language can hardly be overestimated. What started with Frege and Russell as the development of logical tools to help answer philosophical questions about mathematics first transformed into the development of set theory plus metatheories of the predicate calculi. Next, it expanded to incorporate richer logical systems, which in turn, provided the basis for a systematic study of linguistically encoded information, that could, in principle, be applied to all languages. Having reached this stage, we had both a putative answer to the question, *What is the meaning of a sentence S?* and a systematic way of studying meaning. The putative answer is that the meaning of S is its truth conditions, which are modeled by the set of those states w such that if the world were in w, then it would be as S represents it to be. The systematic method for studying meaning is to derive these truth conditions compositionally, from the interpretations of words occurring in the sentences. With this, one has a theoretical framework that can be applied to languages in general.

This is where the philosophically inspired study of linguistically encoded information stood in 1960. Since then, philosophers, philosophical logicians, and theoretical linguists have expanded the framework to cover large fragments of human languages. The research program—to which Saul Kripke, Richard Montague, David Kaplan, Robert Stalnaker, David Lewis, Hans Kamp, Barbara Partee, Angelica Kratzer, Irene Heim, and others have contributed—starts with the predicate calculi and is enriched piece by piece as more constructions found in languages like English, Japanese, and Hindi are added.

I have mentioned modal operators and counterfactual conditionals (*if it had been the case that __, then it would have been the case that __*). Operators involving time and tense can be treated along similar lines. Generalized quantifiers have been added, as have adverbs of quantification, and propositional attitude verbs such as *believe, expect,* and *know.* There are also accounts of adverbial modifiers, intensional transitives, indexicals, and demonstratives. At each stage, a language fragment for which we already have a truth-theoretic semantics is expanded to include more features found in natural language. As the research program advances, and more such features are incorporated, the fragments of which we have a good truth-theoretic grasp become more powerful and more fully natural-language like. Extending results so far achieved, one can imagine a time at which vastly enriched descendants of the original logical languages of Frege and Russell approach, or even match, the expressive power of natural language—allowing us to understand the principles by which information is encoded.

This program is now the dominant semantic approach in theoretical and empirical linguistics. If all that remained were to fill in the gaps and flesh out the details, philosophers would have done most of what was needed to transform initial philosophical questions into more tractable scientific ones. However, we *haven't* reached that point. Rather, we fall short in several ways. One of these involves the relationship between the information semantically encoded by a sentence and the assertions the sentence is used to make or the beliefs it is used to express. Up to now I have oversimplified that relationship by tacitly assuming that, with some exceptions, the semantically encoded information is identical, or nearly identical, with what is asserted and believed by an utterance of the sentence. Although that, indeed, had long been the standard assumption, in recent years that assumption has increasingly been called into question as more and more philosophers and linguists have come to think that meaning, or semantic content, alone doesn't always determine what is asserted but rather interacts, in ways we are just beginning to understand, with relevant contextual information to produce assertive content.

In addition, it has often been assumed that since meaning is semantically encoded information, understanding a sentence is knowing of the sentence that it carries that information. However, this may also be too simple. It is plausible to suppose that to understand a word, phrase, or sentence is to be able to use it in expected ways in communicative interactions with members of one's linguistic community, which may involve graded recognitional and inferential ability that goes beyond our knowledge of a certain content that it is the content of the word, phrase, or sentence. Finally, we have identified semantic content with information that represents the world as being a certain way, but we haven't yet given a plausible story about what a piece of information is. This, in my opinion, is our most urgent task.

The model of the information semantically encoded by a sentence I have so far assumed identifies it with the set of possible world-states in which the sentence is true. In this view, a sentence represents things as being one way or another, and so has truth conditions, *because* the information it encodes—i.e., the proposition it expresses—represents things in that way, and has truth conditions. This is what is identified with the set of world-states in which the sentence is true. But are propositions *really* sets of possible world-states—i.e., sets of maximal properties the world might have had? There are two powerful reasons to think they are not.

First, if they were, then all necessary propositions would be identical with the set of all possible world-states, and so with one another. So there would be only one necessary truth. Moreover anyone who believed a proposition p would believe every necessary consequence of it (provided we take it for granted that whenever one believes the proposition expressed by ⌜P&Q⌝ one believes the proposition expressed by P and the proposition expressed by Q), from which it follows that anyone believing a necessary falsehood would thereby believe every proposition. Since no one could do that, the view has the consequence than no one can believe the impossible. These results are obviously incorrect.

Second, sets of possible world-states aren't the right sorts of things to have truth conditions in the first place. Consider, for example, the set containing world-states 1, 2, and 3. Is it true or false? The question is bizarre no matter which three states we choose. We could answer the question if we could figure what things the set of world-states represents as being one way rather than another. But we can't do that, because the set doesn't represent anything at all. If we wanted, we could use it to represent *the actual state of the world as being in the set*—and so to make the claim that no maximal property of the world *outside* the set is instantiated. But we could equally well use the set to represent the actual state of the world as *not being in the set*—and so to make the claim that no maximal property *inside* the set is instantiated. Independent of interpretation by us, the set of world-states doesn't represent anything, doesn't make any claim, and so doesn't have truth conditions.

What about the *function* that assigns world-states 1–3 *truth* and all others falsity? This doesn't seem to be a piece of information either. Suppose we replace truth and falsity with USC and Lehigh. What does the function that assigns some world-states USC and others Lehigh represent? Without interpretation by us, it doesn't represent anything. Why, then, should the original function assigning truth and falsity be representational? *What, after all, are truth and falsity but properties we grasp primarily through their application to propositions? But if propositions are needed to illuminate truth and falsity, then truth and falsity can't be presupposed as building blocks from which propositions are constructed.*

The illusion that propositions can be identified with functions from world-states to truth values may be fed by illicitly assuming an antecedent conception of propositions. One who does this implicitly associates each assignment of a truth value to a world-state w with *the proposition that predicates that world-state of the universe*, and so is true iff w is the state the universe really is in. A function from world-states to truth values can then be associated with the disjunction of propositions correlated with its assignments of *truth* to such states. It could then be taken to say that the universe is either this way, that way, or the other—which would be fine *if one already had independent accounts of propositions as things that predicate properties*, in this case world-states, of something else, in this case *the universe*. But that is precisely what is lacking when one *identifies* propositions with functions from world-states to truth values. This shows that *possible-worlds semantics* lacks an adequate account of propositions, and so is incomplete.

But, as I will explain, the real problem is far worse; to provide any genuine information about meaning at all, possible-worlds semantics must presuppose the very thing it lacks. The way out of this impasse is to provide a genuinely acceptable conception of what propositions really are. This is the next great stage of philosophical inquiry if we are ever going to succeed in turning the study of language, meaning, and information into a scientific inquiry.

Here is a strategy for getting the job done. We start with the observation that agents *represent objects as being a certain way* when they perceive them or think of them as being that way—e.g., when they perceive this briefcase, call it 'B', as being brown, or think of it as brown. Next, we consider *what the agent does*—namely, *represent B as brown*, which is to predicate the property *being brown* of B. This cognitive act can itself be said to *represent B as being brown* in essentially the same sense in which some acts are said to be intelligent, stupid, thoughtful, or kind. Just as, very roughly, for an act to be intelligent, stupid, thoughtful, or kind is for it to be one the performance of which marks an agent as behaving intelligently, stupidly, thoughtfully, or kindly, so for a cognitive act to represent B as brown is for it to be one the performance of which marks an agent as representing B as brown. We, as agents, use this sense of representation to isolate individual aspects of the thought and perception, of ourselves and others, to assess them for accuracy. When o is such that to perceive or think of o as brown is to represent it accurately, it is enormously useful and very natural to identify an entity—a particular sort of perceiving or thinking—plus a property that entity has when this sort of perceiving or thinking is accurate. The entity is a proposition, which is the cognitive act of representing o as brown. The property is truth, which the act has iff to perform it is for an agent to represent o as o really is.

For an agent to entertain a proposition is, in the simplest case, for the agent to predicate a property of something—which is simply for the agent to perceive the object as having the property or to think of it as having that property. For example to *entertain* the proposition that B is brown is to see it as brown, or to think or imagine it as *being brown*. In all these cases, one predicates *brownness* of the object—either perceptually or cognitively. The proposition itself is *the minimal cognitive or perceptual act* in which one predicates *being brown* of this thing, and so represents it as brown. For this proposition to be true is just for this thing to be as the proposition represents it. Since the B is in fact brown, the proposition is true.

In this simple example, we are introduced to what truth is, and what propositions are. Propositions are individual cognitive acts, or sequences of such, in which an agent represents things as being certain ways. A proposition is true when things are the way it represents them to be. We learn more about truth when we realize that p and the *proposition that p is true* are necessary and apriori consequences of one another, and that any warrant for asserting, denying, believing, or doubting one is warrant for taking the same attitude to the other. Propositions can also be expressed by sentences. When I say, "This is brown," gesturing at my briefcase, *my use of the sentence* is true because the proposition I use it to express is true. Thus we extend the notion of truth to sentences by virtue of the propositions they are used to express. Since my perception and thought also represent the briefcase as brown, they are accurate, or veridical.

There is much more to say about this conception of propositions in my contributions to *New Thinking about Propositions*, by Jeff King, Jeff Speaks, and me, and in my forthcoming monograph *Rethinking Language, Mind, and Meaning*. I end by sketching how it provides what must be added to familiar versions of possible-worlds semantic theories to arrive at genuine theories of meaning. The basic idea is that individual words stand for objects, properties, and functions. Phrases are assigned various combinations of these, and sentences are associated with still larger combinations, from which we can read off the sequences of cognitive acts that are the propositions the sentences express. Given such a sequence, we can specify how it represents things as being. This representational information is combined with the principle that *a proposition p is true at a world-state w iff were w to be instantiated things would be as p represents them to be.* From this combination we generate the truth conditions of propositions, from which the truth conditions of sentences expressing them are inherited.

That, in a nutshell, is how real propositions can be added to possible-worlds semantic theories. In fact, it is *only* by adding such propositions that possible-worlds semantics can, by itself, give us *any information* at all about the meanings of sentences. Since this point has generally *not* been noted, I close by explaining it. As I emphasized earlier, possible-world-state semantics is premised on the idea that the truth conditions of a sentence are intimately related to its meaning. This is reflected in our apriori knowledge that *a sentence that means (or expresses the proposition) that so-and-so is true iff so-and-so.* This knowledge allows us to derive information about meaning from statements about truth conditions. For example, we can derive ⌜'S' doesn't mean that R⌝ from ⌜'S' is true iff Q⌝ when Q and R are known to differ in truth value. This result is strengthened when truth conditions are relativized to world-states. However, doing so requires propositions.

How do we extract information about meaning from the claim *the Spanish sentence 'El presidente habla Inglés' is true at world-state w iff at w the president speaks English*? The first step is to ask what it means to say that x *speaks English* at w. The answer, we are told, is that to say this is to say that *if w were instantiated, then x would speak English.* We next ask, What is it to say that a sentence is true at w? We know that for a sentence to be true is for the proposition it expresses to be true, so we ask, *What is it to say that a proposition p is true at w?* The answer, we are assured, is that it is to say that *if w were instantiated, then p would be true.* For example, to say that the proposition that the president speaks English is true at w is to say that if w were instantiated, then the proposition that the president speaks English would be true, and hence, the president would speak English.

So far so good. However, at this point we face a complication. In possible-worlds semantics we *can't* quite say that for a Spanish sentence S to be true at w is for it to be such that *if w were instantiated, then S would be a true sentence of Spanish (i.e., one which expresses a true proposition).* The reason we can't say that is that in possible-worlds semantics, S can be *true at w* even if S means nothing at w, or means something different at w from what it actually means. This shows that the *dyadic truth predicate of possible-worlds semantics* is a technical substitute for our ordinary notion of truth. Using our ordinary notion, we say that S is true at w iff *at w*, S expresses a proposition that is true. But, since what S could have meant (or expressed) is no help in illuminating what S actually means (expresses), the possible-worlds semanticist needs some other story. Although the strict possible-worlds semanticist is (I think) at a loss, those of us who have real propositions at our disposal are not. To gain information about meaning from a truth-conditional semantics of this sort, we must understand its claim *that S is true at w iff at w, the president speaks English* as stating that *the proposition that S is used by us to express at the actual world-state is true at w iff at w, the president speaks English.*

In short, to directly provide genuine information about meaning, the dyadic truth predicate of possible-world-state semantics must be understood as parasitic on the prior notions: *the proposition actually expressed by a sentence* and the ordinary, unrelativized property *truth* of propositions. It is by taking these for granted that we are able to extract useful information about meaning directly from the truth conditions provided by such a theory. When such a theory gives us ⌜∀w 'S' is true at w iff at w, Q⌝ we derive ⌜'S' doesn't mean that R⌝ when Q and R aren't necessarily equivalent. We do this by tacitly assuming ⌜If 'S' means (or expresses the proposition) that P, then necessarily the proposition 'S' actually expresses is true iff P⌝. Although this doesn't identify what S does mean, it does so up to necessary equivalence, thereby providing information about meaning that restricts the range of acceptable alternatives. What has not formerly been appreciated, but what must now be, is that *without the prior notions of truth and propositions here employed, even this limited information about meaning extracted directly from the semantic theory would be lost.*

This is a core problem for the analysis of propositions as sets of world-states, or functions from world-states to truth values. If world-states are taken to be unexplained primitives, with the goal of using them to provide reductive analyses of properties, propositions, and meaning, then the method just given for extracting claims about meaning from possible-worlds semantic theories is unavailable. *Without prior accounts of propositions, truth, and the connection between meaning and truth, the theorems of such a semantic theory won't, without further supplementation, carry any information about meaning.* What this suggests to me is that the great progress in the scientific study of meaning in human language that has sprung from work in the possible-worlds framework has been premised on our ability to make good on a tacit promise. The promise is to identify what truth, meaning, and, above all, propositions—or pieces of information—really are. This is the task that we are now, after studying this question for more than a century and a quarter, finally in a position to accomplish.

4

For Want of Cognitively Defined Propositions

A HISTORY OF INSIGHTS AND MISSED
PHILOSOPHICAL OPPORTUNITIES

RUSSELL'S STRUGGLES WITH PROPOSITIONS

Propositions were, for the early Russell, meanings of sentences, objects of assertion, belief, and knowledge, and the primary bearers of truth and falsity. They also provided him with propositional functions, which map n-tuples of values of free variables in a formula f onto the proposition expressed by f relative to the assignment. Just as the Fregean concept (which maps arguments to truth values) was the backbone of his account of quantification as higher-order predication, so the propositional function was the backbone of Russell's parallel account. Whereas for Frege the thought expressed by 'Everything is mortal-if-human' predicates *being true of each object* of the concept that assigns truth to x iff x is mortal-if-human, so, for Russell, the proposition expressed predicates *assigning a truth to each object* of the function that assigns each x the proposition that x is mortal-if-human. Thus, we have a plausible account of *what is asserted or believed* when one asserts or believes *that everything is mortal-if-human*. This analysis, which extends to all generalized quantifiers, was the crucial advance in "On Denoting" and the cornerstone of Russell's subsequent philosophical logic.[1]

Since propositions were, for Russell, the *primary* bearers of truth, other things—sentences, utterances, acts of judgment, and states of believing—were taken to be true only in virtue of the relations they bore to true propositions. If a person's beliefs on a given occasion are entirely true, this is so because their contents are true propositions. Propositions themselves were seen as timeless, unchanging entities with which we are acquainted by a kind of passive intellectual awareness. As Russell put it in 1904:

[1] Russell (1905b).

Suppose . . . that our judgment is 'A exists', where A is something that does as a matter of fact exist. Then A's existence [i.e., *the proposition that A exists*], it seems plain, subsists independently of its being judged to subsist. . . . In this case the Objective [proposition] of the judgment—at least in the view of common sense—is as truly independent of the judgment as is A itself. But the peculiarity of the cognitive relation [i.e., the agent's part of the attitude], which is what we wish to consider, lies in this: that one term of the relation *is* nothing but an awareness of the other term.[2]

In this view, the fact that propositions *represent* things as being *so-and-so*, and thus are *true* iff the things are that way, is *not* derivative from conceptually prior cognitive activities of agents who entertain them. On the contrary, since propositions are the *primary* bearers of intentionality, the truth conditions of cognitive acts or states must be explained in terms of quasi-perceptual relations agents bear to them. This difficult doctrine, more than any other, led to the Russellian problem known as "the unity of the proposition."

THE UNITY OF THE PROPOSITION

Since understanding a sentence S requires understanding both its parts and how they are structurally related, it was natural to take S's meaning—the proposition S expresses—to be a structured complex of the meanings of S's constituents. But this raised a problem. Just as sentences aren't collections of unrelated expressions but have a unity that distinguishes them from mere lists and allows us to use them to represent the world truly or falsely, so propositions aren't collections of unrelated meanings but have a unity that endows them with truth conditions that mere aggregations don't have. The problem of "the unity of the proposition" was to explain what this "unity" amounts to.

Elsewhere, I have argued that the problem is *not* to find some relation propositional constituents bear to each other that "holds them together" as parts of a single entity; the problem is to explain the intentionality of propositions.[3] The former, misconceived, problem stems from the idea that for any complex there is a relation in which its parts stand by virtue of which they are all parts of one thing. But since this is

---

[2] Russell (1904, 60).
[3] Chapter 2 of Soames (2010b); chapter 3 of King, Soames, and Speaks (2014); chapters 2, 3, 7, and 9 of Soames (2014).

true of all complexes, it doesn't signal any special problem for propositions. What makes propositions special is that they must, without "interpretation" by us, have truth conditions. Since it is absurd to characterize a mere set, sequence, or abstract tree structure as inherently representing an object as being a certain way, and so as true or false, these things can't be propositions (even if some can be used to *model* propositions).[4] Propositions can't be mental sentences either, since it is only by expressing propositions that sentences have truth conditions. What then, does distinguish propositions from everything that inherits its truth conditions from them?

That was the problem that Russell didn't know how to answer.

> Consider . . . the proposition "A differs from B." The constituents of this proposition . . . appear to be only A, difference, B. *Yet these constituents, thus placed side by side, do not reconstitute the proposition. The difference which occurs in the proposition actually relates A and B, whereas the difference after analysis is a notion which has no connection with A and B.* It may be said that we ought, in the analysis, to mention the relations which difference has to A and B, relations which are expressed by *is* and *from* when we say A is different from B. These relations consist in the fact that A is referent and B relatum with respect to difference. But A, referent, difference, relatum, B, is still merely a list of terms, not a proposition. *A proposition . . . is essentially a unity, and when analysis has destroyed the unity, no enumeration of constituents will restore the proposition. The verb, when used as a verb, embodies the unity of the proposition, and is thus distinguishable from the verb considered as a term, though I do not know how to give a clear account of the precise nature of the distinction.*[5]

As Russell notes, there is more to the proposition *that A differs from B* than the fact that its constituents are A, B, and difference. There is also how A and B occur and how their so occurring *represents* them as being different. Modifying Russell, we may venture that difference is somehow *predicated* of A and B, with the result that they are *represented as being different.* Since in a mere list nothing is *predicated* of anything, the list doesn't *represent* anything as being any particular way. Hence, propositions are true or false, while lists are neither.

[4] Chapter 3 of King, Soames, and Speaks (2014) extends this argument to popular conceptions of propositions as sets of truth-supporting circumstances. Even if such circumstances could—*per impossibile*—be made fine-grained enough to model propositions, sets of them could not be propositions.

[5] My emphasis. Russell (1903, 49–50). Russell's discussion in that work of the problem of the unity of the proposition is treated at length in section 4.5 of chapter 7, Soames (2014).

Russell put the point slightly differently:

> In every proposition . . . we may make an analysis into something asserted and something about which the assertion is made.[6]

What is right about this is that when we assert *that Socrates is human* we may be said to assert the property *being human* of him. Since in so doing *we represent* him as human, what we assert is true iff he is as represented. However, examples like (1) suggest that what Russell needs is not assertion, but predication.

1a. Socrates is human.
1b. If Socrates is human, then Socrates is mortal.
1c. That Socrates is human is widely believed.
1d. I wonder whether Socrates is human.
1e. Is it true that Socrates is human?

One who utters (1a) asserts that Socrates is human, but one who utters (1b–1e) doesn't. Still, there is something common to the cases. In each, the speaker uses the name 'Socrates' to refer to Socrates and the predicate 'is human' to represent him as human. In (1a) Socrates is asserted to be so; in (1b) it is asserted that if he is so, then he is mortal; in (1c) he is asserted to be widely believed to be so; in (1d) I indicate that I wonder whether he is so, and in (1e), I ask whether it is true that he is. In each case, part of what one does in performing the act of asserting or questioning associated with one's use of the sentence is to represent Socrates as being human by predicating humanity of him. Since, for Russell, the intentional properties of the resulting speech acts are derived from the propositions they express, the relation he needs to "unify" the proposition is predication.

But what can it mean to say that *a proposition* predicates something of other things? Propositions don't predicate, people do; so, any sense in which propositions predicate must be derivative from that in which people who entertain them do. In spelling this out, one finds that the early Russellian—as well as the Fregean and early Moorean—conception of entertaining a proposition as somehow making it the object of one's attention is a dead end.[7] Instead of deriving the intentionality of cognitive states from the primary intentionality of proposi-

---

[6] Russell (1903, 43).

[7] The shortcomings of Frege's conception of propositions and his attempt to solve the problem of their "unity" is discussed in section 2 of chapter 2 of Soames (2014). Moore's early view of propositions and its relation to Russell's view are discussed in section 3 of chapter 3 and section 2 of chapter 9 of that volume.

tions agents cognize, we must derive the intentionality of propositions from the intentionality of those who entertain them.

This can be done by taking propositions to be cognitive acts; the proposition that Socrates is human is the act of predicating humanity of Socrates, thereby representing him as human. To entertain this proposition is *not* to think about it, perceive it, or cognize it in any way; it is to perform it. Similarly, understanding S—often called "knowing its meaning"—can't be analyzed in terms of a conceptually prior attitude *knowing of a certain proposition p that S expresses p*. There is, of course, such an attitude, which, in sophisticated language users, often accompanies understanding S. However it is not the analysis of understanding. Understanding S is being disposed to use S in a certain way—to perform the cognitive act that is the proposition S expresses.

From this, we can make sense of the intentionality of propositions. One who predicates humanity of Socrates does something—*represents him as human*. The sense in which this act *itself* represents Socrates as human is related to the sense in which an agent who performs it does. This relationship is similar to that between the sense in which some acts are intelligent or stupid and the sense in which *agents who perform those acts* are such. Roughly, for an act to be intelligent or stupid is for it to be one the performance of which marks one as behaving intelligently or stupidly; for a cognitive act to represent Socrates as human is for it to be one the performance of which guarantees that an agent as so represents him. We need this sense of act-representation because we need to isolate particular aspects of our thought, and that of others, to assess them for accuracy. When to think of o as *so-and-so* is to represent o accurately, it is useful to have an entity—a particular sort of cognizing—plus a property that o has when this cognition is accurate. The entity is a proposition, the cognitive act of representing o as *so-and-so*. The property is truth, which the act has iff to perform it is for an agent to represent o as o really is.[8]

Although this explanation of the unity (i.e., intentionality) of the proposition is commonsensical, the early Russell couldn't see it. To see it, one must recognize that predicating, and hence representing, is something agents do. Properties don't predicate themselves of anything—nor, unless it is explained along something like the lines just sketched, can we make sense of the idea of propositions predicating properties of things, and hence representing things as being certain ways. This is what Russell was up against. He needed predication to make sense of propositions, but his conception of propositions made it

---

[8] For further discussion, see chapter 12 of King, Soames, and Speaks (2014).

impossible for him to find appropriate agents for that predication. It was fundamental to his conception that propositions are abstract, unchanging constituents of reality, the identity and nature of which are independent of the cognitive activity of agents, while also being the source of all intentionality, and hence that from which other representational entities, events, or mental states inherit their truth conditions. This was the deadly combination that fueled Russell's eventual dissatisfaction with propositions, and rendered them ripe for elimination.

ABANDONING PROPOSITIONS: THE MULTIPLE RELATION THEORY OF JUDGMENT

Russell abandons propositions and sketches a new account of truth and propositional attitudes in chapter 12 of *The Problems of Philosophy*.[9] First, he takes the bearers of truth and falsity to be "beliefs," meaning by this something other than *what one believes*. Second, he takes believing, asserting, and other attitudes to be relations, not to a single, unified proposition, but to the very propositional constituents he had come to realize can't be unified in a mind-independent way. Under the old analysis, 'Othello believes that Desdemona loves Cassio' reports a relation between Othello and the proposition he believes. Under the new analysis, it reports a four-place relation that unites Othello with the several objects of his belief—Desdemona, the loving relation, and Cassio. Since he does believe that Desdemona loves Cassio, the belief relation *really does relate* these objects—knitting them together into a complex entity, *Othello's belief that Desdemona loves Cassio,* which Russell takes to be a fact. For this belief to be true would be for the loving relation to *really relate* Desdemona and Cassio (in that order), knitting *them* together into a different complex entity, *Desdemona's love for Cassio,* which would itself be a fact. But, since she doesn't love Cassio, there is no such further fact, and the belief is false. This is taken to be unproblematic because in saying that *the belief is false* we are *not* saying that *what Othello believes* is false; there is no such thing. What is false is the fact that consists of *Othello's believing that Desdemona loves Cassio.* Since this complex entity, which Russell calls the "belief," does exist, he takes the theory to have identified bearers of truth that can also be bearers of falsity.

---

[9] Russell (1912). Russell had already renounced propositions in Russell (1910), where he first advocated the multiple relation theory of judgment. That article, in turn, was preceded by Russell (1906–7), in which he explored, without advocating, the multiple relation theory as a theory of false, but not true, beliefs.

Although the theory does, in the end, contain an important insight, the theory itself clearly fails. Since its problems are so many and so severe, I will merely sketch some of its obvious difficulties.[10]

(i) The theory fails to capture the variety of our ordinary talk of propositions. At most it offers an analysis of ascriptions of the form *x knows/believes asserts (the proposition) that S.* It makes no provision for talk of propositions outside attitude ascriptions, or for ascriptions in which the complement of the attitude verb is a name, singular definite description, variable, or propositional quantifier. Thus, it can't handle examples like (2).

2a. Logicism is a thesis about the relationship between logic and mathematics.

2b. For every true proposition in the report, there are two other propositions in the report that are false.

2c. Bill asserted/denied Church's Thesis/Goldbach's Conjecture.

2d. Susan proved the proposition/several propositions that John denied.

2e. There are many propositions no one has entertained, let alone proved or disproved.

(ii) The theory dispenses with *what one believes/denies/imagines,* without providing a workable replacement. Ordinarily, we would say that the claim that the Earth is round follows from the claims: *John believes/denies/imagines that the Earth is round,* and *What John believes/denies/imagines* is true. According to the new theory, these verbs don't take single objects, the multiple objects they do take aren't bearers of truth value, and their complement clauses are nondesignating "incomplete symbols." We would never take the claim that the Earth is round to follow from the claims *John believes/denies/imagines that the earth is round* and *The fact that John believes/denies/imagines that the Earth is round is true.* Thus, either Russell must accept the incredible claim that our ordinary thought and talk about the truth or falsity of *what one believes/denies/imagines,* and the like, is grotesquely incorrect, or he must find a way of accommodating it in his theory (which he never does).

(iii) Russell's new theory can't accommodate examples like those in (3), in which the complement clause of a belief ascription is a complex sentence.

[10] For fuller discussion, see section 3 of chapter 9 of Soames (2014).

3a. Othello believes that some people are trustworthy.

3b. Othello believes that not many people are trustworthy.

3c. Othello believes that Iago is trustworthy and Desdemona is unfaithful.

3d. Othello believes that either Iago isn't trustworthy or Desdemona loves Cassio.

3e. Othello believes that if Iago is trustworthy, then Desdemona is unfaithful.

3f. Othello believes that it is a necessary truth that if Desdemona loves Cassio, then Desdemona loves Cassio.

First, consider (3a). According to the "On Denoting" analysis of quantification, the constituents of the belief reported by (3a) are the property *assigning a truth to something* and the *propositional function that assigns to any object o the proposition that o is trustworthy* (of which the property is predicated). But this presupposes that *propositions* are values of propositional functions. So, if the aim of the new theory is to dispense with propositions, either it fails to do so, or it must be supplemented by a reanalysis of quantification. No real reanalysis was forthcoming. Russell did, in *Principia Mathematica*, redescribe propositional functions as formulas. But he seemed to think, quite wrongly, that his old, canonical analysis of quantification could survive this redescription. Although he did make suggestive comments in volume 1 of *Principia* that could, in principle, be developed into a different, nonontologically committing, account of quantification, that account would have been a disaster both for his logicist reduction and for aspects of his philosophical logic that he wished to retain.[11]

Next, consider the role of negation in (3b)—where by 'negation' I don't mean a particular symbol (no one of which would be familiar to all believers) but the content shared by the various symbols properly translated by the logician's ' ~ '. With this understanding, the constituents of the belief reported by (3b) are *negation*, something corresponding to the quantifier 'many people', and something corresponding to the formula 'x is trustworthy'. What does Othello do to "unify" these elements, along with himself as agent, in forming his belief? The most plausible answer is that he first does whatever is required to unify the contribution of 'many people' with the contribution of 'x is trustworthy'. Then, he negates what he has just unified. What does he negate? Since for Russell negation was always an operator on a proposition, he would seem to be committed to saying that in forming the belief reported by

[11] This is argued at length in Soames (2014, chap. 10).

(3b), Othello negates *the proposition* that many people are trustworthy. But this can't be the analysis, since it presupposes propositions, which were to have been eliminated. Thus, he needs a new analysis of negation.[12] As the remaining examples in (3) show, this argument can be repeated for all propositional operators, including necessity, plus those for conjunction, disjunction, and the material conditional. Short of a radical reanalysis of most of Russell's previous philosophical logic, his new theory is up to its neck in propositions. Without such a reanalysis, it can't apply to any but the simplest examples.

The final problem with the multiple relation theory brings together all the previous difficulties while illuminating Russell's great missed opportunity. A belief, assertion, or hypothesis *represents* the world as being a certain way and so is capable of being true or false. Ordinarily, what we mean by this is that *what is believed, asserted,* or *hypothesized* represents the world, and so is true or false. Using the familiar name 'proposition', we may ask, *In virtue of what are propositions representational, and so bearers of truth conditions?* This is the unity problem that Russell was unable to solve. One might think, as he apparently did, that in disposing of propositions he was disposing of the problem. He wasn't. Beliefs, assertions, and hypotheses *are* representational. Even though Russell misdescribes them (as facts), he doesn't deny that they exist. Thus, he needs to answer the question, What makes *them* representational, and so bearers of truth conditions? This is the unity problem all over again.

According to Russell's new theory, beliefs, assertions, and hypotheses are facts in which an agent is related by the attitudes of belief, assertion, and hypothesizing to objects, properties, and relations. What makes these facts representational? The answer must be something the agent's cognitive attitude does with the constituents toward which the attitude is directed. When Othello believes that Desdemona loves Cassio, his attitude adds something to the raw material of the belief—Desdemona, loving, and Cassio—that brings it about that the resulting belief represents Desdemona as loving Cassio. What does it add?

---

[12] He realized there was a difficulty here, which he planned to deal with in Russell (1913) (an aborted book manuscript published after his death). Recognizing that in giving up propositions he must *reject* the standard assumption that "when a molecular proposition which is true appears to contain atomic constituents which are false, the apparent atomic constituents must really be constituents," he wrote, "We cannot enter into this question until we come to Part III; for the present, I shall assume by anticipation that a different analysis of such molecular propositions is possible"(Russell 1913, 152–53). Russell never wrote Part III.

Surely, what one agent does to bring it about that his belief represents the world in this way is *the same* as what any other agent does to bring it about that her belief represents the world in exactly that way. The same can be said about what is done when different attitudes are borne to the same content. When agents believe, assert, deny, doubt, hypothesize, or imagine that Desdemona loves Cassio, they take different cognitive stances toward *representing her as loving him*, which is the common element of the different attitudes. What differentiates the attitudes from one another is the cognitive stance taken toward that representation. With this in mind, we can now answer our earlier question. *What the agent does* to bring it about that his or her belief, assertion, or hypothesis *represents* Desdemona as loving Cassio is to *predicate* one constituent, the loving relation, of the other two—Desdemona and Cassio, in that order.

This is the kernel of truth in the multiple relation theory. What unites the elements of a belief, assertion, or hypothesis, giving it representational import, is a cognitive operation agents perform on its constituents. Since this is so no matter what attitude is taken toward the content, we can transform the multiple relation theory back into a propositional theory by collecting the constituents of representationally equivalent instances of believing, asserting, and so forth, into a single structure the entertainment of which requires one to predicate *loving* of Desdemona and Cassio. We then generate the cognitive theory of propositions from the failed multiple relation theory of judgment. The key Russellian insight is that the intentionality of all truth bearers is explained in terms of the intentionality of the cognitive activities of agents, rather than the other way around.

According to the cognitive theory, entertaining a proposition is the most basic attitude we bear to it, the one on which all others are based. To *judge* that Socrates is wise is to predicate wisdom of him while affirming or endorsing that predication. To *believe that he is wise* is to judge, or be disposed to judge, that he is. To *know* that he is wise is, roughly, for him to be wise, to believe that he is, and to be safe, or justified, in so believing. To *assert* that he is wise is to commit oneself, by uttering something, to treating the proposition that he is wise as something one knows. Other attitudes are treated similarly. To say that the proposition that Socrates is wise is true (at a world-state w) is to say that Socrates is, at w, the way he is represented to be by one who entertains (i.e., performs) the proposition (at any world-state). Since it is necessary and sufficient for one to entertain the proposition that one represent Socrates as wise, its truth conditions don't vary from world-state to world-state. Bearing its truth conditions inherently, the proposition can thus be the interpretation of sentences and utterances, without itself being something for which an interpretation is needed.[13]

THE CONSEQUENCES OF RUSSELL'S FAILURE TO CORRECTLY CONCEIVE PROPOSITIONS

Russell's initial embrace of propositions was, though very useful for his philosophical logic, based on a conception of them which, he rightly came to realize, was untenable. His plight was made worse when he failed to see that the insight embodied in the badly flawed theory he hoped would eliminate propositions could have been used to construct a workable cognitive theory of them. Thus, he landed in the unenviable position of repudiating propositions without having an adequate substitute for them. In addition to losing a viable theory of the attitudes, he also lost—without quite realizing it—his powerful treatment of first- and higher-order quantification. Because of this, his discussion of quantification in volume 1 of *Principia Mathematica* is a confused and unsustainable amalgam of (i) his original, objectual, higher-order predication view and (ii) an incipient, incompletely conceptualized, and nonontologically committing, substitutional view. This confusion was intimately connected both to his fanciful attempt to eliminate classes—the infamous "no-class theory"—and to his expressively crippling, ramified (as opposed to simple) theory of types.[14] All of this, along with other confusions extending to his 1918–19 *Philosophy of Logical Atomism*, could have been avoided had he grasped the constructive possibilities inherent in his appeal to the cognition of believers.[15]

Embracing a cognitive theory of propositions rather than the Platonic conception he originally championed would also have helped him avoid an even earlier error. As we now know, the chief impetus of the celebrated theory of descriptions of "On Denoting" came to Russell when he was contemplating an early version of the "Gray's Elegy"

---

[13] The construction of complex propositions and discussion of the existence conditions of cognitive propositions generally, including their truth values at world-states at which they may not exist, are presented in chapters 6 and 12 of King, Soames, and Speaks (forthcoming). The theory is extended to solve semantic and philosophical problems in Soames (2014).

[14] These points are discussed in Soames (2014, chap. 10, sec. 5).

[15] Russell (1918–19) is discussed at length in Soames (2014, chap. 12).

argument given there.[16] The conclusion of the argument is that complex singular terms—including function/argument expressions—like '2 + 2' and '3^2' along with Fregean definite descriptions—are impossible, so no language, natural or artificial, can contain them.

One of the key examples he used in coming to this conclusion was (4), in which 'M' is a Millian name for *the meaning of* 'the first line of Gray's Elegy' (taken, for *reductio*, to be a singular term).

> 4a. The first line of Gray's Elegy is 'The curfew tolls the knell of parting day'.
>
> 4b. 'The first line of Gray's Elegy' means M.
>
> 4c. 'The first line of Gray's Elegy' means the first line of Gray's Elegy.

Since, by hypothesis, 'M' and 'the first line of Gray's Elegy' mean the same thing, Russell reasons that propositions (4b) and (4c) must have the same structure and constituents, and so be identical. But they can't be identical *if the description really means M*. For if that were so, (4b) would be true, even though (4c) is false—since it says that the meaning of the description is the thing it designates (the sentence 'The curfew tolls the knell of parting day'). Thus, Russell thinks, (4b) can't be true and concludes that there is no *true* singular proposition in which *being what 'the first line of Gray's Elegy' means* is predicated of anything. From here it is a short step to the conclusion that no one can *know of* anything that it is what the description means. But surely, Russell thinks, in order for an expression E to mean something it must be possible to know of *what E means* that E means it. Thus, he concludes, it is impossible for meaningful definite descriptions (of any language) to be singular terms. The argument generalizes to all singular terms formed by combining a function symbol with one or more terms serving as arguments—e.g., '3^2'.

This conclusion is clearly false; even if singular definite descriptions in English are generalized quantifiers, it is surely possible for a language to contain complex singular terms. The reason Russell didn't see this is that the distinction between the propositions expressed by (4b) and (4c) (on the supposition that 'the first line of Gray's Elegy' is a complex singular term) is that the predications that distinguish the two propositions differ *cognitively* in a way not easily expressible on the Platonic conception of propositions. For concreteness, let f_{the}

---

[16] The argument comes from the precursor, Russell (1905a) of "On Denoting." Exposition and criticism of the argument, along with an account of its role in leading Russell to his theory of descriptions is found in chapters 7 and 8 of Soames (2014). See also Cartwright (1987) and the seminal discussion in Salmon (2005).

be the function that maps a propositional function f onto the unique object that f assigns a true proposition, if there is one, and is otherwise undefined. Let g map an object o onto the proposition that o is a line in Gray's Elegy that precedes all other lines. The complex constituent f_{the}-*plus-g* will count as the contribution of both 'M' and 'the first line of Gray's Elegy' to the propositions in (4). Thus, we conclude that the constituents of propositions (4b) and (4c) are the complex f_{the}-*plus-g* and the property *being what 'the first line of Gray's Elegy' means,* with the latter predicated of the target provided by the former.[17] Russell's problem was that he could look forever, in his mind's eye, at these constituents standing in whatever mind-independent Platonic structures in which they occur and not see how those propositions differ.[18]

The cognitive conception of propositions allows us to understand what Russell could not see. According to it, the structural relationships in which the constituents of a proposition stand are unlike the relationships in which things occupying certain positions in an n-tuple stand to those occupying other positions, or the relationships that certain nodes in an abstract tree structure bear to other nodes. Although nothing prevents using formal constructions of these or other sorts to model propositional structure, the structures modeled are something else. The structural relationships between the constituents of a proposition are given by the roles the constituents play in the complex cognitive operations performed by an agent who entertains it—roles like *being predicated* (of certain things), *being targets* (of certain predications), *being applied* (to certain arguments), *being arguments* (to which certain things are applied), as well as *being subconstituents* of larger constituents which may themselves play these roles. This is the sense in which propositions (4b) and (4c) differ.

The difference between the two is a difference in the sense in which the property *being what 'the first line of Gray's Elegy' means* is predicated of its argument. In (4b) it is *directly predicated* of the complex that is the meaning of the description; in (4c) it is *indirectly predicated* of whatever is determined by that complex—the value of the function at the argument (which is the referent of the Fregean description). In order for the relation *direct predication* to hold of an agent A (who entertains a proposition p), a property F (to be predicated of something), and an item x (of which F is predicated), A must have x in mind as the thing to be represented as having F. By contrast, the *indirect*

---

[17] For simplicity, I present both propositions as predications of a complex relational property of a predication target rather than predications of the relevant two-place relation of a pair of predication targets. This wrinkle does not affect the discussion.

[18] See sections 2.3 of chapter 8 and 5.5 of chapter 9 of Soames (2014).

predication relation holds between A, F, and an item x *which is the kind of thing (e.g., a function-argument complex) that determines something else (e.g., a value).* In order for this relation to hold, A must have x in mind, and intend to represent whatever, if anything, is determined by x as having F. The *direct predication* is veridical iff x has F; the *indirect predication* is veridical iff there is something uniquely determined by x and that thing has F.[19]

In short, the distinction required to solve the *Gray's Elegy* problem— between what one who entertains proposition (4b) *aims to represent* as having a certain property versus what one who entertains proposition (4c) *aims to represent* as having that property—is a *cognitive* difference encoded in the cognitive acts with which propositions are identified. What made the problem seem insoluble to Russell in 1905 was his conception of propositions as Platonic objects the intentional properties of which are prior to, and independent of, those who entertain them. What makes the problem solvable now is the conception of propositions as cognitive acts.

Tractarian Propositions

By 1922, when Wittgenstein's *Tractatus* was translated and published in English, Russell had adopted an essentially tractarian conception of propositions.[20] In the light of his sad history with propositions, this was, in some ways, an advance. For the young Wittgenstein, propositions were not *sui generis* sources of intentionality in Plato's heaven but interpreted sentences of a logically perfect language. As such, their intentionality was due to the intentionality of agents who used them. This was one of the important strengths of Wittgenstein's conception, which, of course, also had weaknesses.

In the *Tractatus* the simplest propositions are called *elementary*. Likened to mental pictures or maps, they are taken to be combinations of logically proper (Millian) names standing in certain structural relationships. Each name is assumed to stand for an object and every object is assumed to be named. The way names are arranged in an elementary proposition represents a way the objects named could be combined. The elementary proposition is identified with the linguistic fact that such-and-such names stand in so-and-so relation. This linguistic fact is said to be meaningful in virtue of picturing a possible nonlinguistic fact

---

[19] See chapter 6 of King, Soames, and Speaks (2014), or section 5.5 of chapter 9 of Soames (2014).

[20] Russell (1919); Wittgenstein (1922).

in which the objects named stand in a relation corresponding to the relation the names bear to each other in the proposition.

For example, in the interpreted sentence (i.e., proposition) 'Eas'—meaning that Los Angeles is east of San Francisco—the name 'a' stands to the name 's' in the relation _occurring immediately before_and immediately after the symbol 'E'. Putting the names in this relation represents Los Angeles (named by 'a') as bearing the relation being to the east of to San Francisco (named by 's'). An agent who uses this representational system adopts linguistic conventions specifying which objects names are stipulated to designate and which relations R_o (defined over non-linguistic objects) different linguistic relations R_n (holding among the names of a sentence) are stipulated to stand for. An elementary tractarian proposition p is meaningful iff it is possible for the objects named in p to stand in the relation R_o designated by the relation R_n in which the names in p are placed; p is true iff the objects actually stand in R_o.

In a moment, I will turn to Wittgenstein's extension of this account to complex propositions. Before doing so, however, it is useful to make explicit his solution to (a version of) Russell's problem of the unity of the proposition. First, he maintains that what unites the names in an elementary proposition into a single complex entity is the structural relation holding among them. Second, he takes the intentionality of this complex entity to be derived from the cognitive activity of agents who use its names to designate certain stipulated objects while using the structural relation uniting them to predicate a stipulated relation of those objects. This is the explanation of how elementary propositions represent, and so have truth conditions. Finally, since these "propositions" are themselves interpreted sentences, understanding such a sentence does not involve knowing, of any Platonic entity, that the sentence expresses it.

Wittgenstein's incredible doctrine that every proposition is a truth function of atomic sentences/elementary propositions extends this account to all meaningful sentences/propositions. Since there is no upper bound on the number of propositions on which his basic truth-functional operator can operate, he is able to subsume quantification (over a fixed domain) under this heading. Even so, the expressive weakness of the system was crippling.[21] His conception of understanding the meaning of a sentence as knowing its truth conditions was more powerful. Since truth conditions in the Tractatus are possible states of affairs, the discussion there is a clear forerunner of what was to become the immensely popular view that a theory of meaning is a theory of truth relative to a possible world-state. Since Wittgenstein did not claim that sets of such

---

[21] See chapters 10 and 11 of Soames (2003a).

states are themselves meanings of sentences, objects of attitudes, or bearers of truth value, the devastating objections to the later view do not apply directly to his.[22] In the end, however, the Wittgensteinian conception of interpreted sentence types of an ideal language as objects of the attitudes or primary bearers of truth conditions fares no better.[23]

The first problem with this Wittgensteinian view is that the arithmetic of sentences differs from the arithmetic of proper objects of the attitudes in the following ways. (i) Any language containing indexicals (or related forms of context-sensitivity) will either give rise to cases in which multiple attitude-objects are represented by the same (interpreted) sentence, or to cases in which the same attitude-object is represented by different (interpreted) sentences, or to both. Moreover, any language without such context sensitivity will be too impoverished to supply all needed objects of the attitudes.[24] (ii) Any language the sentences of which are *linearly ordered* symbol sequences will contain *different interpreted sentences* and so *different objects of attitudes*, in cases in which the correct (single) object of the attitude involves (a) predication of a two-or-more-place symmetric relation (e.g., identity) of an unordered group of objects or (b) performance of an order-irrelevant operation on propositions like conjunction or disjunction.

The second problem with interpreted sentence types as objects of attitudes is that there is no sentence, or other symbolic representation, with which *every possible* believer of a given proposition—e.g., that a particular object o is red—can be expected to use, understand, or be familiar with. This is problematic because our talk of *every so-and-so* believing, e.g., that o is red, presupposes such a common belief object. The problem can't be avoided by claiming that what the ascription really reports is that each agent understands and accepts *some sentence or other that is true at world-state w iff at w, o is red*. For one thing, this would recapitulate the fatal coarse-grainedness problem for sets of possible world-states as objects of belief within the sentential theory. For another, it begs the empirical question by assuming, without evidence, that every possible belief by every possible believer (and by extension other propositional attitude) must be mediated by a symbol system of some sort.

---

[22] Recent statements of these objections are found in Soames (2006, 2008b) and chapter 3 of King, Soames, and Speaks (2014).

[23] Although this Wittgensteinian view is a natural construction from materials provided in the *Tractatus*, it abstracts away from Wittgenstein's seemingly skeptical remarks about propositional attitude reports discussed in section 2 of chapter 11 of Soames (2003a).

[24] Issues of this sort are discussed in Soames (1990) in connection with the proposal in Fodor (1981, 71) that "propositional attitudes are relations between organisms and internal representations."

Nor can the problem be sidestepped by taking the relevant tractarian sentence/proposition to be a mere tool, invented by the theorist, to track psychologically real cognitive acts, operations, and states in the mental lives of agents—without the "propositional trackers" themselves being psychologically real. As I argue elsewhere, the psychologically real cognitive acts and operations tracked by ascribing attitudes to complex propositions involve acts and operations that agents perform on simpler propositions, which must themselves be psychologically real.[25]

The third, and most fundamental, problem is that propositions can't be interpreted sentences because sentence interpretation requires an antecedent conception of cognitively real propositions. Consider the proposition that a certain object o_1 is redder than a given object o_2. In the tractarian account, this proposition is an interpreted sentence, which we may suppose consists in the symbol 'R' followed by the symbols 'O_1' and 'O_2', in that order. Let us further suppose that those who understand the language interpret the sentence (a) by taking 'O_1' to name o_1 and 'O_2' to name o_2, (b) by taking the relation _occurring immediately after 'R' and immediately before_, which 'O_1' bears to 'O_2' in the sentence, to stand for being redder than, and (c) by using the sentence to predicate being redder than of the pair o_1, o_2 (in that order).

Let us further grant two things for which Wittgenstein makes no room in the Tractatus—(i) that a person B who had never seen red things, might pick up the symbol 'R' from someone A who used it with the stipulated interpretation, and (ii) that by virtue of standing in a chain of communication with A, B might use 'RO_1O_2' to predicate being redder than of the order pair o_1, o_2, and, endorsing that predication, might to come to believe that o_1 is redder than o_2. Such an agent uses the sentence to make a predication and acquire a belief that he or she is unable to make or acquire without it. Surely, however, no one would be in a position to use the sentence to make that predication and acquire that belief were it not for the fact that some agents had made similar predications, and presumably acquired similar beliefs, without using that sentence.

More generally, it is overwhelmingly likely that some agents make such predications and acquire such beliefs without using, or understanding, any sentence. How could languages get started, if this were not so? Consider predications of the property being red. To predicate this property of an object is just to represent it as red, which is how the perceptual experiences of many creatures with color vision routinely

---

[25] Chapter 5 of Soames (2010b) and chapter 6 of King, Soames, and Speaks (forthcoming).

represent some things. Can't some nonlinguistic creatures *see things as red* and, in many cases, *believe that they are red*? If they can, then they are bearers of propositional attitudes the objects of which are nonlinguistic, and so are not tractarian "propositions." Although the case is a bit more complex for predications of *being redder than,* and the outcome not quite as obvious, the end result is, I think, similar.

This conclusion is, of course, uncongenial to advocates of "the language of thought."[26] Although some cognition is linguistic, and the extent of our linguistic versus nonlinguistic cognition is an empirical matter, there is no compelling reason to suppose that all propositional attitudes *must be,* at bottom, linguistic. The common idea to the contrary is roughly (i) that mental states and processes the contents of which are propositions represent things in the world as being certain ways; (ii) that for this to be so, they must incorporate representational entities the systematic nature of which requires them to be compositional; and (iii) that this is all that is meant by claiming that they are linguistic in nature. The chief flaw in this reasoning is (ii). As I explained earlier, cognitive acts and operations—and dispositional mental states defined in terms of them—can be inherently and systematically representational without necessarily involving other "representations." Often, the performance of such acts or operations involves crucial linguistic intermediaries. It is conceivable that empirical research may expand this class of cases in surprising ways. But the mere requirement that attitudes systematically represent doesn't guarantee linguistic representations.

For want of a cognitive theory of propositions, many philosophers are pushed into prematurely and implausibly postulating a linguistic basis of all propositional attitudes (of all possible agents). Of course, the young Wittgenstein was no cognitive scientist. However, the aprioristic basis of the *Tractatus* saddled him with a conception of propositions as interpreted sentences which suffered from problems similar to those that can be raised against contemporary theorists like Jerry Fodor.[27]

Still, the tractarian conception of propositions had its virtues. In the *Tractatus* Wittgenstein rejected Platonic propositions as unexplanatory and correctly regarded the analysis of understanding a sentence S as knowing, of some proposition p, that S expressed p as simply wrong. He also rightly took propositions to be structured entities the unity and intentionality of which are due to the cognitive activity of agents.

---

[26] See Fodor (1975).
[27] See the critique of Fodor in Soames (1990).

Lacking a cognitive theory of propositions, he unfortunately but understandably saw no alternative to identifying them with sentences of a hidden "logically perfect" language. Later, when the inadequacy of that view became apparent to him, he gave them up altogether.

TRUTH, MEANING, AND PROPOSITIONS IN ORDINARY-LANGUAGE PHILOSOPHY

From the late 1940s through the mid 1960s the ordinary-language school of philosophy—led by John Austin, Gilbert Ryle, Peter Strawson, and the later Wittgenstein—placed the study of language at the center of philosophy. Advancing under the slogan "Meaning is use," these philosophers attempted, in one form or another, to extract large philosophical lessons from attention to how words are used in nonphilosophical settings. But how was language to be studied? Although there was considerable variation in the ways in which these philosophers appealed to language, they were more or less united about certain repudiations. Chief among the views repudiated was the idea that understanding expressions is, at bottom, knowing certain semantic facts about them—e.g., that name n refers to object o, that predicate F stands for property P, and that sentence S expresses proposition p. Instead, understanding a word, phrase, or sentence was thought to consist of *knowing how to use it.*

There is much to be said both for this repudiation and for the admittedly vague and schematic appeal to *use* in replacing it.[28] However, there are also elements to contest, including the abandonment of propositions, which appears to have been virtually universal among these philosophers. Insofar as this abandonment repudiated traditional Platonic conceptions of propositions, the repudiators were on the side of the angels. Nor can they be faulted for not seeing that the then-unknown cognitive theory of propositions endorses their connection between understanding a sentence and using it to do something—maintaining, as it does, that to understand S is to be disposed to use S to perform the cognitive act that *is* the proposition S expresses. Where the ordinary language philosophers chiefly can be faulted was in failing to appreciate the important theoretical roles played by propositions, and so in not looking for a conception of propositions capable of playing those roles. I will illustrate this error with a few examples of serious mistakes

---

[28] Regarding the repudiation, see Soames (1989b).

that could have been avoided, had a worked-out conception of cognitive propositions been available.[29]

STRAWSON ON STATEMENTS, CONTEXT SENSITIVITY, AND PRESUPPOSITION

The distinctions drawn between properties of expressions and properties of uses of expressions in Peter Strawson's classic 1950 article, "On Referring," were among the most important of the period. The central theses of the article are paraphrased by $T1_S$–$T5_S$.

$T1_S$ *Meaning* is a property of expressions; *referring, being true or false,* and *saying something* are properties of uses of expressions in contexts.

$T2_S$ A sentence is meaningful iff it can be used to say something true or false.

$T3_S$ To give, or to know, the meaning of S is to give, or to know, a rule for determining the contexts in which S is used to say something true and those in which it is used to say something false.

$T4_S$ The semantic function of a singular term (e.g., a name, demonstrative, or singular definite description) in its primary referring use is to refer to an entity which the rest of the sentences is used to say something about. The meaning of such an expression is a rule for determining its referents in different contexts.

$T5_S$ If a singular term n in a sentence ⌜Fn⌝ is used referringly in the course of using the sentence in a context C, then this use of the sentence says something true (false) in C iff, in C, the referent of n has (doesn't have) the property that F is used to express in C. If the use of n fails to refer to anything, then the use of the sentence doesn't say anything true or false.

To appreciate the virtues and vices of these theses, it is instructive to compare them to corresponding theses incorporating a version of the distinction in David Kaplan (1989) between the meaning (character) of

---

[29] A related obstacle to the adoption of any cognitive theory of propositions was a powerful anti-mentalist strand running through much ordinary-language philosophy—evident in Wittgenstein (1953) and Ryle (1949, 1954)—that would probably not have found the explanatory appeal to cognitive acts and operations congenial. For more on this anti-mentalism, see chapters 2, 3, and 4 of Soames (2003b), plus the discussion of Ryle's "behaviorism" in Soames (2007).

an expression and the content of that expression relative to a context of utterance.

T1$_K$ Meaning (character) is a property of expressions; *saying something* is a property of uses of sentences in contexts, and *what is said* is the proposition that is semantically determined by the use of the sentence in the context. Being true and or false, at different possible world-states, is a property of propositions, and hence derivatively of uses of sentences in contexts. Designating something, relative to possible world-states, is a property of uses of expressions in contexts.

T2$_K$ A sentence is meaningful iff it can be used to say something, i.e., iff its use semantically determines a proposition in some context of utterance.

T3$_K$ To give, or to know, the meaning of a sentence is to give, or to know, a rule for determining *what it is used to say* (the proposition semantically determined by its use) in an arbitrary context; propositions are true or false at different possible world-states.

T4$_K$ The propositional constituent corresponding to a referring use of a *directly referential singular term* n in a context C is the referent of n at the world-state of C. This is what is contributed by uses of n in C to the propositions semantically determined by uses of sentences containing n in C. The meaning of n is a rule for determining its referent in different contexts.

T5$_K$ If a *directly referential singular term* n is used in a context C in which it designates o, in the course of using a sentence ⌜Fn⌝, and F is used in C to express a property P, then the proposition semantically determined by this use of ⌜Fn⌝ in C (and, derivatively, the use itself) will be true (false) at a possible world-state w iff o has (doesn't have) P at w. *If the use of n in C fails to refer to anything (in C), then there is no propositional constituent corresponding to that use, and the use of ⌜Fn⌝ in C fails to (semantically) determine (express) a proposition.*

Although the two sets of theses are broadly similar, there are important differences between them, including the now familiar relativization of truth conditions to world-states in the latter. But the crucial difference is the introduction, in the second set, of *contents* of uses of expressions in contexts, *including propositions expressed by uses of sentences.* In this picture, it is in virtue of expressing these contents that uses of expressions refer to objects (at world-states), and that uses of sentences are true or false (at such states).

The significance of this difference shows up clearly in the contrast between $T3_S$ and $T3_K$. Whereas $T3_S$ suggests that sentences are synonymous if uses of them agree in truth value in every context, $T3_K$ does not—and would not, even if one wrongly took propositions true at the same world-states to be identical. The point is illustrated by (5).

5a. I exist.
5b. I am using a sentence.
5c. Someone is using a sentence.
5d. Something exists.
5e. I am here now.

For any possible context C of utterance, an agent's use of any of these sentences would express a truth. But the truths expressed would be different. For example, if I were to use the sentences in (5), the propositions in (6) *which I would assert or express* would have little more in common than the fact that each is true.

6a. that Scott Soames exists
6b. that Scott Soames is using a sentence
6c. that someone is using a sentence
6d. that something exists
6e. that Scott Soames is in Santa Monica on December 31 of 2012

This shows, as clearly as anything could, that the sentences in (5) are not synonymous, and that $T3_S$ is false. The fault lies in Strawson's refusal to credit *what is said*, the proposition asserted or expressed, by a use of a sentence. It is this error, more than any other, that indelibly mars his otherwise prescient discussion of the connection between meaning and use in "On Referring."[30]

The fruits of this error also infect the other theses. $T1_S$ rightly takes meaning to be a property of one kind of thing while taking truth and reference to be properties of things of a different sort (insofar as Strawson recognizes truth to be a property at all). $T1_S$ also rightly takes *saying (expressing) something* to be a property of uses of sentences. But this turns out to be no advantage, because Strawson refuses to take *something said (expressed)* seriously. Realizing that "statements," in the

---

[30] This contrast between $T3_S$ and $T3_K$, as well as between $T4_S$, $T5_S$ and $T4_K$ and $T5_K$ was originally made in Soames (1989a). In exploring these contrasts here, I will continue to acquiesce, as I did there, in the idea that *what is said* by a use of a sentence S in a context is *semantically determined* by the meaning of S plus objective features of the context. Although this is an oversimplification, which I discuss at length in Soames (2005a), (2009c), and chapter 7 of (2010a), the complications can here be held in abeyance unless otherwise indicated.

sense of *what is said* (*expressed*), can't be sentences, he also plausibly holds that they can't be uses of, occurrences of, utterance tokens of, or acts of uttering, sentences, either.[31] In fact, he uses the word 'statement' ubiquitously—*for what is said, asserted or expressed* and *what is true or false*—while insisting that no entities whatsoever can play these roles.[32] Thus, although he rightly holds that uses of sentences may be properly called true, he has no way of making good on the thought that this is so only when *the propositions they are used to assert or express* are true.

His problem with singular terms is similar, though more subtle. Yes, we do use them to refer, which is more or less all that needs to be said when the terms are simple and directly referential. However, when they are complex function/argument combinations, their reference or, perhaps better, their designation, may (sometimes) vary from world-state to world-state—which means that their designata must be relativized.[33] In these cases, there is something connected with a use of the term in a context C—its content in C—that determines its designation at a world-state in a manner not unlike the way in which the proposition semantically determined by a use of a sentence determines the truth value of that use at a world-state.

There was, of course, no way Strawson could have seen this in 1950. However, his hostility to propositions was surely a big part of what he missed. This is obvious in the case of his struggles with "statements" and "what is said." But it also played a role in his discussion of reference/designation. The distinction between simple directly referential and complex nondirectly referential singular terms is, at bottom, a distinction between (i) the objects contributed by uses of the former versus (ii) the contents—which determine designated objects relative to possible world-states—contributed by uses of the latter, to the propositions expressed by uses of sentences containing the terms. If you don't have a conception of propositions as objects of the attitudes (and bearers of truth), you will have a hard time seeing this distinction. Having despaired of finding an acceptable conception of propositions, it is not surprising that Strawson didn't properly distinguish directly referential singular terms like names and demonstratives from complex

[31] See Richard Cartwright (1962) for classic arguments that statements can't be any of these things. Though I believe that some of these arguments require modification in light of the cognitive theory of propositions, they do, I think, continue to embody important insights.

[32] This is connected with his ill-fated performative theory of truth to be discussed later.

[33] When no such relativization is explicit we take the designation to be relative to the world-state of the context of utterance.

nondirectly referential terms, including singular definite descriptions (of the Fregean variety).

The failure to do so is reflected in $T4_S$ and $T5_S$. The former speaks of the meaning of a singular term—*in its primary referring use*—as being a rule for determining the referents of uses of the term at different contexts of utterance. This account is fine for simple, directly referential singular terms, but it doesn't work for complex function/argument terms or Fregean singular definite descriptions. Strawson doesn't see this because his conception of meaning as a function from uses of an expression to *extensional semantic values*—e.g., reference and truth value—leaves out content as the crucial intermediary. Hence he goes as badly wrong with descriptions as he does with sentences. Without any conception of propositions, and hence of the contents contributed to them by subsentential expressions, this failure could hardly have been avoided.

In reality, meanings of Fregean descriptions or other complex singular terms are functions from contexts to contents, which determine designations at world-states. It won't do to object that this isn't true of descriptions used referentially. Meaning is a property of expressions, not their uses. One may, to be sure, use a description in the manner of Donnellan (1966) to single out something about which the speaker asserts a singular proposition. But the proposition asserted is not the meaning of the sentence uttered, and the contribution to that proposition made by the use of the description is not its rule-governed semantic content relative to the context of utterance.[34]

It is important to note in this connection that despite the restriction in $T4_S$ to "the function of a singular term *in its primary referring use*," Strawson himself posited no semantic ambiguity corresponding to the difference between Donnellan's referential and attributive uses. In "On Referring," *a (uniquely) referring use of a singular term* is one in which the term is used to mention a particular individual. Strawson intended this restriction to rule out generic use of 'the whale' in 'The whale is a mammal' and predicative use of 'the greatest French soldier' in 'Napoleon was the greatest French soldier' (to predicate *being greater than any other French soldier* of Napoleon). Whereas Strawson's notion of a uniquely referring use is meant to *include* all genuinely singular, non-predicative uses of definite descriptions, Donnellan's notion of a referential use is meant to *exclude* nondemonstrative uses of this sort that can be understood in an essentially Fregean fashion. "On Referring" is oblivious to this distinction.

For that reason, $T5_S$ goes wrong in a way that both implicates $T2_S$ and seriously detracts from the interesting and influential theory of presupposition presented in Strawson (1950a, 1952). When n is directly

---

[34] Kripke (1977), Neale (1990), Salmon (1982), Soames (1994, 2005b).

referential, the proper thesis is $T5_K$; when n is nondirectly referential, it is $T5_{K+}$.

$T5_{K+}$ If a nondirectly referential singular term n in a sentence ⌜Fn⌝ is used in a context C, in the course of using the sentence, and F is used in C to express a property P, then the proposition semantically determined by this use of ⌜Fn⌝ in C (and, derivatively, the use itself) will be true at a possible world-state w iff the content of n in C uniquely determines a designated object o at w, and o has the property P at w; it will be false at w iff o doesn't have P at w. On a Fregean conception, this proposition, though expressed, will fail to be true or false at w if n fails to uniquely designate anything at w; thus, it will fail to be true or false at C if the content of n fails to determine a unique referent at the world-state of C.

The upshot for $T2_S$—which claims that S is meaningful iff it can be used to say something true or false—is that the thesis now becomes hostage to fortune. While it is clearly reasonable to claim that a sentence is meaningful iff it can be used to express a proposition in some contexts (and hence is not meaningful iff its use never expresses a proposition in any context), whether it is reasonable to require meaningful sentences be those that can be used to express propositions that are *true or false* depends on whether there are genuine propositions that are neither. If there are, then there may be some propositions which, though neither true nor false at any context, may be the meanings of sentences, thereby falsifying $T2_S$.[35] The reason Strawson is oblivious to this risk is, in part, that he doesn't take *what is said* seriously.

This brings me to his theory of presupposition, which, when properly reconstructed, is ambiguous between a theory of *expressive proposition* and a theory of *propositional presupposition*.[36]

EXPRESSIVE PRESUPPOSITION

A use of S in a context C presupposes$_E$ a proposition p iff the truth of p is a necessary condition for that use of S to express a proposition conforming to all semantic constraints given by the meaning of S.

---

[35] Candidates for such propositions include: the proposition *that the largest prime number is odd*, the proposition *that the element other than hydrogen and oxygen in water molecules is nitrogen*, plus certain propositions expressed by sentences containing partially defined predicates in the sense of chapters 6 and 7 of Soames (1999) and Soames (2003c).

[36] See Soames (1989a).

PROPOSITIONAL PRESUPPOSITION

A proposition p presupposes$_p$ a proposition q iff the truth of q is a necessary condition for p to be either true or false.

Propositional presupposition, which is often associated with Frege, is illustrated by the propositions expressed by uses of the positive and negative versions of (7), both of which were taken by him to presuppose$_p$ that France has one and only one king.

> 7. The king of France is (isn't) wise.
> Pre$_p$: France has one and only one king.

The basic idea is that since for Frege the truth value of ⌜Ft⌝ is the value of the concept designated by F at the individual designated by t, failure of t to designate will lead to failure of the sentence to be true or false— even in cases in which, like 'the king of France', t is meaningful, and so expresses a sense. Since negation for Frege denotes a function from truth values to truth values, ⌜~Ft⌝ will also be truth valueless. In such cases, the propositions expressed by ⌜Ft⌝ and ⌜~Ft⌝ will presuppose$_p$ any proposition q the truth of which is necessary for the sense expressed by t to determine a referent. Hence the proposition that the king of France is (isn't) wise will presuppose$_p$ that France has one and only one king. Frege's model can easily be expanded to include (8a) and (8b).[37]

> 8a. John (didn't) realize that time was running out.
> Pre$_p$: Time was running out.
> 8b. (Not) all graduate students in the class wrote term papers.
> Pre$_p$: There were graduate students in the class.

Expressive presupposition is illustrated by the examples in (9).

> 9a. That man is wise.
> Pre$_E$: The user of the sentence demonstrates, and refers to, a man.
> 9b. This is a fine red one.
> Pre$_E$: The user of the sentence refers to, and demonstrates, a fine red one of an understood kind.
> 9c. You are late.
> Pre$_E$: Some person or persons are addressed by the user of sentence.
> 9d. We saw those three other men.
> Pre$_E$: There are two contextually salient groups, one containing the user of the sentence and the other containing three men not in the first group.

---

[37] Fregean propositional presupposition, including this extension, is explained on pp. 76–80 of the reprinting in Soames (2009a) of Soames (1989a).

9d. Socrates is dead.

Pre$_E$: The user of the sentence refers to Socrates.

In each of these cases, a use of S by an agent A will express a proposition that conforms to semantic constraints on uses of S only if the expressively presupposed proposition is true.[38]

Sometimes, when the expressively presupposed proposition isn't true, extrasemantic features of the context may provide a substitute propositional constituent; in such cases A may assert a proposition, albeit not one of the sort semantically associated with S—as when A uses (9a), demonstrating, and referring to, a woman, or when A uses (9d) pointing at a photo of three men, one of whom is, unbeknown to A, a member of the group containing A whose past visual experience A is reporting. In other cases, however, no substitute proposition is available, and the utterance misfires. Strawson gives such an example in "On Referring":

> I advanced my hands, cautiously cupped towards someone, saying, as I do, 'This is a fine red one'. He, looking into my hands and seeing nothing there, may say: 'What are you talking about?' Or perhaps, 'But there is nothing in your hands.'[39]

The significant point for us is not just that the utterance is neither true nor false, as Strawson rightly notes, but that the reason it is neither is *not* that it asserts or expresses a (Fregean) proposition that is neither true nor false but rather that *it fails to assert or express any proposition at all.*

This is especially important in light of Strawson's unfortunate assimilation of this sort of failure with the kind that occurs when one uses a definite description that doesn't uniquely denote anything. His discussion leading up to his "fine red one" example concerns a contemporary use of 'The king of France is wise', which, like the demonstratively empty use of 'this' in (9b), is supposed to be "spurious" and "nongenuine"—a "pseudo" use of the term and sentence.[40] Strawson's point is that both cases involve presupposition failure *of the same sort*

That they don't is shown by the contrast between (10a) and (10b).

10a. Mary says/believes that the King of France is wise.

10b. Mary says/believes that this is a fine red one.

---

[38] The idea of a sentence being used to assert or otherwise express a proposition that meets all the requirements deriving from the meaning of the sentence is touched on in Soames (2005a, 2005b, 2008a, 2009c) and chapter 7 of (2010a).

[39] Strawson (1950a, 333).

[40] Ibid., 328–32.

Whereas my use of (10a) may be true even though 'the King of France' is nondenoting, my use of (10b) accompanied by an empty Strawsonian demonstration is as problematic as his original example. This contrast is naturally explained on the assumption that 'say' and 'believe' stand for relations between agents and propositions expressed by uses of the complement clauses of those verbs. Since my use of the complement in (10a) expresses a proposition, *there is something* which my use of the ascription truly reports Mary as saying or believing. Since my use of the complement in (10b) fails to express a proposition, nothing is so reported. Strawson misses this contrast because he doesn't think that there are entities of any sort for uses of sentences to assert, or for agents to believe.

The broader failure of the theory of presupposition offered in Strawson (1950a) and (1952) can clearly be seen by focusing on the examples in (11).

11a. That F is G
11b. The F is G.

Whereas a use of (11a) in a context in which the speaker is demonstrating, and referring to, a particular individual x, would presuppose$_E$ that x "is F," a use of (11b) by one who had merely surmised that something or other "was F" would not bear that presupposition. Moreover, if a speaker failed to demonstrate, or refer to, anyone, then the assertive utterance of (11a) might fail to assert anything. This would not be true of an assertive utterance of (11b)—even though a Fregean might claim, rightly or wrongly, that the asserted proposition presupposed$_P$ that something "was F."

The problem with Strawson's theory, and his discussion of definite descriptions, is that he treats uses of (11b) on the model of uses of (11a) while also treating them on the model of uses of (12a–d)—each of which is said to "presuppose" the truth of (12e).

12a. All F's are G.
12b. Some F's are G.
12c. No F's are G.
12d. Some F's are not G
12e. There is at least one F.

This incoherence of this pair of assimilations is hidden by Strawson's slippery use of the term "statement" in his definition of presupposition: *A statement S presupposes a statement R iff the truth of R is necessary for S to be true or false.* If we read 'statement' as 'proposition', then the theory of presupposition will be propositional, without any counterpart of Frege's semantics to explain how presuppositions are supposed to arise. If, however, we read 'for S to be true or false' as 'for S to express a proposition', then we have an informal statement of expressive proposition, which can't be applied to (11b) or (12a–d) but which does apply to (11a) and the examples in (9).

The failure of Strawson's theory of presupposition is that he ended up with neither expressive presupposition, propositional presupposition, nor any other framework capable of doing justice to his attempt to understand how meaning and context are related in understanding language use. The most important cause of failure was his inability to identify or properly conceptualize entities closely related to the meanings of sentences capable of playing the roles of objects of the attitudes and bearers of truth value. Though unfortunate, this inability is understandable. Nowhere in the philosophical tradition with which he was familiar was there any workable conception of the entities he needed. More recent theorists have done better, either by invoking flawed conceptions of propositions (which are better than none at all) or by taking propositions seriously without attempting to explain what they are. Now that the cognitive theory of propositions is available, we can give a more plausible foundational account of the entities so clearly needed in our theories of language and mind.

TRUTH, COGNITIVE PROPOSITIONS, AND THE AUSTIN/STRAWSON DEBATE

"On Referring" appeared just one year after Strawson (1949)—in which Strawson presented his performative theory of truth—and in the same year as Strawson (1950b), in which he savaged the valiant, though flawed, attempt in Austin (1950) to rehabilitate a version of the correspondence theory of truth. The key to both was the rejection of propositions indicated in the following remarkably bold passage from Strawson (1950b).

> The words 'assertion' and 'statement' have a parallel and convenient duplicity of sense. 'My statement' may be either what I say or my saying it. My saying something is certainly an episode. What I say is not. It is the latter, not the former, we declare to be true. . . . *It is futile to ask what thing or event I am talking about (over and above the subject matter of the statement) in declaring a statement to be true; for there is no such thing or event.* The word 'statement' and the phrase 'what he said,' like the conjunction 'that' followed by a noun clause are convenient, grammatically substantival devices, which we employ, on certain occasions . . .

notably (but not only) the occasions on which we use the word 'true'. . . . *To suppose that, whenever we use a singular substantive, we are, or ought to be, using it to refer to something is an ancient, but no longer respectable, error.*[41]

The logic leading here to the performative theory of truth is clear. Since there are no propositions, or indeed any class of entities which are (i) *that which is said, asserted, or believed* or (ii) the bearers or truth and falsity, there are no properties *truth* and *falsity*, either. Hence, the grammatical predicates 'is true' and 'is false' are *not* used to predicate anything of anything else. Instead, they are used to perform speech acts like 'conceding', 'confirming', 'endorsing', 'denying', and 'rebutting'. This theory was fleshed out in Strawson (1949). The lesson to be learned from its failure—which ranks among the most spectacular failures of any theory of truth ever offered—is that truth *is* a property of some things.[42] What neither Strawson nor many others could see was what they are.

One such philosopher was John Austin. Recognizing that truth is a property, he begins his classic, though much maligned article, Austin (1950) by attempting to identify what it is a property of. After correctly rejecting some obvious candidates, he concludes that statements are the bearers of truth, where a statement is "*an historic event, the utterance by a certain speaker or writer of certain words (a sentence) to an audience with reference to an historic situation.*"[43] A statement, so identified, is said to be true iff the historic situation to which the speaker, employing demonstrative linguistic conventions, refers is one of the general type required by the descriptive linguistic conventions associated with the meaning of the sentence uttered.[44] Since neither Austin's account of the bearers of truth value nor his analysis of the property *truth* are remotely correct, many of the criticisms in Strawson (1950b) are on the mark.

Thus, the two main theories of truth offered by leading ordinary language philosophers failed miserably. In both cases, the failure stemmed from an appreciation of why many initially plausible candidates could not, in fact, be primary bearers of truth, without any adequate conception of what things could fill the bill. By now this pattern should be familiar. Propositions have played important roles at pivotal moments throughout the analytic tradition. Because of this, the lack, until now,

---

[41] My emphasis; Strawson (1950b) at pp. 33–34 of its reprinting in Pitcher (1964).
[42] See the detailed critique in chapter 5 of Soames (2003b).
[43] Page 20 of the reprinting in Pitcher (1964) of Austin (1950).
[44] Ibid., 22.

of an adequate conception of what they are has distorted, inhibited, or prevented philosophical progress on many issues. For this reason, the benefits to be reaped from an adequate conception of propositions should be far reaching.

References

Austin, John. 1950. "Truth." *Proceedings of the Aristotelian Society, Suppl. Vol.* 24:111–29; reprinted in Pitcher 1964, 18–31.

Cartwright, Richard. 1962. "Propositions," in *Analytical Philosophy, First Series*, Oxford: Blackwell, 81–103.

———. 1987. "On the Origins of Russell's Theory of Descriptions," in R. J. Butler, ed., *Philosophical Essays*, Cambridge, MA: MIT Press, 95–133.

Donnellan, Keith. 1966. "Reference and Definite Descriptions." *Philosophical Review* 75:281–304.

Fodor, Jerry. 1975. *The Language of Thought.* New York: Crowell.

———. 1981. "Propositional Attitudes," in *RePresentations: Philosophical Essays on the Foundations of Cognitive Science*, 117–203. Cambridge, MA: MIT Press. Originally published in *Monist* 61 (1978).

Kaplan, David. 1989. "Demonstratives: An Essay on the Semantics, Logic, Metaphysics, and Epistemology of Demonstratives and Other Indexicals," in Almog, Perry, and Wettstein, eds., *Themes from Kaplan*, 481–563. New York: Oxford University Press.

King, Jeff, Scott Soames, and Jeff Speaks. 2014. *New Thinking about Propositions*, Oxford University Press.

Kripke, Saul. 1977. "Speaker's Reference and Semantic Reference," in French, Uehling, and Wettstein, eds., *Contemporary Perspectives in the Philosophy of Language*, 6–27. Minneapolis: University of Minnesota Press.

Neale, Stephen. 1990. *Descriptions.* Cambridge, MA: MIT Press.

Pitcher, George. 1964. *Truth.* Englewood Cliffs, NJ: Prentice Hall.

Russell, Bertrand. 1903. *Principles of Mathematics.* New York: Norton.

———. 1904. "Meinong's Theory of Complexes and Assumptions." *Mind* 13:204–19, 336–54, 509–24; reprinted in Russell 1973, *Essays in Analysis*, ed. Lackey, 21–76. New York: George Braziller.

———. 1905a. "On Fundamentals. Written in June 1905; first published in Urquhart and Lewis, eds., *The Collected Papers of Bertrand Russell*. Vol. 4: *Foundations of Logic*. London: Routledge, 1994.

———. 1905b. "On Denoting." *Mind* 14:479–93.

———. 1906–7. "On the Nature of Truth." *Proceedings of the Aristotelian Society, New Series* 7:28–49.

———. 1910. "On the Nature of Truth and Falsehood," in *Philosophical Essays*. London: Allen and Unwin.

———. 1912. *The Problems of Philosophy*. London: Williams and Norgate; New York: Henry Holt; reprinted New York and Oxford: Oxford University Press, 1997.

———. 1913. *Theory of Knowledge*, in E. Eames, ed., *The Collected Papers of Bertrand Russell*, vol. 7. London: George Allen and Unwin, 1989.

———. 1918–19. "The Philosophy of Logical Atomism." *Monist* 5 (no. 28): 495–527; continued in *Monist* 5 (no. 29): 32–63, 190–222, 345–80; reprinted in *The Philosophy of Logical Atomism*. With an introduction by David Pears. Peru, IL: Open Court, 1985.

———. 1919a. "On Propositions: What They Are and How They Mean." *Proceedings of the Aristotelian Society, Suppl. Vol.* 2:1–43.

———. 1973. *Essays in Analysis*. Edited by Douglas Lackey. New York: George Braziller, 21–76.

Russell, Bertrand, and Alfred North Whitehead. 1910. *Principia Mathematica*, vol. 1. Cambridge: Cambridge University Press.

Ryle, Gilbert. 1949. *The Concept of Mind*. Chicago: University of Chicago Press.

———. 1954. *Dilemmas*. Cambridge: Cambridge University Press.

Salmon, Nathan. 1982. "Assertion and Incomplete Descriptions." *Philosophical Studies* 42:37–45.

———. 2005. "On Designating," *Mind* 114:1069–1133.

Soames, Scott. 1989a. "Presupposition," in D. Gabby and F. Guenthner, eds., *Handbook of Philosophical Logic*. Vol. 4: *Topics in Philosophy of Language*. Dordrecht: Reidel, 553–616; reprinted in Soames 2009a, 73–130.

———.1989b. "Semantics and Semantic Competence," in James Tomberlin, ed., *Philosophy of Mind and Action Theory*, 575–96. Philosophical Perspectives 3. Atascadero, CA: Ridgeview; reprinted in Soames 2009a, 182–201.

———. 1990. "Belief and Mental Representation," in Philip P. Hanson, ed., *Information, Language, and Cognition*, 217–46; reprinted in Soames 2009b.

———. 1994. "Donnellan's Referential/Attributive Distinction." *Philosophical Studies* 73:149–68; reprinted in Soames 2009a, 360–76.

———. 1999. *Understanding Truth*. New York: Oxford University Press.

———. 2003a. *Philosophical Analysis in the Twentieth Century*, vol. 1. Princeton, NJ, and Oxford: Princeton University Press.

———. 2003b. *Philosophical Analysis in the Twentieth Century*, vol. 2. Princeton, NJ, and Oxford: Princeton University Press.

———. 2003c. "Higher-Order Vagueness for Partially Defined Predicates," in J. C. Beall, ed., *Liars and Heaps: New Essays on Paradox*, 128–50. New York: Oxford University Press; reprinted in Soames 2009b, 340–61.

———. 2005a. "Naming and Asserting," in S. Zabo, ed., *Semantics vs. Pragmatics*, 356–82. New York: Oxford University Press; reprinted in Soames 2009a, 251–77.

———. 2005b. "Why Incomplete Descriptions Do Not Defeat Russell's Theory of Descriptions." *Teorema* 24:7–30; reprinted in Soames 2009a, 377–400.

———. 2006. "Understanding Assertion," in Judith Thomson and Alex Byrne, eds., *Themes from the Philosophy of Robert Stalnaker*, 222–50. Oxford: Oxford University Press; reprinted in Soames 2009b.

———. 2007. "What We Know Now that We Didn't Know Then." *Philosophical Studies* 135:461–78.

———. 2008a. "Drawing the Line between Meaning and Implicature—and Relating Both to Assertion. *Nous* 42:440–65; reprinted in Soames 2009a, 298–326.

———. 2008b. "Why Propositions Can't Be Sets of Truth-Supporting Circumstances." *Journal of Philosophical Logic* 37:267–76; reprinted in Soames 2009b.

———. 2009a. *Philosophical Essays*, vol. 1. Princeton, NJ: Princeton University Press.

———. 2009b. *Philosophical Essays*, vol. 2. Princeton, NJ: Princeton University Press.

———. 2009c. "The Gap between Meaning and Assertion: Why What We Literally Say Often Differs from What Our Words Literally Mean," in Soames 2009a, 278–97.

———. 2010a. *Philosophy of Language*. Princeton, NJ: Princeton University Press.

———. 2010b. *What is Meaning?* Princeton, NJ: Princeton University Press.

———. 2014. *The Analytic Tradition in Philosophy*, vol. 1. Princeton, NJ: Princeton University Press.

———. Forthcoming . *Language, Mind, and Meaning: The Hempel Lectures.* Princeton, NJ: Princeton University Press.

Strawson, Peter. 1949. "Truth." *Analysis* 9:83–97.

———.1950a. "On Referring." *Mind* 59:320–44.

———. 1950b. "Truth." *Proceedings of the Aristotelian Society, Suppl. Vol.* 24: 129–56; reprinted in Pitcher 1964, 32–53.

———. 1952. *Introduction to Logical Theory*. London: Methuen.

Wittgenstein, Ludwig. 1922. *Tractatus Logico-Philosophicus*, trans. by C. K. Ogden. London: Routledge and Kegan Paul; reprinted in 1999 by Dover; re-translated by D. Pears and B. McGuinness. London: Routledge, 1961.

———. 1953. *Philosophical Investigations*. Edited by G.E.M. Anscombe and R. Rhees. Translated by G.E.M. Anscombe. Oxford: Blackwell.

5

The Place of Willard Van Orman Quine in Analytic Philosophy

W.V.O. Quine was born on June 25, 1908, in Akron, Ohio. From 1926 to 1930 he attended Oberlin College, from which he graduated with a BA in mathematics that included reading in mathematical philosophy. He received his PhD from Harvard in 1932 with a dissertation on *Principia Mathematica* advised by Alfred North Whitehead. Quine spent the next year traveling on fellowship in Europe, where he interacted with Carnap, Tarski, Lesniewski, Lukasiewicz, Schlick, Hahn, Reichenbach, Gödel, and Ayer. Between 1933 and 1936 Quine was a Junior Fellow at the Harvard Society. In 1936, he joined the Harvard faculty, where he remained for 42 years, except for the 3 years he served in the navy in World War II. Returning after the war, he was promoted to Professor in 1948. Although he retired in 1978, he retained his office and remained active through much of the 1990s. Quine died on Christmas Day 2000.

The Harvard faculty he joined in 1936 included Whitehead, Ralph Barton Perry (who edited the papers of William James), Henry Sheffer (of the "Sheffer stroke"), and C. I. Lewis. An eclectic thinker, Lewis combined the perceptual realism of Perry with the Kantianism of Josiah Royce and the pragmatism of Peirce. Like Perry, Lewis believed that perception and knowledge require an independent reality given in experience. Like Royce, Lewis believed experience to be structured by concepts added by the mind. Like Peirce, Lewis held that these concepts are revisable in light of experience and that the "meanings" of concepts and thoughts lie in their success in predicting new experience and grounding successful action.[1] Despite having some commonalities with logical empiricists, Lewis was never one of them. While sharing their scientific naturalism, their emphasis on analysis, and their view

---

[1] These ideas were developed in Lewis (1929) and (1946), which were widely read—the former being the subject of a seminar at Oxford led by J. L. Austin and Isaiah Berlin in 1936–37.

of testable consequences as the basis of empirical significance, he opposed their noncognitivism about value, their physicalism, and their "linguistic turn." For him, the primary bearers of meaning and truth were thoughts, a point on which he differed from Quine. Lewis also differed from Quine in embracing analyticity and modal logic, to which he contributed the axiomatic S-systems.

This was the milieu into which Quine stepped as a young professor. It wasn't until after the war that his impact was widely felt. Even in 1948 his influence on his own department was too weak to secure the proposed appointment of his friend Rudolf Carnap. By 1953, when Lewis retired, Quine was ready to lead the first great analytic department in America. With the publication of Quine (1948, 1951a, 1951b, 1953a, 1953b, 1953c, 1956), he was recognized as a world leader in philosophy. The first American to achieve this status, Quine changed analytic philosophy by transcending the limitations of logical empiricism and replacing it with a more thoroughly empiricist view.

THE LOGICAL EMPIRICIST BACKGROUND

The logical empiricism of Quine's predecessors was built on (i) the Frege-Russell rejection of the Kantian synthetic apriori in favor of a notion of analyticity encompassing logic, arithmetic, and mathematics (except for geometry about which Frege followed Kant, but which the logical empiricists took to be an empirical theory); (ii) the Russellian version of Humean empiricism in which material objects were said to be *logical constructions* out of perceptual experience; and (iii) the tractarian idea that a test for meaning, or intelligibility, is central to philosophy. By 1934 Carnap had synthesized and extended these ideas into a new version of empiricism developed in Carnap (1928a, 1928b, 1930, 1931, 1932a, 1932b, 1934).

To the logicist program of Frege and Russell, Carnap added Wittgenstein's conception of logical truths as tautologies, guaranteed to be true by the meanings of their logical terms. Accepting logicist definitions as explicating the meanings of arithmetical terms, Carnap extended this status to all of mathematics, thereby attributing the apriority and necessity of logic and mathematics to analyticity. Correct philosophical analyses were treated similarly. Having said, "Philosophy is to be replaced by the logic of science—that is to say by the logical analysis of the concepts and sentences of the sciences,"[2] Carnap maintained that analyticity was philosophy's stock-in-trade. To him, the point seemed

[2] Page 277 of the 1937 translation of Carnap (1934).

obvious. If a truth is apriori, the reason it can be known without justifying empirical evidence *must be* that it places no constraint on the world but rather is true in virtue of meaning. Since a necessary truth provides no information about which possible state the world is in, it too must be analytic, and empty of empirical content. Finally, experience can tell us only about the way the world actually is; so anything we *know to be necessary* must be something that doesn't constrain the world at all, again because it is true in virtue of meaning.

By contrast, the aposteriori, contingent, and synthetic were subject to Carnap's version of Wittgenstein's intelligibility test. In the *Tractatus*, empirical descriptions of the world are meaningful, but other (nonanalytic, noncontradictory) claims are not, including those of traditional (metaphysical or moral) philosophy. Whereas Wittgenstein's test maintained that the truth/falsity of all empirical statements is determined by the totality of atomic facts (which correspond to atomic truths), Carnap dropped talk of correspondence, and characterized empirical meaningfulness in terms of verifiability or falsifiability. Unlike the *Tractatus*, which offered an ineffable metaphysical parallel between language and the world, Carnap's early writings rejected talk of relations between words and things (a position he revised after encountering Tarski's theory of truth).

This is where things stood on the eve of Quine's first major article, "Truth by Convention," which attacked Carnap's linguistic theory of the apriori. Although Quine's critique was powerful, for many years it didn't attract much attention or change many minds—probably because its target seemed undeniably correct to its proponents. Nevertheless, central tenets of the target theory are clearly problematic. Most obviously, the bearers of analyticity are sentences, whereas the bearers of apriority and necessity seem not to be. When one says that *it is necessary, and knowable apriori, that all squares are rectangles*, what is said to be necessary and knowable apriori is not the sentence 'All squares are rectangles,' or any other. How, in light of this, is one supposed to move from the claim that S is analytic to the truth of the claim ⌜it is necessary/knowable apriori that S⌝?

Although this wasn't a worry to which Quine or the logical empiricists paid much attention, it's not obvious how a proponent of the linguistic theory of the apriori (and the necessary) should deal with it. Here is one line of thought, the failure of which may be instructive. Let S be an analytic truth expressing p.

> (i) Since S is analytic, one can know that S expresses a truth by learning what it means.

(ii) One will thereby know the metalinguistic claim q—*that S expresses a truth*—on the basis of the evidence E provided by one's experience in learning the meaning of S.

(iii) Since one has come to understand S, one will also know, on the basis of E, that S expresses p (and only p).

(iv) Combining (ii) and (iii), one will thereby know, on the basis of E, that p is true. Since p is an apriori consequence of this claim, one will be in position to come to know p.

(v) However, the claim that E *justifies*—by ruling out possibilities in which it is false—is not p, but q.

(vi) Since p can be known without justifying evidence ruling out possibilities in which it is false, there must be no such possibilities.

(vii) So, if S is analytic, p must be necessary, and capable of being known to be so (by the present reasoning); p is also apriori, since knowledge of p doesn't require evidence justifying it.

Though one might be fooled by this reasoning, if it were left implicit, the problems with it—apart from (i), which we here accept for the sake of argument—are evident.[3] The most obvious difficulty concerns the knowledge of p reached at (iv). Anyone who comes to know p by this route will know it *aposteriori*—whether or not p is *knowable* apriori. Worse, p will be knowable apriori only if there is a *different* route to such knowledge—which threatens to undermine the point of the linguistic theory. Further, the reasoning described, by which one comes to know both p and the necessity of p, requires one to employ apriori logical knowledge independent of the linguistic conventions in question. So, even if there were no other problems with it, the argument would presuppose much of what the linguistic theory purports to explain. Finally, (vi) falls afoul of the contingent apriori.

QUINE'S "TRUTH BY CONVENTION"

The theory under attack holds that logical truths are true by convention, and so are analytic, apriori, and necessary. Let us begin by taking the language L under discussion to be a first-order language with an infinite set LT of sentences true in all models of L. Quine observes that speakers cannot have adopted a separate convention for each member of LT. Rather, the proponent of the linguistic theory must maintain,

---

[3] See Williamson (2007, chaps. 3 and 4) for a catalog of well-taken worries about (i).

L-speakers have adopted a finite set of conventions from which the truth of every member of LT *follows*. But this won't do. If the linguistic theory of logic, apriority, and necessity must presuppose logical, apriori, and necessary consequence, then it can't explain them. The point can be illustrated in an example.

1. All sentences of the form 'S or ~S' are true.
2. The sentence 'Los Angeles is in California or it isn't' is of the form 'S or ~S'
3. So, 'Los Angeles is in California or it isn't' is true.

Suppose that (1) is the statement of a convention, and so is true by stipulation. Since (2) is obviously true, (3) must also be true, where the sentence mentioned is a logical truth. Imagine that every other logical truth is similarly treated. Although this is supposed to establish the analyticity/apriority/necessity of all such logical truths, it doesn't.

First, notice a problem Quine doesn't mention. For the argument to explain agents' knowledge of (3), agents must know *that all sentences of the form 'S or S' are true* by virtue of knowing *that linguistic convention stipulates that they are*. Surely, this is *aposteriori knowledge* of an empirical fact about the linguistic community. So, we have a problem at the outset. The problem on which Quine does focus is that to derive (3) one must recognize the inference from (1) and (2) to (3) to be truth preserving, which requires knowing *that if all F's are G, and a is an F, then a is G*. Since this logical knowledge is required for one to come to know (3) on the basis of (1) and (2), *any appeal to knowledge of linguistic conventions to explain (apriori) logical knowledge will presuppose (apriori) logical knowledge that is not explained by knowledge of those conventions*. It is no good to object that one can derive (3) from (1) and (2) without thinking to oneself *"if all F's are G, and a is an F, then a is G."* This makes no difference. If there was *nothing* behind A's moving from (1) and (2) to (3), other than a blind process *insufficient to credit A with knowledge of the rule,* we wouldn't credit A's accepting (3) as showing that A *knew it* by virtue of knowing (1) and (2). So, the critique stands.

Quine's second objection is that since logical words are needed to state the conventions, some logical words must get their meanings independently, and some logical truths must not be true by convention. To the objection that we can be guided by conventions that are never formulated, he replies that an explanation that appeals to *truth by unstated conventions* is empty without a compelling story of what such conventions amount to:

> In dropping the attributes of deliberateness and explicitness from the notion of linguistic convention we risk depriving the latter of

any explanatory force and reducing it to an idle label. We may wonder what one adds to the bare statement that the truths of logic and mathematics are *a priori*, or to the still barer behavioristic statement that they are firmly accepted, when he characterizes them as true by convention in such a sense.[4]

To this we add that *if* the imagined conventions by which words are introduced rely on prior beliefs and intentions to guide later linguistic behavior, then presumably those attitudes will have negative, disjunctive, and quantified contents. This confronts the defender of the linguistic theory of the apriori with a dilemma. To insist that *none* of the propositions toward which prelinguistic agents are capable of having attitudes are knowable apriori—and hence that none is identical with the (apriori) proposition that *either o is red or o isn't red*—would be to cast doubt on the idea that such agents have contentful attitudes at all (thereby undermining the account of how unstated conventions arise). To admit that such agents *do* grasp propositional contents that are knowable apriori is to invite questions to which the linguistic theory has no answers.

(i) How, if the truth of a sentence depends on the truth of what it expresses, can introducing sentences expressing contents one can already entertain possibly enable one to know apriori things one could not know apriori before they were linguistically expressed?

(ii) Why suppose that prelinguistic agents who already have the concepts of negation, disjunction, and quantification introduce words for them by stipulating that 'not', 'or', and 'all' will mean whatever they must to make certain sentences true, rather than by simply resolving to use them to express the concepts they already possess?

QUINE'S BATTLE AGAINST QUANTIFIED MODAL LOGIC

Although Quine was critical of the linguistic theory of the *apriori*, he shared two presuppositions of its proponents—that necessity is apriority and that both are defensible only if they are reducible to analyticity. Having rejected the reduction of apriority to analyticity, he concluded that there is no apriori knowledge and no necessary truths. But his attack on the later still hadn't been made explicit. When it came it proceeded in two stages. The first stage—in Quine (1943, 1947, 1953a,

---

[4] Quine (1936) at Quine (1966, 99).

1953b)—attacked quantified modal logic as developed in the 1940s by Ruth Marcus and Rudolf Carnap. The second, in Quine (1951b), was directed at analyticity/ necessity itself. In this section, I discuss the first stage of the attack.

At this stage Quine was willing (for the sake of argument) to take the notion *analyticity* for granted—defined as a sentence that can be turned into a logical truth by replacing synonyms with synonyms. Interpreting necessity as analyticity, taking S to be possible iff its negation isn't analytic, and assuming logicism, he could make sense of claims like (4) and (5), which are instances of the first grade of modal involvement.

    4. '9 is an odd number' is necessary.
    5. 'The number of planets is even' is possible.

The second grade is illustrated by (6) and (7).

    6. It is necessary that 9 is an odd number.
    7. It is possible that the number of planets is even.

Quine's strategy was to reduce this grade of modal involvement to the first. When modal operators aren't iterated, the truth conditions of (6) and (7) are those of (4) and (5). When they are, he assigns sentences to a hierarchy, depending on the number of modal operators embedded under such operators. Each level is governed by a definition of logical truth and analyticity, with the truth conditions of ⌜It is necessary that S⌝ (which is of level $n+1$, when S is of level n) being given in terms of the definitions of logical truth and analyticity at level n.[5]

At the third level of modal involvement '□' and '◊' are operators (expressing necessity and possibility) that can be prefixed to open formulas, allowing quantifying in.

    8. ∃x □ x is an odd number.
    9. ∃x (x is the number of planets & ◊ x is even)

Even if we understand analyticity and objectual quantification, this doesn't guarantee that we can assign intelligible truth conditions to sentences like these. If necessity is analyticity, it is a property of *sentences*. To make sense of (8) and (9) we must decide whether *an open formula relative to an assignment of an object to a variable is a logically true sentence or one that can be turned into a logical truth by replacing synonyms with synonyms*. Since open formulas are *not* sentences, and variables relative to assignments are *not* terms with meanings or definitions, it is puzzling what the truth conditions of (8) and (9) are supposed to be. Quine did *not* foist this puzzle on the modal logicians of his

---

[5] Section 2 of Quine (1947).

time; they brought it on themselves by sharing the identification of necessity with analyticity that generated it. Quine was right to insist that if quantified modal logic was to progress, it had to solve this puzzle or give up that identification.

From here, he developed two lines of argument that neither he nor his opponents consistently distinguished. One was that if necessity is analyticity, there is no way of solving this puzzle. The other was that, the interpretation of necessity aside, quantified modal logic violates fundamental logical and semantic principles, and so must be rejected.

The second, more ambitious, attack depends on A1, which is true; A2 and A3, which are false; plus the definitions D1–D3.[6]

A1. The modal operators '□' and '◊' are referentially opaque.

A2. Occurrences of objectual variables in the scope of referentially opaque operators are not purely referential.

A3. Bindable occurrences of objectual variables must be purely referential.

D1. An occurrence of a term in a formula or sentence S is *purely referential* iff what it contributes to the truth or falsity of S (relative to an assignment) is simply what it designates or denotes (relative to the assignment).

D2. A position in S is *referentially transparent* iff for any pair of terms t and t*, the results S(t) and S(t*) of substituting these terms into that position will have the same truth values (relative to an appropriate assignment) iff ⌜t = t*⌝ is true (relative to that assignment). A position is *referentially opaque* iff it is not referentially transparent.

D3. A sentential operator is *referentially transparent* iff any referentially transparent position in a sentence remains so when the operator is prefixed to the sentence. A sentential operator is *referentially opaque* iff it is not referentially transparent.

The idea behind A2 is this: Let 'O' be a referentially opaque operator, let ⌜O F(x)⌝ be a formula in which 'x' occurs free (in position p), and let ⌜O F(t)⌝ and ⌜O F(t*)⌝ be sentences that differ in truth value that arise from substituting distinct terms t and t* designating the same object o for 'x' (at p). (There must be such terms if 'O' is referentially opaque.) The truth value of ⌜O F(x)⌝ relative to an assignment A of o to 'x' differs from the truth value of *one* of these two sentences even though

---

[6] The explication of this argument given below is of the reasoning, implicit and explicit, in Quine (1943, 1953b). The category of "terms" in D1, D2 includes definite descriptions (whether Fregean or Russellian).

⌜t = t* = x⌝ is true relative to A. Suppose ⌜O F(t*)⌝ differs in truth value from ⌜O F(x)⌝ (relative to A). Then, Quine concludes, occurrences of t in the former and 'x' in the latter both fail to be purely referential, verifying A2. As noted in section III of Kaplan (1986) and Kazmi (1987), this argument is fallacious. From the fact that ⌜O F(t*)⌝ differs in truth value from ⌜O F(x)⌝ (relative to A), we can conclude that either the occurrence of t* in the former or the occurrence of 'x' in the latter is not *purely referential*, but we cannot conclude that the occurrence of 'x' isn't. Also, one can construct opaque operators, as Kaplan does in sections IV, VII, and VIII–XIII, for which occurrences of variables in their scope *are* purely referential, and bindable from outside by objectual quantifiers. So A2 is false.[7]

Kaplan introduces the notion of the *valuated sentence* associated with F(x) relative to an assignment of o to 'x'. It is what one gets by substituting o for 'x' in the syntactic structure F(x). Given this, one can define referentially opaque operators that allow quantifying in and have extensions that include both ordinary and valuated sentences. For example, we might define an operator O_1 that maps an ordinary sentence S onto truth iff Ralph utters S, while mapping a valuated sentence VS onto truth iff he utters any complete sentence that results from replacing an occurrence of an object o in VS with an occurrence of any proper name of o. So understood, occurrences of variables under O_1 are *purely referential*, and the standard "law" (10) of quantification theory is retained. ('F' is used as a schematic letter in (10).)

   10. ∀x,y [x = y ⊃ (O (Fx) ⊃ O (Fy))]

There is, however, nothing in the nature of quantification that requires (10) to be true. Let a *finely valuated sentence* be just like a valuated sentence except that instead of replacing 'x' with o, we replace 'x' with <'x',o>. Now, we stipulate that O_2 maps a finely valuated sentence FVS onto truth iff Ralph utters any complete sentence that results from replacing all occurrences of each variable/object pair <v,o> in FVS with occurrences of a proper name of o, *provided different occurrences of the same pair are replaced by occurrences of the same name.* Quantification

---

[7] Quine (1947) uses different reasoning in attempting to establish A2. Quine notes that if O is a referentially opaque operator, there will be truths ⌜t = t* & O (S(t) & ~ O S(t*)⌝. If t and t* occupy positions open to objectual quantification, and if existential generalization is universally truth preserving, then ⌜∃x ∃y (x = y & Sx & ~Sy)⌝ must also be true. Since this violates "the law of the substitutivity of identity for variables" and requires some occurrences of variables to be nonpurely referential, he thinks this is impossible. Later, I argue that Quine is wrong about this. The other flaw is his incorrect assumption that existential generalization is fundamental to objectual quantification. Although it is always truth preserving in certain contexts, it fails to be so in others.

into contexts governed by O_2 is as intelligible as quantification into contexts governed by O_1, even though (10) fails with O_2. So (10) *isn't* really a law of quantification, and bindable occurrences of variables need not be purely referential.

To understand this one must *not* confuse schema (11a) with the indiscernibility principle that may be formulated by (11b) or (11c).[8]

11a. $\forall x,y \ [x = y \supset (S(x) \supset S(y))]$
11b. $\forall x,y \ (x = y \supset$ every property of x is a property of y)
11c. $\forall x,y \ [x = y \supset \forall P(Px \supset Py)]$

The instance of (11a) that arises from replacing '$S(x) \supset S(y)$' with '$O_2(x{\neq}y) \supset O_2(y{\neq}y)$' is false if Ralph has uttered 'Hesperus ≠ Phosphorus' but not ⌜n ≠ n⌝ for any name designating Venus. This is consistent with the truth of (11b) and (11c), since the property Venus must have iff $O_2(x \neq y)$' is true (relative to an assignment A of Venus to 'x', 'y') is *being designated by some pair of names* t_1 *and* t_2 *such that Ralph utters* ⌜$t_1 \neq t_2$⌝, while the property Venus must have iff '$O_2(x \neq x)$' is true (relative to A) is *being designated by some name t such that Ralph utters* ⌜$t \neq t$⌝. In short, the failure of Quine's principle A3 does not threaten the indiscernibility of identicals.[9]

However, the failure of this Quinean argument—that quantifying into referentially opaque constructions violates fundamental semantic and logical principles—doesn't resolve Quine's worries about the quantified modal logic of his day. To do that, one must make positive sense of quantifying into modal contexts *when necessity is identified with analyticity*. Quine argues, in (1947, 1953b), that this is impossible because the truth conditions of sentences of the third grade of modal involvement can't be specified in terms of the truth conditions of those of the second grade. As he notes, it is natural to appeal to (i) and (ii) in attempting to do so.

(i) $\exists x \ldots x \ldots$ is true only if $\ldots a \ldots$ is true for some term a.
(ii) $\exists x \ldots x \ldots$ is true if $\ldots a \ldots$ is true for some term a.

Principle (i) is problematic because there will typically be no guarantee that unnamed, or even unnamable, objects might be the only ones underwriting the truth of an existence claim. Principle (ii) is also problematic. Suppose there are two names, a and b, such that (12a) and (13a) are both true. Then, by (ii), (12b) and (13b) must also be true.

---

[8] See Kazmi (1992).
[9] Two interesting analyses of propositional attitude verbs that lead to violations of (11a) are Mark Richard (1987) and Kit Fine (2007). These are critically discussed in Soames (1987; 2012; 2002, chap. 7).

12a. $a = b \, \& \, \square \, aRa$
12b. $\exists x \, [x = b \, \& \, \square \, xRa]$

13a. $b = b \, \& \sim \square \, bRa$
13b. $\exists x \, [x = b \, \& \sim \square \, xRa]$

But, since (12b) and (13b) are contraries, they can't both be true. So, in order to prevent (ii) from being falsified, one must restrict the terms used to specify the truth conditions of quantified sentences to members of a class T of terms coreferential members of which are *analytically equivalent.*

   (iii) If a and b are members of T, then ⌜a = b⌝ is analytic if true, and substitution of one for the other in any analytic sentence preserves analyticity.

If this restriction is observed, (12a) and (13a) can't be jointly true, which in turn will block the erroneous characterization of (12b) and (13b) as jointly true.

   However, to adopt (iii) as the means of specifying the truth conditions of third-grade modal sentences in terms of second-grade sentences requires one to drastically limit the domain of objects and the class of terms designating them. As cases involving 'Hesperus'/'Phosphorus' and 'Cicero'/'Tully' illustrate, ordinary proper names of empirically given objects must be excluded. That's not all. As Quine notes in (1947, 1953b), the severity of the needed restrictions would undercut any significant philosophical interest in quantified modal logic. Nor does there seem to be another way of specifying truth conditions of the third grade in terms of those of the second. Quine was right: *if necessity is nothing more than analyticity,* then quantified modal logic is of little interest. His error, as well as that of most of those against whom he argued, was in taking it for granted that if there is such a thing as necessity, it must be analyticity.[10]

ANALYTICITY, NECESSITY, AND MEANING

"Two Dogmas of Empiricism" (1951), which was among the most widely influential works in philosophy of its time, changed the self-conception of analytic philosophy in two ways. By undermining the analytic/synthetic distinction, as then understood, it decisively challenged the picture of philosophy as conceptual analysis; by embracing

---

[10] The discussion in this section has profited greatly from the contributions of Ali Kazmi.

a holistic view of empirical confirmation, it drove the final nail in the coffin of the logical empiricists' verificationist criterion of meaning. Though in retrospect Quine's moves were simple, they were essential to freeing philosophy from the once liberating but by then confining "linguistic turn."

The first phase of the attack on analyticity was the circle argument in sections 1–4 of "Two Dogmas." A sentence is characterized as analytic iff it is a logical truth or can be turned into one by replacing synonyms with synonyms. Synonymy is intersubstitutivity that always preserves truth value. In what environments? The answer, in contemporary terms, is that for A and B to be synonymous, substitution of one for the other must preserve truth value in *intensional* constructions (though not necessarily in hyperintensional ones). These constructions are identified with those in the scope of a modal operator. But this requires an independent conception of necessity that Quine's targets didn't have. Rather, they insisted, it is only by explicating necessity as analyticity that the former can be made defensible. Quine agreed, while insisting that the proposed explication was worthless, because we can't explain analyticity without presupposing necessity. Far from vindicating necessity, he argued, the logical empiricists' treasured reduction infused analyticity with necessity's fatal defects.

Although Quine's attack succeeded against its intended targets, today we realize that analyticity and necessity need not be yoked together. His failure to see what others of his time also failed to see was connected to his rejection in "Two Dogmas" of synonymy, and his later rejection, in Quine (1960), of hyperintensionality. As for analyticity, the jury is still out. Despite the trenchant criticism in Williamson (2007) of recent attempts to rehabilitate epistemic conceptions of analyticity, it is not obvious that no such conception can be sustained. What is clear is that no conception of analyticity with the broad philosophical significance accorded to it by Quine's opponents will ever be forthcoming. On this crucial matter, he was right.

After giving the circle argument, Quine devotes the last two sections of "Two Dogmas" to improving the logical empiricists' faulty conception of meaning. His second "dogma" was the view that every meaningful sentence S is associated with sets C and D of observational claims such that the truth of any member of C would add to the degree to which S is confirmed, while the truth of any member of D would add to the degree to which S is disconfirmed. This dogma is connected to the dogma that there is an analytic/synthetic distinction by a conception that identifies the meaning of a synthetic sentence with the sets of experiences that would confirm/disconfirm it. As Quine observes, if S1 and S2 are confirmed/disconfirmed by the same experiences, they are synonymous, and their biconditional will be analytic. So, one who rejects analyticity (and synonymy) must reject the second dogma too.

Quine's reason for so doing is rooted in the Duhemian idea that what counts as confirmation or disconfirmation of a hypothesis H depends on the background assumptions we hold fixed in testing H. Because he thinks we often have a wide range of choice in deciding which background assumptions to appeal to, and which to give up when they plus H entail a falsehood, he rejects the idea that H's meaning determines the evidence that would confirm or disconfirm H. If that idea were correct, the meaning of H would underwrite analytic truths specifying which experiences would confirm, or disconfirm, H. But if understanding H were sufficient to determine when it was confirmed, or disconfirmed, we wouldn't have the range of theoretical choice of when to hold onto H, and when not, that we know we do have.

To this plausible criticism of Carnap, Quine adds two more dubious claims: (i) that only entire theories, rather than individual hypotheses, are confirmed or disconfirmed by empirical evidence; (ii) that the meaning of a theory is the totality of empirical evidence that would confirm or disconfirm it. In short, he agreed with logical empiricists that meaning (empirical significance) is verifying or falsifying experience while insisting that "the unit [of meaning] accountable to an empiricist critique" is not the individual sentence but "the whole of science."[11]

In the final section of "Two Dogmas" Quine sketches the following theses of this holistic version of logical empiricism.

QT1. Holistic Verificationism
    1a. The meaning of a theory = the class of possible observations it fits.
    1b.Two theories have the same meaning iff they fit the same class of possible observations.

QT2. The totality of our beliefs is a "man-made fabric which impinges on experience only along the edges."

QT3. Any statement can be held true come what may (by making adjustments elsewhere).

QT4. Any statement can be rejected, or held to be false (by making adjustments elsewhere). Thus, no statement is immune from revision.

QT5. Underdetermination

    For any consistent theory T_1, and class of possible observations O that fit it, there is a theory T_2 incompatible with T_1 which also fits O.

---

[11] Quine (1951b), p. 42 of the 1980 reprinting of Quine (1953a).

In QT1 and QT5, we take the class of possible observations a theory fits to be the class of observational conditionals, $\ulcorner O_1 \supset O_2 \urcorner$ it entails. (O_1 and O_2 specify observable events.) For the theory to be true, it is necessary that all these conditionals be true. For two theories to mean the same thing, it is necessary and sufficient that they entail the same observational conditionals.

One who accepts this view can identify (putative) mistakes made by defenders of the analytic/synthetic distinction. For Quine, their mistakes were to have accepted (14a–c) instead of (15a–c).

14a. Experience is relevant to the confirmation of individual synthetic, but not analytic, sentences.

14b. Analytic sentences can, without error or change of meaning, be held true in the face of any experience. Synthetic sentences cannot be.

14c. Analytic sentences cannot be rejected without error, unless we change what we mean by them. Synthetic sentences can be so rejected.

15a. Experience is not relevant to the confirmation of individual nonobservation statements taken in isolation. It is relevant to their confirmation taken in their role as contributing to our total theory of the world.

15b. Any nonobservation sentence, can, without error, be held true in the face of any experience—by making compensatory changes elsewhere in one's theory.

15c. Insofar as it makes sense to talk of the meanings of individual sentences at all, changes in one's total theory (which involve changes in which sentences one accepts and which one rejects) should be seen as implicitly changing the meanings of all one's sentences.

Although Quine takes no sentences to be immune from revision in light of experience, he does recognize that the degree to which we are ready to revise them varies from sentence to sentence, depending on how central they are to our conceptual framework. There is, he thinks, a continuum on which sentences that have traditionally been characterized as analytic typically occur at one end, while those that have been characterized as synthetic often occur at the other.

One cannot, in evaluating Quine's holistic verificationism, avoid the role played by the underspecified wild card—observation—in his system. In Quine (1948, 1951b) he spoke of "sense experiences" as observational touchstones of theories. This is what underlay his perversely even-handed comparison of phenomenalistic versus physicalistic ontologies, including his characterization of physical objects as mythic intermediaries, "comparable epistemologically to the gods of Homer,"[12] that are imported into theories as aids in predicting future experience in light of past experience. As I have argued elsewhere, to combine holistic verification with this conception of observation is to reproduce some of the worst absurdities of the earlier empiricist systems.[13] Fortunately, his sensory conception of evidence was temporary, to be dropped in later years along with the pseudoprofundity of his earlier talk about myths and the gods of Homer.

Nevertheless, observation remained a problem. If, for the holistic verificationist, statements reporting the contents of ordinary, unaided observations can play the role of data statements that give empirical content to theories, how far should we go? Do observations using magnifying glasses count? How about binoculars, telescopes, microscopes, radar, electron microscopes, ratio-telescopes, and CT scans? The more we include in the observational base of theories, the less radical, but also less interesting, holistic verificationism becomes. Is there a principled way to draw the line between the observational and the nonobservational that would render even a weakened holistic verificationism plausible? It will, with some justice, be objected that Quine himself was no friend of a sharp distinction between the two. But this is less a defense of holistic verificationism than recognition that no definite thesis about meaning and verification can be extracted from his discussion. Rather than attempting to extract such a view, one might do better by rejecting his gestures in this direction as too imprecise and global to have a chance of success. We simply have no clear idea what a comparison of two theories that differ radically in their ideologies might amount to.

Another reason to be suspicious of holistic verificationism is that it leads to paradox. Suppose, according to QT1 and QT5, that a certain consistent theory T_1 means the same as T_2 while being logically incompatible with T_2. Since two theories that mean the same thing must make the same claim about the world, they must agree in truth value.

> (i) If two theories mean the same thing, then they make the same claim about the world, in which case they cannot differ in truth value. Hence one is true iff the other is.

It follows that either T_1 and T_2 are both true or both false. Since they are logically incompatible, they can't both be true. So, they both must be false. But surely there are *some* true theories of *some subject matters*.

> (ii) Some theories of some subject matters are true.

---

[12] Page 44 of the 1980 reprinting of Quine (1951b).
[13] Soames (2003a, 398–405).

Given this, we may simply select some *true* theory T_1 and run the argument again. But now we get the result that T_1 and T_2 must *both* be true, because they have the same meaning, while also getting the result that they *can't* both be true, because they are logically incompatible. So either holistic verificationism or underdetermination, or both, must be rejected. Although this conclusion is unassailable, it is not clear whether it shows Quine's view to be irretrievably wrong or merely to need some modification. Quine (1975) discusses this difficulty. But the best defense of his view is the modification proposed in Harman (1979), which is critically discussed in Soames (2003a).

ON WHAT THERE IS: QUINE, CARNAP, AND ONTOLOGY

The connection between Quine's ontology and his theory of meaning is more fully displayed in Quine (1948), the first part of which sets out his criterion of ontological commitment. One is not, he argues, committed, merely by using a name, to the existence of something named. Nor is one committed, in using any meaningful term, to their being some thing it means. It is a substantive theoretical position, which Quine rejects, that words are meaningful only if there exist entities they mean. In using the predicate 'is red' or the adjective 'seven', one is not thereby committed to the existence of colors or numbers, though one is committed when one says that there exist primary colors, or prime numbers between 6 and 12. One is committed to the existence of *so-and-so's* only when one says there exist *so-and-so's*.

That is the idea behind the slogan "To be is to be the value of a bound variable." The point is *not* that to exist amounts to being the value of a variable, but that to *commit* oneself to the existence of something is *to say* that there exists such a thing. To commit oneself to the existence of Fs is to say something the proper regimentation of which is, or entails, ⌜∃x Fx⌝—the truth of which requires the existence of an object o that makes ⌜Fx⌝ true when o is assigned as value of 'x'. The qualification about regimentation is crucial to avoid unwanted commitments. Quine had no problem saying that *there is a possibility that S*, without thereby committing himself to the existence of possibilities.[14] The justification of his nonchalance is that proper regimentation of the remark involves no quantification over possibilities but simply recognition that *it may be true that S*. Using the flexibility provided by such regimentation, he held that the *only* way to commit oneself to the existence of Fs is

---

[14] In this example 'S' is used as a schematic letter.

by asserting something the proper regimentation of which entails the existentially quantified claim that there exist Fs.[15]

Quine puts this idea to use in discussing abstract objects:

> When we say that some zoological species are cross-fertile we are committing ourselves to recognizing as entities the several species themselves, *abstract though they are.* We remain so committed at least until we devise some way of so paraphrasing the statement as to show that seeming reference to species . . . was an avoidable manner of speaking. . . . Classical mathematics . . . is up to its neck in commitments to an ontology of abstract entities. Thus it is that the great mediaeval controversy over universals has flared up anew in the modern philosophy of mathematics. . . . The three main mediaeval points of view regarding universals are designated by the historians as *realism, conceptualism,* and *nominalism.* Essentially these same three doctrines reappear in twentieth-century surveys of the philosophy of mathematics under the new names *logicism, intuitionism,* and *formalism. Realism* . . . is the Platonic doctrine that universals or abstract entities have being independently of the mind; the mind may discover them but cannot create them. *Logicism,* represented by Frege, Russell, Whitehead, Church, and Carnap, condones the use of bound variables to refer to abstract entities known and unknown, specifiable, and unspecifiable.[16]

Quine suggests that Carnap's commitment to numbers is a form of Platonism. Though the label may seem apt, Carnap, who had long repudiated metaphysics as meaningless nonsense, resented having it applied to him. He devoted Carnap (1950) to explaining why the charge is unfair.

Carnap's key thesis was that ontological questions are intelligible only within a framework for describing the world. Such a framework is a formalizable language with semantic rules interpreting its expressions and assigning truth conditions to its sentences. Ordinary English contains terms for observable physical objects and events. Carnap assumes that rules constituting their meanings specify possible observations that would confirm or disconfirm sentences containing them. So, he thinks, whether there are things of a given sort reduces to whether observable events occur that, as a matter of linguistic rule, confirm the relevant sentences. Since these *internal questions* can be answered by evidence, they aren't metaphysical. He contrasts *internal questions*

---

[15] Page 12 of the 1980 reprinting of Quine (1948).
[16] Ibid., 13–14.

with *external questions*, which can't be settled by evidence but nevertheless purport to be about the world. Traditional metaphysical questions about the reality of the external world are of this sort. ⌜Are there Fs?⌝ is properly understood to be an internal question, resolvable by empirical evidence of the kind given by the semantic rule governing F. However, philosophers have traditionally misunderstood the question as not being settled by such evidence. Their mistake has been to divorce the application of F from the linguistic rules that constitute its meaning. In this way, they have been led to ask cognitively meaningless pseudoquestions that can't be answered.

This mistake is compounded by another one that disguises it. Philosophers are prone to run together the proper, though often trivial, internal *theoretical* question ⌜Are there Fs?⌝ with the nontrivial *practical* question of whether to adopt a theoretical framework incorporating F. Regarding physical objects, Carnap says:

> Those who raise the question of the reality of the thing world itself have perhaps in mind not a theoretical question . . . but rather a practical question, a matter of a practical decision concerning the structure of our language. . . . [W]e are free to choose to continue using the thing language or not; in the latter case we could restrict ourselves to a language of sense-data and other "phenomenal" entities. . . . If someone decides to accept the thing language, there is no objection against saying that he has accepted the world of things. But this must not be interpreted as if it meant his acceptance of a *belief* in the reality of the thing world; there is no such belief or assertion or assumption, because it is not a theoretical question.[17]

We are asked to imagine a choice between our ordinary physical-object framework and a Berkeleyan alternative that speaks only of minds and "sense data." This, we are told, is *simply* a choice between two linguistic schemes for describing experience. There is, we are assured, no belief, assertion, or assumption *in the reality of the thing world* that one adopts when one opts for the physical, rather than the phenomenal, framework. If there were, what would it be? Not an unverifiable and unfalsifiable pseudostatement, since they lack cognitive content. It would have to be an empirical statement of some sort. But then the assertion, belief, or assumption would require empirical justification—in which case the choice between frameworks would be genuinely *theoretical*, rather than the purely *practical* decision Carnap takes it to be.

---

[17] Carnap (1950) at pp. 207–208 of its 1956 reprinting; my emphasis.

From here it is a short step to the conclusion that the cognitive contents of empirically equivalent theories stated in the two languages are the same. Since they have the same content, there is no fact on which they differ, and no claim about the world made by one of them that isn't made by the other. This is why Carnap insists that the choice between the two theories is "not cognitive in nature" but to be made solely on practical grounds.[18] We are justified in adopting the physicalistic theory because (i) we find it more efficient to use than the phenomenalistic one, and (ii) it doesn't make any contentious claims about the world beyond those made by the phenomenalistic theory.

Ontological questions about abstract objects are treated similarly. When F is a predicate applying to physical objects or events, Carnap takes its meaning to supply analytic truths specifying empirical evidence that would confirm or disconfirm statements containing F. The internal question ⌜Are there Fs?⌝ is answered by gathering this evidence, while the external ontological question is dismissed as meaningless. When F is a predicate of abstract objects, empirical evidence is often irrelevant, and the meaning of F is given by rules specifying logical properties of sentences containing it. In these cases, the answer to the internal question ⌜Are there Fs?⌝ is analytic, while the external question is meaningless. Since, ⌜There are numbers⌝ is analytic, it makes no claim about the world, and so cannot be metaphysical.

That, in a nutshell, was Carnap's response to Quine. Quine's reply to Carnap was the rejection of analyticity in "Two Dogmas." Although this was fine as far as it went, it didn't go far enough. Since at this stage Quine was a holistic verificationist, he agreed with Carnap that it makes no difference to the empirical contents of whole theories, and hence to their truth or falsity, how they differ on *any nonobservational statements*, so long as their observational consequences coincide. Hence, it makes no difference what their ontologies are. Theories that "posit" numbers, sets, physical objects, propositions, and properties do not differ in content from theories that don't, *as long as the theories are observationally equivalent*. This is the counterintuitive bedrock of agreement between Carnap and Quine.

The contrast between physicalist and phenomenalist ontologies is a case in point. For Carnap, physicalist and phenomenalist theories compatible with the same sense experience have the same content, and so make the same claims about the world. So, the choice between them must be made on practical grounds. Quine agrees:

As an empiricist I continue to think of the conceptual scheme of science as a tool, ultimately, for predicting future experience

---

[18] Ibid., 208.

in the light of past experience. Physical objects are conceptually imported into the situation as convenient intermediaries . . . as irreducible posits comparable, epistemologically, to the gods of Homer. . . . [I]n point of epistemological footing the physical objects and the gods differ only in degree and not in kind. The myth of physical objects is epistemologically superior to most in that it has proved more efficacious than other myths as a device for working a manageable structure into the flux of experience.[19]

Quine stresses that the "myth of physical objects," though useful, is not indispensable for making predictions about sense experience. The same predictions could, in principle, be made by a phenomenalistic theory. He makes this point with an analogy in which the phenomenalistic theory of nature is said to stand to the physicalistic theory as the algebra of the rational numbers stands to the algebra of the reals. He notes that in the algebra of the rationals, functions like square root sometimes go undefined, complicating the laws. "Then," Quine says:

it is discovered that the rules of our algebra can be much simplified by conceptually augmenting our ontology with some *mythical entities*, to be called irrational numbers. *All we continue to be really interested in, first and last, are rational numbers*; but we find that we can commonly get from one law about rational numbers to another much more quickly and simply by *pretending* that the irrational numbers are there too. Now I suggest that experience is analogous to the rational numbers and that the physical objects, in analogy to the irrational numbers, are posits which serve *merely* to simplify our treatment of experience. . . . The salient differences between the positing of physical objects and the positing of irrational numbers are, I think, *just two*. First the factor of *simplification* is more overwhelming in the case of physical objects than in the numerical case. Second, the positing of physical objects is far more archaic, being indeed coeval, I expect, with language itself. (my emphasis)[20]

Quine's point was (i) that the phenomenalistic theory tells us the whole truth and nothing but the truth about nature; (ii) that what it talks about are "all that we are really interested in first, and last;" and (iii) that since

---

[19] Quine (1951b), p. 44 of the 1980 reprinting.

[20] Ibid., 41–42 of the *original 1951 version* of "Two Dogmas" printed in *Philosophical Review*. Quine tells us, in the section "On the Origins of These Essays" in Quine (1953a), that the passage was deleted from later reprintings because it overlapped with a passage from "On What There Is" that also appears in the collection. This is unfortunate, since though there is such an overlap, the original passage from "Two Dogmas" is more revealing. For further discussion, see Soames (2003a, 401–3).

the physical theory adds nothing new about the world, the *only* reason to prefer it is that it makes the needed predictions about sense experience more simply and conveniently. Carnap couldn't have said it better.

THE ROAD TO WORD AND OBJECT

The view that emerged from "Two Dogmas" was unstable, not because of anything inherent in the rejection of analyticity, but because of the rejection of synonymy to which Quine's argument committed him. Since synonymy is sameness of meaning, it is hard to reject it without rejecting meaning itself. And if meaning is rejected, can reference be far behind? Surely, it was objected—in Grice-Strawson (1956), and in Carnap (1955)—we can't do without meaning and reference. No matter that the notion of synonymy rejected by Quine in "Two Dogmas" was an artificial one, according to which for expressions to be synonymous was for them to be substitutable *salva veritate* in modal (rather than hyperintensional) constructions. The fact that this isn't the ordinary notion of sameness of meaning didn't prevent the parties from writing as if meaning in the ordinary sense, and perhaps reference too, would be vulnerable, if the notion of synonymy that Quine rejected was to go. Since, in the end, this road led to *Word and Object* and "Ontological Relativity," the objectors were vindicated.

The argument in Grice-Strawson (1956) was that it is absurd to reject synonymy, because doing so would require rejecting meaning altogether, which was taken to be obviously untenable. If expressions can be meaningful at all, it was argued, there must be true answers to the question, *What does this, or that, expression mean?* But if there are such answers, we can identify synonymous expressions as those for which the answers are the same.

> To say that two expressions x and y are cognitively synonymous seems to correspond . . . to what we should ordinarily express by saying . . . that x means the same as y. If Quine is to be consistent . . . then it appears that he must maintain not only that the distinction we suppose ourselves to be marking by the use of the terms "analytic" and "synthetic" does not exist, but also that the distinction we suppose ourselves to be marking by the use of the expressions "means the same as," and "does not mean the same as" does not exist either. . . . Yet the denial that the distinction . . . really exists, is extremely paradoxical. . . . For we frequently talk of the presence or absence of relations of synonymy between kinds of expressions . . . where there does not appear to be any obvious substitute for the ordinary notion of

synonymy. . . . *Is all such talk meaningless? Is all talk of correct or incorrect translation of sentences of one language into sentences of another meaningless?* It is hard to believe that it is. . . . *If talk of sentence-synonymy is meaningless, then it seems that talk of sentences having a meaning at all must be meaningless too. For if it made sense to talk of a sentence having a meaning, or meaning something, then presumably it would make sense to ask "What does it mean?" and if it made sense to ask "What does it mean?" of a sentence, then sentence-synonymy could be roughly defined as follows: Two sentences are synonymous if and only if any true answer to the question "What does it mean?" asked of one of them, is a true answer to the same question, asked of the other.* (my emphasis)[21]

This powerful argument—that one can give up synonymy only if one gives up meaning and translation too—turned out to be prophetic. Four years later, this is what Quine proposed to do.

Carnap also turned out to be prophetic. In Carnap (1955) he tried to show that the meaning of a term, over and above its reference, can play a role in empirical theorizing about language users. He argued that although there are empirical uncertainties in establishing the meaning and reference of a term, there are sound empirical methods for bringing evidence to bear on both questions. As a result, he concluded, meaning and reference are in the same boat. Thus, he thought, Quine was wrong to dismiss intensional notions like meaning and synonymy while apparently retaining extensional ones like reference (and truth). For Carnap, the intensional and the extensional were scientifically on par—both required and both respectable. Quine's response came in *Word and Object*, which he dedicated to Carnap. There, he agreed that meaning and reference are on a par but upped the ante by (in effect) rejecting both.

MEANING AND TRANSLATION

In *Word and Object* Quine argues that *meaning*, as ordinarily understood, plays no empirical fact-stating role. He uses theories of translation between languages spoken by different communities to illustrate his point. Although translation is a useful practical activity, we cannot, he argues, take its claims about meaning to be genuine truths. Assuming that no other empirical theory can provide such truths, he concludes that the ordinary notion of *meaning* has no role to play in serious descriptions of the world.[22]

---

[21] Grice-Strawson (1956, 141–58) at pp. 145–46.
[22] Quine (1960, 221).

His two main theses are as follows:

UNDERDETERMINATION OF TRANSLATION BY DATA

Let L_1 and L_2 be arbitrary languages, and D be the set of all observational truths (known and unknown) relevant to translation from L_1 to L_2. For any theory of translation T for L_1, L_2, compatible with D, there is a theory T′, incompatible with T, that is equally well supported by D.

INDETERMINACY OF TRANSLATION

Translation is not determined by the set N of all truths of nature, known and unknown. For any pair of languages and theory of translation T for those languages, there are alternative theories of translation, incompatible with T, that accord equally well with N. All such theories are equally true to the facts; there is no objective matter of fact on which they disagree, and no objective sense in which one is true and the other is not.

To reconstruct Quine's argument for these theses, we need some understanding of what theories of translation are, what evidence they are answerable to, and what empirical predictions they make. Quine understands them along roughly the following lines.

THEORIES OF TRANSLATION

A theory of translation for two languages correlates individual words of each with words or phrases of the other; this correlation is then used to correlate the sentences of the two languages. Any system of establishing such correlations can be counted as a translation manual, or theory. We may take such a theory as yielding (infinitely many) theorems of the form:

Word or phrase w in L_1 means the same as word or phrase w* in L_2.
Sentence S in L_1 means the same as sentence S* in L_2.

EMPIRICAL DATA

Empirical data relevant to theories of translation are statements about the behavior of language users. More specifically, they are statements about the *stimulus meanings* of certain classes of sentences.

STIMULUS MEANING

The stimulus meaning of a sentence S (for a speaker at a time) is a pair of classes—the class of situations in which the speaker would assent to S and the class of situations in which the speaker would dissent from S.

OCCASION SENTENCES

S is an occasion sentence for a speaker x iff x's assent to or dissent from S depends on what x is observing.

OBSERVATION SENTENCES

S is an observation sentence in a language L iff (i) S is an occasion sentence for speakers of L, and (ii) the stimulus meaning of S varies very little from one speaker of L to another. (Sameness of the stimulus meaning of such a sentence S across the members of a population is taken to be a reasonable approximation of the maximal degree to which assent to S, or dissent from S, is dependent on observation alone, free of contextually varying background assumptions.)

EMPIRICAL PREDICTIONS

(i) Translation of observation sentences must preserve stimulus meaning. If a translation theory states that an observation sentence S_1 in L_1 means the same as a sentence S_2 in L_2, then the theory predicts that S_1 and S_2 have the same stimulus meanings in their respective linguistic communities.

(ii) Translation must preserve the stimulus synonymy of pairs of occasion sentences. If S_1 and S_2 are occasion sentences of L_1, and if a translation theory states both that S_1 means the same in L_1 as P_1 in L_2 and that S_2 means the same in L_1 as P_2 in L_2, then the theory predicts that S_1 and S_2 have the same stimulus meaning for speakers of L_1 iff P_1 and P_2 have the same stimulus meaning for speakers of L_2.

(iii) Translations of truth functional operators—*and, or, not* etc.—have recognizable effects on stimulus meaning. For example, if a theory translates an expression n of a language L as meaning the same as *not* in English, then the theory predicts that adding n to sentences of L reverses stimulus meaning. Similar claims hold for other truth functional operators.

In addition, Quine sometimes talks as if these predictions might be augmented by a fourth kind defined in terms of his notions of *stimulus analyticity* and *stimulus contradiction*.

S is stimulus analytic in L iff virtually all speakers of L assent to S in all stimulus situations.

S is stimulus contradictory iff virtually all speakers of L dissent from S in all stimulus situations.

(iv) Translation must preserve stimulus analytic and stimulus
contradictory sentences. If S_1 is a stimulus analytic (contradictory) sentence of L_1, and if a theory of translation states
that S_1 means the same in L_1 as S_2 in L_2, then the theory
predicts that S_1 is stimulus analytic (contradictory) iff S_2 is.

Because Quine conceives of (i)–(iv) as exhausting all possible evidence
for theories of translation, he accepts the underdetermination thesis.
In arguing for it, he imagines trying to translate some language L into
English that has never previously been encountered by outsiders. (He
calls this "radical translation.") Suppose the linguist can discover how
questions in L, as well as assent and dissent to them, are expressed. The
linguist might then discover that L-speakers will assent to the one-word
sentence 'Gavagai?' in roughly the same situations in which an English
speaker would assent to 'Rabbit?' This would support the hypothesis
that the two sentences have the same stimulus meaning, and so are
intertranslatable. But, Quine thinks, once we go beyond observation
sentences, the limitations on behavioral data will never provide an empirical basis capable of ruling out different incompatible theories of
translation, each compatible with all the evidence.

His point is illustrated by the difficulty moving from translations of
the *sentence* 'Gavagai!' by 'Rabbit!' to a translation of the *word* 'gavagai'
by 'rabbit'. He observes:

For, consider 'gavagai'. Who knows but what the objects to which
this term applies are not rabbits after all, but mere stages, or brief
temporal segments, of rabbits? In either event the stimulus situations that prompt assent to 'Gavagai' would be the same as for
'Rabbit'. Or perhaps the objects to which 'gavagai' applies are all
and sundry undetached parts of rabbits; again the stimulus meanings would register no difference.[23]

Does it seem that the imagined indecision between rabbits,
stages of rabbits, integral parts of rabbits . . . must be due merely
to some special fault in our formulation of stimulus meaning, and
that it should be resoluble by a little supplementary pointing and
questioning? Consider, then, how. Point to a rabbit and you have
pointed to a stage of a rabbit, to an integral part of a rabbit. . . .
Nothing not distinguished in stimulus meaning itself is to be distinguished by pointing, unless the pointing is accompanied by

---

[23] Quine (1960, 51–52).

questions of identity and diversity: 'Is this the same gavagai as that?', 'Do we have here one gavagai or two?'[24]

For Quine, the question of whether 'gavagai' means the same as, and refers to (i.e., is true of) the same things as 'rabbit'—as opposed to meaning the same as, and referring to the same things as, our expressions "undetached spatial part of a rabbit" or "temporal stage of a rabbit"—depends on what expression of L, if any, means what "is the same thing as" means in English. Evidence about stimulus meaning won't decide this question. Imagine "squiggle" to be a word in L that is a candidate for expressing our notion of identity. Pointing at different spatial or temporal parts of the same rabbit we might ask "Gavagai (point) squiggle gavagai (point)?" with the thought that if the L-speaker assents, we will know that 'gavagai' *doesn't* mean what 'undetached spatial part of a rabbit' or 'temporal stage of a rabbit' mean in English, since the spatial or temporal parts pointed at are different. But, as Quine observes, such a conclusion wouldn't be justified; for as far as the evidence goes, 'squiggle' might be translated 'is the same thing as', 'is an undetached spatial part of the same extended whole as', or 'is a temporal stage of the same enduring complex as'. The choice of a translation for 'gavagai' depends on a choice for 'squiggle', and vice versa. We can, if we like, translate 'gavagai' as 'rabbit' and 'squiggle' as 'is the same thing as', or we can translate 'gavagai' as 'undetached spatial rabbit part' and translate 'squiggle' as 'is an undetached spatial part of the same extended whole as'—or we can make other choices, always adjusting our translations of 'gavagai' and 'squiggle' as a pair. Seeing these different translation theories as *incompatible* with each other, while being equally compatible with all possible evidence, Quine takes himself to have established the Underdetermination of Translation by Data.[25]

But how does one move from this to the Indeterminacy of Translation? Not being clear about this in *Word and Object*, Quine left himself open to an objection made in Chomsky (1969). As Chomsky observed, interesting empirical theories are always underdetermined by the data against which they are tested. If one is not already a behaviorist, one won't regard the mundane fact that theories of translation are underdetermined by Quine's behavioral data to be any more threatening to those theories, and the notion of meaning they employ, than similar underdetermination is threatening to theories in physics, chemistry,

---

[24] Ibid., 52–53.

[25] Although Quine doesn't clarify in what sense the theories are supposed to be incompatible, I suspect he intends logical incompatibility. If so, we must think of translation theories as being augmented by certain claims that go beyond those he specifies. This complication is addressed at Soames (1999, 326–28; 2003b, 238–40) .

and biology. Since Quine *was* a behaviorist, this may not have worried him, but he did need a route to Indeterminacy that didn't presuppose behaviorism to convince the rest of us. In Quine (1969), he offered one. Recognizing that many might agree with him that facts about stimulus meanings won't resolve indeterminacies about meaning, he suggested that adding *any other physical* facts won't help. After all, if one can't deduce from an L-speaker's behavior that his word "gavagai" means the same as "rabbit," how would it help to add that certain neurons in his brain fire when he uses the word? We can no more read off the contents of a person's words from neurological claims than we can read off the contents of his words from statements about the sounds he emits in different environments. So, if nonintensional descriptions of linguistic behavior don't determine meaning, adding neurological—or any other physical facts—won't help.

These thoughts led to Quine's most powerful route to the Indeterminacy of Translation, which was to derive the thesis from the following (roughly stated) doctrines.[26]

PHYSICALISM

All genuine truths (facts) are determined by physical truths (facts).

THE UNDERDETERMINATION OF TRANSLATION BY PHYSICS

Translation is not determined by the set of all physical truths (facts), known and unknown. For any pair of languages and theory of translation T for those languages, there are alternative theories of translation, incompatible with T, that accord equally well with all physical truths (facts).

If these doctrines are correct, then claims about what our words mean— e.g., *that word$_1$ used by person$_1$ means the same as word$_2$ used by person$_2$* (for different persons and words)—never express genuine truths. Hence, the Indeterminacy of Translation. However, to properly assess this argument, the *determination relation* between sets of potential truth bearers must be carefully specified. When one does this, one encounters a serious problem: determination relations that make the Underdetermination of Translation by Physics most plausible make Physicalism implausible, and vice versa. To date, no clearly specified relation has been offered that makes both plausible. Although, this doesn't show that none ever will be, it raises a worry. Perhaps, the initial plausibility

---

[26] Soames (1999) contains a more nuanced discussion.

of Quine's argument for the Indeterminacy of Translation lies in equivocation about the determination relation.[27]

THE INSCRUTABILITY OF REFERENCE

The upshot, for Quine, of the indeterminacy thesis is that no claim that L-speakers use 'gavagai' to mean the same as what I mean by w (for any word in my language) expresses a truth. Similar reasoning leads to the result that no claim that they use 'gavagai' to refer to the same thing I use w to refer to is true. From here it is not far to the conclusion that they don't use it to refer to anything.[28] Although this sounds extreme, and Quine doesn't explicitly say it, what he does say in a crucial passage in "Ontological Relativity" is tantamount to it. Earlier in the article, he notes that the Indeterminacy of Translation, according to which it is indeterminate whether 'gavagai' means the same as 'rabbit', is inextricably linked to the Inscrutability of Reference, according to which it is indeterminate whether 'gavagai' refers to rabbits. He notes that if it is indeterminate whether the native's word 'gavagai' refers to rabbits, then it is indeterminate whether *my neighbor* uses 'rabbit' to refer to rabbits. At this point he considers the possibility of making the same claim about himself:

> I have urged . . . that the inscrutability of reference is not the inscrutability of a fact; there is no fact of the matter. But if there is really no fact of the matter, then the inscrutability of reference can be brought even closer to home than the neighbor's case; we can apply it to ourselves. If it is to make sense to say even of oneself that one is referring to rabbits . . . and not to rabbit stages . . . then it should make sense equally to say it of someone else. . . . We seem to be maneuvering ourselves into the absurd position that there is no difference on any terms, interlinguistic or intralinguistic, objective or subjective, between referring to rabbits and referring to rabbit parts or stages. . . . Surely this is absurd, for it would imply that there is no difference between the rabbit and each of its parts or stages. . . . Reference would seem now to become nonsense not just in radical translation but at home.[29]

The implicit argument here can be reconstructed as follows:

[27] See Soames (1999) and (2003b, chap. 10).
[28] See Soames (2003b, 260–64).
[29] Quine (1968, 47–48) of the version in *Ontological Relativity and Other Essays*.

R1. It is indeterminate (hence there is no fact of the matter) regarding whether the native uses 'gavagai' to refer to rabbits, temporal stages of rabbits, etc. It is similarly indeterminate whether my neighbor uses 'rabbit' to refer to rabbits, rabbit stages, etc.

R2. If (R1), then it is indeterminate (hence there is no fact of the matter) regarding whether I use 'rabbit' to refer to rabbits, temporal stages of rabbits, etc.

R3. So it is indeterminate whether I use 'rabbit' to refer to rabbits, temporal stages of rabbits, etc. More generally, it is never determinate that a word (used by anyone) refers to (i.e., is true of) all and only rabbits, as opposed to all and only temporal stages of rabbits, all and only undetached rabbit parts, etc.

R4. But if that (R3) is so, then there is no difference between referring to all and only rabbits and referring to all and only temporal stages of rabbits, or to all and only undetached rabbit parts—i.e., *for any word w, it is true that w refers to all and only rabbits only if it is equally true that w refers to all and only temporal stages of rabbits, and to all and only undetached rabbit parts.*

R5. If the consequent of R4 is true, then there is no difference between rabbits, temporal stages of rabbits, undetached rabbit parts—i.e., something is a rabbit iff it is a temporal stage of a rabbit iff it is an undetached rabbit part.

R6. So, there is no difference between rabbits, temporal stages of rabbits, undetached rabbit parts, and so on.

Since R6, is false, at least one of R1, R2, R4, or R5 must also be false.

In selecting the offending premise it is important to remember that the indeterminacy and inscrutability theses are ontological, not epistemic. They claim that all physical truths don't determine the truth of statements about meaning and reference. Since the physical truths don't distinguish between L-speakers, my neighbors, and me, they must determine reference for all of us if they determine truths for any. So, one can't avoid the absurd R6 by rejecting R3. Nor can Quine reject R1, which is his own doctrine. This leaves R4 and R5. What, from his point of view, is wrong with them? The passage quoted contains a comment on R4 suggesting that the previous steps require us to accept its "absurd" consequent. He concludes with the comment, "Reference would seem now to become nonsense not just in radical translation but at home." Two paragraphs later he adds that reference *really is nonsense*, if taken "absolutely," but it isn't nonsense if it is relative to a background theory or language.

Quine sees his indeterminacy theses as requiring us to reject our ordinary "absolute" notion of reference, which is employed in the reductio throughout. Although Quine himself isn't clear about this, properly understood, this rejection blocks R6 by allowing him to reject R5, the consequent of which is the absurd conclusion to be avoided. This is possible only if the conditional of which the antecedent of R5 predicates truth is itself true by falsity of antecedent—i.e., only if no word refers to (is true of) all and only rabbits. Since the same argument could be repeated for any class of things, Quine must deny that any word ever refers to anything, in the ordinary sense of 'refer' ('is true of').

From here we move to Quine's reconstruction. Just as he doesn't simply reject ordinary meaning, but replaces it with 'stimulus meaning', so he doesn't simply reject ordinary reference but replaces it with 'Tarski-reference' in his own present language, $L_{Quine\ Now}$. The "reference" of others, as well as his own reference at other times, is then taken to be the product of translation of their or his words onto expressions of $L_{Quine\ Now}$, plus Tarski-reference for that language. In this view, when one says that x's use of word w at t refers to (is true of) Fs, one is saying that *relative to some underdetermined theory T of translation from x's words at t onto the words of one's own present language*, x's use of w at refers to Fs—which is to say that there is some word or phrase P in one's own present language such that (i) according to T, w, as used by x at t, means the same as P, and (ii) P (as one now uses it) refers to (is true of) Fs. As for Tarski-reference, it is strictly disquotational and can, in principle, be defined along the following lines.

TARSKI-REFERENCE OF MY PRESENT WORDS:

For all names n of my present language and objects o, n refers to o iff n = 'Alfred' and o is Alfred, or n = 'Willard' and o is Willard, or . . .
For all predicates P of my present language and objects o, P refers (applies) to o iff P = 'rabbit' and o is a rabbit, or P = 'dog' and o is a dog, or P = 'white' and o is white, or . . . .

Just as Tarski-reference replaces ordinary reference, so Tarski-truth replaces ordinary truth for one's own present language. Thus, neither the claims one makes about the Tarski-referents of the words of one's own present language nor the claims one makes about the Tarski-truth or Tarski-falsity of its sentences are relativized to underdetermined theories of translation. Underdetermination arises only when reporting the speech of others, or of oneself at other times.[30]

---

[30] Replacement of the rejected ordinary notions of reference and truth by language-relativized Tarski-reference and Tarski–truth is discussed at Soames (2003b, 270–77).

QUINE'S SELF-REFUTING ELIMINATIVISM

As I have explained, the Indeterminacy of Translation and the Inscrutability of Reference lead to eliminativism about (i) our ordinary notion of meaning, including the notion of a sentence's meaning that P; (ii) our ordinary notion of reference or application—*being true of*. In addition, as Quine himself notes, this eliminativism requires him to reject standard propositional attitudes, such as believing and asserting that P. He says:

> For, using the intentional words 'believe' and 'ascribe', one could say that a speaker's term is to be construed as 'rabbit' if and only if the speaker is disposed to ascribe it to all and only the objects that he believes to be rabbits. Evidently, then, the relativity to non-unique systems of analytical hypotheses [which give rise to indeterminacy] invests not only translational synonymy but intentional notions generally. Brentano's thesis of the irreducibility of intentional idioms is of a piece with the thesis of indeterminacy of translation. One may accept the Brentano thesis either as showing the indispensability of intentional idioms and the importance of an autonomous science of intention, or as showing the *baselessness* of intentional idioms and the *emptiness* of a science of intention. My attitude . . . is the second. To accept intentional usage at face value is, we saw, to postulate translation relations as somehow objectively valid though indeterminate in principle relative to the totality of speech dispositions. Such postulation promises little gain in scientific insight if there is no better ground for it than that the supposed translation relations are presupposed by the vernacular of semantics and intention. Not that I would forswear daily use of intentional idioms, or maintain that they are practically dispensable. But they call, I think, for bifurcation in canonical notation. Which turning to take depends on which of the various purposes of a canonical notation happens to be motivating us at the time. If we are *limning the true and ultimate structure of reality*, the canonical scheme for us is the austere scheme that knows no quotation but direct quotation and no propositional attitudes but only the physical constitution and behavior of organisms.[31]

The message can't be missed. If claims about propositional attitudes were determinate, translation would also be. Since translation is indeterminate, claims about propositional attitudes are, too. Strictly

---

Though not explicit in "Ontological Relativity," such replacement and relativization becomes so in section 20 of Quine (1992).

[31] Quine (1960, 220–21); my emphasis.

speaking there are no facts about attitudes like belief and assertion, just as there are no facts about translation. Whatever the practical utility of such notions, they have no place in a properly scientific description of the world. This is icing on the cake, further underlining Quine's rejection of our ordinary notions *truth* and *being true of,* which are conceptually connected with the eliminated notions of meaning, reference, what is said, and what is believed. Our ordinary notion of truth, which applies to these things, as well as to sentences of arbitrary different languages, must be replaced with Tarski-truth, which is restricted to one's own present language.

With this, Quine's position has become not just implausible but self-defeating. Elimination of ordinary semantic notions undermines the Quinean's ability to formulate and argue for indeterminacy and inscrutability. Consider the claim that biology is determined by the physical truths, but semantics and nonbehaviorist psychology are not. In speaking of truths, the Quinean has to be speaking of Tarski-truths of his present language. Thus, we have a thesis that a certain set of physical sentences of his present language determines a certain set of biological sentences of his present language but does not determine a third set of semantic and psychological sentences of that language. But why should this matter? Suppose present physics lacks some concepts needed for an accurate and comprehensive scientific description of the world. *If the physics capable of being expressed in one's present language is incomplete in this way, then the fact that some set S of claims is not determined by one's Tarski-true physical sentences won't provide any compelling reason to doubt the genuine truth of members of S.* If someone three hundred years ago had maintained that the set of Tarski-true physical sentences of his or her then present language failed to determine the set of Tarski-true biological sentences of that language, nothing of philosophical interest would have followed. So, Quine faces a dilemma. Either his theses of physicalism, underdetermination, indeterminacy, and inscrutability state something about the totality of physical truths in the ordinary sense, in violation of his eliminativism, or they state something only about the totality of Tarski-truths of his present language, in which case physicalism and indeterminacy are indefensible, while underdetermination is uninteresting. This is the sad end of Quine's long flight from both intension and intention.

ANALYTIC PHILOSOPHY AFTER QUINE

The failure of Quine's eliminativist project does not detract from the value of his earlier work pointing out the shortcomings, and correcting the errors, of his logical-empiricist predecessors. He was right to attack their linguistic theory of the apriori, to observe that quantified modal logic could not succeed as long as necessity was identified with analyticity, and to reject their use of analyticity as an all-purpose philosophical tool. He was similarly effective in moving philosophy away from conceptual analysis and toward something continuous, though not identical, with science. Today's conception of the overlap of philosophy of language with linguistics, of philosophy of mind and epistemology with psychology, of philosophy of physics and biology with physics and biology, and of metaphysics with science more generally, owes much to his influence. To be sure, his behaviorism was a dead end, and his flights from intension and intention were mistaken. Fortunately, they were spectacular mistakes that couldn't be ignored. Just as his own era progressed by correcting the fundamental errors of the logical empiricists, so the era succeeding his—led by his sometime students Saul Kripke and David Lewis—progressed by correcting his errors about meaning and modality.

REFERENCES

Ayer, A. J. 1959. *Logical Positivism*. Glencoe, IL: Free Press.

Carnap, Rudolf. 1928a. *Der logische Aufbau der Welt*. Berlin-Schlachtensee, Weltkreis-Verlag; translated by Rolf A. George as *The Logical Structure of the World*. Berkeley and Los Angeles: University of California Press, 1967.

———. 1928b. *Scheinprobleme in der Philosophie*. Berlin-Schlachtensee: Weltkreis-Verlag. Translated by Rolf A. George as *Pseudoproblems in Philosophy*. Berkeley and Los Angeles: University of California Press, 1967.

———. 1930. "Die alte und die neue Logik." *Erkenntnis* 1:12–26; translated by Isaac Levi, "The Old and the New Logic," in Ayer 1959.

———. 1931. "Die logizistische Grundlegung der Mathematik." *Erkenntnis* 2: 91–105; translated as "On the Logicist Foundations of Mathematics," in Paul Benacerraf and Hilary Putnam, eds., *Readings in the Philosophy of Mathematics*. Englewood Cliffs, NJ: Prentice Hall, 1964.

———. 1932a. "Überwindung der Metaphysik durch logische Analyse der Sprache." *Erkenntnis* 2:219–41; translated by Arthur Pap as "The Elimination of Metaphysics through the Logical Analysis of Language," in Ayer 1959.

———. 1932b. "Die physikalische Sprache als Universalsprache der Wissenschaft." *Erkenntnis* 2:432–65; translated by Max Black as "The Unity of Science," in *Psyche Miniatures, General Series*, no. 63. London: Kegan Paul.

———. 1934. *Logische Syntax der Sprache*. Vienna: Springer; translated by A. Smeaton as *The Logical Syntax of Language*. London: Kegan Paul Trench, Trubner, 1937.

———. 1950. "Empiricism, Semantics, and Ontology." *Revue Internationale de Philosophie* 4:20–40; revised and reprinted in Carnap 1956.

———. 1955. "Meaning and Synonymy in Natural Languages." *Philosophical Studies* 6:33–47; reprinted in Carnap 1956.

———. 1956. *Meaning and Necessity*, 2nd ed. Chicago: University of Chicago Press.

Chomsky, Noam. 1969. "Quine's Empirical Assumptions," in Davidson and Hintikka 1969.

Davidson, D., and J. Hintikka. 1969. *Words and Objections*. Dordrecht: Reidel.

Fine, Kit. 2007. *Semantic Relationism*. Oxford: Blackwell.

Grice, Paul, and Peter Strawson. 1956. "In Defense of a Dogma." *Philosophical Review* 65:141–58.

Harman, Gilbert. 1979. "Meaning and Theory." *Southwestern Journal of Philosophy* 9:9–20.

Kaplan, David. 1986. "Opacity," in L. E. Hahn and P. A. Schilpp, eds., *The Philosophy of W. V. Quine*. La Salle, IL: Open Court.

Kazmi, Ali. 1987. "Quantification and Opacity." *Linguistics and Philosophy* 10: 77–100.

———. 1992. "Some Remarks on Indiscernibility." *Canadian Journal of Philosophy Supplement* 18:167–78.

Lewis, C. I. 1929. *Mind and the World Order*. New York: Scribner.

———. 1946. *An Analysis of Knowledge and Valuation*. La Salle, IL: Open Court.

Quine, W.V.O. 1936. "Truth by Convention," in O. H. Lee, ed., *Essays for A. N. Whitehead*. New York: Longmans; reprinted in Quine 1966.

———. 1943. "Notes on Existence and Necessity." *Journal of Philosophy* 40: 113–27.

———. 1947. "The Problem Interpreting Modal Logic." *Journal of Symbolic Logic* 12:43–48.

———. 1948. "On What There Is." *Review of Metaphysics* 2:21–38.

———. 1951a. "On Carnap's Views on Ontology." *Philosophical Studies* 2:65–72.

———. 1951b. "Two Dogmas of Empiricism." *Philosophical Review* 60:20–43; reprinted in Quine 1953a.

———. 1953a. *From a Logical Point of View*. Cambridge, MA: Harvard University Press.

———. 1953b. "Reference and Modality," in Quine 1953a.

———. 1953c. "Three Grades of Modal Involvement." *Proceedings of the XI International Congress of Philosophy* 14:65–81.

———. 1956. "Quantifiers and Propositional Attitudes." *Journal of Philosophy* 53:177–87.

———. 1960. *Word and Object*. Cambridge, MA: MIT Press.

———. 1966. *The Ways of Paradox*. New York: Random House.

———. 1968. "Ontological Relativity." *Journal of Philosophy* 64: 185–212; reprinted in *Ontological Relativity and Other Essays*. New York: Columbia University Press, 1969.

———. 1969. "Reply to Chomsky," in Davidson and Hintikka 1969.

———. 1975. "On Empirically Equivalent Systems of the World." *Erkenntnis* 9:313–28.

———. 1980. *From a Logical Point of View*, 2nd rev ed. Cambridge, MA: Harvard University Press.

———. 1992. *In Pursuit of Truth*. Cambridge, MA: Harvard University Press.

Richard, Mark. 1987. "Quantification and Leibniz's Law." *Philosophical Review* 96:555–78.

Soames, Scott. 1987. "Substitutivity," in J. J. Thomson, ed., *On Being and Saying*. Cambridge, MA: MIT Press.

———. 1999. "The Indeterminacy of Translation and the Inscrutability of Reference." *Canadian Journal of Philosophy* 29:321–70.

———. 2002. *Beyond Rigidity*. New York: Oxford University Press.

———. 2003a. *Philosophical Analysis in the Twentieth Century*, vol. 1. Princeton, NJ: Princeton University Press.

———. 2003b. *Philosophical Analysis in the Twentieth Century*, vol. 2. Princeton, NJ: Princeton University Press.

———. 2012. "Two Versions of Millianism," in W. Kabasenche, M. O'Rourke, and M. Slater, eds., *Reference and Referring: Topics in Philosophy*, vol. 10. Cambridge, MA: MIT Press.

Williamson, Timothy. 2007. *The Philosophy of Philosophy*. Oxford: Blackwell.

6

David Lewis's Place in Analytic Philosophy

By the early 1970s, David Lewis and Saul Kripke had taken over W.V.O. Quine's leadership in metaphysics, epistemology, philosophy of language, and philosophical logic in the English-speaking world. Their dominance continued through 2001. Quine, in turn, had inherited his position in the early 1950s from Rudolf Carnap, who had been the leading logical positivist—first in Europe, then, after 1935, in America. A renegade positivist himself, Quine eschewed apriority, necessity, and analyticity while (for a time) adopting a holistic version of verificationism. Like Carnap, Quine placed philosophical logic and the philosophy of science at the center of philosophy. While not entirely avoiding metaphysics and epistemology, he tried to "naturalize" both. By contrast, Lewis and Kripke embraced the modalities Quine rejected.[1] They also had no sympathy for his early verificationism or for his twin flights from intension and intention. As for philosophy of science, it was transforming itself into specialized philosophies of the several sciences and did not lend itself to unified treatment. Although Lewis had deep interests in scientific issues, and was commendably a realist about science in general, science itself was not the center of his own distinctive approach to philosophy.

Despite similarities in their opposition to Quine, the differences between Lewis and Kripke were large—especially in the semantics and metaphysics of modality. They also had different philosophical styles. Whereas Lewis was a wide-ranging thinker who pieced together a systematic philosophical worldview, Kripke gave little thought to system, focusing instead on a few central topics. There is, therefore, no conflict between the two on many of the issues on which Kripke was silent. However, the modal, semantic, and metaphysical issues on which they

---

[1] Though they did so in very different ways. Whereas Lewis continued the Quinean identification of necessity with analyticity, Kripke did not. In Lewis (1969, 1970a, 1975b) analyticity is necessity, which, in light of his "modal realism," is explained in terms of ordinary quantification *over everything that is*. By contrast, for Kripke necessity is primitive but linked to the traditional metaphysical doctrine of essentialism.

differed were so central to the philosophy of their era that their deep differences had widespread repercussions.

I begin with one such difference, broached in Lewis (1973a):

> I believe that there are possible worlds other than the one we happen to inhabit. If an argument is wanted, it is this. It is uncontroversially true that things might be otherwise than they are. . . . But what does this mean? Ordinary language permits the paraphrase: there are many ways things could have been besides the way they actually are. On the face of it, this sentence is an existential quantification. It says that there exist many entities of a certain description, to wit 'ways things could have been.' I believe things could have been different in countless ways: I believe permissible paraphrases of what I believe: taking the paraphrase at its fact value, I therefore believe in the existence of entities that might be called '*ways things could have been*'. I prefer to call them 'possible worlds'. (84; my emphasis)

Although there is much here with which to agree, there is also a point of Kripke-inspired contention. There are many ways my desk could have been but isn't; e.g., it could have been clean and uncluttered. These "ways"—*being clean* and *uncluttered*—are not themselves *desks* existing somewhere else, numerically distinct from mine; they are *properties* my desk could have had but doesn't. To call them "possible desks" would not be to respect common sense and ordinary language but to flout them. Similarly, the "ways" posited in modal semantics are *not* alternative concrete universes but *properties* (treated as maximal) that could have been instantiated. Metaphysically possible worlds or, better, *world-states*, are properties that the (or a) universe *could have had*. For a proposition p to be true *at* w is for it such that *had w been instantiated, p would have been true*. For a sentence S to be true at w is for S to (actually) express a proposition that is true at w.[2]

The contrast with Lewis's "modal realism" is illustrated by (1), drawn from Lewis (1986a):

1. Hubert Humphrey could have been so-and-so.

According to the Kripke-inspired view just sketched, (1) is true iff there is a world-state the instantiation of which would have made the proposition *that Humphrey is so-and-so* true. By contrast, Lewis takes (1) to be true only if there is a concrete universe w causally disconnected from ours, and an individual HH who is both *so-and-so* and *an inhabitant*

---

[2] See Soames (2007a; 2010a, chap. 5; and 2010b).

of w.[3] Humphrey inhabits our universe and is, we may suppose, *not* so-and-so. Since HH is, while Humphrey is not, so-and-so, Humphrey and HH are *not* the same person.[4] Rather, HH is Humphrey's *counter-part*, sharing the characteristics of him we wish to keep fixed when evaluating (1).

This is already shocking. How could the truth of the claim that Humphrey could have won the 1968 U.S. presidential election require the existence of an *alternative universe* in which *someone similar to Humphrey* wins an election similar to the U.S. presidential election of 1968? Surely, if the truth of our original claim did require that, we would be in no position to know or justifiably accept it. Lewis, implausibly, thought otherwise; worse, he took his metaphysical story to be *what we mean* when we say that Humphrey could have won. The "incredulous stare" (as he put it) that was regularly evoked by his claim is evidence that it isn't what we mean.

Lewis thought that incredulous staring should cease, because *any analysis of modal truth* must identify Humphrey's being so-and-so at w with something, potentially other than him, being a constituent of w and bearing some property potentially other than being so-and-so.

> I think counterpart theorists and ersatzers [Lewis's derogatory name for those whose modal metaphysics differs from his] are in perfect agreement that there are other worlds (genuine or ersatz) *according to* which Humphrey . . . wins the election. And we are in equal agreement that Humphrey . . . is not *part* of these other worlds. Somehow, perhaps by containing suitable constituents . . . but anyhow not by containing Humphrey himself, the other world represents him as winning. . . . Counterpart theory does say . . . that someone else . . . enters into the story of how it is that another world represents Humphrey as winning. . . . Insofar as the intuitive complaint is that someone else gets into the act, the point is rightly taken. But I do not see that is any objection, any more than it would be an objection against ersatzism that some abstract whatnot gets into the act. What matters is that someone else, or the abstract whatnot, should not crowd out Humphrey himself. And there all is well. Thanks to

---

[3] At Lewis (1986a, 5–6) Lewis says that the operator *in w* is like the operator *in Australia*; 'In w, HH is having dinner' is like 'In Australia, Hubert is having dinner'. Just as the latter says that Hubert is located in Australia and is having dinner, so the former says that HH inhabits w and is having dinner.

[4] See Lewis (1986a, 199–201), where he argues in this way that the idea that an individual might have different intrinsic properties at different worlds is unintelligible.

the victorious counterpart, Humphrey himself has the requisite modal property.[5]

Suppose it is false at the actual world (state) that Humphrey is so-and so. Still, it may be true at w. For this to be so, Lewis argued, it can't be required that Humphrey be both a genuine constituent of w and so-and-so (since he isn't so-and-so). So, Lewis assumed, what is required must be either (i) that something other than Humphrey is both so-and-so and a constituent of w, or (ii) that Humphrey has some property related to *being so-and-so,* while also being, somehow, a constituent of w, or (iii) that something other than Humphrey is a constituent of w that has a property related to *being so-and-so.* (i) is counterpart theory;[6] (iii) is exemplified by an "ersatz view" in which "worlds" are sets of sentences, some expression denoting Humphrey is a constituent of one of the sentences of w, and the property it has *is referring to an individual said by the w-sentences to be so-and-so;* (ii) is a variant of (iii) that Lewis illustrates with the idea that Humphrey might be treated as a word that denotes itself, and *occurs in a sentence that says of its referent that it is so-and-so.*[7] 'n each case, Humphrey's having the modal property *being one who could have won the election* is constituted either by someone else's having that property, or by something's having some other property. Hence, it is no objection to counterpart theory that it views modal properties as indirectly constituted; every theory must.

Really? According to the Kripke-inspired alternative just sketched, Humphrey could have won the election iff some maximal property W, of which he himself is a constituent, could have been instantiated, and if it had been, would have assured his victory. Is this an instance of Lewis's variant (ii), in which the related property is *being such that one would have been so-and-so if w had been* instantiated? Call it what you like. The key point is that the Kripke-inspired analysis does *not* attempt to explain how Humphrey's having the property *being one who could have won the election* is constituted. Instead, it takes the modal notions used to state (1)'s commonsensical truth conditions to be primitive.

This is no more objectionable than using quantifiers to state the truth conditions of quantificational sentences. It isn't a requirement on a semantic analysis of a construction that "the analysis" constitute a reductive definition. Why, then, should we require modal semantics

[5] Ibid., 196.

[6] (i) is counterpart theory if *being so-and-so* is a "pure" property that doesn't itself involve any individuals; if it does involve an individual o, then the property had by the Humphrey counterpart at w will involve an o counterpart and so will not be identical with *being so-and-so.*

[7] Lewis (1986a, 197).

to allow us to *reduce* modal to nonmodal notions? Although Lewis had what was for him an important reason for doing so, Kripke and many others regard the escape from Lewis's unacceptable alternatives to be itself a compelling reason not to go down that road. The way to make this escape is *not* to retreat to fictionalism about possible worlds, which is attractive only by comparison with Lewis's unrealistic "realism."[8] The way to escape Lewis's metaphysical jungle is to take certain modal notions to be primitive and to use them to construct a plausible conception of possible world-states.

For the Kripkean, world-states are properties ascribable to the universe. Just as we recognize properties ordinary objects don't have, but could have had, so we should recognize (maximal) properties— metaphysically possible world-states—the universe doesn't have, but could have had. For any such property W, the universe *could* have had W, and if did, certain propositions *would have* been true. Note the use of modal notions—*what could have been,* and *what would have been true if such and such had been so-and-so.* Possible world-states are not defined in nonmodal terms. Nor is there any attempt to reduce these two modal notions to nonmodal notions. Nothing rules out such a subsequent reduction, but nothing requires it either.

The chief reason Lewis couldn't, or wouldn't, adopt this nonreductionist approach came from his commitment to an ambitious version of philosophical naturalism, the goal of which was to reduce the mental to the physical, causation to counterfactuals, counterfactuals to possible worlds, and possibility and necessity to quantification over ordinary (though very large) objects. The desired destination was a homogeneous reality consisting of momentary point-sized objects (given in physics) instantiating purely qualitative universals—natural properties and relations (also given in physics)—related by similarity, difference, and spatiotemporal relations across multiple universes, but *not* related by "occult," empirically unexplainable forces or connections. To those attracted by this vision, one may say, "Wishing doesn't make it so." For the faithful, however, the final reduction (of necessity and possibility to quantification over the large but ordinary) is indispensable, since without it the other reductions don't lead to any exciting or satisfying system.

Here we see what appears to have been the enduring influence of Lewis's teacher, Quine, the great champion of naturalism and extensionalism, and the uncompromising scourge of the modalities. The underlying philosophical purpose of modal realism and counterpart theory was to reduce an intensional object-language to a purely extensional semantic metalanguage, in the service of an antecedently desired

---

[8] See Gideon Rosen (1990, 1995).

conception of reality. Whereas Quine taught that vindicating naturalism and extensionalism required eliminating intensional facts and rejecting intensional constructions, his student, David Lewis, tried to show that intensional facts are just a species of extensional facts, and that intensional constructions in language are no threat to the integrity of an austere, naturalistic vision of reality.

With this in mind, consider the following passage from section 45 of *Word and Object*:

> If we are limning the true and ultimate structure of reality, the canonical scheme for us is austere scheme that knows no quotation but direct quotation and no propositional attitudes but only the physical constitution and behaviour of organisms.[9]

Although Quine's immediate topic was propositional attitudes, the intent of his remark went much further: no indirect quotation, no intentional operators on *that*—clauses (including 'it is possible/necessary that'), austere extensional systems of representation, and, in the reality to be described, only the physical constitution of things and the behavior of organisms. Whereas Quine married metaphysical naturalism to overtly extensional systems of representation, Lewis strove to save the former by divorcing it from the latter, using extensional descriptions of a metaphysically stupefying reality to interpret superficially intensional systems of linguistic representation.

The parallel between Lewis and Quine was not limited to their metaphysical outlook; it also included their mature views of physics. After his marked holistic verificationist period, the author of Quine (1969, 1970) wrote mostly as a scientific realist, as illustrated in a passage from the former:

> theory in physics is an ultimate parameter. There is no legitimate first philosophy, higher or firmer than physics, to which to appeal over physicists' heads. . . . [A]dopt for now my fully realistic attitude toward electrons and muons and curved space-time, thus falling in with the current theory of the world despite knowing that it is in principle methodologically under-determined. Consider, from this realistic point of view, the totality of truths of nature, known and unknown, observable and unobservable, past and future. The point about indeterminacy of translation is that it withstands even all this truth, the whole truth about nature.[10]

[9] Quine (1960, 220–21).

[10] Quine (1969, 303). Although Quine was willing to accept physical theories at face value, he never explicitly repudiated holistic verificationism, and was, it would appear, never fully the scientific realist that Lewis was.

For Lewis, as for the later Quine, physical science was the ultimate parameter, which no philosophical theory could afford to contradict, radically reinterpret, or diminish the epistemic and metaphysical significance of. Unlike Russell (1914, 1918–19), or Carnap (1928), Lewis did not favor any attempt to translate or reinterpret science in phenomenalistic terms. Unlike Quine (1948, 1951) or Carnap (1950), Lewis never dreamed of identifying the content of a scientific theory with the totality of observational statements supporting it. Unlike Van Fraassen (1980), Lewis didn't merely *accept* physical theory as way of producing reliable observational results; he believed it, and took it to be our most accurate conception of reality.

In keeping with his scientific realism, Lewis didn't attempt to explain away theoretical terms but took them to stand for genuine realities. For him, their referents were determined by Ramsification; electrons and muons, for example, are whatever elements of reality best fill the 'electron' and 'muon' roles in our theories (making them at least approximately true). In this he diverged from Kripke. For the latter, many theoretical terms—including 'heat', 'light', and 'electricity'—refer to natural kinds with which we are cognitively acquainted (through their instances) in a way that secures reference, without tying it to the approximate truth of any theory in which the terms occur.[11] While versions of Kripke's story have won widespread acceptance (for many such terms), it is not unreasonable to suppose that some highly theoretical terms may best be understood roughly along the lines Lewis suggests.[12] Kripkeans needn't have a problem in accepting a version of this limited friendly amendment. Whether followers of Lewis can afford such eclecticism is less clear. His own commitment to descriptive reference fixing was nothing if not ferocious and pervasive. In addition to covering all natural kind terms and ordinary proper names, it was also embedded in his thoroughgoing analytic functionalism.[13]

Returning to Lewis's audacious attempt to reduce the modal to the nonmodal—as the capstone of the reductions implementing his grand naturalistic program—I note his parallel treatment of temporal modification. What is it for o to have been *so-and-so* at a past time t (where *being so-and-so* is an intrinsic property o now lacks)? As in the modal case, Lewis thinks it must be for some object different from, but related to, o to be both *so-and-so* and located (i.e., existing) at t. Thus, he takes it to be incoherent to suppose that o might itself bear different (intrinsic) properties at different times, in the same way he takes it to be

[11] See lectures 2 and 3 of Kripke (1980).
[12] For one such version of the Kripke story see Soames (2007c).
[13] See, for example, Lewis (1966, 1970c, 1974, 1997).

incoherent to suppose that o itself might (without the help of counter-parts) bear different such properties at different possible worlds. The chief difference is that the temporal counterpart of o is a time slice of o, while o is itself supposed to be a parade of time slices. By contrast, the modal counterpart of o is an entity on a par with, but nonidentical with, o.

As before, this move from mundane semantics to revisionary meta-physics is, I think, unfortunate. The first step in avoiding it is to trade the time-relativized object for the time-indexed property *being so-and-so at t*. But, Lewis rightly objects, that property is relational rather than intrinsic, just as *being so-and-so at w* is. The key to overcoming this objection is to define the world-state- and time-indexed properties in terms of the intrinsics (rather than *vice versa*). For o to be *so-and-so at w* is for it to be the case that *if w were instantiated, then o would have the property so-and-so*. For o to be *so-and-so at t* (where t is a past time) is for it to have been true when t occurred that *o had the property so-and-so*. Temporal semantics does not, contra Lewis, require time slices.

Viewing world-states as properties the instantiation of which *would* make various propositions true, Kripkeans don't take counterfactuals to be *defined* by, or reduced to, conceptually prior world-states. This may seem to flout the orthodox view of counterfactuals in Lewis's (1973a). However, the appearance of heterodoxy is exaggerated; much of Lewis's influential treatment of the truth conditions of sentences of the form (2) can be accepted.

> 2. If it had been the case that A, then it would have been the case that B (A □ → B)

Lewis's idea was that (2) is true at w iff either there are no A-states (world-states at which A is true), or some A-states at which B is true are more similar to w than any A-states at which B is false. His semantics differs from one developed independently in Stalnaker (1968) in not validating conditional excluded middle—(A □ → B) v (A □ → ~ B).[14]

What is it for one world-state to be similar to another? Lewis doesn't say much about this in *Counterfactuals,* beyond noting that what counts as similarity can vary from one context of utterance to another. Chal-lenged by counterexamples to the analysis when similarity is under-stood to be *overall similarity* of the world-states,[15] he responded in Lewis

---

[14] If one is worried that some counterfactuals with metaphysically impossible ante-cedents should come out false, while others are really true, the Kripkean may go beyond Lewis by including world-states that are epistemically, but not metaphysically, possible in stating the truth conditions of counterfactuals. More on such world-states later.

[15] See Fine (1975).

(1979b) with default rules for determining similarity. Since then there has been much back and forth concerning what relation S_C is needed to complete the account of counterfactuals. Although there is reason to believe that Lewis originally did think that some kind of qualitative similarity was central to the semantics of counterfactuals (just as it was to his counterpart relation), the subsequent literature, including his own later contributions, makes it clear that the fact that S_C was originally called "similarity" was merely a distraction.

At this point, we do well to reflect again on the grand naturalistic reduction for which Lewis was striving. In addition to *reducing* possible worlds to other universes, it required *reducing* counterfactuals to possible worlds plus similarity. But once simple qualitative similarity went by the boards, there was no real *analysis* on offer but only the relatively innocuous statement that in order for it to be true (at w) that *if A were true, then B would be true*, B must be true at those worlds (if any) at which A is true which also bear some further unspecified relation to w. Whatever its merits, this is no definition, analysis, or reduction.

The next stage in the saga—finding the relation S_C needed to complete the "analysis" of counterfactuals—produced both genuine progress and a further threat to Lewis's grand plan. Recent work—including Jonathan Bennett (2003), Dorothy Edgington (2004), Jonathan Schaffer (2004), and Boris Kment (2006)—suggests that similar facts in w_1 and w_2 contribute to the worlds' being closely related by S_C, only if the facts have the same, often causal, explanation in both. Although this extends Lewis's story, and provides needed content, it also raises a worry. Which, if either, of causation and counterfactual dependence is to be analyzed in terms of the other? According to Lewis (1973b), causation is defined in terms of *causal dependence*, which is a form of *counterfactual dependence*. Roughly put, an event b *causally depends* on a distinct, nonoverlapping event a iff *if a were to occur, then b would occur* (and if a were not to occur, then b would not occur). A* is *a cause* of a distinct, nonoverlapping event b* iff b* is causally dependent on A*, or there is an event c* which both causes b* and is causally dependent on A*.

In the decades after this analysis appeared, many objections were raised, leading Lewis to further modifications—the last of which are found in Lewis (2004). But the direction of analysis remained constant: causation is analyzed in terms of counterfactuals. This is threatened by the idea that causal explanation might itself be needed to explain the S_C-relation in terms of which counterfactuals are to be "analyzed." If, as Lewis intended, these analyses are to express conceptual and explanatory priorities, then either counterfactuals are *not analyzable* in terms of S_C, or S_C is *not analyzable* in terms of the causal features of worlds, or causation is *not analyzable* in terms of counterfactuals—or all three. As I write, the jury seems to be out on this. Perhaps the best strategy is to acknowledge interdependence among these, even though to admit this is to give up the idea of *reducing* causality to anything involving counterfactuals.

Such a loss would be no minor matter. In the context of Lewis's grand naturalistic reduction, the role of his counterfactual analysis of causation was to solve Hume's problem by reconciling (i) the way in which our thought and talk of causation is embedded in counterfactual reasoning with (ii) an ultimately Hume-like constant-conjunction analysis of causation—in terms of spatiotemporal relations among events involving point-sized counterpart time slices instantiating natural properties across universes.[16] If, however, there is no such payoff in the offing, then there will be no philosophical treasure to pay the high price of Lewis's modal realism and his embrace of counterparts and temporal parts as explanatorily basic.

Earlier, in outlining the structure of his grand naturalistic project, I mentioned the reduction of the mental to the physical. The *locus classicus* for this reduction is Lewis (1980a), the precursor of which was Lewis (1966). In both, he self-consciously adopted a version of the contingent identity theory of the relation between mind and body. By 1980, this implicitly involved a counterattack against Kripke's celebrated attempt to refute such theories. To understand Lewis, it is helpful to understand the Kripkean position it repudiated.

Kripke's discussion in *Naming and Necessity* focuses on (3) and (4).

3. Heat = mean molecular kinetic energy
4. Pain = C-fiber stimulation

We here treat the expressions flanking ' = ' as designating kinds and the statements as ordinary identities. Initially, both (3) and (4) appear to be contingent, if true. However, Kripke argues, with (3) this impression is illusory. Suppose that 'heat' and 'mean molecular kinetic energy' are rigid designators—i.e., that the state that is heat couldn't have existed without being heat, and similarly for the state of having such-and-such mean molecular kinetic energy. Then, it is thought, (3) will be necessary, if true. Since it *is* true, it is also necessary.

What, then, is responsible for the illusion that it isn't? Kripke's answer focuses on how we identify or "fix the referent of" 'heat'. Since our primary means of identifying heat is by the sensations it causes, he imagines us using the description 'the cause of such-and-such sensations'. The illusion that (3) is contingent comes from mistaking this

---

[16] See the discussion in Lewis (1986b), e.g., at p. ix.

(nonrigid) description for a synonym of 'heat', thereby confusing the necessary truth expressed by (3) with the contingent truth expressed by (3*).

    3*. The cause of such-and-such sensations in us = mean molecular kinetic energy.

One who makes this mistake wrongly takes genuinely possible world-states at which kinetic energy exists without the usual accompanying sensations to be world-states with kinetic energy but no heat. Hence, the illusion of contingency.

Kripke finds (4) to be different. As before, he takes the terms flanking '=' to be rigid, in which case (4) is necessary, if true. However, he argues, there is no way of dismissing the initial impression of contingency. With (3), the impression is (allegedly) caused by our reliance on sensations to detect what causes them. With (4), the sensation itself is what we use 'pain' to talk about. We don't think: *What a horrible sensation! Let's use 'pain' to talk about whatever causes it.* Instead, we use the word to designate the sensation itself. Thus, whereas one can dispel the illusion that (3) is contingent by appealing to the contingent connection between heat and the sensation by which we recognize it, one can't dispel the impression of contingency of (4) that way. Since he sees no other way to do so, Kripke concludes that (4) *must be contingent, if it is true at all.* But, it can't be contingent, since its terms are rigid. So, he suggests, it isn't true.

This argument, which fails to distinguish epistemic from metaphysical possibility, is unconvincing. Although Kripke may have identified one source of the impression that (3) is contingent, he neglected another. Imagine a man who doesn't take 'heat' to be synonymous with any term for our sensations, because he recognizes that heat could exist without us. He might still be under the impression that (3) is contingent because it is *conceivable* for heat to be something other than the motion of molecules. After all, he may reason, it was an empirical discovery that how hot something is depends on how fast its molecules are moving. Since empirical evidence was needed *to rule out possibilities in which this is not so,* it must be *possible* for heat *not* to be molecular motion. Hence, he may (wrongly) conclude, (3) must be contingent. The same reasoning applies to (4). The error is in confusing epistemic with metaphysical possibility. Once it is corrected, the flaw in the argument becomes obvious. Having dismissed only one of two sources of the impression that (4) is contingent, if true, Kripke is not entitled to his conclusion that it's not true.[17]

[17] Soames (2006a).

This objection to Kripke, relying on sharply distinguishing epistemic from metaphysical possibility, would not have appealed to Lewis. For him, contingent theoretical identities involving natural kind terms are unproblematic.[18] In his analysis, pain, for an organism x, is the physical state which, in *normal* members of x's kind, plays a certain functional role; it is typically caused by injuries, it interferes with one's activities, and it is something the avoidance of which motivates action. The theory, articulated in Lewis (1980a), is designed to accommodate normal pain plus "mad" and "Martian" pain.

MAD PAIN

There might be a strange man . . . whose pain differs greatly from ours. . . . Our pain is typically caused by cuts, burns, pressure, and the like; his is caused by moderate exercise on an empty stomach. Our pain is generally distracting; his turns his mind to mathematics, facilitating concentration on that but distracting him from anything else. Intense pain has no tendency whatever to cause him to groan or writhe. . . . He is not in the least motivated to prevent pain or get rid of it. In short, he feels pain but his pain does not at all occupy the typical causal role of pain.[19]

MARTIAN PAIN

Also, there might be a Martian . . . whose pain differs greatly from ours in its physical realization. His hydraulic mind contains nothing like our neurons. Rather, there are varying amounts of fluid in many inflatable cavities, and the inflation of any one of these cavities opens some valves and closes others. . . . When you pinch his skin you cause no firing of C-fibers—he has none—but rather you cause the inflation of many smallish cavities in his feet. When these cavities are inflated, he is in pain. And the effects of his pain are fitting: his thought and activity are disrupted, he groans and writhes, he is strongly motivated to stop you from pinching

---

[18] To the extent that Kripkean intuitions about rigid designation need to be accommodated, Lewis came (by the 1990s) to see rigidified descriptions plus Chalmers/Jackson style two-dimensionalist analyses as the way to do so. The appeal of this strategy was, as explained in Soames (2005, 2006a), to preserve a pre-Kripkean conception of conceptual possibility as the only possibility. For Lewis (and the others) the distinction between epistemic and metaphysical modalities which allows a single proposition to be conceivable though necessarily false is replaced by a system in which a pair of propositions (associated with the same sentence) can receive different modal evaluations.

[19] Page 122 of the version reprinted in Lewis (1983a).

him. . . . In short, he feels pain but lacks the bodily states that either are pain or else accompany it in us.[20]

While "Martian pain" is easily imaginable, "mad pain" isn't. Is it really possible? Here, we must distinguish epistemic from metaphysical possibility. Let's say that p is epistemically possible iff we can't know apriori that p isn't true. Since the connection between neurological states and behavior is aposteriori, it is *epistemically possible* for one to be in the neurological state we are in when feeling pain while having the madman's behavior and motivation. It is also epistemically possible to be in that state and not *feel pain*. However, when one adds that the madman *feels pain*, despite lacking normal *pain behavior* and *pain-avoiding motivation*, it is natural not only to doubt that *mad pain* is metaphysically possible but also to question whether it is epistemically so. It is conceivable, and presumably possible, for agents to exhibit *some* behavioral and motivational responses to pain that differ from the norm. But this doesn't mean that the wholesale difference exhibited by Lewis's "madman" is either possible or coherently conceivable. By contrast, the epistemic possibility of Martian pain is beyond doubt. As for its metaphysical possibility, caution is in order. While it is very plausible that actual and possible organisms can feel pain despite having physiologies quite different from ours, the limits of these differences are unknown, and likely to fall well short of what we can pretheoretically conceive. Presumably, however, Lewis could accept this.

He disagrees with Kripke about 'pain' being a rigid designator. Since most general terms are rigid (whether or not they designate natural kinds), his claim that 'pain' isn't rigid is counterintuitive.[21] Could *pain* have existed without being *pain*? Could anything other than *pain* have been that state? Like (5), but unlike (6), the answers to these questions seem to be no.

5. Could the color *blue* have existed without being (the color) *blue*? Could anything other than *blue* have been that color?
6. Could the color of a cloudless sky at noon have existed without being the color of a cloudless sky at noon? Could anything other than the color of a cloudless sky at noon have been the color of a cloudless sky at noon?

One way out is to take 'pain' to be equivalent to 'the state of an individual that plays such-and-such functional role'. To do so is to lose the madman while gaining rigidity—whether or not different physical

---

[20] Ibid., 123.
[21] For discussion of the rigidity of general terms see Soames (2007c).

states *realize* pain states (at different times/worlds). True, one loses something, since pain may no longer be *identified* with any one physical-state type among all those that may realize it. True also, Lewis would have regarded this as insufficient for his ambitious naturalistic reduction. By now, however, it is not clear that this is a serious worry.[22]

Reviewing my discussion of the core components of Lewis's grand naturalistic reduction—of the mental to the physical, of causation to counterfactuals, of counterfactuals to the similarity relation on worlds, and of worlds to existing physical universes—I have found them all to fall short. They are not, I think, genuine reductions of one class of things to another. Nevertheless, all but the last (the modal to the nonmodal) contained much of value that moved the discussion of the issues with which they were concerned forward. Even the grand reductive attempt was not without value, being the first real effort by a leading figure of analytic philosophy to construct a comprehensive view of the whole of reality since Russell (1918–19) and Carnap (1928).[23]

Because metaphysics was the center of Lewis's philosophy, this mixed verdict is not a happy one for such a gifted thinker. There were, however, other projects to which he contributed much more successfully. His first book, *Convention*, made an important contribution to the study of equilibriums arising as solutions to certain kinds of coordination problems and multiagent games. His work on conditional probability

[22] It is important to distinguish the question whether 'pain' is a rigid designator from the question whether being a pain is an essential property of anything that has it. Although Kripke seems to run them together in his discussion of pain in *Naming and Necessity* (1980, 148–49), they are distinct. (See Soames 2006a, 181–82; 2002, 252–53.) Having dealt with the rigidity issue, we may wonder whether, as Kripke thinks, *being a pain* is an *essential property* of anything that has it. Consider, the intense headache I had last night. Could it have existed without being a pain? It's mildly bizarre to suppose it could—while being pleasurable or unfelt. Lewis seems to allow both. Suppose at w, I exist with all my C-fibers, but my brain has been altered by the addition of genetically designed D-fibers that make the C-fiber stimulation pleasurable. At w, the same C-fibers firing that constituted my headache at @ are experienced as a pleasurable tickling. It seems, in Lewis's account, that the thing which is my headache at @ also exists at w. Is it a pain? If others of my kind haven't had the benefit of the procedure, Lewis's theory will count me as feeling mad pain, even though it is enjoyable. That seems wrong. Suppose I am the only one of my kind at w, or that all the others have new D-fibers, too. In both cases, my headache, which for Lewis is identical with a certain firing of C-fibers, exists and is *not a pain*, but rather is a pleasurable sensation. Not, I think, a convincing counterexample to Kripke's essentiality thesis. By contrast, the example causes no problem for our final, purely functionalist reformulation of Lewis, since in this analysis the pain state is *realized* by, but not *identified* with, the C-fiber firing.

[23] Russell's system is examined in detail in chapter 12 of volume 1 of Soames (2014). I don't put the metaphysical system of the *Tractatus* in the same category because of its subservience to the larger themes of the work, which were devoted to turning philosophy away from genuine metaphysics.

and its distinctness from the probability of any conditional sentence, in Lewis (1976), was path breaking.[24] He was also one of the leading contributors to the grand project to which many analytic philosophers have devoted themselves—moving the study of language, information, and cognition from unsystematic philosophical speculations to a (still future) stage in which solid and comprehensive frameworks for genuine scientific investigation are in place. It is to this broad project that I now turn.

Lewis's (1970b) was one of the cutting-edge texts of its time—along with work by Richard Montague, David Kaplan, and Robert Stalnaker. Together, they laid out a powerful framework for the use of intensional logic in semantic theories of natural language. In his paper, Lewis used a categorial grammar to generate deep structures, mappable onto surface structures by Chomsky-like transformations (in a manner then being investigated by his colleague Barbara Partee at UCLA). Deep structures were interpreted by a version of Montague's one-semantic-rule-for-each-syntactic-rule approach. The resulting system assigned intensions (functions from indices to truth values) to sentences.[25] Although his system was both powerful and fruitful, it was also resolutely intensional, with no room for hyperintensional operators. In keeping with the assumptions of the time, propositions were identified with intensions of sentences—which, for our purposes, we may take to be functions from "worlds" to truth values, or, more simply, sets of "worlds." Though many today still adhere to this approach, others have come to see it as incorporating limitations that Lewis never transcended, as demonstrated by his discussion and individuation of propositions in such late works as Lewis (1996).

Historically, the three main attempts to deal with hyperintensionality in intensional semantics have been (i) to substitute finer-grained circumstances for world-states, (ii) to distinguish the proposition semantically expressed by S from what one asserts by uttering S, and (iii) to adopt a 2D semantic theory which associates *pairs* of

---

[24] In addition to establishing this result, the article also offers an analysis of indicative conditionals on which ⌜If A, then B⌝ has the truth conditions of a material conditional while having assertability conditions requiring the conditional probability B given A to be high. In the postscript, Lewis (1986c), he gives up the details of this view in favor of a related account given in Frank Jackson (1979, 1981).

[25] The demonstration, in Hans Kamp (1971), that times and worlds must be double-indexed had not been widely recognized. David Kaplan's reconceptualization (including his distinction between character and content) was also not yet in place. The indices in Lewis (1970b) each consisted of a single time, place, world, and assignment of objects to variables. In Lewis (1980b, 1983b) he noted the work of Kamp, Stalnaker, and Kaplan, and recognized various ways in which his original parameters might be enriched.

coarse-grained propositions with sentences. The high-water mark for
(i) (never favored by Lewis) was the system of situation semantics developed by Barwise and Perry (1983). It failed because the hyperintensionality problem is reconstructable for all theories of propositions
as sets of truth-supporting circumstances (satisfying certain minimal
assumptions).[26] The high-water mark for (ii), pioneered by Stalnaker
(1978) and endorsed by Lewis, identified propositions with sets of
metaphysically possible world-states while combining the distinction
between semantic and assertive content with a 2D strategy of "diagonalization" to breathe informativeness into utterances of sentences that
express necessary consequences of propositions already in the context.
It fails for various reasons, including its inability to accommodate attitudes to singular propositions that predicate essential properties of
things.[27] The high-water mark for (iii) is a semantic view, suggested by
David Chalmers (1996) and Frank Jackson (1998), called "strong two-
dimensionalism" in Soames (2005). The basic idea is that sentences
express propositions dubbed "primary" and "secondary" intensions,
the former being the arguments of hyperintensional operators and the
latter being the arguments of modal operators. Since the primary intension of S says, roughly, that S's Kaplanian character expresses a truth,
primary and secondary intensions diverge when S contains indexicals
or indexically rigidified descriptions (which names and natural kind
terms are taken to be).[28] The chief technical problem is that strong

---

[26] See Soames (1987, 2008).

[27] See Soames (2006b) and King, Soames, and Speaks (2014, chap. 3).

[28] In Lewis (1997), we are given the following account of the descriptions to be rigidified in the case of names.

> Did not Kripke and his allies refute the description theory of reference, at
> least for names of people and places? . . . I disagree. What was well and
> truly refuted was a version of descriptivism in which the descriptive senses
> were supposed to be a matter of famous deeds and other distinctive pe-
> culiarities. A better version survives the attack: *causal descriptivism*. The
> descriptive sense associated with a name might for instance be 'the place
> I have heard of under the name "Toromeo"' or maybe 'the causal source
> of this token: Toromeo', and for the account of the relation being invoked
> here, just consult the writings of causal theorists of reference. (332n22).

The final clause of this passage is problematic. There is no precise theory of how the
referent of one's use of a name is inherited from other uses. Since it is inherited, the description 'the referent of the uses from which my use of 'Toromeo' somehow inherits its
reference' picks out the right object, but can't, on pain of circularity, be what *determines*
my referent. The problem for causal descriptivism is that speakers have no other, noncir-
cular, descriptive means of fixing reference. For more on this and related problems with
attempts to fix the referents of names descriptively see my reply to Jackson in Soames
(2007b).

2D can't account for sentences containing both modal and hyperintensional operators, one embedded under the other. Rescue attempts that appeal to weaker versions of 2D semantics suffer from similar shortcomings.[29]

Though Lewis didn't himself pioneer this failed approach, he did embrace it.[30] Moreover, the problems with propositions as sets of "possible worlds" are not limited to the coarse-grained nature of the latter. It is crucial to any account of propositions that, as bearers of truth conditions, they represent the universe as being certain ways (without requiring interpretation by us). No set is inherently representational in this way. What does the set containing "worlds" 1, 2, and 3 represent? Is it true or false? These questions make no sense. If we wanted, we could use the set to represent the "actual world" as being in the set—and so to make the claim that no "world" *outside* the set is actual. But we could equally use it to represent the "actual world" as *not* being in the set—and so to make the claim that no "world" *inside* the set is actual. Independent of interpretation by us, the set doesn't represent anything, and so has no truth conditions.[31]

This brings me to the necessary aposteriori, where several fault lines dividing Lewis and Kripke meet.[32] No theory identifying necessarily equivalent propositions can distinguish necessary propositions that are knowable apriori from those that aren't. If I am right, there is also no acceptable 2D reanalysis of Kripke's data supporting the necessary aposteriori. Lewis's treatment of metaphysically possible worlds as *concrete universes* rather than *maximal properties* exacerbates the problem. The latter simply generalizes to the universe the platitude that some things could have had properties they don't have. The further platitude that sometimes a property something couldn't have had can be known not to be had by it *only by appeal to empirical evidence*, allows a further extension. In addition to including maximal properties the universe could have had but doesn't (metaphysically possible worldstates), the analysis can accommodate those the universe couldn't have

[29] See Soames (2005).

[30] Throughout the 1999–2000 academic year David and I jointly taught a graduate seminar on *Naming and Necessity* and its aftermath. In it, he identified propositions with sets of worlds and used diagonalization plus a Jackson/Chalmers–like distinction between primary and secondary intension to deal with attitude ascriptions.

[31] The function that assigns "worlds" 1–3 truth, and all others falsity, isn't intentional either. What, after all, are truth and falsity but properties we grasp primarily through their application to propositions? But surely, if propositions are needed to illuminate truth and falsity, they can't be among the building blocks for constructing propositions. See chapters 3 and 6 of King, Soames, and Speaks (2014).

[32] See Soames (2006a).

had but can't be known apriori not to have (metaphysically impossible but epistemically possible world-states). With such states, the function of evidence needed to know an empirical proposition p can be just what Lewis (1996) says it is—namely, to rule out relevant *possibilities* in which p is false—even when there are no *metaphysical possibilities* to rule out because p is necessary.[33] By contrast, when one thinks of possible worlds as concrete universes (that exist but don't "actually exist") the idea of metaphysically impossible, but epistemically possible, worlds will, wrongly, seem incoherent.

Mention of actuality highlights another problem with modal realism. Most philosophers agree that ⌜Actually S⌝ is necessarily true when S is contingently true. Less widely recognized is the fact that assertively uttering either sentence typically commits one to the propositions expressed by both. Lewis's counterpart theory prevents him from recognizing these things. Although Hubert Humphrey's counterpart, HH, exists and is so-and-so, according to Lewis he doesn't *actually exist* and is not *actually so-and-so* (because he doesn't exist and is not so-and-so *in our universe*).[34] The right result—that anything that exists and is so-and-so, *actually exists* and *actually is so-and-so*—is readily explainable when 'Actually' is taken to indexically refer to the *world-state* of the context, and ⌜Actually S⌝ is seen as equivalent to ⌜At this very world-state S⌝[35]

As I have emphasized, Lewis was a systematic philosopher. Sometimes I wish he hadn't been quite so. One of his most influential papers, Lewis (1979a), contains insights that must be separated from the modal realism that deeply informs it. The insights concern a problem about "first-person" (*de se*) attitudes previously raised and addressed in Hector-Neri Castaneda (1966, 1968) and John Perry (1977, 1979). Here is Lewis's statement of the problem:

---

[33] See Soames (2011).

[34] The semantics of 'actual' is discussed in Lewis (1970a). Although the analysis there is called "indexical," it doesn't take into account the then-unrecognized need for double indexing of times and worlds. Because of this, only one of the two meanings he assigns to 'is actual' (and to 'the actual world') is genuinely indexical—the reading on which 'is actual' is true of a world iff it is identical with the world of the context (assuming double indexing). The other, nonindexical, reading is one in which 'is actual' is true (relative to a context and a circumstance of evaluation) of a world w iff w is the world of the circumstance. The obvious truths that Lewis is forced to deny are those involving the genuine indexical reading. He is forced to deny them by the basic tenet of modal realism that for Hubert to possibly exist, or be so-and-so, is for an inhabitant HH, of a merely possible world, to exist, or be so-and so. That is the key mistake; adopting an approximately correct indexical semantics for 'actual' merely helps reveal it.

[35] See Soames (2007a) and (2010a, chap. 6).

Consider... two gods. They... know every proposition that is true at their world.... Still... [n]either one knows which of the two he is.... One lives on top of the tallest mountain, and throws down manna; the other lives on top of the coldest mountain and throws down thunderbolts. Neither one knows whether he lives on the tallest mountain or on the coldest mountain, nor whether he throws manna or thunderbolts. Surely their predicament is possible. (The trouble might perhaps be that they have an equally perfect view of every part of their world, and hence cannot identify the perspectives from which they view it.) *But if it is possible to lack knowledge and not lack any propositional knowledge, then the lacked knowledge must not be propositional.* If the gods came to know which was which, they would know more than they do. But they wouldn't know more propositions.... Rather... [o]ne... would correctly self-ascribe the property of living on the tallest mountain.[36]

The gods know that the manna-thrower lives on the tallest mountain, and the thunderbolt-thrower lives on the coldest mountain. Each also knows, of the manna-thrower M, *that he lives on the tallest mountain*—i.e., each knows the singular proposition expressed by '"x" lives on the tallest mountain' relative to an assignment of M to 'x'. The same is true of the singular proposition expressed by ' "x" lives on the coldest mountain' relative to an assignment of the other god, T, to 'x'. Nevertheless, they seem to lack knowledge. If M or T were to say "I don't know whether I live on the tallest/coldest mountain," we would judge him to have spoken truly. This suggests *there are some things they don't know.* Since there are no propositions they don't know, Lewis concludes that not all knowledge is propositional; sometimes what is known is a property that one could correctly self-ascribe. The main alternative at the time was Perry's, according to which the gods already know all there is to know; they simply fail to recognize certain known propositions when presented to them in a first-person way. I believe Lewis is closer to the truth.

Still, there are challenges to be met. The first is illustrated by Perry's (1977) example of the amnesiac Lingens, who is trapped in the Stanford library reading a fact-filled biography of Lingens that includes a description of his predicament. Although Lingens believes, and even knows, all the propositions learned from reading, we naturally describe him as "not knowing that *he* is Lingens," and "not knowing that *he* is trapped in the Stanford Library." Which propositions are these? Not the propositions *that Lingens is Lingens* and *that Lingens is trapped in the Stanford Library.* Everyone who has heard of Lingens knows the former, and

---

[36] Page 139 of the 1983a reprinting of Lewis (1979a), my emphasis.

Lingens himself knows the latter because the book told him. Despite this, Lewis maintains, Lingens is in no position to self-ascribe *being Lingens* and *being in the Stanford library*. So far, so good. Now consider an extension in which Lingens looks in the mirror and says "That's me!" or "I am identical with him," self-ascribing *being him* (demonstrating himself). Since this *is* the property *being Lingens*, it seems we should conclude that Lingens now *knows that he is Lingens*. But we wouldn't naturally say that. Is Lewis's account therefore incorrect, or unmotivated, because it allows us to re-create a version of the very problem it was designed to solve? Perhaps, but I doubt it. Since Frege's puzzle has been laid on top of the *de se* puzzle, getting the right result involves combining what is needed for both—Lewis's self-ascription plus, e.g., Perry's, or Salmon's, ways of believing/ascribing.[37]

The next challenge is similar, except that the property self-ascribed is necessarily empty. In this case, adapted from (Perry 1979), Perry is shopping in the supermarket, when he looks up at two differently placed security mirrors and says to himself, "I am nearer to him [demonstrating the man seen in mirror 1] than I am to him [demonstrating the man seen in mirror 2]." Since he is the man seen in both mirrors, he thereby self-ascribes *being nearer to Perry than to Perry*. Because this property is necessarily empty, self-ascription of it will, for Lewis, result in believing the impossible, which, for him, is itself impossible.[38] Since this is wrong, salvaging the Lewisian *de se* requires embracing hyperintensionalism. Not surprising.

Next, notice that John and Mary express *different beliefs* by sincerely uttering, "I am hungry"—despite the fact that they self-ascribe the *same property*. How does this fit the idea that *de se* belief is the self-ascription of properties? Pretty well, if we add that an agent x who *self-ascribes P* counts as *ascribing* P of *x* (but not conversely). Whereas both involve predicating P of x, the former requires *thinking of the predication target in the first-person way* (whatever that amounts to), while that latter doesn't. It will then follow that, in addition to their identical *de se* beliefs, John and Mary also have different *de re* beliefs. (I will return to the question of whether they really do also express *identical* beliefs.)

The same idea allows us to recognize that Lingens and his friend Lola express the same (*de re*) belief when Lingens sincerely says, "This book is about me," and Lola, agrees, saying "That book is about you."

---

[37] Salmon (1986).

[38] For Lewis, when S is necessarily false, ⌜A believes that S⌝ is necessarily equivalent to ⌜A believes that S & P⌝ for every P. Since 'believe' distributes over conjunction, the truth of the former guarantees the truth of ⌜A believes that P⌝ *for every P*. Since it is impossible for any agent to simultaneously believe everything (and its negation), it must be impossible for ⌜A believes that S⌝ to be true when S is necessarily false.

A state of *de se* believing something is always also a state of *de re* believing something closely related. Innocent enough, this idea worsens the problems posed by Lewis's antihyperintensionalism—making it impossible for Lingens, prior to his epiphany, to coherently take himself *not to be Lingens*. Since doing that would involve both self-ascribing *not being Lingens* and believing the necessary falsehood *that Lingens is not Lingens*, Lewis must, by the assumptions in the previous footnote, (wrongly) disallow the possibility that Lingens might wrongly believe *that he isn't Lingens*. To avoid this, hyperintensionality must (again) be embraced.

So far, I have written as if Lewis took the objects of *de se* beliefs to be properties and the objects of other beliefs to be propositions. He didn't. Rightly wanting a unified analysis, and judging propositions not to be objects of *de se* beliefs, he took properties to be the objects of all beliefs. In this view, to believe that the earth moves is to self-ascribe *being such that the earth moves* (a property everything has). This is artificial at best and problematic at worst. First, Lewisian properties aren't true or false; second, agents who self-ascribe *being hungry* don't thereby express identical beliefs. To me, this suggests the need for a new conception of propositions that explains how genuine *de se* propositions (the entertaining of which require Lewisian self-ascription) can be distinct from, but representationally identical with, corresponding *de re* propositions. Elsewhere, I argue for such a conception, which preserves the virtues of Lewis's solution without its drawbacks.[39]

Another brilliant and highly influential paper is Lewis (1975b). Marrying Lewis (1970b, and 1969), it reconciles two ways of thinking about language. According to one, languages are sets of well-formed, interpreted expressions; according to the other, they are social practices. As Lewis persuasively argues, both perspectives are needed. By distinguishing the question, *What is a language?*—an abstract object with semantic properties—from the question, *What facts are necessary and sufficient for a population to speak it?* he puts the two perspectives into a single frame. In the simplest case (ignoring ambiguity and indexicality, and considering only declarative sentences) he takes a language L to be a set of well-formed sentences paired with their meanings— which are sets of worlds at which they are true. (Meanings of constituents of sentences are not part of the specification because Lewis shared Quine's worries about referential indeterminacy.) For L to be used by a population P is for *a convention of truthfulness and trust in L* to exist in P. To be *truthful in L* is, to a first approximation, to assertively utter a sentence S of L only when one believes S to be *true in L*. To be *trusting in*

---

[39] See King, Soames, and Speaks (2014, chap. 6); also chap. 3 of Soames forthcoming.

L is, roughly, to be disposed to believe that others in P are *truthful in L*, and so will assertively utter S only if they believe S to be *true in L*. From this it follows that the trusting hearer h will be disposed to believe that S is *true in L* to the extent h has reason to believe that the speaker s knows what s is talking about. Finally, to say that there is a *convention* of *truthfulness and trust in L* is to say, very roughly (i) that there is a regularity of such among members of P; (ii) that members of P realize this; (iii) that the expectation that others conform to the regularity gives one a good reason to conform; (iv) that there is a general preference, given that most conform, for all (including oneself) to conform; and (v) that members of P could, in theory, satisfy their interests in communication by conforming to an alternative regularity of truthfulness and trust in a different language.

These are, of course, just the bare bones of Lewis's theory, without his many complex elaborations. It is, however, enough to raise two questions:

Q1 Is it essential that something like his regularities be *conventions*?

Q2 Does the framework require individuating meanings/propositions so coarsely, or it is compatible with a genuinely hyperintensional conception of both?

First Q1. Conditions (iii) and (iv) are crucial to Lewis's analysis of convention and to his view that the solution to the coordination problem provided by *linguistic conventions* gives members of P good practical and epistemic *reasons* for action and belief. In what sense does a regularity of truthfulness and trust in L provide each speaker with such reasons? Let's grant that speaker x has an abiding interest in communication and in the conformity of others to the policy of being *truthful and trusting in L*. Presumably, the fact that they do conform gives x a good reason to trust that they do. Does it also give x a good reason to be *truthful in L*? Although it may give x a moral reason, this is not the type of reason Lewis emphasizes, any more than the fact that there is a moral reason—to avoid injuring or inconveniencing others—to conform (when driving in the United States) to the regularity of driving on the right-hand side of the road, is the main sort of interest served by the convention of driving on the right. In the driving case, anyone interested in getting safely and swiftly from point A to point B has reason to conform, independent of a concern for others. Although the issue is delicate in the linguistic case, it would seem that Lewis needs a similarly compelling reason that comes from x's interest in communication. Is there such a reason for x to speak *truly in L?* Pending an answer to this question, it is not easy to say whether conditions (iii) and (iv) of Lewis's definition of a convention are met.[40]

The answer to Q2 is more direct. Substituting hyperintensional propositions for Lewis's intensional ones strengthens the analysis. Suppose, what I take to be obvious, that necessarily equivalent sentences may differ both in meaning and in the beliefs they are used to express. It follows naturally that L and L* may differ in the hyperintensional propositions they assign to the same sentences, even though the truth conditions of sentences resulting from those assignments are necessarily equivalent. This in turn requires an adjustment in the statement of the convention of truthfulness and trust. We now say (again very roughly): to be truthful in L is to assertively utter a sentence S of L only when one believes the proposition S expresses in L, and to be trusting in L is to be disposed to believe that other members of P are truthful in L, too. With this modest reformulation, none of the attractiveness of Lewis's guiding idea is lost.

Lewis (1979c) is a similarly brilliant and even more influential discussion of the nuanced relationship between meaning, context, and assertion. The article develops two leading ideas. First, various linguistic items and constructions place requirements on contexts in which sentences containing them can acceptably be uttered—requirements regarding what must be assumed or presupposed by conversational participants prior to the utterance, what is taken by them to be under discussion, what possibilities are relevant for conversational exploration, the standards of precision governing the discussion of certain topics and the uses of certain words, the objects most saliently available for conversational reference, and the like. Second, when an utterance requires some aspect of the context to meet one of these requirements which is not, in fact, met prior to the utterance, there is a general, though defeasible, presumption that the conversational participants will *accommodate* the speaker by updating the context so as to bring it into line with what the speaker's remark requires (if doing so is unobjectionable and doesn't involve violating their other commitments). Lewis applies this idea with considerable effect to presuppositions, uses of singular definite descriptions, uses of pronouns seemingly (but not really) anaphoric on prior uses of quantifiers, the reference points of narratives, uses of vague predicates, the choice of different and varying modal domains for terms like 'can' and 'must', the choice of relevant alternatives that must be ruled out to verify claims to know a proposition to be true, the use of language in developing complex

---

[40] See Lewis (1983a, 184–85) for his interesting and nuanced discussion of this issue.

plans, and the use of explicit performatives that are verified (made true) by that very use.[41] The influence of this article in epistemology, philosophy of language, and linguistic semantics can hardly be overestimated.

Lewis was, of course, the author of many more influential articles in the philosophy of language. A final one that must be mentioned is Lewis (1975a). In it, he argues that sentence adverbs such as 'always', 'usually', 'often', sometimes', and 'never' are unselective quantifiers that bind all free variables in their scope. For example, in 'Usually (x likes y iff y likes x)' 'usually' binds occurrences of both 'x' and 'y', so the sentence is true iff for most pairs of people the first likes the second iff the second likes the first. In addition to being attractive, this analysis has also been extremely influential in the literature in linguistic semantics. For example, as noted in Richard Holton (2003), it is cited in Irene Heim (1990) as providing important inspiration for Discourse Representation Theory.

In sum, despite what I judge to be the less than successful outcome of David's overarching metaphysical project, there can be no scanting his many large and lasting contributions to a variety of areas, including, but not restricted to, philosophical logic, the philosophy of language, and linguistic semantics. Nor was his influence limited to the dazzling corpus of his published work. For thirty years he was, during the era of its greatness, a pillar of the Princeton philosophy department. A cooperative and influential colleague, as well as a dedicated and conscientious teacher, his impact on the PhD program there was profound. Always one of the chief draws in recruiting graduate students and one of the strongest influences on their education, he was, for nine years, a model Director of Graduate Studies. His dissertation students are spread far and wide across the profession, and his personal influence on individual philosophers in the United States, "Down Under," and throughout the English-speaking world (and beyond) was simply unmatched during his far too short a time on Earth.[42]

---

[41] Lewis acknowledges Stalnaker (1973, 1974) on presupposition, Kratzer (1977) on relative modality, and Lemmon (1962) on performatives. According to Lemmon and Lewis, declarative sentences like 'I promise to arrive on time' and 'I order you to leave' are used to express propositions that are made true by asserting them (in the right circumstances). To assert them in such circumstances is to perform the speech acts of promising and ordering. In addition to further elaborating these and other analyses, Lewis is responsible for bringing them together under the common head of *accommodation*.

[42] Thanks to Ali Kazmi for very helpful comments on this paper.

REFERENCES

Barwise, Jon, and John Perry. 1983. *Situations and Attitudes*. Cambridge, MA: MIT Press.

Bennett, Jonathan. 2003. *A Philosophical Guide to Conditionals*. Oxford: Clarendon Press.

Carnap, Rudolf . 1928. *Der logische Aufbau der Welt*. Leipzig: Felix Meiner Verlag; translated by Rolf A. George as *The Logical Structure of the World*: *Pseudoproblems in Philosophy*. Berkeley and Los Angeles: University of California Press, 1967.

———. 1950. "Empiricism, Semantics, and Ontology." *Revue Internationale de Philosophie* 4:20–40; revised and reprinted in *Meaning and Necessity*, 2nd ed. Chicago: University of Chicago Press, 1956.

Castaneda, Hector-Neri. 1966. "He: A Study in the Logic of Self-Consciousness." *Ratio* 8:130–57.

———. 1968. "On the Logic of Attributions of Self-Knowledge to Other." *Journal of Philosophy* 65:439–56.

Chalmers, David. 1996. *The Conscious Mind*. New York: Oxford University Press.

Edgington, Dorothy. 2004. "Counterfactuals and the Benefit of Hindsight," in P. Dowe and P. Noordhof, eds., *Causation and Counterfactuals*, 12–27. London: Routledge.

Fine, Kit. 1975. "Critical Notice of *Counterfactuals. Mind* 84:451–58.

Harper, W. L., R. Stalnaker, and G. Pearce. 1981. *If's*. Dordrecht: Reidel.

Heim, Irene. 1990. "E-Type Pronouns and Donkey Anaphora." *Linguistics and Philosophy* 13:137–77.

Holton, Richard. 2003. "David Lewis's Philosophy of Language." *Mind and Language* 18:286–95.

Jackson, Frank. 1979. "On Assertion and Indicative Conditionals." *Philosophical Review* 88:565–89.

———. 1981. "Conditionals and Possibilia." *Proceedings of the Aristotelian Society* 81:125–37.

———. 1998. *From Metaphysics to Ethics*. Oxford: Oxford University Press.

Kamp, Hans. 1971. "Formal Properties of 'Now'." *Theoria* 37:227–74.

King, Jeff, Scott Soames, and Jeff Speaks. 2014. *New Thinking about Propositions*. Oxford: Oxford University Press.

Kment, Boris. 2006. "Counterfactuals and Explanation." *Mind* 115:261–310.

Kratzer, Angelika. 1977. "What 'Must' and 'Can' Must and Can Mean." *Linguistics and Philosophy* 1:337–55.

Kripke, Saul. 1980. *Naming and Necessity*. Cambridge, MA: Harvard University Press; originally published in D. Davidson and G. Harman, eds., *Semantics of Natural Language*. Boston: Reidel. 1972.

Lemmon, E. J. 1962. "On Sentences Verifiable by Their Use." *Analysis* 22:86–89.

Lewis, David. 1966. "An Argument for the Identity Theory." *Journal of Philosophy* 63:17–25; reprinted in Lewis 1983a.

———. 1969. *Convention*. Cambridge, MA: Harvard University Press.

———. 1970a. "Anselm and Actuality." *Nous* 4:175–88; reprinted in Lewis 1983a.

―――. 1970b. "General Semantics." *Synthese* 27:18–67; reprinted in Lewis 1983a.

―――. 1970c. "How to Define Theoretical Terms." *Journal of Philosophy* 67: 427–46; reprinted in Lewis 1983a.

―――. 1973a. *Counterfactuals*. Cambridge, MA: Harvard University Press.

―――. 1973b. "Causation." *Journal of Philosophy* 70:556–67; reprinted in Lewis 1986b.

―――. 1974. "Radical Interpretation." *Synthese* 23:331–44; reprinted in Lewis 1983a.

―――. 1975a. "Adverbs of Quantification," in Edward L. Keenan, ed., *Formal Semantics of Natural Language*. Cambridge: Cambridge University Press; reprinted in Lewis 1998.

―――. 1975b. "Languages and Language," in Keith Gunderson, ed., *Minnesota Studies in the Philosophy of Science*, vol. 7. Minneapolis: University of Minnesota Press; reprinted in Lewis 1983a.

―――. 1976. "Probabilities of Conditionals and Conditional Probabilities." *Philosophical Review* 85:297–315; reprinted in Lewis 1986b.

―――. 1979a. "Attitudes *De Dicto* and *De Se*." *Philosophical Review* 88:13–43; reprinted in Lewis 1983a.

―――. 1979b. "Counterfactual Dependence and Time's Arrow." *Nous* 13:418–46; reprinted in Lewis 1986b.

―――. 1979c. "Scorekeeping in a Language Game." *Journal of Philosophical Logic* 8:339–59; reprinted in Lewis 1983a.

―――. 1980a. "Mad Pain and Martian Pain," in Ned Block, ed., *Readings in the Philosophy of Psychology*, vol. 1. Cambridge, MA: Harvard University Press; reprinted in Lewis 1983a.

―――. 1980b. "Index, Context, and Content," in Stig Kanger and Sven öhman, eds., *Philosophy and Grammar*, 79–100. Dordrecht: Reidel; reprinted in Lewis 1998.

―――. 1983a. *Philosophical Papers*, vol. 1. New York: Oxford University Press.

―――. 1983b. "Postscript to 'General Semantics'," in Lewis 1983a.

―――. 1986a. *On the Plurality of Worlds*. Oxford: Blackwell.

―――. 1986b. *Philosophical Papers*, vol. 2. New York: Oxford University Press.

―――. 1986c. "Postscript to 'Probabilities of Conditionals and Conditional Probabilities'," in Lewis 1986b.

―――. 1996."Elusive Knowledge." *Australasian Journal of Philosophy* 74:549–67; reprinted in Lewis 1999.

―――. 1997. "Naming the Colors." *Australasian Journal of Philosophy* 75:325–42; reprinted in Lewis 1999.

―――. 1998. *Papers in Philosophical Logic*. Cambridge: Cambridge University Press.

―――. 1999. *Papers in Metaphysics and Epistemology*. Cambridge: Cambridge University Press.

―――. 2004. "Causation as Influence," in J. Collins, E. Hall, and L. Paul, eds., *Causation and Counterfactuals*, 75–106 . Cambridge, MA: MIT Press.

Perry, John. 1977. "Frege on Demonstratives." *Philosophical Review* 86:474–97.

―――. 1979. "The Problem of the Essential Indexical." *Nous* 13:3–21.

Quine, W.V.O. 1948. "On What There Is." *Review of Metaphysics* 2:21–38; reprinted in Quine 1980.

———. 1951. *Philosophical Review* 60:20–43; reprinted in Quine 1980.

———. 1960. *Word and Object*. Cambridge, MA: MIT Press.

———. 1969. "Reply to Chomsky," in D. Davidson and J. Hintikka, eds., *Words and Objections*. Dordrecht: Reidel.

———. 1970. "On the Reasons for Indeterminacy of Translation." *Journal of Philosophy* 67:178–83.

———. 1980. *From a Logical Point of View*, 2nd ed. Cambridge, MA: Harvard University Press.

Rosen, Gideon. 1990. "Modal Fictionalism." *Mind* 99:327–54.

———. 1995. "Modal Fictionalism Fixed." *Analysis* 55:67–73.

Russell, Bertrand. 1914. *Our Knowledge of the External World*. Chicago and London: Open Court; 2nd ed. London: Allen and Unwin, 1926.

———. 1918–19). "The Philosophy of Logical Atomism." *Monist* 5 (no. 28): 495–527; continued in *Monist* 5 (no. 29): 32–63, 190–222, 345–80; reprinted in *The Philosophy of Logical Atomism*, with an introduction by David Pears. Peru, IL: Open Court Publishing, 1985.

Salmon, Nathan. 1986. *Frege's Puzzle*. Cambridge, MA: MIT Press.

Schaffer, Jonathan. 2004. "Counterfactuals, Causal Independence and Conceptual Circularity." *Analysis* 64:299–309.

Soames, Scott. 1987. "Direct Reference, Propositional Attitudes, and Semantic Content." *Philosophical Topics* 15:44–87; reprinted in Soames 2009.

———. 2000. *Beyond Rigidity*. New York: Oxford University Press.

———. 2005. *Reference and Description*. Princeton, NJ: Princeton University Press.

———. 2006a. "The Philosophical Significance of the Kripkean Necessary Aposteriori," in Ernest Sosa and Enrique Villanueva, eds., *Philosophical Issues* 16:288–309; reprinted in Soames 2009.

———. 2006b. "Understanding Assertion," in J. J. Thompson and A. Byrne, eds., *Content and Modality: Themes from the Philosophy of Robert Stalnaker*. New York: Oxford University Press; reprinted in Soames 2009.

———. 2007a. "Actually." *Aristotelian Society Supplement* 81:251–77; reprinted in Soames 2009.

———. 2007b. "The Substance and Significance of the Dispute over Two-Dimensionalism. *Philosophical Books* 48:34–49.

———. 2007c. "What Are Natural Kinds?" *Philosophical Topics* 35:329–42.

———. 2008. "Why Propositions Can't Be Sets of Truth-Supporting Circumstances." *Journal of Philosophical Logic* 37:267–76; reprinted in Soames 2009.

———. 2009. *Philosophical Essays*, vol. 2. Princeton, NJ: Princeton University Press.

———. 2010a. *Philosophy of Language*. Princeton, NJ: Princeton University Press.

———. 2010b. "True At." *Analysis* 71:124–33.

———. 2011. "Kripke on Metaphysical and Epistemic Possibility: Two Routes to the Necessary Aposteriori," in Alan Berger, ed., *Saul Kripke*. Cambridge, MA: Cambridge University Press.

————. 2014. *The Analytic Tradition*, vol. 1. Princeton, NJ: Princeton University Press.

————. Forthcoming. *Rethinking Language, Mind, and Meaning*. Princeton, NJ: Princeton University Press.

Stalnaker, Robert. 1968. "A Theory of Conditionals," in *Studies in Logical Theory. American Philosophical Quarterly Monograph Series*, no. 2. Oxford: Blackwell; reprinted in Harper, Stalnaker, and Pearce 1981.

————. 1973. "Presuppositions." *Journal of Philosophical Logic* 2:447–57.

————. 1974. "Pragmatic Presuppositions," in Milton K. Munitz and Peter K. Unger, eds., *Semantics and Philosophy*. New York: New York University Press.

————. 1978. "Assertion," in Peter Cole, ed., *Syntax and Semantics*, vol. 9: *Pragmatics*. New York: Academic Press; reprinted in Stalnaker 1999, 78–95.

————. 1999. *Context and Content: Essays on Intentionality in Speech and Thought*. New York: Oxford University Press.

Van Fraassen, Bas C. 1980. *The Scientific Image*. Oxford: Oxford University Press.

7

Kripke on Epistemic and Metaphysical Possibility

TWO ROUTES TO THE NECESSARY A POSTERIORI

Saul Kripke's discussion of the necessary a posteriori in *Naming and Necessity* and "Identity and Necessity," laid the foundation for distinguishing epistemic from metaphysical possibility, and explaining the relationship between the two.[1] My aim is to extract the enduring lessons of his discussion and to disentangle them from certain difficulties which, alas, can also be found there. I will argue that there are two Kripkean routes to the necessary a posteriori—one correct and far-reaching, the other incorrect and philosophically misleading.[2] After distinguishing these routes, I will apply the lessons learned to his discussion of mind-body identity.

PROPOSITIONS

Although Kripke avoids the word "proposition" in *Naming and Necessity*, and tries to keep his theoretical commitments to a minimum, he speaks repeatedly of necessary or contingent "statements," and "truths" knowable a priori or a posteriori, that sentences are used to express . Evidently, then, he thinks there are things expressed by sentences that are both bearers of truth value and objects of attitudes like knowledge. Since this is what propositions are supposed to be, his discussion can be understood as implicitly involving propositions, while avoiding, as far as possible, substantive theoretical commitments about what they are. Thus, it should be safe to introduce the word into our discussion, so long

---

[1] Saul Kripke, *Naming and Necessity* (Cambridge, MA: Harvard University Press, 1980); "Identity and Necessity," in Milton Munitz, ed., *Identity and Individuation* (New York: NYU Press, 1971).

[2] For a discussion of the philosophical significance of a correct understanding of this matter, see my *Philosophical Issues* 16 (2006): 288–309; reprinted in *Philosophical Essays*, vol. 2 (Princeton, NJ: Princeton University Press, 2009).

as we limit our assumptions about propositions to those that are least objectionable and most in tune with Kripke's implicit presuppositions.

A1. Some things are asserted, believed, and known. For an agent to assert, believe, or know something is for the agent to stand in a relation to that thing.

A2. The things asserted, believed, and known, are bearers of (contingent or necessary) truth and falsity. These things, which we may call "propositions," can also be expressed by sentences. The proposition expressed by S is designated expressions such as ⌜the proposition that S⌝, ⌜the statement/ claim/assertion/belief that S⌝, or simply ⌜that S⌝—e.g., the proposition expressed by 'Hesperus is Phosphorus' is the proposition that Hesperus is Phosphorus.

A3. Since different sentences may be used to assert the same thing, or express the same belief, and different beliefs or assertions may result from accepting, or uttering, the same sentence, propositions are not identical with sentences used to express them. Intuitively, they are what different sentences that are used to say the same thing have in common, whatever that may turn out to be.

A4. Attitude ascriptions—⌜x asserts, believes, knows, knows a priori, or knows a posteriori that S⌝—report that an agent bears a certain attitude to the proposition expressed by S (in the context).

Kripke's central thesis about the necessary a posteriori is that for some propositions p, p is both necessarily true and knowable only on the basis of empirical evidence.

ESSENTIALISM AND THE DISTINCTION BETWEEN EPISTEMIC AND METAPHYSICAL POSSIBILITY

Kripke's first, and most compelling, route to the necessary a posteriori is illustrated by (1)–(4).

1. Greg Soames ≠ Brian Soames
2. If Saul Kripke exists, then Saul Kripke is a human being.
3. This desk (pointing at the one in my office) was not made out of metal.
4. If this desk exists, then it is made of molecules.

Since these propositions are true, they are, according to Kripke, necessarily true. However, it is obvious that they are knowable only a posteriori. How can this be? How can a proposition that is necessary, and known to be so, also be knowable only a posteriori? Kripke's answer appeals to our knowledge of essential properties and relations.[3] We know a priori that being human, being a desk that was not (originally) made out of metal, and being a desk made out of molecules are essential properties of anything that has them. We also know a priori that being nonidentical is a relation that holds essentially of any pair it relates. So, we know a priori that if any objects have these properties, or stand in this relation, then they have, or stand in, them in any genuinely possible circumstance in which they exist. Hence, we know a priori that propositions (1)–(4) are necessary, if true.[4] Still, discovering that they are true requires empirical investigation. This means that to discover whether certain things are true in all states that the world could, genuinely, have been in, and other things are true in no such states, we sometimes must first discover what is true in the state that the world actually is in. Sometimes, to discover what could and could not be, one first must discover what is.

Implicit in this route to the necessary a posteriori is a sharp distinction between epistemic and metaphysical possibility—between ways things could *conceivably* be versus ways things could *really* be (or have been). It is natural to draw this distinction in terms of the notion of a *possible world* or, better, a *possible world-state*. For Kripke, possible states of the world are *not* alternative concrete universes but abstract objects. Metaphysically possible world-states are maximally complete ways the real concrete universe could have been—maximally complete properties that the universe could have instantiated. Epistemically possible world-states are maximally complete ways the universe can coherently be conceived to be—maximally complete properties that the universe can be conceived of as instantiating, and that one cannot know a priori that it doesn't instantiate. These two sets of properties are different. Just as there are properties that ordinary objects could possibly have had and other properties they couldn't have had, so there are certain maximally complete properties the universe could have had—metaphysically possible world-states—and other maximally complete properties the universe couldn't have had—metaphysically impossible world-states. Just as some of the properties that objects couldn't have had are properties that one can conceive them as having, and that one

---

[3] When speaking of (Kripkean) "essential" properties and relations, I mean simply *properties and relations that hold necessarily of objects (in all genuinely possible world-states in which the objects exist)*.

[4] More properly, in the case of (2) and (4) we know a priori that they are necessary if their consequents are true. Thanks to Teresa Robertson for pointing this out.

cannot know *a priori* that they don't have, so some maximally complete properties that the universe couldn't have had—some metaphysically impossible world-states—are properties that one can conceive it as having, and that one cannot know a priori that it doesn't have. These states of the world are epistemically possible. In this picture—which Kripke did not make explicit, but could have—empirical evidence required for knowledge of necessary truths like (1)–(4) is needed to rule out metaphysically impossible, but epistemically possible, world-states in which they are false.

According to Kripke, some things that are coherently conceivable are not genuinely possible. How, then, are conceivability and possibility related? Here, in effect, is his answer:

> If the essentialist view is correct, it can only be correct if we sharply distinguish between the notions of a posteriori and a priori truth on the one hand, and contingent and necessary truth on the other hand, for although the statement that this table, if it exists at all, was not made of ice, is necessary, it certainly is not something that we know a priori. . . . This looks like wood. It does not feel cold and it probably would if it were made of ice. Therefore, I conclude, probably this is not made of ice. Here my entire judgment is a posteriori. . . . [G]iven that it is in fact not made of ice, in fact is made of wood, one cannot imagine that under certain circumstances it could have been made of ice. So we have to say that though we cannot know a priori whether the table was made of ice or not, given that it is not made of ice, it is *necessarily* not made of ice. In other words, if P is the statement that the lectern is not made of ice, one knows by a priori philosophical analysis, some conditional of the form "if P, then necessarily P." If the table is not made of ice, it is necessarily not made of ice. On the other hand, then, we know by empirical investigation that P, the antecedent of the conditional is true—that this table is not made of ice. We can conclude by *modus ponens*:
>
> P ⊃ Necessarily P
> P
> Necessarily P
>
> The conclusion—'Necessarily P'—is that it is necessary that the table not be made of ice, and this conclusion is known a posteriori, since one of the premises on which it is based is a posteriori. ("Identity and Necessity," 152–53)

Though not put in terms of the distinction between conceivability and genuine possibility, or between two different, but related, types of world-states, the lesson of the passage can easily be so stated. In Kripke's argument, the fact one cannot know that P a priori means that one cannot know a priori that a world-state in which it is false that P is not instantiated. Hence, such states are coherently conceivable, and so epistemically possible. The fact that one knows a priori that if P, then necessarily P, means that one knows a priori that if a world-state in which it is true that P is instantiated, then no world-state in which it is false that P could have been instantiated. Thus, when one finds, empirically, that it is true that P, one learns a posteriori that epistemically possible world-states in which it is false that P are metaphysically impossible.

In this picture, the objects of conceivability—the things we conceive when trying to determine what is metaphysically possible—include not only individual world-states but entire *systems* of metaphysical possibility, each with a designated "actual" world-state and a space of related states. Someone seeing my desk for the first time who doesn't know what it was (originally) made of can conceive of a world-state in which it was made of mahogany, a world-state in which it was made of oak, and perhaps even a world-state in which it was made of metal. One can conceive of each of these states being instantiated. Accompanying each state, one can conceive of related states that will be genuine metaphysical possibilities if the initial, designated, state is instantiated. So, accompanying the designated (actual) state in which the desk was made of reddish-brown mahogany, one can conceive of related world-states in which it was made of mahogany stained another color. But given the supposition that the original state is instantiated, one can conceive of *no* state possible relative to it in which that very desk was made of some other material—e.g., oak or metal. A similar point holds for other epistemically possible world-states in which the desk *was* made of those things. When they play the role of the designated "actual" world-state—i.e., when one considers them as instantiated and asks which states are possible relative to them—one regards world-states in which the desk was made of mahogany as impossible *relative to those states.*

So, we have a set of epistemically possible world-states, each of which can coherently be conceived as being instantiated. Along with each such state w_1, we have (epistemically possible) world-states w_2 which we recognize to be metaphysically possible, if the initial, designated "actual" state w_1 is instantiated—i.e., we recognize that if w_1 was instantiated, then w_2 would be a property that the universe could have had. Moreover, for each such state w_2 there are (epistemically possible) world-states w_3 which we recognize to be metaphysically possible if w_2 is instantiated—i.e., we recognize that if w_1 was instantiated, then

w_3 would be (metaphysically) possibly possible. Repeating this process indefinitely, we generate a coherently conceivable system of metaphysical possibility. Collecting all such systems together, we have a set of epistemically possible systems of metaphysical possibility. Roughly, for a world-state to be genuinely metaphysically possible (or possibly possible) is for it to be a metaphysically possible (or possibly possible) member of some epistemically possible system of metaphysical possibility, *the designated world-state of which is the state that the world really is in.*

Obviously, this is not a definition of metaphysical possibility in non-modal terms (something Kripke would never countenance). Rather, it is a way of thinking about the relationship between conceivability and possibility using the primitive notion of a property that the universe could instantiate. In this picture, conceivability is a fallible, but useful, guide to metaphysical possibility. It is fallible because before we know much about what is actual, there are many epistemically possible world-states that appear to be genuinely possible, and so remain candidates for being metaphysically possible. The more we learn about the world, the more we whittle down this field of candidates, and the better able we are to identify the scope of genuine metaphysical possibility. In short, our guide to metaphysical possibility is conceivability plus knowledge of actuality. Whether this is a *complete* guide is a further question. If, somehow, we could discover all actual, nonmodal facts, would we know precisely which world-states were metaphysically possible, possibly possible, and so on? Once ignorance of actuality is factored out, are facts about which world-states are metaphysically possible relative to other world-states always knowable a priori? Neither anything I have said, nor any doctrine of Kripke's that I know of, settles the issue.

THE SCOPE OF KRIPKE'S ESSENTIALIST ROUTE TO THE NECESSARY A POSTERIORI

The Essentialist Route to the Necessary A posteriori (ERNA)

Let P be a true proposition that attributes a property (or relation) F to an actually existing object o (or to a series of objects), conditional on the object (or objects) existing (while not attributing any further properties or relations to anything). Then, p will be an instance of the necessary a posteriori if (a) it is knowable a priori that F is an essential property of o, if F is a property of o at all (or a relation that holds essentially of the objects, if F holds of them at all); (b) knowledge of o that it has F, if it exists (or of the objects that they are related by F, if they exist) can only be had a posteriori; and (c) knowing p involves knowing of o (or of the objects) that it (they) have F, if it (they) exist at all. (o can be an individual or a kind.)[5]

Instances of ERNA like (2) and (4) are basic cases from which other instances can be derived. For example, since nonidentity essentially relates any pair of objects it actually relates, an argument of this pattern establishes the necessary aposteriority of the proposition that Greg Soames is nonidentical with Brian Soames, if Greg and Brian exist. But since this proposition is trivially equivalent to the proposition expressed by (1), that proposition is also necessary and a posteriori. Similar remarks apply to (3).

Although Kripke's essentialist paradigm explains many putative instances of necessary aposteriority, certain simple identity sentences raise problems. Such sentences are standardly taken to be paradigmatic instances of the Kripkean necessary a posteriori, but their status is doubtful. Let o and o* be objects to which the identity relation actually applies, and p be a proposition that (merely) attributes identity to the pair. Then, although conditions (a) and (c) of ERNA are satisfied, condition (b) is not, since knowledge of the pair—i.e., of ‹o,o›—that identity truly applies to it can surely be had a priori. Thus, p is an example of the necessary a priori, not the necessary a posteriori. This point is illustrated by (5).

5. [∃x: x = Hesperus] [∃y: y = Phosphorus] it is a necessary truth that x = y.

Since (5) is true, the proposition expressed by 'x = y', relative to an assignment of Venus to 'x' and 'y', is a necessary truth. However, since this proposition (merely) predicates identity of Venus and itself, it is knowable a priori, if anything is.

Of course, not all identities pose this difficulty. For example, let 'a' and 'b' name the sperm and egg from which Saul Kripke actually developed. The possibility of identical twins aside, his doctrine of the essentiality of origin will then characterize (6a, 6b) as instances of the necessary a posteriori.

6a. Saul Kripke = the individual who developed from a and b (if Kripke exists).

---

[5] If one wishes to generate instances of the necessary a posteriori, like 'No man is human, if he exists' about a merely possible man, while avoiding a similar characterization of 'No man is an elephant, if he exists' clause (b) needs to be changed. One way of doing this is to have it read: knowledge of o that it would have F, if it were to exist, can be had, but only a posteriori. In what follows I will ignore such niceties. Thanks again to Teresa Robertson for the underlying observation.

6b. λx [$\forall y$ (y developed from a and b $\leftrightarrow$ y = x)] Saul Kripke (if Kripke exists).

If Kripke is right about the essentiality of origin, then the proposition p expressed by (6b) fits his essentialist account—since (a) it is knowable a priori that the property expressed by the lambda predicate is essential to any individual that has it, (b) knowledge of Kripke that he has this property (if he exists) can only be had a posteriori, and (c) knowing p involves knowing of Kripke that he has the property (if he exists). Hence, p is an instance of the Kripkean necessary a posteriori. Since proposition (6a) is trivially equivalent to p, it is, too.

Similar explanations cover (7) and (8).

7. gold = the element with atomic number 79 (if gold exists).
8. water = the substance molecules of which consist of two hydrogen atoms and one oxygen atom (if water exists).

Here, 'gold' and 'water' are treated as designating (abstract) natural kinds k_g and k_w (rather than their concrete instances). Thus, the proposition expressed by (7) is trivially equivalent to the proposition p_g that predicates of k_g the property of being a unique element instances of which have a certain atomic structure (if k_g exists), and the proposition expressed by (8) is trivially equivalent to the proposition p_w that predicates of k_w the property of being a unique substance instances of which are made up of molecules consisting of two hydrogen atoms and one oxygen atom (if k_w exists). Supposing, with Kripke, that these properties are knowable a priori to be essential properties of any kind that has them, even though empirical evidence is needed to justify their attribution to any particular kind, we conclude that p_g and p_w are examples of the necessary a posteriori. Since the propositions expressed by (7) and (8) are equivalent to them, they, too, fall under this heading.

Examples (9a)–(9c) also fit the essentialist paradigm, even though they are not strictly *identities*.

9a. Cats are animals.
9b. Lightning is electricity.
9c. Light is a stream of photons.

Kripke calls these *theoretical identification statements* and gives a clue to their correct analysis when he suggests (10b) as the analysis of (10a).[6]

10a. Heat is mean molecular kinetic energy.
10b. $\forall x \forall y$ (x is hotter than y $\leftrightarrow$ the mean molecular kinetic energy of x is greater than that of y)

---

[6] *Naming and Necessity*, p. 138.

Applying this idea to (9) yields (11):

11a. ∀x (x is a cat ⊃ x is an animal)
11b. ∀x (x is (an instance of) lightning ⊃ x is (an instance of) electricity)
11c. ∀x (x is (an instance of) light ⊃ x is a stream of photons)

Proposition (11a) is equivalent to one that predicates of the species cat the property of having only instances that are also instances of genus animal. If this property can be known a priori to be an essential property of any species that has it (even though knowing that a species has it requires empirical investigation), then (11a) falls under Kripke's essentialist paradigm. Analogous remarks hold for (11b), (11c), and (10b).[7]

In sum, Kripke's essentialist paradigm explains a great many genuine instances of the necessary a posteriori. It may even seem that all his putative examples of the necessary a posteriori fall into this category. However, they don't. Sentences of the form (12a), where m and n are simple, coreferential names, do not fit the paradigm; nor do sentences of the form (13a), where K and K* are simple natural kind terms (rigidly) designating the same kind k, and ⌜is a K⌝ and ⌜is a K*⌝ are predicates applying to all and only instances of k.

12a. n = m
12b. Hesperus is Phosphorus

13a. ∀x [x is a K ↔ x is a K*]
13b. Woodchucks are groundhogs (and conversely)

Since, according to Kripke, names don't have descriptive senses, it is natural to take a sentence consisting of names plus a relational predicate R to semantically express a proposition that predicates the relation expressed by R of the referents of the names, without any further predication. In this model, the proposition expressed by (12b) merely predicates identity of Venus and itself. Although this proposition is necessary, it seems to be knowable a priori. One could, of course, avoid this conclusion by adopting the assumption (foreign to Kripke) that—in addition to predicating identity of Venus and itself—the proposition expressed by (12b) also predicates the properties of being visible in the evening and being visible in the morning of Venus. However, then the

---

[7] For discussion, see chapters 9–11 of my *Beyond Rigidity* (New York: Oxford University Press, 2002); "Knowledge of Manifest Kinds," *Facta Philosophica* 6 (2004): 159–81; and chapter 4 of *Reference and Description* (Princeton, NJ, and Oxford: Princeton University Press, 2005). See also, Nathan Salmon, "Naming, Necessity, and Beyond," *Mind* 112 (2003): 475–92; Bernard Linsky, "General Terms as Rigid Designators"; and my reply to Linsky in "Reply to Critics," *Philosophical Studies* 128:711–38.

proposition will be *contingent*.[8] Thus, although Kripke gives (12b), and other instances of (12a), as paradigmatic examples of the necessary a posteriori, one cannot arrive at this result by his standard essentialist route. Analogous remarks apply to instances of (13).

KRIPKE'S SECOND (ATTEMPTED) ROUTE TO THE NECESSARY A POSTERIORI: HESPERUS AND PHOSPHORUS

The argument for the a posteriority of (12b) given in the last few pages of lecture 2 of *Naming and Necessity* is based on the observation that the evidence available to a speaker who understands 'Hesperus' and 'Phosphorus' is insufficient to determine that they are coreferential. Kripke illustrates this by noting that there are possible world-states w in which competent users of 'Hesperus' and 'Phosphorus' are in evidentiary situations qualitatively identical to ours (prior to the astronomical discovery), and yet, in w, the names refer to different things.

> The evidence I have before I know that Hesperus is Phosphorus is that I see a certain star or certain heavenly body in the evening and call it 'Hesperus', and in the morning and call it 'Phosphorus'. I know these things. There certainly is a possible world in which a man should have seen a certain star at a certain position in the evening and called it 'Hesperus' and a certain star in the morning and called it 'Phosphorus'; and should have concluded—should have found out by empirical investigation—that he named different stars, or two different heavenly bodies. . . . And so it's true that given the evidence that someone has antecedent to his empirical investigation, he can be placed in a sense in exactly the same situation, that is a qualitatively identical epistemic situation, and call two heavenly bodies 'Hesperus' and 'Phosphorus', without their being identical. So in that sense we can say that *it might have turned out either way*. (103–4; my emphasis)

Kripke rightly takes his example to show that the evidence available to us, simply by being competent users of the names, doesn't establish (12c) or (12d).

12c. 'Hesperus' and 'Phosphorus' are coreferential.
12d. 'Hesperus is Phosphorus' expresses a truth.

---

[8] Including these properties in the contents of 'Hesperus' and 'Phosphorus', and rigidifying using the actuality operator, would preserve the necessity of (12b) (or near enough). However, such an analysis fails on independent grounds. See chapter 2 of *Beyond Rigidity*.

Thus, these propositions are not knowable a priori.

However, the lesson he explicitly draws is that the proposition expressed by (12b) is not knowable a priori.

> So two things are true: first, that we do not know a priori that Hesperus is Phosphorus, and are in no position to find out the answer except empirically. Second, this is so because we could have evidence *qualitatively indistinguishable* from the evidence we have and determine the reference of the two names by the positions of the two planets in the sky, without the planets being the same. (104; my emphasis)

This conclusion is unwarranted. Since the proposition expressed by (12b) is true in all metaphysically possible world-states, it is true in all such states in which agents are in epistemic situations qualitatively identical to ours—even when the proposition *they* use (12b) to express is false. Although both we and they need evidence to rule out the falsity of (12c) and (12d), it has *not* been shown that when (12b) does express a true proposition p, evidence is needed to rule out the possible falsity of p. Since it has *not* been shown that evidence is needed to rule out the possible falsity of the proposition *actually* expressed by *our* use of (12b), it has *not* been shown that we can know that Hesperus is Phosphorus only a posteriori.

To derive Kripke's conclusion, one needs a premise that Kripke leaves implicit. In the passage, he exploits a familiar connection between speakers' understanding and acceptance of sentences and our ability to use those sentences to report what they believe. Before the astronomical discovery, speakers understood but didn't accept sentence (12b); hence, it is natural to conclude, they didn't believe that Hesperus was Phosphorus. Since they wouldn't have been *justified* in accepting (12b), based on the evidence then, it is plausible to suppose that they wouldn't have been justified in believing that Hesperus was Phosphorus. But then, the proposition that Hesperus is Phosphorus must require empirical justification, in which case it must not be knowable only a priori—exactly as Kripke says.

Here is the argument:

(i) One who understands 'Hesperus is Phosphorus' (a) accepts it and believes it to be true iff one believes that Hesperus is Phosphorus, and (b) would be justified accepting it and believing it to be true iff one would be justified in believing that Hesperus is Phosphorus.

(ii) To be justified in accepting 'Hesperus is Phosphorus' and believing it to be true, one needs evidence that the two names refer to the same thing. Given that one knows that 'Hesperus' designates the heavenly body seen in the evening and that 'Phosphorus' designates the heavenly body seen in the morning, one needs evidence that these are one and the same.

(iii) Since one needs empirical evidence to be justified in believing that Hesperus is Phosphorus, it is knowable only a posteriori.

When expressed in the framework of propositions, this argument presupposes the following premise.

STRONG DISQUOTATION AND JUSTIFICATION (SDJ)

If x understands S, uses S to express p, and knows that S expresses p, then (a) x believes p iff x accepts S (and believes it to be true), and (b) x would be justified in believing p on the basis of evidence e iff x would be justified in accepting S (and believing it to be true) on the basis of e.

One who understands 'Hesperus is Phosphorus', while associating the names with 'the heavenly body seen in the evening', and 'the heavenly body seen in the morning', will justifiably accept the sentence and believe it to be true only if one justifiably believes that the heavenly body seen in the evening is the heavenly body seen in the morning. This descriptive belief doesn't involve any *de re* belief about Venus, and so is the sort that Kripke is looking for in his argument. Since justification for this belief rests on empirical evidence, justification for accepting 'Hesperus is Phosphorus' requires this evidence. SDJ transfers this requirement to one's belief in the proposition one uses the sentence to express— presumably, in our case, the proposition that Hesperus is Phosphorus. Hence, our knowledge of this proposition can only be a posteriori.

EXTENSION OF THE ARGUMENT TO OTHER INSTANCES OF THE NECESSARY A POSTERIORI

In lecture 3, Kripke generalizes this explanation to all cases of the necessary a posteriori. After summarizing his analysis of natural kind terms, and illustrating their role in expressing instances of the necessary a posteriori, he takes up a challenge. Up to now, when describing these instances, he emphasizes that although they are necessary, for all we knew prior to empirically discovering their truth, *they could have turned out otherwise.* Realizing that this may sound puzzling, he gives voice to the following objection:

Now in spite of the arguments I gave before for the distinction between necessary and a priori truth, the notion of a posteriori necessary truth may still be somewhat puzzling. Someone may well be inclined to argue as follows: "You have admitted that heat might have turned out not to have been molecular motion, and that gold might have turned out not to have been the element with the atomic number 79. For that matter, you also have acknowledged that . . . this table might have turned out to be made from ice from water from the Thames. I gather that Hesperus might have turned out not to be Phosphorus. What then can you mean when you say that such eventualities are impossible? If Hesperus might have *turned out* not to be Phosphorus, then Hesperus might not have *been* Phosphorus. And similarly for the other cases: if the world could have *turned out* otherwise, it could have *been* otherwise." (140–41; my emphasis)

The objection covers all instances p of the necessary a posteriori. Since p is a posteriori, its falsity must be conceivable, and so, it would seem, knowledge of p must require empirical evidence ruling out possibilities in which p is false. Without such evidence, *it could turn out that p is false.* But, the objector maintains, if p is necessary, there are no such possibilities to be ruled out, since no matter what possible state the world is in, it is a state in which p is true. Thus, if p is necessary, we don't require empirical evidence to know p after all, and if p is a posteriori, then p isn't necessary. Either way, the necessary a posteriori is an illusion.

Kripke begins his reply by invoking an idea central to his account of (12b). According to that account, the function of empirical evidence needed for knowledge that Hesperus is Phosphorus is *not* to rule out possible world-states in which the proposition is false. There are no such states. Rather, evidence is needed to rule out possible states in which we use the *sentence* (12b) to express something false. Ruling this out involves putting aside our *de re* beliefs about Venus and determining whether our justified *descriptive* beliefs are up to the task. If they fail to rule out the possibility of an epistemic state *qualitatively identical* to ours in which the names refer to different things, then we can't rule out the falsity of the sentence we accept, and so, the thought goes, we can't justify the belief we use the sentence to express. Kripke's task is to extend this explanation of (12b) to all instances of the necessary a posteriori:

The objector is correct when he argues that if I hold that this table could not have been made of ice, then I must also hold that it could not have turned out to be made of ice; *it could have turned out that P* entails that P could have been the case. What, then, does the intuition that the table might have turned out to have been made of ice or of anything else, that it might even have turned out not to be made of molecules, amount to? I think that it means simply that there might have been *a table* looking and feeling just like this one and placed in this very position in the room, which was in fact made of ice. In other words, I (or some conscious being) could have been *qualitatively in the same epistemic situation* that in fact obtains, I could have the same sensory experience that I in fact have, about *a table*, which was made of ice. (141–42; my emphasis)

Suppose I encounter a table. I examine it and come to know that it is made of wood, not ice. For all I knew, prior to my investigation, *it could have turned out* that the table was made of ice. Kripke tells us that this intuition—that *it could have turned out* that the table was made of ice—is simply the recognition that it is genuinely possible for an agent to be in a situation qualitatively identical to mine prior to my investigation, and be facing a table that *is* made of ice. He generalizes this point in the next paragraph:

The general answer to the objector can be stated, then, as follows: Any necessary truth, whether *a priori* or *a posteriori*, could not have turned out otherwise. In the case of some necessary a posteriori truths, however, we can say that under appropriate qualitatively identical evidential situations, an appropriate corresponding qualitative statement might have been false. The loose and inaccurate statement that gold might have turned out to be a compound should be replaced (roughly) by the statement that it is logically possible that there should have been a compound with all the properties originally known to hold of gold. The inaccurate statement that Hesperus might have turned out not to be Phosphorus should be replaced by the true contingency mentioned earlier in these lectures: two distinct bodies might have occupied, in the morning and the evening, respectively, the very positions actually occupied by Hesperus-Phosphorus-Venus. (142–43)

Here we have the generalization of (12b). In pointing at the table and saying 'This table is not made of ice', I express a necessary truth—since *this very table* could not have been made of ice. However, I would not accept, and would not be justified in accepting, the sentence uttered, unless I *also* believed, and was justified in believing, the (general) descriptive proposition DP that *a unique table directly in front of me is not made of ice*. It is my justified belief in DP (shared by agents in qualitatively identical states) that rules out possible situations in which my utterance fails to express a truth. DP is, of course, contingent rather than necessary and hence not to be confused with the (singular) proposition expressed by the indexical sentence uttered. Still, since I am justified in believing DP only on the basis of empirical evidence, and since this evidence is required for my utterance to be justified, my justification for accepting the sentence uttered requires empirical evidence. From SDJ, it follows that although it is a necessary truth that *this table* is not made of ice, my knowledge of this truth requires empirical justification, and so is a posteriori.

This is Kripke's second route to the necessary a posteriori. All his examples contain names, natural kind terms, or demonstratives, and semantically express propositions knowledge of which involves *de re* knowledge of the individuals or kinds those terms designate. The *necessity* of these propositions is explained by their attribution of essential properties and relations to those individuals or kinds. Their aposteriority is explained—in his *first* route to the necessary a posteriori—by the fact that the properties and relations can be known to apply to particular individuals and kinds only a posteriori. This explanation, though general, excludes simple identities. Thus, it applies to (1)–(4) and (6)–(11), but *not* to (12) and (13). Kripke's *second* (attempted) explanation is meant to apply not only to these stragglers but to the other cases, as well. In the second route, knowledge of a necessary proposition p is linked to acceptance of a sentence S used to express p—which in turn is linked to knowledge of a descriptive proposition DP for which empirical evidence is required. Since justification for accepting S, and believing DP, requires empirical evidence, this evidence is also required for knowledge of p.

The two routes to the necessary a posteriori differ as follows:

  (i) The first route applies to a proper subset of cases to which the second is meant to apply.

 (ii) Only the first route leads to the recognition of epistemically possible world-states over and above those that are metaphysically possible.

(iii) Only the first takes the empirical evidence needed for a posteriori knowledge of p to rule out epistemic possibilities in which p is false.

There is also another important difference. The first route is, as I have indicated, sound. The second is not.

THE UNSOUNDNESS OF KRIPKE'S SECOND ROUTE TO THE NECESSARY A POSTERIORI

The problem with Kripke's second route to the necessary a posteriori is that the principle, SDJ, on which it depends, requires an unrealistic degree of transparency in the relationship between sentences and the propositions they express. S_1 and S_2 may mean the same thing, or express the same proposition p, even though a competent speaker who understands both, and knows of each that it expresses p, does *not* realize that they express the same proposition. Such an agent may accept S_1, and believe it to be true, while refusing to accept S_2, or believe it to be true, thereby falsifying SDJ. One such agent is Kripke's Pierre.[9] Although he understands both 'Londres est jolie' and 'London is pretty', he does not realize that they mean the same thing, and so accepts one while rejecting the other. Since SDJ yields the contradictory result that Pierre both believes and does not believe that London is pretty, it cannot be accepted.

A similar result can be reached using Kripke's example of Peter, who encounters different occurrences of (14), wrongly believing that they are about two different men named 'Paderewski'.

14. Paderewski had remarkable musical talent

Since neither the name nor the sentence is ambiguous, the proposition semantically expressed doesn't change from one occasion, in which Peter accepts (14) because he takes it to be about a musician, to another occasion, in which he rejects (14) because he takes it to be about a statesman. Since Peter understands (14) without realizing that Paderewski the musician is Paderewski the statesman, his acceptance of (14) in one case, and rejection of it in another, leads, by SDJ, to contradiction. Similar results involving indexicals are easily obtained.[10] For these reasons, both SDJ and Kripke's second route to the necessary a posteriori must be rejected—unless some other principle can be found to take the place of SDJ.

When SDJ is applied to Kripke's examples, belief in singular propositions (about individuals or kinds) is linked to acceptance of specific sentences (containing names, indexicals, or natural kind terms) that express them – which, in turn, is linked to belief in certain descriptive propositions related to the original singular propositions. This suggests the possibility of dropping the problematic SDJ and linking the singular propositions directly to their descriptive counterparts. In the case of (12b) my belief that Hesperus is Phosphorus might be linked to (something like) my belief that the heavenly body visible in the evening is the heavenly body visible in the morning, while in the case of Kripke's example about the table, my belief that it is not made of ice might be linked to (something like) my belief that a unique table over there is

[9] Saul Kripke, "A Puzzle about Belief," in *Meaning and Use*, ed. A. Margalit (Dordrecht: Reidel, 1979).

[10] See chapter 1 of *Beyond Rigidity* and chapter 15 of *Philosophical Analysis in the Twentieth Century*, vol. 2 (Princeton, NJ, and Oxford: Princeton University Press, 2003).

not made of ice. The idea, in each case, is that the linked beliefs are related in two ways: (i) my coming to have the descriptive belief, in the circumstances in question, is necessary and sufficient for me to come to believe the singular proposition, and (ii) my justification for believing the singular proposition rests on my justification for the descriptive belief. Since in each case, justification of the descriptive belief requires empirical evidence, my belief in the putative instance of the necessary a posteriori is taken to require the same evidence.

The resulting nonmetalinguistic substitute for SDJ that emerges from this line of thought is, roughly, the following.

THE STRONG DESCRIPTIVE ORIGIN AND JUSTIFICATION OF *DE RE* BELIEF (SDOJ)

If an agent x in a circumstance C is capable of believing a singular proposition p by virtue of believing a certain related descriptive proposition DP, then (a) x believes p in C iff x believes DP in C, and (b) x would be justified in believing p in C on the basis of e iff x would be justified in believing DP in C on the basis of e.

SDOJ can be used in Kripke's second route to the necessary a posteriori in essentially the same way that SDJ was. Thus, if one accepts the idea that belief in singular propositions about individuals or kinds always results from (or is accompanied by) believing certain related descriptive propositions, one can substitute SDOJ for SDJ, while preserving the structure of Kripke's second route to the necessary a posteriori.

However, one cannot save the route in this way, since the same counterexamples that falsify SDJ also falsify SDOJ. In the case of Pierre, a proponent of the idea that belief in singular propositions always arises from belief in associated descriptive propositions must admit that there are several ways that Pierre can come to believe singular propositions about London. He may, for example, come to believe that London is pretty either by believing that the city he lives in is pretty or by believing that the city on the picture postcards brought from Paris is pretty. SDOJ will then give the results that he believes that London is pretty (i) iff he believes that the city he lives in is pretty and (ii) iff he believes that the city on the picture postcards brought from Paris is pretty. Since in fact he believes that the city in the pictures is pretty while failing to believe that the city he lives in is pretty, SDOJ leads to the contradictory conclusion that Pierre both believes and does not believe that London is pretty. The case of Peter and Paderewski yields a similar, unacceptable conclusion. For this reason, SDJ, SDOJ, and Kripke's second route to the necessary a posteriori must all be rejected. Fortunately, this rejection does not diminish the correctness of his first route to the necessary a posteriori. The only thing cast into doubt is the aposteriority of (12) and (13).

Origins of SDJ and SDOJ

Although SDJ and SDOJ are false, each may be seen as an incorrect generalization of a defensible idea. The guiding idea behind SDJ is that many of our beliefs (including those in singular propositions) are the result of understanding and accepting sentences (or other representations) that express them. The guiding idea behind SDOJ is the view (i) that thinking of an individual or kind always involves thinking of it in a certain way—as the bearer of a certain descriptive property—and (ii) that because of this, believing the bare singular proposition that o is F always involves also believing a related, descriptive proposition in which some further property is used to think about o.[11] These ideas—behind SDJ and SDOJ—have considerable plausibility, and nothing said here shows them to be false.

The two ideas may be formulated roughly as follows.

The Metalinguistic Origin and Justification of (Some) Belief (MOJB)

Let A be a certain class of agents (including us), C a certain class of contexts, and P a certain class of propositions (including singular propositions about individuals or kinds). For any member x of A, c of C, and p of P, (i) x believes p in c iff there is a sentence (or representation) s such that x understands s, x knows that s expresses p in c, and x accepts s in c (thereby believing p), and (ii) x would be justified in believing p in c on the basis of evidence e iff there is some sentence (or representation) that x understands and knows to express p in c that x would be justified in accepting in c on the basis of e.

The Descriptive Origin and Justification of De Re Belief (DOJB)

Let A be a certain class of agents (including us), C a certain class of circumstances, and P a class of singular propositions about individuals or kinds. For any member x of A, c of C, and p of P, (i) x

---

[11] Two illuminating sources of this amalgam of Fregean and Russellian ideas are David Kaplan, "Quantifying In," in *Words and Objections*, ed. D. Davidson and J. Hintikka (Dordrecht: Reidel, 1969); and Nathan Salmon, "Three Perspectives on Quantifying In," in *Singular Thought*, ed. R. Jeshion (Oxford: Oxford University Press, 2010).

believes p in c iff there is a descriptive proposition DP— related, in c, to x and to p in a certain way—that is such that x believes p in c by virtue of believing DP in c, and (ii) x would be justified in believing p in c on the basis of evidence e iff there is a descriptive proposition DP related, in c, to x and to p as in (i), and x would be justified in believing DP in c on the basis of e.[12]

We need not here try to determine the truth or falsity of either of these principles (for specified classes of agents, contexts, and propositions). There are, however, two important points to notice. First, the reason they are *not* falsified by Pierre-type examples is that they allow an agent x to believe a singular proposition p by virtue of accepting a sentence S, or believing a descriptive proposition DP, of a certain type—even if x fails to accept other sentences S*, or believe other descriptive propositions DP*, of the very same type (acceptance of, or belief in, which would also be sufficient for believing p). Thus, Pierre believes that London is pretty because he understands and accepts 'Londres est jolie', and believes that the city in the picture postcards is pretty, even though he understands but *doesn't* accept 'London is pretty', and *doesn't* believe that the city he lives in is pretty. The second point to notice is that the very feature of the principles that renders them compatible with Pierre-type examples also renders them *incapable* of playing the roles of SDJ and SDOJ in Kripke's second route to the necessary a posteriori. It does, of course, follow from MOJB and DOJB that any knowledge of the proposition p expressed by 'Hesperus is Phosphorus', that arises *solely* from understanding and accepting that very sentence, or believing that the heavenly body visible in the evening is the heavenly body visible in the morning, is justified by the empirical evidence needed for one's accepting the sentence, or believing the descriptive proposition, to be justified. However, this is not enough to show that p is knowable *only* a posteriori. Unless it can be shown that belief in p can *never* arise from acceptance of some other sentence S* or from belief in some other descriptive proposition DP*—the justification of which does *not* require empirical evidence—the possibility that p is knowable a priori cannot be ruled out. Nothing in Kripke's discussion does this.[13]

Moreover, the prospect of achieving this result by supplementing Kripke's discussion is not promising. Suppose, for example, that Pierre is accompanied in his odyssey from Paris to London by a band of similar unfortunates who share his epistemic fate. One can easily imagine

---

[12] It is natural to take the relation between x, p, and DP in (i) to involve some sort of (perceptual, causal, or historical) acquaintance relation connecting x's epistemic attitudes toward DP with the objects or kinds that are constituents of p.

[13] Kripke seems to show an implicit awareness of essentially this point in footnote 44 of "A Puzzle about Belief."

them learning a dialect of English in which the name 'Londres' is imported from French, and in which (15a) semantically expresses the same proposition as (15b).

15a. Londres is London.
15b. London is London.

In this scenario, one way for Pierre to know the proposition p expressed by both sentences would be by understanding and justifiably accepting (15a), while knowing that the city in the picture postcards is the city he lives in. Another way of knowing the same thing would be by understanding and justifiably accepting (15b) while knowing that the city he lives in is the city he lives in. Although the first way of knowing p might properly be regarded as a posteriori, the second way of knowing p is a priori.[14] Thus, the proper answer to the question of whether p is an instance of the necessary a posteriori—and the answer supported by MOJB and DOJB—seems to be 'no', since although p is necessary, it is possible to know p a priori. Given the clear parallel between this example and the Hesperus/Phosphorus example, as well as other instances of (12a) and (13), we can accept neither Kripke's characterization of these examples nor his second route to the necessary a posteriori.[15]

A FINAL WORD ABOUT STRONG DISQUOTATION AND JUSTIFICATION

Although the original principle, SDJ, cannot bear the weight placed on it by Kripke's second route to the necessary a posteriori, it does have

---

[14] For purposes of simplicity, here and throughout, I ignore questions concerning the existential commitments of identity statements. Depending on which view of this matter one takes, the necessary complications can easily be added.

[15] Example (15) is similar to a number of less artificial examples in the literature. One involves Nathan Salmon's character Sasha, who learns the words 'catsup' and 'ketchup' from independent ostensive definitions, in which bottles so labeled are given to him to season his foods at different times. The words are, of course, synonymous, though no one ever tells Sasha that. As a result, he does not accept 'Catsup is ketchup'—because he suspects that there may be some, to him indiscernible, difference between the things the two words refer to. Nevertheless he understands both words. As Salmon emphasizes, nearly all of us learn one of the words ostensively, the order in which they are learned doesn't matter, and if either term may be learned ostensively, then someone like Sasha could learn both in that way. But then there will be synonymous sentences S1 and S2 which differ only in the substitution of one word for the other, which Sasha understands while being disposed to accept only one—just as with Pierre. Nathan Salmon, "A Millian Heir Rejects the Wages of Sinn," in *Propositional Attitudes: The Role of Content in Logic, Language, and Mind*, ed. C. A. Anderson and J. Owens (Stanford, CA: CSLI, 1990). See also Kripke on 'furze' and 'gorse', p. 134 of "A Puzzle about Belief"; and Stephen Rieber, "Understanding Synonyms without Knowing that They Are Synonymous," *Analysis* 52 (1992): 224–28.

intuitive appeal, and versions of it play a role in our belief-reporting practices. Thus, it is worth separating what is correct about it from what isn't. The key to doing this is, as I have argued elsewhere, to recognize that an utterance often results in the assertion and communication of more than the proposition semantically expressed by the sentence uttered.[16]For example, (14) might be used in a context in which musicians are being discussed to assert or communicate the proposition p_M—*that the musician Paderewski had remarkable musical talent*—while being used in a context in which politicians are the topic of conversation to assert or communicate the proposition p_S—*that the statesman Paderewski had remarkable musical talent.* The same is true of other attitudes. Sometimes Peter uses (14) to entertain p_M, and sometimes he uses it to entertain p_S (in addition to the bare proposition that simply attributes the property of having remarkable musical talent to Paderewski). This one-many relationship between sentences and propositions affects the application of SDJ. When we apply it to an agent A who uses (14) first to entertain p_M and later to entertain p_S, no contradiction results from A's acceptance of (14) in the first case and rejection of it in the second—provided we let p_M play the role of 'p' in the first case, and p_S play this role in the second. However, if we let the semantic content of (14) play the role of 'p' in both cases, we do get a contradiction. Hence, particular applications of SDJ can be either unproblematic, or clearly incorrect, depending on how, precisely, it is formulated, and whether or not contextual enrichment is involved.[17]

With this in mind, suppose we take Kripke's implicit reliance on SDJ at the end of lecture 2 to involve a modestly *enriched* proposition that speakers might naturally use (12b) to assert or entertain—e.g., the proposition that the heavenly body, Hesperus, that is visible in the evening, is the heavenly body, Phosphorus, that is visible in the morning. *This proposition* is, of course, knowable only a posteriori, and the relevant application of SDJ is unproblematic. However, this way of taking the case does not advance Kripke's argument, since the *enriched* proposition is *not* necessary. If, on the other hand, we are asked to focus on the necessary proposition that (12b) *semantically* expresses, then we need a clear account—which Kripke doesn't provide—of precisely which proposition this is.

---

[16] See chapter 9 "Naming and Asserting," in *Semantics versus Pragmatics*, ed. Z. Szabo (Oxford: Oxford University Press, 2004); "Beyond Rigidity, Reply to McKinsey," *Canadian Journal of Philosophy* 35 (2005): 169–78; and "The Gap between Meaning and Assertion: Why What We Literally Say Often Differs from What Our Words Literally Mean," in Soames, *Philosophical Essays*, vol. 1 (Princeton, NJ: Princeton University Press, 2009).

[17] This idea is used to illuminate and resolve central issues raised by Kripke's puzzle about belief in Mike McGlone, "Assertion, Belief, and Semantic Content"(unpublished PhD diss., Princeton University, 2007).

The semantic theory most in harmony with Kripke's thoroughgoing antidescriptivism—contemporary Millian-Russellianism—won't save his argument, since, according to it, the proposition semantically expressed by (12b) is the a priori proposition also expressed by (12e).

12e. Hesperus is Hesperus

In this theory, neither (12b) nor instances of (13) are examples of the necessary a posteriori. Of course, Millian-Russellianism cannot be attributed to Kripke. However, if it isn't, then it is mysterious what his positive view is. Being in the dark about this, we are in no position to accept either his argument for the necessary aposteriority of (12b) or his second route to the necessary a posteriori. Fortunately for us, and for the practice of philosophy in the post-Kripkean era, one sound route to the necessary a posteriori remains.

PART TWO

Historical Problems and Controversies

8

What Is the Frege/Russell Analysis of Quantification?

The Frege-Russell analysis of quantification was a fundamental advance in semantics and philosophical logic. Abstracting away from details idiosyncratic to each, the key idea is that quantifiers express higher-level properties that are predicated of lower-level properties. The two philosophers express this *properties of properties* analysis slightly differently. Whereas Russell talks of properties of propositional functions (which are functions from objects to structured propositions), Frege speaks of senses that present higher-level concepts that are predicated of lower-level concepts. Since the issues I will raise are neutral between these different frameworks, I will confine the discussion to property talk.[1]

The analysis is illustrated by claims P1–C3 about sentence 1.

1. $\forall x\ Fx$/Everything is F.
P1. The proposition expressed by (1) consists of two constituents—the property *being true of everything* and the property *being F*—the first of which is predicated of the second.
P2. If a proposition p consists of two constituents—*being so-and-so* and *being such-and-such*, the first of which is predicated of the second, then p = the proposition *that such-and-such is so-and-so*.
C1. The proposition expressed by (1) = the proposition *that being F is true of everything*. (Call this proposition 'Prop 1'.)
P3. Prop 1 is also expressed by sentence (1a).
1a. The property *being F* is true of everything.
C2. So, (1) and (1a) express the same proposition.

The first thing to notice about my illustration is that although I have called the account of quantification "an analysis," the sentences used to

---

specify the proposition expressed by sentence (1) themselves contain the universal quantifier being analyzed. That may seem strange. Indeed, it may seem worse than strange, as the following argument shows.

P4. The expression 'is true of' that occurs in sentence (1a) is a two-place predicate that expresses the relation *being true of*, which holds between properties and objects. Since the quantifier 'everything' stands in the second argument-place of this predicate, (1a) is a universally quantified sentence that expresses the same proposition as (1∀).

1∀. Everything is such that *the property being F is true of it*. (∀x: *the property being F is true of x*.)

P5. So, the Frege/Russell analysis of quantification applies to (1a/1∀), yielding a proposition that has two constituents the first of which—*being true of everything*—is predicated of the second—*being an object of which the property F is true*.

P6. This proposition (described in P5), is the proposition *that the property being an object of which the property being F is true is true of everything*. Call it 'Prop 2'.

C3. The proposition expressed by (1a/1∀) is Prop 2.

C4. Since (1) and (1a) each express just one proposition, Prop 1 = Prop 2.

The cycle can be repeated, producing a hierarchy of propositions each of which is identified with all the others:

Prop 1: The proposition that *being F* is true of everything.

Prop 2: The proposition that *being an object of which (being F) is true* is true of everything.

Prop 3: The proposition that *being an object of which (being an object of which being F is true) is true* is true of everything.

Is this result problematic? The propositions in the sequence are necessarily and apriori equivalent to one another. There is even some temptation to think that anyone who asserts or believes Prop 1 should be counted as also asserting or believing Prop 2. After all, it might be argued, anyone who *explicitly* accepted, and thereby believed, the former would be *disposed* to accept, and rightly be counted as believing, the latter. Even so, however, we don't get the needed result—namely, that the propositions in the hierarchy are *identical* with one another. We don't even establish that anyone who believes or asserts one of them believes or asserts all the others. Although there is some justification for thinking that one who *explicitly* asserts or judges, and hence *occurrently* believes, p may be counted as *implicitly* asserting and believing *obvious* necessary and apriori consequences of p, this doesn't justify taking assertion and belief to be closed under obvious necessary and apriori consequence. Of course, if it is in the nature of propositions that those that are necessarily and apriori equivalent are *identical*, then the hierarchy I have generated is simply a harmless multiple repetition of the same proposition. However, since Frege and Russell were proponents of structured propositions, this wouldn't have impressed them.

Those like me who share their belief in structured propositions face a more serious problem. The constituents of Prop 1 are the properties *being true of everything* and *being F*. The constituents of Prop 2 are *being true of everything*, and *being an object of which the property being F is true*. Note, the property *being F* is itself a constituent of the property *being an object of which the property being F is true,* and so is a subconstituent of Prop 2. However, *being F* is not the predication target in Prop 2, as it is in Prop 1. In Prop 2, the target, of which *being true of everything* is predicated, is *being an object of which the property being F is true.* Since the predication target is *being an x such that the property being F is true of x*, identifying Props 1 and 2 would require identifying the simple property *being F* with a relational property of which *it* is merely a constituent. Since this is absurd, proponents of structured propositions must distinguish the two propositions, along with all others in the hierarchy. But this is intolerable; the unique proposition expressed (1) can't be identical with infinitely many different propositions.

Consequently, the proponent of structured propositions can accept the Frege/Russell analysis only by rejecting the conclusion C4 that identifies Props 1 and 2. This, in turn, requires blocking the argument before it reaches C3 (which leads to the identification). How did we land in this fix? We started off by accepting an analysis of quantification that identifies the proposition p expressed by an arbitrary sentence 'Everything is F' with one that predicates *being true of everything* of the property *F*. However, since the analysis *uses* the very quantifier being analyzed, we were tempted to apply the analysis again to the sentences used to identify p. When we did this, we arrived at a new proposition p* different from p. This is intolerable if—as we have been assuming—sentence (1) expresses a single proposition. The challenge for the proponent of structured propositions is to explain why the Frege/Russell analysis of quantification can't be applied to its own output.

The natural thought is that we went wrong in using the quantifier 'everything' in the analysis of sentences containing it. When Frege and Russell analyzed numerical concepts they were careful not to employ those concepts but, rather, to define them in terms of what they took to be purely logical concepts. The same is true of Russell's analysis of descriptions. If his analysis of definite descriptions is correct, then someone who has mastered universal quantification, negation, and identity should be able to acquire the definite article by being given its analysis. Russell seems to have understood his analysis of indefinite descriptions in the same way. His stock examples involve substitution of an adjective functioning as a predicate for the nominal in the description. Thus, 'I met a man' is always said to express the proposition *that for some x, I met x and x is human*, not *for some x, I met x and x is a man*. This is noteworthy, since for many indefinite descriptions—like 'a tiger' and 'a large and rowdy man' there is no corresponding adjectival form. There is, presumably, a reason Russell avoids examples like these, in which there is no obvious way of stating the analysis without using the expression being analyzed. The worry—whether substantial or merely a distracting complication to be avoided in presenting the theory—is that such examples don't fit a certain conception of *analysis* that he invokes in some other cases.

This point is reinforced by his analysis of quantification, summarized by R.

> R A sentence S_E containing 'everything' in a position capable of being occupied by a singular term expresses the proposition *that fs_x is always true*—where fs_x is the propositional function (from objects to propositions) designated by the formula that results from replacing 'everything' in S_E with a free occurrence of the variable 'x'. A sentence $S_\exists$ containing 'something' in a comparable position expresses the proposition *that it is not the case that fs_x is always false*.

The key point about Russell's formulation, which was surely no accident, is that it *does not use* the universal quantifier 'everything' in specifying the constituent that the quantifier contributes to propositions expressed by sentences containing it. Instead of employing the predicate 'is true of everything', Russell employs the adverbially modified predicate 'is always true', which is short for the more elaborate, but still putatively primitive, predicate 'always assigns a true proposition to an argument'. This predicate designates a genuine property of propositional functions that is a constituent of propositions expressed by universally quantified sentences. What then does the predicate 'is true of everything'—which is short for 'assigns a true proposition to every argument'—designate? The answer, I imagine, is that it is a Russellian incomplete symbol, and so doesn't designate anything. If so, then sentence (1) will express Prop 1_R, while sentences (1a/1∀) will express Prop 2_R.

Prop 1_R: the proposition that *being F* is always true
Prop 2_R: the proposition that *being an object of which the property being F is true* is always true

(Here I revert to property rather than propositional function talk.) Although these propositions are different, no paradox results, because the second is not generated from the analysis that produced the first. One can, of course, still generate a sequence of necessarily and apriori equivalent propositions, but the basis for identifying them has been eliminated.

Russell extends his analysis to (2) —'Something is F'—by defining 'something' in terms of the universal quantifier plus falsity and negation. This is fine when giving a system of logic. Since any choice of standard primitives plus the usual definitions yields the same truth-preserving relations among sentences, one can adopt Russell's suggestions, or make different choices, as one wishes. But since logical equivalence doesn't track identity of propositions expressed, and since there are often facts to be captured about which of the different but equivalent propositions an agent asserts or believes, semantic analyses of quantified propositions require more. For these purposes, we are better off identifying the proposition *that something is F* with the proposition that *being F is sometimes true.*

But this is only the beginning. The Russellian analysis must be extended to all generalized quantifiers, including those in (3) and (4).

3a. Some F is G.
3b. Every F is G.
3c. No F is G.

4a. Most F's are G's.
4b. Exactly two F's are G's.
4c. At least seven F's are G's.
4d. Many F's are G's.
4e. Few F's are G's.

The properties predicated of the propositional function (or property) G by the propositions expressed by the sentences in (3) are *being sometimes true of F's, being always true of F's,* and *never being true of F's.* Reductio *by hierarchy* is avoided as before.

The predicates 'is sometimes/always/never true of F's' stand for genuine properties that are predicated of lower-level properties in propositions expressed by quantified sentences. The predicates 'is true of some/every/no F's', designate nothing but, rather, are incomplete symbols to be eliminated by analysis. Though necessary and apriori equivalents, the propositions expressed by (5) and (6) are different, with the former being primary and grasped independently of the latter.

5. So-and-so is *sometimes/always/never true of F's*.
6. So-and-so *is true of some/every/no F*.

The quantifiers in (4) are treated similarly. The properties predicated of the propositional function (or property G) in (4a) and (4b) are *being most times true of F's* and *being exactly two times true of F's*. In the case of (4c)–(4e) the quantificational properties are *being true at least seven times of F's, being many times true of F's,* and *being few times true of F's*. The *reductio*-avoiding explanation is the same as before.

Although elaborating the Frege/Russell analysis of quantification in this way avoids the original *reductio*, I think it is a sham. Imagine being told, without benefit of the argument here, that "*Being G is a property that is few times true of F's,*" or that "*The propositional function that assigns to any object o the proposition that o is G is few times truth-assigning for F's.*" Far from being transparent, these remarks border on the bizarre. The natural reaction is to assimilate them to more familiar quantified forms. "Oh, I see," one is inclined to think, "You're saying that being G is a property that is true of *few F's,*" or "You're saying that the propositional function that assigns to any object o the proposition that o is G assigns a true proposition to *few F's* (or to *few things that are F*)." The worry is not that the Russellian can't admit the speaker said this. The worry is that the proffered Russellian explanation gets things backward. According to it, the speaker *implicitly* said that being G is a property that is true of few F's—or that the propositional function that assigns to any object o the proposition that o is G assigns a true proposition to few things that are F's—*by virtue of having explicitly asserted* the allegedly different, adverbially expressed proposition of which the proposition implicitly asserted is a trivial consequence. Not so, one is inclined to object; it is our understanding of the Russellian adverbial formulations that is *parasitic* on our prior understanding of the quantificational locutions, not the other way around. Nor is this simply a matter of empirical facts about language learning. The *fundamental notions* are the ordinary quantificational ones, not the adverbial forms.

Although I take this objection to be correct, it is stronger than needed. The adverbial strategy for avoiding the *reductio* requires the notions *being every time true of F's, being at least one time true of F's,* and *being few (or most) times true of F's* to be primitive, conceptually and explanatorily prior to, and used in the analysis of, *being true of every F, being true of at least one F,* and *being true of few (or most) F's*. Surely this is misguided. If one set of notions is to be explained in terms of the other, the objector is right in taking the adverbial formulations to be derivative rather than primary. But we need not insist on this. It is enough to note that *if* the adverbially expressed notions can be taken to be explanatorily primitive, then those expressed using the ordinary quantifiers 'every F', 'at least one F', and 'few F's' can, too.

With this I put aside the adverbial strategy for blocking the *reductio* and return to the practice of using quantifiers undergoing analysis to specify the propositions expressed by sentences containing them. This involves accepting the original argument up to C2.

P1. The proposition expressed by (1) consists of two constituents— the property *being true of everything* and the property *being F*— the first of which is predicated of the second.

P2. If a proposition p consists of two constituents—*being so- and-so* and *being such-and-such,* the first of which is predi- cated of the latter, then p = the proposition *that such-and- such is so-and-so.*

C1. The proposition expressed by (1) = the proposition *that being F is true of everything.* (Call this proposition 'Prop 1'.)

P3. Prop 1 is also expressed by sentence (1a).

1a. The property *being F* is true of everything.

C2. So, (1) and (1a) express the same proposition.

At this point, we need to find a new way of challenging P4, so as to block *reductio*-generating conclusion C3.

P4. The expression 'is true of' that occurs in sentence (1a) is a two-place predicate that expresses the relation *being true of,* which holds between properties and objects. Since the quantifier 'everything' stands in the second argument-place of this predicate, (1a) is a universally quantified sentence that expresses the same proposition as (1∀).

1∀. Everything is such that *the property being F* is true of it. (∀x: *the property being F* is true of x.)

P5. So, the Frege/Russell analysis of quantification applies to (1a/1∀), yielding a proposition that has two constituents the first of which—*being true of everything*—is predicated of the second—*being an object of which the property F is true.*

P6. This proposition (described in P5), is the proposition *that the property being an object of which the property being F is true* is true of everything. Call it 'Prop 2'.

C3. The proposition expressed by (1a/1∀) is Prop 2.

To block this reasoning, we must prevent the analysis from reapplying to (1a) in the manner indicated by P4 and P5. We must either allow the analysis to apply in a *different* way that does *not* produce the original hierarchy, or explain why applying it again would be a mistake.

Let's try the former. We ask, What is the property *being true of everything*? Suppose it is *being a property P such that for every x, P is true of x*—i.e., λP (*for every x: P is true of x*). So understood, the proposition expressed by (1a) is *not* identical with that expressed by (1∀)—as claimed by P4. The two are merely equivalent. On this new view, the predicate 'is true of everything' is *not* an incomplete symbol; it expresses a genuine property that is predicated of *being F*. This improvement, which is squarely in line with the fundamental idea behind the Frege/Russell analysis, was *not* captured by taking (1∀) to express the proposition expressed by sentences (1) and (1a). According to the present suggestion, these two sentences express the proposition given by (1aλ). With this change, the previous hierarchy is no longer generated.

However, this doesn't help. Since (1aλ) contains 'every x' we simply get a new and equally worrisome hierarchy. We start with (1), which we are told expresses the same proposition as (1a), which, by the route just taken, expresses the same proposition as (1aλ).

1.   Every x: Fx.
1a. The property *being F* is true of everything.
1aλ. λP [Every x: P is true of x] the property *being F*
       The property of *being F* is true of everything.

This is trouble. Because (1aλ) contains a quantified clause, it is structurally and computationally more complex than (1a), which is itself reason to doubt that the two sentences express the same proposition. The case is strengthened by applying the analysis again inside the clause, which results in (1aλλ).

1aλλ. [λQ (Every x: Q is true of x) *being an object of which P is true*] the property *being F*
        The property *being F is a property P such that the property being an object of which P is true* is true of everything

This proposition is even more complex, containing new and more complex constituents than proposition (1a)/(1aλ). Since it isn't identical with that proposition, we still have a *reductio*.

The problem, I suggest, is that we have misconstrued the Frege/Russell analysis of quantification from the outset. The point of the analysis is *not* to *define* quantificational locutions like 'everything', 'at least seven F's', and 'Most F's' in other terms. As we saw in pursuing the adverbial strategy, the proposed substitutes are no advance on the originals. Their only virtue is that because they don't contain the quantifiers under analysis, there is no temptation to reapply the analysis, and so generate a hierarchy. But surely, taking *them* to be primitive is no better than taking *being true of everything, being true of at least seven F's,* and *being true of most F's* to be primitive.

The correct way of understanding the Frege/Russell analysis is to see it as a theory of logical form. Instead of specifying the propositions expressed by *every sentence* containing quantificational locutions, the analysis targets a *subclass* of these sentences to be explained using quantifier-containing sentences *outside the class*. The sentences outside the class are the analysis-giving ones. In these sentences, a quantifier Q occurs in a predicate ⌜is true of Q⌝ the argument of which is a term designating a property or propositional function applying to the entities over which Q ranges. Sentences of this form are *antecedently intelligible without further analysis,* and express propositions in which the property expressed by the predicate containing the quantifier is predicated of the property or propositional function designated by its argument. The point of the analysis is *not* to analyze the *contents* of quantifiers but to indicate the semantic role quantifiers play as constituents of higher-level predicates.

This is a theory of *logical form* the goal of which is to reveal the structure of the propositions expressed by sentences containing quantifiers. The analysis tells us that even when a quantifier appears in a sentence in which no higher-level predication is explicit, the true *logical form* of the sentence is one in which the quantifier is used to predicate a higher-level property of the property, or propositional function, designated by the formula that results from extracting the quantifier from the original sentence. When this is understood, the explanation of why the analysis doesn't reapply to the logical form of the original sentence is evident. It doesn't apply because once we have arrived at the logical form of a sentence, there is nothing further to do.

9

No Class

RUSSELL ON CONTEXTUAL DEFINITION

AND THE ELIMINATION OF SETS

Michael Kremer complains that my first-order presentation of Russell's logicist reduction in Soames (2003) "misrepresents the technical achievement of Russell's theory of classes"—which he identifies with the "ontological economy" of eliminating commitment to classes (sets). I disagree. Russell did attempt to eliminate classes, and he connected this attempt to other interesting projects. These projects aside, however, the purported elimination was not, in my opinion, a genuine achievement, and the relevant issues have little to do with first-order versus second-order symbolizations.

Kremer's discussion focuses on what he calls Russell's "contextual definition of classes," the purpose of which is "to eliminate the notion of classes":

1. $F(\{x: Gx\}) =_{df} \exists H(\forall y(Hy \leftrightarrow Gy) \& F(H))$

This characterization of the definition is tendentious. What (1) defines is a notation containing complex singular terms for classes. By identifying contents of sentences containing such terms with those of sentences that don't, Russell eliminates the terms from the primitive vocabulary of his theory. Whether an ontological reduction is achieved depends on how predicate quantifiers are understood. In standard second-order interpretations, there is no reduction, since they range over sets. By contrast, Russell took the quantifiers to range over "propositional functions." Kremer tells us little about what these are—for good reason. Russell's discussion vacillates between taking them to be formulas, properties, or functions from nonlinguistic arguments to nonlinguistic propositions. Mostly, he seems to have inclined to the former.[1] So, if

---

[1] To take two, albeit retrospective, indicators: "In the language of the second order, variables denote symbols, not what is symbolized," Russell (1940, 192), and "Whitehead

strict historical fidelity is the issue, then Russell should be taken to have seen himself as reducing classes to expressions. But this is problematic.

First, the ontology of formulas isn't innocent. Since there are infinitely many that will never be produced, they must be types—abstract sequences of existing simple expressions. And what are sequences if not the set-theoretic constructions they are standardly taken to be? In this account, the ontological "achievement" of the "no-class theory" is to have eliminated classes in favor of classes. Nor would matters be helped by contending that sequences are *sui generis*, since their formal and ontological features parallel those of classes.

Then, there is the logical problem. To treat predicate variables as ranging over formulas is to risk artificially limiting their range. If, as is natural, the formulas are those of a single language, then, on the standard assumption that no formula is infinitely long, the range of the variables will be restricted to a denumerable infinity—with crippling results on set theory and the expressive power of the logic.[2] Far from being a "technical achievement," this would be a technical slip. One could, of course, relax the usual assumptions. But then the ontology of formulas would become even more contentious, and the resulting logic more complex—with no gain in historical accuracy, since Russell didn't foresee any of this. Finally, there is the semantic problem. Arithmetical sentences aren't about language, which, in Russell's account, they would be if his predicate quantifiers ranged over formulas. For all these reasons, something else is needed as the value of a predicate variable.

Since Russell's semantics identifies the meanings of subsentential expressions—including predicates—with nonlinguistic entities they denote, such entities are a natural choice. A basis for implementing this idea is given in Soames (2003, vol.1, chap. 5). Let 'x is green' denote the propositional function g, which assigns to any object o the proposition expressed by 'x is green' relative to an assignment of o to 'x'. This proposition is a structured complex in which the property of being green is predicated of o. '∃x x is green' says that g "is sometimes true"—i.e., that g assigns a true proposition to at least one argument. '∃F (F grass)' says the same thing about the propositional function denoted by '(F grass)'—which assigns to any propositional function f the proposition that f assigns to grass. How one thinks of the metaphysical

---

and I thought of a propositional function as an expression," Russell (1959, 124). See Sainsbury (1979, 278–95) for a good discussion of Russell's view of quantification into predicate position, plus Sainsbury's take on how he could have improved it.

[2] The expressive distinctiveness of second-order logic—e.g., the completeness of second-order arithmetic and the impossibility of complete second-order proof procedures—depends on the ability of second-order quantifiers to range over the nondenumerable infinity of subsets of a denumerable domain.

nature of such functions—set theoretically or in some other way—is not crucial. Nor, contrary to Kremer, is there any semantic reason not to identify functions that agree on the values of all arguments. In this conception, g is *the* function that assigns to any o the proposition that o is green. Knowing that it assigns a truth to something is a fairly good approximation to knowing that something is green.

With propositional functions as values of predicate variables, (1) stipulates that to say that the class of G's is F is to say that there is a propositional function h which is both F and equivalent to g (where g/h are denoted by 'Gy'/'Hy', and the functions are equivalent iff they assign true propositions to the same things). Talk of propositional functions can, in this way, be substituted for talk of classes. However, this is not a genuine reduction. If one recognizes functions of this sort from objects to propositions, one can hardly refuse to recognize similar functions from objects to other entities, including truth values. But the distinction between the class of G's and the function that assigns truth to all and only G's is a distinction without a difference. So, in this interpretation, the "no-class theory" achieves no real "ontological economy."

It appears that Kremer doesn't accept this conception of propositional functions. Although he agrees that Russellian propositional functions should, ultimately, be understood as nonlinguistic, he regards them as "intensional." What does that mean? In one sense, *extensional functions* are correlations of arguments and values that are identical whenever they map the same arguments onto the same values. Since Kremer denies that propositional functions are extensional in this sense, it is tempting to interpret him as taking *intensional functions* to be correlations that can differ in such cases, when the same values are reached by different procedures. But in this interpretation, his position is untenable. Since *intensional functions* in this sense are just *extensional functions*, plus the murky notion of a procedure (when are two of them the same?), eliminating the latter (which are interdefinable with sets) in terms of the former makes little sense.

The fundamental problem is that Kremer is confused about the intensional/extensional distinction. The notion "intensional function" is obscure, and Kremer's "one thing that is certain is that Russell's propositional functions are *intensional* entities" is worse. It is clear what it is for a linguistic construction to be intensional or extensional but unclear what it is for an arbitrary *entity* to be one or the other. Sometimes, as with properties versus classes, it is easy to determine what the contrast is supposed to be. The pair <property, instantiation-relation> differs from the pair <class, membership-relation> in that properties with the same instantiators can differ, while classes with the same members can't. But this is fortuitous. Since arbitrary entities don't come with obvious analogs of the membership relation, the general notion of an intensional (or extensional) *entity* has no definite sense.

Russell does, of course, speak of intensional versus extensional functions. But this talk is obscured by his habitual conflation of formulas with the nonlinguistic functions they denote. Typically, he has in mind a linguistic construction that is intensional/extensional but leaves the relation between the function and the construction in his usual muddle. For example, in *Principia* *20, p. 187, he says, " 'I believe (x) ϕx' is an *intensional* function, because even if (x) (ϕx $\leftrightarrow \psi$x), it by no means follows that I believe (x) ψx provided I believe (x) ϕx." Here a *sentence* is said to be both intensional, which it is, and a function, which it isn't. To make sense of this, one must tread carefully. If one wishes to distinguish formulas from the functions they denote while continuing to apply the labels "intensional" and "extensional" to the latter, one must explicitly state what the distinction comes to.

Kremer's failure to do this leads him to make a critical mistake. He assumes that Russell's distinction between intensional and extensional functions *of functions* requires propositional functions that are not mere correlations of arguments and values. It doesn't. Let *extensional*$_2$ and *intensional*$_2$ stand for the notions relevant to Russell's distinction. When 'F' is a predicate variable, the functions denoted by '~(Fa)' and 'I believe Fa' are functions from functions to propositions. The former is *extensional*$_2$, and the latter is *intensional*$_2$, because the former always maps *equivalent propositional functions* onto *equivalent propositions*, while the latter doesn't. (Propositions are equivalent iff they agree in truth value; propositional functions are equivalent iff the same arguments are always mapped to equivalent propositions.) Nevertheless, *both* functions are mere pairings of arguments and values—and so, extensional *in the sense defined earlier*. Thus, when Kremer wrongly concludes that since (some) Russellian propositional functions are *intensional*$_2$, they can't be *extensional*$_1$, he conflates two fundamentally different understandings of *extensional* versus *intensional*. Since even *intensional*$_2$ *functions* are extensional in the sense that characteristic functions of sets are, Kremer's admission that trading sets for their characteristic functions yields no ontological economy undermines his central claim. If (i) the propositional functions that Russell's predicate quantifiers range over are *extensional*$_1$, and (ii), one who is committed to these functions can't plausibly avoid commitment to other functions that are *extensional*$_1$, including characteristic functions (which Kremer admits are on a par with sets), then Russell can't have achieved an ontological economy by adopting his contextual definition.[3]

---

[3] There are, of course, advantages to second-order quantification over Russellian propositional functions rather than sets—especially if one wants to make room for belief,

Can one salvage such an economy by abandoning Russellian propositional functions, and identifying values of predicate variables with *properties* that are the meanings of predicates, and open sentences? Though this seems to be more of a revision than an interpretation of Russell, such a system makes sense. According to it '∃x x is green' says that being green has the property *combining with some (appropriate) argument to form a truth*, while '∃F (F grass)' says that the property *being instantiated by grass*—denoted by '(F grass)'—also has that property. The idea works fine. However, to use it in Russellian semantics, one needs a way of specifying the compound properties expressed by complex formulas. That, of course, was just what propositional functions were made for. Given an open formula . . . v_1 . . . v_n . . . , we identify the compound property it denotes with the function that maps n-tuples of arguments onto the structured propositions expressed by the formula relative to assignments of those n-tuples to the variables. Nothing could be easier. If, in the name of salvaging the "no-class theory," such functions are forbidden, then something else must take their place.

Here's a thought. Since the meanings of complete sentences are structured propositions, the meanings of open sentences—the compound properties they express—can be identified with structured propositional matrices—propositions with gaps in them. To say that such a matrix "is sometimes true" is to say that there is a way of filling the gaps that results in a truth. This works as an account of quantification in essentially the way that propositional functions do. However, the no-class theory is still in trouble. For what is a propositional matrix? It would seem, at the very least, to be a kind of sequence (with gaps) the elements of which are either individual meanings or sequences of meanings. But now we are back to an earlier objection. For what are sequences if not set-theoretic constructions, or something so similar as to be ontologically on a par with sets? No matter how we twist and turn, the requirements of Russellian semantics seem to preclude using the language of *Principia* to eliminate sets.[4] Hence, even in the most favorable interpretation, the "no-class theory" remains dubious.

---

or other intensional, operators. Such systems need not explicitly invoke sets and may even, as Russell shows, use (1) to simulate certain kinds of talk of sets. However, one who adopts such a system does not achieve a genuine ontological reduction, because the propositional functions one is committed to make it impossible to deny the existence of characteristic functions, which are acceptable iff sets are.

[4] If, as might be maintained, our mastery of Russell's language—including our recognition of (1) as defining the contents of one set of sentences in terms of another (as opposed to simply being a true biconditional)—requires being given a systematic semantics, then the attempt to use that language to eliminate sets requires a set- and sequence-free ontology not only of compound properties but also of sentences.

This is one main reason I didn't discuss Russell's ideas about eliminating classes in Soames (2003): too many problems for too little result. The entities to which classes are supposed to be reduced—propositional functions—are more taken for granted by Russell than seriously investigated. As already indicated, he speaks confusingly and inconsistently about them, and the view that seems to be uppermost in his mind—that they are expressions—is obviously inadequate. Although other choices—*extensional*₁ functions and gappy propositions—make more sense, Russell doesn't systematically explore them, and as we have seen, they aren't promising candidates for achieving ontological economies anyway. In addition, the "no-class theory" has been more or less historically inert—central figures in logic, mathematics, and formal semantics haven't adopted it. Thus, it should be clear why there was no room for Russell's ideas about the eliminability of sets in the history I aimed to write. It should be equally clear why I presented the reduction in a simple first-order system of naïve set theory. Since sets weren't going to be eliminated anyway, there was little point in putting readers through the extra complexity of a second-order system.[5] Russell's most important achievement was in showing how numbers can be identified with sets and how Russell's Paradox can be avoided. Since these are issues that all students of the analytic tradition need to know the rudiments of, they are what I tried to explain.

Evidently, this evaluative perspective irritates Kremer and those on whose behalf he purports to write. They are deeply suspicious of my attempt to evaluate which ideas of past philosophers marked the most significant advances and therefore merit the most attention. That's fine, so long as they identify fruitful philosophical truths I missed or misleading falsehoods to which I succumbed. In the case of the "no-class theory," they haven't done so. On the contrary, Kremer's assumption that it was a "technical achievement" resulting in an "ontological economy" is a serious mistake. That, of course, doesn't mean that Russell's ideas on the subject aren't interesting or that they aren't connected to other ideas that are more significant. In fact, they are intertwined with his dauntingly complex and far-reaching ideas about predicativity,

---

[5] The important expressive differences between first- and second-order quantification were unknown (and unimportant) to Russell. If the values of the predicate variables are taken to be properties or propositional functions, then his second-order sentences can be rewritten using many sorted, first-order quantification. For example, '∃F(Fx)' can be taken to say that for some property p, x instantiates p. (See Sainsbury [1979, 283, 290–92], for a defense of this procedure as true to Russell.) Further, if we give up the fruitless attempt to eliminate sets, then '∃F(Fx)' can (for purposes of the reduction) be taken to say that for some set s, x is a member of s—and so can be symbolized '∃s (x ε s)'—as it is in my volumes.

the semantic paradoxes, and the ramified versus the simple theory of types—all of which are fascinating, and some of which involve real technical achievements.[6] Kremer and others may feel that at least some hint of this should have found its way into my history. If so, I agree. I also agree with Kremer that Russell's "no-class theory" can be used to shed light on the thinking behind (what I believe to be) his disastrous attempt, in *Our Knowledge of the External World,* to reduce talk of physical objects to talk of sense data. I will try to correct these shortcomings in the expanded edition of my history.[7]

REFERENCES

Burgess, J. 2005. *Fixing Frege.* Princeton. NJ: Princeton University Press.

Russell, B. 1914. *Our Knowledge of the External World.* Chicago, IL: Open Court; 2nd ed., London: Unwin, 1926.

———. 1940. *An Inquiry into Meaning and Truth.* London: Unwin.

———. 1959. *My Philosophical Development.* London: Unwin.

Sainsbury, M. 1979. *Russell.* London: Routledge and Kegan Paul.

Soames, S. 2003. *Philosophical Analysis in the Twentieth Century.* 2 vols. Princeton: Princeton University Press.

Whitehead, A. N., and B. Russell. 1910–13. *Principia Mathematica.* 3 vols; 2nd ed., 1927. Cambridge: Cambridge University Press.

[6] See Burgess (2005, chap. 1) for an explanation of Russell's leading technical result about the relationship between higher-order logic with an axiom of extensionality and higher-order logic without such an axiom.

[7] Thanks to John Burgess for comments on an earlier draft.

10

Ontology, Analyticity, and Meaning

THE QUINE-CARNAP DISPUTE

In the middle of the twentieth century a dispute erupted between the chief architect of logical empiricism, Rudolf Carnap, and logical empiricism's chief reformer, Willard Van Orman Quine—who was attempting to save what he took to be its main insights by recasting them in a more acceptable form. Though both philosophers eschewed metaphysics of the traditional apriori sort, and both were intent on making the investigation of science the center of philosophy, they disagreed about how to do so. Part of the disagreement involved the nature of ontological disputes. The following are the central documents in the debate:

(i) Quine's 1948 article "On What There Is," which tells us how to discern ontological commitments, what such commitments amount to, and how to evaluate them;[1]

(ii) Carnap's 1950 article "Empiricism, Semantics, and Ontology," which—with the help an ambitious analytic/synthetic distinction—attempts to reconcile his promiscuous commitment to a rich ontology of abstract objects with his puritanical devotion to empiricism by distinguishing scientifically tractable ontological issues from the unintelligible "pseudo-questions" of traditional ontology;[2]

(iii) Quine's 1951 article "Two Dogmas of Empiricism"—which attacks Carnap's analytic/synthetic distinction and offers a holistic reconstruction of logical empiricism.[3]

---

[1] Quine, "On What There Is," *Review of Metaphysics* 2 (1948): 21–38; reprinted in Quine, *From a Logical Point of View*, rev. 2nd ed. (Cambridge, MA: Harvard University Press, 1980). Citations are to the latter.

[2] Carnap, "Empiricism, Semantics, and Ontology," *Revue Internationale de Philosophie* 4 (1950): 20–40; revised and reprinted in *Meaning and Necessity*, 2nd ed. (Chicago: University of Chicago Press, 1956). Citations are to the latter.

[3] Quine, "Two Dogmas of Empiricism," *Philosophical Review* 60, no. 1 (1951): 20–43; revised and reprinted in *From a Logical Point of View*. Citations are to the original.

Although these documents make up the core of the debate, they don't exhaust it. For example, in 1951, Quine responded briefly in "On Carnap's Views of Ontology."[4] In "Meaning and Synonymy in Natural Languages" (1955), Carnap criticized Quine's rejection of intension as opposed to extension, arguing that the former is legitimate if the latter is.[5] In *Word and Object* (1960), Quine conceded the point, noting that indeterminacy of reference goes hand in hand with the indeterminacy of translation and meaning.[6] Though I will touch on this later material, I will mainly focus on the three core documents.

The debate in these papers is about how to understand ontological commitment, and what ontology to adopt. The central dispute is over abstract objects. Though both Quine and Carnap recognize the existence of numbers, Quine is unhappy with Carnap's commitment to properties, propositions, and meanings. Even in the case of numbers, Quine's acceptance is grudging. Since numbers are abstract, he takes commitment to them to be a regrettable form of Platonism. Though inherently suspect, numbers are apparently unavoidable, since they seem to be required by our best physical theory. The same cannot, he thinks, be said for other abstract objects.

Carnap disagrees. For him, properties and propositions are no more problematic than numbers. Each is scientifically useful, and commitment to them doesn't involve any form of Platonism. On the contrary, when properly understood, these commitments are nothing more than uncontentious consequences of an optimal theoretical framework for science. Philosophers haven't seen this because, he believes, they have approached ontology in a confused and unscientific way—failing to distinguish theoretical questions that arise within a framework for describing the world from practical questions about which framework is best. This is his famous distinction between theory-internal and theory-external questions. Since his use of the distinction depends on a strong doctrine of analyticity, it is subject to Quine's critique. Although Carnap has a response to the critique, I will argue that it is not enough to save his ambitious conception of analyticity.

How much this matters to Carnap's ontological views depends on whether his account of the cognitive content of empirical theories is retained. At the time, both he and Quine were verificationists about such contents—despite disagreeing over whether the content of a theory

---

[4] Quine, "On Carnap's Views of Ontology," *Philosophical Studies* 2 (1951): 65–72.

[5] Carnap, "Meaning and Synonymy in Natural Languages," *Philosophical Studies* 7 (1955): 33–47; reprinted as *Appendix D* of *Meaning and Necessity*. Citations are to the reprinted version.

[6] Quine, *Word and Object* (Cambridge, MA: MIT Press, 1960).

could be parceled out to its individual statements. In the presence of their shared verificationism, the essence of Carnap's ontological position survives the loss of analyticity, and Quine's victory is pyrrhic. However, that isn't the end of the story. If verificationism about the contents of theories is dropped, the ontological import of Quine's critique of analyticity is reinstated. Though Carnap's ontology is still attractive, the argument for it must be modified. That, in brief, is what I will argue.

ONTOLOGICAL COMMITMENT AND ABSTRACT OBJECTS IN "ON WHAT THERE IS"

The opening shot in the conflict was Quine's "On What There Is," the first part of which sets out his criterion of ontological commitment. One is not, he argues, committed, merely by using a name, to there being a referent of the name. Nor is one committed, merely by using a meaningful term, to their being an entity that is its meaning. It is a substantive theoretical position—which Quine sees no reason to accept—that words are meaningful only if there are entities that they mean. In using the predicate 'is red' or the adjective 'seven', one is not thereby committed to the existence of colors or numbers, though one is committed when one says that there are primary colors from which the others can be generated, or that there are prime numbers between 6 and 12. In general, one is committed to the existence of F's when, and only when, one says that there are F's.

This is the simple idea behind Quine's slogan "To be is to be the value of a bound variable." The point is *not* that to exist amounts to nothing more than being the value of a bound variable, but that to *commit* oneself to the existence of something is nothing more than *to say* that there is such a thing. To commit oneself to "things that are F" is to say something the proper regimentation of which is, or entails, a quantificational sentence—⌜∃x Fx⌝—the truth of which requires the existence of at least one object o that makes ⌜Fx⌝ true when o is assigned as value of 'x'. The qualification about regimentation is a crucial device Quine uses to avoid unwanted ontological commitments that violate his preference for desert landscapes. He has no problem, for example, saying that *there is a possibility that S*, without thereby committing himself to the existence of possibilities. The justification of his ontological nonchalance is that the proper regimentation of the remark involves no quantification over possibilities but simply the recognition that *it may be true that S*. With the flexibility provided by this kind of philosophically motivated regimentation, Quine holds that the *only* way to commit oneself to the existence of so-and-so's is by asserting something the proper regimentation of which is, or entails, the existentially quantified claim that there are so-and-so's.[7]

So far, it might appear that there is nothing in Quine's position to which Carnap could object. However, toward the end of the essay—when illustrating potentially problematic ontological commitments, Quine gives us a hint that things might be otherwise. He starts out uncontroversially, noting that in saying that some dogs are white, one commits oneself to there being dogs and white things, but not to the existence of doghood or whiteness. "On the other hand," he says:

> When we say that some zoological species are cross-fertile we are committing ourselves to recognizing as entities the several species themselves, *abstract though they are.* We remain so committed at least until we devise some way of so paraphrasing the statement as to show that seeming reference to species on the part of our bound variable was an avoidable manner of speaking.[8]

His next illustration of commitment to abstract objects involves mathematics:

> Classical mathematics, as the example of primes larger than a million illustrates, is up to its neck in commitments to an ontology of abstract entities. Thus it is that the great mediaeval controversy over universals has flared up anew in the modern philosophy of mathematics. . . . The three main mediaeval points of view regarding universals are designated by the historians as *realism, conceptualism,* and *nominalism.* Essentially these same three doctrines reappear in twentieth-century surveys of the philosophy of mathematics under the new names *logicism, intuitionism,* and *formalism.* *Realism,* as the word is used in connection with the mediaeval controversy over universals, is the Platonic doctrine that universals or abstract entities have being independently of the mind; the mind may discover them but cannot create them. *Logicism,* represented by Frege, Russell, Whitehead, Church, and Carnap, condones the use of bound variables to refer to abstract entities known and unknown, specifiable, and unspecifiable.[9]

Quine here suggests that Carnap's commitment to numbers is *a form of Platonism.* The label seems apt. After all, Carnap does say there are numbers while admitting that they are abstract, and not limited to

---

[7] Page 12.
[8] Page 13; my emphasis.
[9] Pages 13–14; italics in original; my (underlined) emphasis.

those we can specify. However, he cannot have liked being called a Platonist, since Platonism is among the traditional metaphysical views he consistently dismissed as cognitively meaningless nonsense. It was Carnap who, in *The Logical Syntax of Language*, proclaimed that "Philosophy is to be *replaced* by the logic of science—that is to say by the logical analysis of the concepts and sentences of the sciences."[10] His logical empiricism was supposed to leave traditional metaphysics behind, replacing it with something better. If someone as sympathetic as Quine could misread Platonism into his project, Carnap would have to state his position more clearly and explain why he wasn't guilty of metaphysical backsliding.

ONTOLOGY AND THE REJECTION OF METAPHYSICS IN "EMPIRICISM, SEMANTICS, AND ONTOLOGY"

This was the task of "Empiricism, Semantics, and Ontology," which begins as follows:

> Empiricists are in general rather suspicious with respect to any kind of abstract entities. . . . As far as possible they try to avoid any reference to abstract entities and to restrict themselves to what is sometimes called a nominalistic language, i.e., one not containing such references. However, within certain scientific contexts it seems hardly possible to avoid them. . . . Recently the problem of abstract entities has arisen again in connection with semantics. . . . Some semanticists say that certain expressions designate certain entities, and among these designated entities they include not only concrete material things but also abstract entities, e.g., properties as designated by predicates and propositions as designated by sentences. *Others object strongly to this procedure as violating the basic principles of empiricism and leading back to a metaphysical ontology of the Platonic kind.* It is the purpose of this article to clarify this controversial issue. *The nature and implications of the acceptance of a language referring to abstract entities will first be discussed in general; it will be shown that using such a language does not imply embracing a Platonic ontology but is perfectly compatible with empiricism and strictly scientific thinking.*[11]

---

[10] Carnap, *The Logical Syntax of Language* (London: Kegan Paul, 1937); translation of *Logische Syntax der Sprache* (1934); my emphasis.

[11] Ibid., 205–6; my emphasis.

The message here is as clear as it is perplexing. Despite his acceptance of abstract objects, Carnap is no Platonist. Instead, he sees himself as an unreconstructed empiricist who rejects metaphysics in favor of science and wishes to transform the misguided metaphysical debate between realists and nominalists into scientifically tractable terms. Doing so will, he believes, show why his commitment to abstract objects is unproblematic.

His key thesis is that ontological questions are intelligible only within a scientific framework for describing the world. Such a framework is a formalized (or formalizable) language, with semantic rules interpreting its expressions and assigning truth conditions to its sentences.[12] Among these expressions are terms and predicates referring, or applying, to postulated objects. For example, our ordinary language contains terms for observable physical objects and events. Carnap assumes that the rules constituting their meanings specify possible observations that would confirm or disconfirm sentences containing them.[13] The question of whether there are things of a given sort, therefore, reduces to the question of whether observable events occur that would, as a matter of linguistic rule, confirm the relevant sentences. Since these *internal (ontological) questions* can, in principle, be answered by appeal to evidence, they are empirical, rather than metaphysical. For example, the internal question of whether there are physical objects is answered by consulting the semantic rules of our ordinary theoretical framework and noting the occurrences of experiences needed to justify physical-object sentences.[14]

Carnap contrasts *internal ontological questions*—which he takes to be about the possible evidence that would answer them—with *external ontological questions*—which can't be settled by evidence, while nevertheless purporting to be about the world. Traditional questions

---

[12] Ibid., 206–7.

[13] Once we have accepted the thing language . . . we can raise and answer internal questions, e.g., "Is there a white piece of paper on my desk?" . . . "Are unicorns and centaurs real or merely imaginary?" . . . These questions are to be answered by empirical investigations. Results of observations are evaluated according to certain rules as confirming or disconfirming evidence for possible answers. (The evaluation is usually carried out . . . as a matter of habit rather than a deliberate, rational procedure. But it is possible . . . to lay down explicit rules for evaluation. . . .) (207).

[14] "The concept of reality occurring in these internal questions is an empirical, scientific, nonmetaphysical concept. To recognize something as a real thing or event means to succeed in incorporating it into the system of things . . . so that it fits together with the other things recognized as real, according to the rules of the framework." (207)

of metaphysics, including questions about the reality of the external world, are of this sort.

> From these [internal] questions we must distinguish the external question of the *reality of the thing world itself.* In contrast to the former questions, this question is raised neither by the man in the street nor by scientists, but only by philosophers. Realists give an affirmative answer, subjective idealists a negative one, and the controversy goes on for centuries without ever being solved. And it cannot be solved because it is framed in the wrong way. *To be real in the scientific sense means to be an element of the system; hence this concept cannot be meaningfully applied to the system itself.*[15]

Although imperfectly put, the message is clear. The question ⌜Are there F's?⌝ is properly understood by everyone except philosophers to be an internal question, resolvable by empirical evidence of the kind given by the semantic rule governing F. Philosophers, however, have traditionally misunderstood the question as not being settled by this evidence. Their mistake has been to divorce the application of F from the evidential rules that constitute its meaning. As a result, they have been led to ask cognitively meaningless pseudoquestions that can't be answered.

This mistake is compounded by another one, which serves to disguise it. Philosophers are prone to run together the proper, though often trivial, internal *theoretical* question ⌜Are there F's?⌝ with the nontrivial *practical* question of whether to adopt a theoretical framework incorporating F, as opposed to other terms. Regarding physical objects, Carnap says:

> Those who raise the question of the reality of the thing world itself have perhaps in mind not a theoretical question as their formulation seems to suggest, but rather a practical question, a matter of a practical decision concerning the structure of our language. . . . [W]e are free to choose to continue using the thing language or not; in the latter case we could restrict ourselves to a language of sense-data and other "phenomenal" entities. . . . If someone decides to accept the thing language, there is no objection against saying that he has accepted the world of things. But this must not be interpreted as if it meant his acceptance of a *belief* in the reality of the thing world; <u>there is no such belief or assertion or assumption</u>, because it is not a theoretical question. <u>To accept the thing world means nothing more than to accept a certain form of language</u>, in other words, to accept rules for

---

[15] Ibid.; my emphasis.

forming statements and for testing, accepting, or rejecting them. The acceptance of the thing language leads, on the basis of observations made, also to the acceptance, belief, and assertion of certain statements. But the thesis of the reality of the thing world cannot be among these statements, because it cannot be formulated in the thing language, or, it seems, in any other theoretical language.[16]

The contrast is striking. We are asked to imagine a choice between our ordinary physical-object framework and a (suitably elaborated) Berkeleyan alternative that speaks only of minds and "sense-data." We are told that this is *simply* a choice between two linguistic schemes for describing experience. There is, we are told, "no belief or assertion or assumption" *in the reality of the thing world* that one adopts when one opts for the thing, rather than the phenomenal, framework.

How are we to understand this? Part of the point is that the metaphysical pseudostatement that physical objects exist in reality has no intelligible content.[17] Hence, there is nothing in that statement to believe or assume. But there is more to the position than this. According to Carnap, there is *no assertion whatsoever* that one makes, or belief or assumption one adopts, in opting for theories in the thing language rather than in a suitably elaborated Berkeleyan framework. If there were, what would it be? Not a pseudostatement, since they lack cognitive content.[18] It would have to be an empirical statement of some sort. But then the assertion, belief, or assumption would require empirical justification—in which case the choice between the frameworks would be a genuine theoretical matter, rather than the purely practical decision he takes it to be. As Carnap puts it,

---

[16] Ibid., 207–8; my (underlined) emphasis.

[17] On page 214, he says that the "alleged statement of the reality of the system of entities is a pseudo-statement *without cognitive content*." My emphasis.

[18] Carnap's long-standing position was that statements with no cognitive content can't be objects of thought or assertion:

> A statement asserts only so much as is verifiable with respect to it. Therefore a sentence can be used only to assert an empirical proposition, if indeed it is used to assert anything at all. If something were to lie, in principle, beyond possible experience, it could neither be said, nor thought nor asked." ("The Elimination of Metaphysics through the Analysis of Language," in A. J. Ayer, ed. *Logical Positivism* [New York: Free Press, 1959], 76; originally published in 1932.)

Though by 1950 Carnap analyzed meaning in terms of confirmation rather than verification, his view of statements with no cognitive content remained fundamentally the same.

we take the position that the introduction of the new ways of speaking does not need any theoretical justification *because it does not imply any assertion of reality.*[19]

From here it is a short step to the conclusion that the cognitive contents of empirically equivalent theories couched in the two languages are the same. Since they have the same content, there is no objective fact of the matter on which they differ, and no genuine claim about the world made by one of them that isn't made by the other. This is why Carnap insists that the choice between the two theories is purely pragmatic, "not cognitive in nature," and to be made solely on practical grounds.[20] We are justified in adopting the physicalistic theory, because (i) we find it simpler and more efficient to use to use than the phenomenalistic one, and (ii) it doesn't make any contentious claims about the world beyond those made by the phenomenalistic theory.

ABSTRACT OBJECTS AND THE ROLE OF ANALYTICITY IN "EMPIRICISM, SEMANTICS, AND ONTOLOGY"

Ontological questions about abstract objects are treated similarly. When F is a predicate applying to physical objects or events, Carnap takes its meaning to supply analytic truths specifying empirical evidence that would confirm, or disconfirm, statements attributing F to something. The internal question ⌜Are there F's?⌝ is answered by gathering this evidence, while the external ontological question is dismissed as a metaphysical pseudoquestion. By contrast, when F is a predicate of abstract objects, empirical evidence is often irrelevant, and the meaning of F is given by rules specifying logical properties of sentences containing it. In these cases, the answer ⌜There are F's⌝ to the internal question ⌜Are there F's?⌝ is analytic, while the external question is cognitively meaningless, as before.

Numbers and properties are good examples. About the former Carnap says:

Here again there are internal questions, e.g., "Is there a prime number greater than a hundred?" Here, however, the answers are found, not by empirical investigation based on observations, but by logical analysis based on the rules for the new expressions. Therefore the answers are here analytic, i.e., logically true.[21]

---

[19] "Empiricism, Semantics, and Ontology," p. 214; my emphasis.
[20] Ibid., 208.
[21] Ibid., 208–9.

As for the external question about "the reality of numbers," philosophers who raise this question are guilty of essentially the same fallacy pointed out earlier—namely, of divorcing the application of F from the rules that constitute its meaning. As a result, their "external ontological question" about numbers lacks clear sense.[22] The case of properties is similar:

> The thing language contains words like "red," "hard," "stone," "house," etc., which are used for describing what things are like. Now we may introduce new variables, say "f," "g," etc., *for which those words are substitutable* and furthermore the general term "property." New rules are laid down which admit sentences like "Red is a property," "Red is a color," "These two pieces of paper have at least one color in common" (i.e., "There is an *f* such that *f* is a color, and . . ."). *The last sentence is an internal assertion. It is of an empirical, factual nature.* However, the external statement, the philosophical statement of the reality of properties—a special case of the reality of universals—is devoid of cognitive content.[23]

For Carnap, the ontological status of properties is on a par with that of numbers. In this case, the internal statement he cites, "These two pieces of paper have at least one color in common," is empirical, rather than analytic. To confirm it, it is sufficient to establish, e.g., 'These two pieces of paper are white'. It *follows analytically* from this that there is a color (property) that the pieces of paper share. The same framework-internal rules governing property words that generate this entailment also render his other examples— "Red is a property" and "Red is a color"—analytic, along with the overtly ontological statements 'There are properties' and 'There are colors'.

There is, however, a puzzle here. How can the mere introduction of *words,* with rules governing their meaning, guarantee the existence of *entities*—properties and colors—required to make these ontological

---

[22] Carnap says that these philosophers

> have so far not given a formulation of their question in terms of the common scientific language. Therefore our judgment must be that *they have not succeeded in giving to the external question and to the possible answers any cognitive content.* Unless and until they supply a clear cognitive interpretation, we are justified in our suspicion that their question is a pseudo-question, that is, one disguised in the form of a theoretical question while in fact it is non-theoretical; in the present case it is the practical problem whether or not to incorporate into the language the new linguistic forms which constitute the framework of numbers." (209; my emphasis)

[23] Ibid., 211–12; my emphasis.

statements true?[24] For Carnap, the answer lies in a proper understanding of analyticity. Since the truth of an analytic statement is supposed to be due entirely to its meaning, whatever facts there may be in the world are irrelevant. *An analytic truth places no constraints on the way the world is, and therefore makes no genuine claim about it, including no claim about what exists in it. Hence, it can't be ontologically worrying.* This is the classical Tractarian doctrine of analyticity, which identifies the necessary and the apriori with the analytic while maintaining that such statements tell us nothing about the world. It had been Carnap's doctrine since the early 1930s.[25]

---

[24] Note, in the preceding passage, that when Carnap talks about introducing new variables, he doesn't speak of introducing new entities as their values, but of specifying the general terms for which they may substitute.

[25] From *The Logical Syntax of Language* (London: Kegan Paul, 1937), 41; my (underlined) emphasis:

> In material interpretation, an <u>analytic sentence</u> is absolutely true whatever the empirical facts may be. <u>Hence, it does not state anything about the facts</u>. . . . A synthetic sentence is sometimes true—namely, when certain facts exist, and sometimes false; hence it says something as to what facts exist. *Synthetic sentences are the genuine statements about reality.*

From "The Elimination of Metaphysics through the Analysis of Language," in *Logical Positivism*, 76; a translation of "Überwindung der Metaphysik durch logische Analyse der Sprache," *Erkenntnis* 2 (1932); my (underlined) emphasis:

> If a compound sentence is communicated to us, e.g. "It is raining here and now or it is snowing," we learn something about reality. This is so because the sentence excludes certain of the relevant states-of-affairs and leaves the remaining ones open. . . . If, on the other hand, we are told a tautology, no possibility is excluded but they all remain open. <u>Consequently, we learn nothing about reality from the tautology</u>, e.g., "It is raining (here and now) or it is not raining." <u>Tautologies, therefore, are empty. They say nothing; they have, so-to-speak, zero content.</u> . . . Mathematics, as a branch of logic, is also tautological. In Kantian terminology: The sentences of mathematics are analytic. They are not synthetic *a priori*. Apriorism is thereby deprived of its strongest argument. Empiricism, <u>the view that there is no synthetic apriori knowledge</u>, has always found the greatest difficulty in interpreting mathematics. . . . This difficulty is removed by the fact that mathematical sentences are neither empirical nor synthetic *a priori* but analytic.

From "The Old and the New Logic," in *Logical Positivism,* 142–43; a translation of "Die alte und die neue Logik," *Erkenntnis* 1 (1930–31); my emphasis:

> (Meaningful) statements are divided into the following kinds. First there are statements which are true solely by virtue of their form ("tautologies" according to Wittgenstein; they correspond approximately to Kant's "analytic judgments"). *They say nothing about reality.* The formulae of logic and mathematics are of this kind. *They are not themselves factual statements*, but serve for the transformation of such statements.

For logical empiricists, this doctrine functioned not only to fend off worries about abstract objects but also to accommodate necessary and apriori truths to their uncompromising empiricism. In their view, all knowledge of the world comes from, and is justified by, experience. Thus, if there are necessary truths about the world, the necessity of which is knowable, this knowledge must somehow come from, and be justified by, experience of the world as it actually is. This presented a problem. It is easy to see how experience provides knowledge of which features the world actually has. But how could it provide knowledge that the world has certain features in every possible circumstance? In the face of this apparent mystery, the logical empiricists concluded that necessary truths must not be about the world in any genuine sense, after all. Apriori truths were, of course, in the same boat.[26]

This was the context in which analyticity was used to explain and legitimate necessity and apriority. If all necessity and apriority is linguistic, then, it was thought, the truth of such statements is due to their meaning, rather than to the world. Since this truth doesn't constrain the way the world is, these statements are not, it was concluded, *about* the world. In addition, knowledge of them seemed to pose no problems for empiricism. Since we can surely know both what meanings we have assigned to our words and what follows from those assignments, it was assumed that explaining apriori knowledge of necessity would be no problem. Unfortunately, the explanation was never worked out in detail, with the result that serious problems were overlooked.[27]

For our purposes, the most important problem dates to Quine's incisive, but at the time underappreciated, article "Truth by Convention."

It is clear from the 1957 postscripts Carnap added to the two articles in *Logical Positivism* that he retained the strong view of analyticity, and its relevance to his theses about abstract objects. Although he uses the postscripts to make minor changes, he leaves his doctrine of the emptiness of analytic truths intact, and notes the similarity between his 1932 treatment of ontological theses and his treatment of abstract objects in "Empiricism, Semantics, and Ontology."

[26] This reasoning is illustrated in chapter 4 of Ayer, *Language, Truth, and Logic* (London: Gollancz, 1936); 2nd ed.,1946.

[27] Here is one possible (but problematic) line of thought. Let S be an analytic sentence that expresses the proposition p. (i) Since S is analytic, one can know that S expresses a truth simply by learning what it means. (ii) One will thereby know the metalinguistic claim q—that S expresses a truth—on the basis of the evidence E provided by one's experience in learning that meaning. (iii) Since one has come to understand S, one will also know, on the basis of E, that S expresses p. (iv) Combining (ii) and (iii), one will thereby know—on the basis of E—that p is true. (v) However, the claim that E *justifies*—by ruling out possibilities in which it is false—is not p, but q. (vi) Since p can be known without any justifying evidence ruling out possibilities in which it is false, there must be no such possibilities. (vii) So, if p is analytic, p must be necessary, and—by the present reasoning—capable of being known to be so; p is also apriori, since knowledge of p doesn't require evidence justifying it.

There, he questions the idea that one can know a sentence to be true simply by knowing the linguistic conventions that govern it, and thereby understanding it.[28] His point, in a nutshell, is that often the passage from understanding meaning to knowing truth must be mediated by reasoning that involves tacit knowledge of the principles of logic—which are known apriori, if anything is. For believers, like Carnap, in the linguistic explanation of all apriori knowledge, this objection is fatal—since, if Quine is right, Carnap's explanation tacitly appeals to what he takes to be a kind of apriori knowledge that is conceptually prior to the linguistic knowledge being explained. This objection—to which no effective response was ever given—remained in the background of Quine's dispute with Carnap in the 1940s and 1950s.[29]

"TWO DOGMAS" AND BEYOND: QUINE AND CARNAP ON MEANING, REFERENCE, AND ANALYTICITY

Quine's attack on analyticity takes center stage in "Two Dogmas of Empiricism." The circle argument, in the first four sections of the paper, is aimed precisely at the ambitious conception of analyticity Carnap uses to explain and legitimate necessity and apriority. The persuasive point

---

[28] Quine, "Truth by Convention," first published in O. H. Lee (ed.), *Philosophical Essays for A. N. Whitehead* (New York: Longmans, 1936); reprinted in *The Ways of Paradox* (New York: Random House, 1966).

[29] What was not in the background was the continuity of Carnap's views of meaning, analyticity, and ontology—as he makes clear at the end of section 3 of "Empiricism, Semantics, and Ontology," pp. 214–15:

> Thus, it is clear that the acceptance of a linguistic framework must not be regarded as implying a metaphysical doctrine concerning the reality of the entities in question. It seems to me due to a neglect of this important distinction that some contemporary nominalists label the admission of variables of abstract types as "Platonism." [Carnap here footnotes Quine's "On What There Is".] This is, to say the least, an extremely misleading terminology. It leads to the absurd consequence, that the position of everybody who accepts the language of physics with its real number variables . . . would be called Platonistic, even if he is a strict empiricist who rejects Platonic metaphysics. A brief historical remark may here be inserted. The noncognitive character of the questions which we have called here external questions was recognized and emphasized already by the Vienna Circle. . . . Influenced by ideas of Ludwig Wittgenstein, the Circle rejected both the thesis of the reality of the external world and the thesis of its irreality as pseudo-statements [Here Carnap inserts a reference to his "Scheinprobleme in der Philosophie," 1928]; the same was the case for both the thesis of the reality of universals (abstract entities, in our present terminology) and the nominalistic thesis that they are not real and that their alleged names are not names of anything.

of the argument is that analyticity can't play this role because the analytic/synthetic distinction presupposes the very notions it is supposed to explain. Although this argument may have little effect on other, less philosophically ambitious, conceptions of analyticity, this concession is of little help to Carnap—whose version of empiricism requires a linguistic explanation of necessity and apriority, and a deflationary understanding of the allegedly analytic truths used to assert the existence of abstract objects. This is what Quine effectively argued that Carnap cannot have.[30]

Carnap replies in "Meaning and Synonymy in Natural Languages," where he argues that meaning and reference play comparable, and complementary, roles in empirical theorizing about natural language. Although facts about them are not strictly *determined* by observational facts about how speakers use words, this isn't required for a notion to be scientifically respectable.[31] Taking it to be obvious that reference (extension) is respectable, he argues that meaning (intension) is equally so.[32] His strategy is to show that the meanings of coextensive predicates are often empirically distinguishable—e.g., 'horse'/'horse or unicorn', and 'goblin'/'unicorn'. His method is to ask speakers to apply the words to *merely possible circumstances*, pictorially or verbally represented. Since one can often use this method to determine that

---

[30] For a discussion of the strengths and weakness of the circle argument see sections 2-4, chapter 16, volume 1, of my *Philosophical Analysis in the Twentieth Century* (Princeton, NJ, and Oxford: Princeton University Press, 2003).

[31] On p. 236 of "Meaning and Synonymy in Natural Languages," Carnap discusses a hypothesis purporting to give a complete specification of the reference of a term used by a speaker. He says:

> The latter hypothesis cannot, of course, be completely verified, but every single instance of it can in principle be tested. On the other hand, it is also agreed that this determination of extension involves uncertainty and possible error. But since this holds for all concepts of empirical science, nobody regards this fact as a sufficient reason for rejecting the concepts of the theory of extension."

[32] The purpose of this paper is to defend the thesis that the analysis of intension for a natural language is a scientific procedure, methodologically just as sound as that of extension. . . . The intensionalist thesis in pragmatics [the study of natural languages], which I am defending, says that the assignment of an intension is an empirical hypothesis which, like any other hypothesis in linguistics, can be tested by observations of language behavior. On the other hand, the extensionalist thesis asserts that the assignment of an intension, on the basis of the previously determined extension, is not a question of fact but merely a matter of choice. The thesis holds that the linguist is free to choose any of those properties which fit the given extension . . . there is no question of right or wrong. Quine seems to maintain this thesis . . . (Ibid., 236–37)

coextensive words mean different things, he concludes that there is more to meaning than extension. But if words have meanings (over and above their extensions), then the notion of sameness of meaning must be empirically legitimate, and analyticity can be defined. Thus, Carnap says, two expressions are synonymous iff they have the same intension, and a sentence is analytic iff "its intension comprehends [is true in] all possible cases."[33]

Much of this is surely right. We often bring empirical evidence about speakers to bear on hypotheses about both reference and meaning. If the former hypotheses are empirically respectable, then the latter are, too. Quine himself came to see this in *Word and Object* but drew the wrong conclusion from it, going down the disastrous path leading to his essentially eliminativist theses—the indeterminacy of translation and inscrutability of reference.[34] However, the fact that Carnap was on the right side of that issue does nothing to blunt Quine's success-ful attack on his philosophically ambitious notion of analyticity. Since Carnap's defense of intension rests heavily on modal claims about what a predicate *would* apply to, or what truth value a sentence *would* have, were certain *possible circumstance* to obtain, it is not even clear that his definition of analyticity escapes the circle argument. A more promis-ing strategy would be to give up the attempt to reduce necessity and apriority to analyticity, and try to formulate a narrower conception of analyticity according to which many nonanalytic, necessary truths are made true by essential features of things, and much of our apriori knowledge isn't a species of knowledge of meaning. The problem for Carnap is that although one might thereby salvage a narrow notion of analyticity, it is dubious that it could be used to legitimate his ontology of abstract objects. In the new picture, the fact that statements assert-ing the existence of such objects may be necessary or apriori, if true, won't confer on them the uncontentious status he requires. It would have to be shown both that these statements are analytic in the new sense and that this renders them philosophically unproblematic. That is a tall order. What Carnap needs is for statements proclaiming that there are abstract objects to be "empty of content," and so "to say noth-ing about the world." Once necessity is allowed to outstrip analyticity, the familiar Carnapian staple—the idea that statements that don't dis-tinguish between different possible ways the world could be say noth-ing about it—is no longer available to support this deflationary idea

---

[33] Ibid., 243.

[34] For an explanation of Quine's advocacy of these theses, plus an argument that they are ultimately self-undermining, see chapters 10 and 11 of volume 2 of *Philosophical Analysis in the Twentieth Century*.

about content. He could, in principle, appeal to a straightforwardly verificationist account of analyticity according to which truths immune from falsifying experience say nothing about the world. However, the difficulties with the statement-by-statement form of verificationism underlying this account had become legion by the time of "Two Dogmas."[35] It is to the alleged lessons of these difficulties that Quine turns in sections 5 and 6.

The Relevance of Quine's Holism to the Dispute over Analyticity and Ontology

He begins section 5 by summarizing the history of Carnap's reductionist project, as a prelude to his own holism about confirmation:

> Radical reductionism . . . sets itself the task of specifying a sense-datum language and showing how to translate the rest of significant discourse, *statement by statement*, into it. Carnap embarked on this project in the *Aufbau*. . . . Carnap did not seem to recognize, however, that his treatment of physical objects fell short of reduction not merely through sketchiness, but in principle. . . . Carnap seems to have appreciated this point afterward; for in his later writings he abandoned all notion of the translatability of statements about the physical world into statements about immediate experience. . . . But the dogma of reductionism has, in a subtler and more tenuous form, continued to influence the thought of empiricists. *The notion lingers that to . . . each synthetic statement there is associated a unique range of possible sensory events such that the occurrence of any of them would add to the likelihood of truth of the statement, and that there is associated also another unique range of possible sensory events whose occurrence would detract from that likelihood*. . . . The dogma of reductionism survives in the supposition that each statement, *taken in isolation from its fellows*, can admit of confirmation or infirmation at all. My countersuggestion . . . is that our statements about the external world face the tribunal of sense experience not individually but only as a corporate body.[36]

[35] See Alonzo Church, "Review of *Language, Truth, and Logic: Second Edition*," *Journal of Symbolic Logic* 14 (1949): 52–53; Carl Hempel, "The Empiricist Criterion of Meaning," originally published in 1950, and reprinted in *Logical Positivism*; plus the discussion of these in chapter 13 of *Philosophical Analysis in the Twentieth Century*, vol. 1.

[36] "Two Dogmas of Empiricism," pp. 36–38; my emphasis. When reprinted in *From a Logical Point of View* (Cambridge: Harvard University Press, 1953), Quine added a

Quine makes two significant points here. The first is a variant of the Duhemian idea that what counts as confirmation or disconfirmation of a hypothesis H depends on the background hypotheses we hold fixed in testing it. Because he thinks that we often have a wide range of choice both in deciding which background assumptions A to appeal to, and in selecting which claim to give up when A plus H yields an empirical falsehood, Quine rejects Carnap's supposition that the conventional meaning of H dictates the evidence that would confirm, or disconfirm, it. This criticism is of a piece with Quine's rejection of Carnap's ambitious conception analyticity. If Carnap were right, then the very meaning of H would generate analytic truths telling us which experiences count as confirming, and which disconfirming, it. However, if simply understanding H were sufficient to determine when it was confirmed, and when disconfirmed, we wouldn't have the range of theoretical choice regarding when to hold onto it, and when not, that we know we have.

Quine's second point is more dubious—namely, that what are confirmed or disconfirmed by evidence are not individual hypotheses but entire theories. Though it is easy to see why he says this, the fact that it's not the way that those who produce empirical hypotheses normally think, or talk, about them might well give us pause. Not Quine, however. For him, holism about confirmation is a mere way station on the way to holism about meaning—or, as the logical empiricists put it, *empirical significance,* or *cognitive content:*

> We lately reflected that in general the truth of statements does obviously depend both upon language and upon extralinguistic

---

footnote to Duhem at the end of this passage. The reader can verify the essential accuracy of Quine's summary of Carnap by reviewing (i) sections 8 and 9 of "The Old and the New Logic," 1930–31 (pp. 143–45 in *Logical Positivism*) and (ii) the postscript Carnap added in 1957 (p. 146). In (i) he maintains that all scientific concepts can be "reduced" to observable properties of physical objects and events, and that these, in turn, can be "reduced" to "the content of immediate [sense] experience." (143–44). In (ii) he says:

> The position explained in sections 8 and 9 of the foregoing paper was modified in the years following its publication. The reduction of scientific concepts to the concepts of either of the two bases indicated (viz., to the given, i.e., sense-data, or to observable properties of physical things) cannot generally be carried out in the form of explicit definitions. Therefore, scientific sentences are in general not translatable into sentences of either of the two bases. . . . Consequently a scientific sentence is not simply decidable as true or as false; it can only be more or less confirmed on the basis of given observations. Thus the earlier principle of verifiability . . . was replaced by the weaker requirement of confirmability. (146)

fact. . . . The factual component must, if we are empiricists, boil down to a range of confirmatory experiences. . . . My present suggestion is that it is nonsense, and the root of much nonsense, to speak of a linguistic component and a factual component in the truth of any individual statement. Taken collectively, science has its double dependence upon language and experience; but this duality is not significantly traceable into the statements of science taken one by one. . . . The unit of empirical significance is the whole of science.[37]

Elsewhere, I have explained Quine's holistic verificationism more fully while documenting the problems with it.[38] Here, I limit myself to how it undermines his ontological critique of Carnap.

It is striking that, in "Two Dogmas," Quine has no problem with Carnap's identification of the empirical (i.e. cognitive) contents of our theories with their observational consequences, or—even more radically—with his willingness to take those consequences to be statements about sense experience. Although Quine objects mightily to parceling out cognitive content to sentences one by one, he agrees with Carnap about the contents of whole theories. Thus, he agrees that there is no genuine theoretical difference between empirically equivalent theories with different so-called ontologies. Since they have the same cognitive content, they make the same claims about the world. There is, therefore, no objective matter of fact on which they differ, and the choice between them is, as Carnap insisted, purely practical. It's no wonder that Carnap, while puzzled about being labeled a proponent of "Platonic realism," expresses confidence in "Empiricism, Semantics, and Ontology," that, in the end, Quine agreed with him about the fundamental nature of ontological disputes.[39]

The contrast between physicalist and phenomenalist ontologies is a case in point. It is clear, for Carnap, that physicalist and phenomenalist theories compatible with the same sense experience have the same content, and so make the same claims about the world. Since there is

---

[37] Ibid., 38–39.

[38] Chapter 17 of volume 1 of *Philosophical Analysis in the Twentieth Century*. See, in particular, pp. 380–84 for a line-by-line explication of how the preceding passage, and related remarks, lead to Quine's holistic version of verificationism.

[39] On p. 215n5, he says:

> With respect to the basic attitude to take in choosing a language form (an "ontology" in Quine's terminology, which seems to me misleading), there appears now to be agreement between us: "the obvious counsel is tolerance and an experimental spirit." [a quote from the penultimate paragraph of "On What There Is"]

no fact of the matter on which they differ, the choice between them is to be made entirely on practical grounds.[40] In "Two Dogmas," Quine agrees. He says:

> As an empiricist I continue to think of the conceptual scheme of science as a tool, ultimately, for predicting future experience in the light of past experience. Physical objects are conceptually imported into the situation as convenient intermediaries . . . as irreducible posits *comparable, epistemologically, to the gods of Homer*. . . . [I]n point of epistemological footing the physical objects and the gods differ only in degree and not in kind. . . . The *myth of physical objects* is epistemologically superior to most in that it has proved more efficacious than other myths as a device for working a manageable structure into the flux of experience.[41]

Quine stresses that the "myth of physical objects," though useful, is not indispensable for making predictions about sense experience. The same predictions could, in principle, be made by a phenomenalistic theory. He makes this point with an analogy in which the phenomenalistic theory of nature is said to stand to the physicalistic theory as the algebra of the rational numbers stands to the algebra of the reals. He notes that in the algebra of the rationals, functions like square root sometimes go undefined, complicating the laws. "Then," Quine says:

> it is discovered that the rules of our algebra can be much simplified by conceptually augmenting our ontology with some *mythical entities,* to be called irrational numbers. *All we continue to be really interested in, first and last, are rational numbers*; but we find that we can commonly get from one law about rational numbers to another much more quickly and simply by *pretending* that the irrational numbers are there too. . . . Now I suggest that experience is analogous to the rational numbers and that the physical objects, in analogy to the irrational numbers, are posits which serve *merely* to simplify our treatment of experience. . . . The salient differences between the positing of physical objects and the positing of irrational numbers are, I think, *just two*. First the factor of *simplification* is more overwhelming in the case of physical objects than in the numerical case. Second, the positing of physical

---

objects is far more archaic, being indeed coeval, I expect, with language itself.[42]

Colorfully put, Quine's point is (i) that the phenomenalistic theory tells us the truth, the whole truth, and nothing but the truth about nature; (ii) that the elements it talks about are "all that we are really interested in first, and last"; and (iii) that since the physical theory adds nothing new about the world, the *only* reason to prefer it to the phenomenalistic theory is that it makes the needed predictions about sense experience more simply and conveniently. Carnap couldn't have put it better.

So, where does Quine differ with Carnap about ontology? Here is how he sums it up:

> Ontological questions . . . are on a par with questions of natural science. Consider the question whether to countenance classes as entities. . . . Carnap has maintained that this is a question not of matters of fact but of choosing a convenient language form . . . for science. *With this much I agree, but only on the proviso that the same be conceded regarding scientific hypotheses generally.* Carnap has recognized that he is able to preserve a double standard for ontological questions and scientific hypotheses only by assuming an absolute distinction between the analytic and the synthetic . . . which I reject.[43] (my emphasis)

According to both Quine and Carnap, it makes no difference to the empirical contents of whole theories, and hence to their truth or falsity, how they differ on *any nonobservational statements*, so long as their observational consequences are the same. Hence, it makes no difference what their ontologies are. Theories that posit numbers, sets, physical objects, propositions, and properties do not differ on any fact of the matter from theories that don't, *as long as the theories are observationally equivalent.* This is the stunningly counterintuitive bedrock of ontological agreement between Carnap and Quine. Their only difference is over whether *individual sentences* asserting the existence of various objects are analytic in Carnap's ambitious sense—and so, empty of content.

---

[42] Ibid., 41–42; my emphasis. Quine closes his discussion of the analogy by saying:

> The overall algebra of rational and irrational numbers is underdetermined by the algebra of rational numbers, but is smoother and more convenient; and it includes the algebra of rational numbers as a jagged or gerrymandered part. Total science, mathematical and natural and human, is similarly but more extremely underdetermined by experience. The edge of the system must be kept squared with experience; the rest, with all its elaborate *myths or fictions*, has as its objective the simplicity of laws. (my emphasis)

[43] Ibid., 43.

Though one can imagine philosophical systems in which different answers to this question would have significant consequences for ontology, the shared commitment of Carnap and Quine to a version of holistic verificationism about theories obliterates such consequences. If a total Carnapian theory is observationally equivalent to a total Quinean one, then, by holistic verificationism, Carnap's expansive ontology has, as he insists, zero effect on the claims his theory makes about the world. In this way he wins the ontological battle, despite suffering a minor setback in the skirmish over analyticity.

Extracting Positive Lessons about Ontology from the Debate

The situation changes if we drop holistic verificationism and suspend judgment on grand theories of the cognitive contents of entire theories. Then, Quine's view that ontological questions "are on a par with questions in natural science," and his opposition to Carnap's contention that statements asserting the existence of abstract objects are analytic (in the relevant sense) is an advance. If Carnap were right, such statements would be empty of significant content and so would not require theoretical justification. Since they do, in fact, require such justification, Quine's point is reinstated.

What kind of justification, and how much they require, are vexing matters. Think again about numbers, properties, and propositions. Quine wants to know if they are eliminable—if talk about them can be paraphrased away without significant loss. But loss of what? Suppose it were shown that physics could, by highly complex and technical reconstruals, be reformulated without quantification over numbers. Would this justify abandoning our commitment to them? I don't see why. If the complexity of the numberless theories precluded their actual use by physicists, a case could be made that the simplicity achieved by positing numbers constituted evidence of their existence. Alternatively, one might put aside physics altogether, and base the case on arithmetic alone. Forget about reconstrual. Can there be any serious doubt that *there are prime numbers greater than a million, and hence that there are numbers*? Surely not. Perhaps, then, what needs to be abandoned is the idea that the existence of abstract objects is especially questionable, requiring an unusually demanding justification. This idea was, I would argue, one of Quine's central unexamined presuppositions. It is worth reexamining. Here, my sympathies are with Carnap. Though wrong in thinking that statements asserting the existence of numbers, properties, and propositions are trivially analytic, he was, I suspect, right in thinking that our ready appeal to them in mathematics and semantics is all the justification they need. Pinpointing precisely why this is so is something that very much requires an explanation.[44]

[44] An abbreviated version of this paper appears under the title "The Quine, Carnap Debate on Ontology and Analyticity" in the *Soochow Journal of Philosophical Studies* no. 16 (2007): 17–32. Thanks to Jeff King, Nate Gadd, and William Dunaway for helpful comments and discussion.

PART THREE

Current Topics

11

Two Versions of Millianism

With the addition of Kit Fine's *Semantic Relationism* to the mix, there are now two main versions of Millianism on offer.[1] Both maintain

    (i) that the semantic contents of names, indexicals, and variables (appropriately relativized) are their referents;

    (ii) that the semantic contents of sentences (so relativized) are the propositions they express;

    (iii) that attitudes like assertion and belief are relations to propositions; and

    (iv) that the semantic contents of attitude reports ⌜A asserts/believes that S⌝ represent the agent as bearing the attitude to the proposition expressed by S (relative to the context of utterance and any relevant assignment of values to variables).

While these versions of Millianism both assign the standard Russellian propositions in P1 to the sentences in (1), relationism adds a *coordination scheme* to (P1c) (which nonrelationism also assigns to (2)) to produce the structure (P2R), which relationism assigns to (2).

    1a. Delia Fara is a Princeton philosopher.
    1b. Delia Graff is an MIT PhD.
    1c. Delia Fara is a Princeton philosopher and Delia Graff is an MIT PhD.

    P1a. ‹DGF, *being a Princeton philosopher*›
    P1b. ‹DGF, *being (one with) an MIT PhD*›

---

[1] In what follows, I use 'relationism' for a view based on, and inspired by, Fine (2007), which, nevertheless, does not follow him in every detail. The view here is what I take to be the simplest, most plausible version of the relational ideas he introduces. I will discuss, in footnotes, in the text, and in an appendix points about which the view I focus on may differ from his. The reader should also be aware of a relational view that differs in some important details (most notably involving quantification) that is sketched by David Kaplan in an unpublished lecture, "Word and Belief," given in the late 1980s.

P1c. «‹DGF, *being a Princeton philosopher*›, ‹DGF, *being (one with) an MIT PhD*›», CONJ›

2. Delia Fara is a Princeton philosopher and Delia Fara is an MIT PhD.

P2R. «‹D̲G̲F̲, *being a Princeton philosopher*››, ‹D̲G̲F̲, *being (one with) an MIT PhD*››, CONJ›[2]

Sentences (1c) and (2) both predicate *being a Princeton philosopher* and *being an MIT PhD* of the same person. However, understanding (1c) (which contains two names) doesn't require one to recognize this, whereas (it may be argued) understanding (2) (which contains two occurrences of the same name) does.[3] For relationism this putative difference is reflected in the propositions expressed. Since understanding a sentence involves grasping the proposition it expresses, entertaining the coordinated proposition (P2R) requires recognizing the individual it represents as a Princeton philosopher as the same as the one it represents as having an MIT PhD. Since understanding sentence (1c) doesn't require this, entertaining the uncoordinated proposition (P1c) that it expresses doesn't either. So, relationism maintains, (P2R) is epistemically equivalent to (P3) —which is expressed by (3a, 3b)—but (P1c) is not.

3a. Delia Fara is both a Princeton philosopher and an MIT PhD.
3b. λx (x is a Princeton philosopher & x is an MIT PhD) Delia Fara

P3. ‹DGF, *being a Princeton philosopher and (one with) an MIT PhD*›

The coordinated dyadic proposition (P2R) and the uncoordinated monadic proposition (P3) are truth-conditionally equivalent to, but not inferable from, the uncoordinated dyadic proposition (P1c); while being trivially inferable from one another. They differ in that while (P3) predicates a compound one-place property of a single individual, (P2R) predicates two simple properties of a pair of individuals that are, in Fine's words "represented as the same" (2007, 39–41).

As a rule, the two versions of Millianism assign different, epistemically nonequivalent propositions to sentences the understanding of which typically involves recognition of multiple occurrences of terms as standing for the same thing. However, there are exceptions, like (4a, 4b), involving pronominal anaphora:

---

[2] Throughout, underlining of two or more occurrences indicates that they bear the semantic relation that Fine calls "coordination" to one another.

[3] Although I will not here contest the claim that understanding a sentence that contains multiple occurrences of the same name requires recognizing the name as *recurring* in the sentence, I do contest it in my *Rethinking Language, Mind, and Meaning*, Soames (forthcoming).

4a. *John* harmed *himself*.
4b. *John* thinks that Mary likes *him*.

In my version of nonrelationism, anaphoric relations are semantically significant structures, the pronouns in (4) function as occurrences of bound variables as in (5), and the propositions expressed are (6a, 6b) Soames (1994).

5a. λx (x harmed x) John
5b. λx (x thinks that Mary likes x) John

6a. ‹John, self-harming›
6b. ‹John, *thinking that Mary likes one*›

By contrast, Fine assimilates (4a, 4b) to (7a, 7b), which contain multiple occurrences of the same name, and so express the coordinated propositions (8a, 8b).[4]

7a. John harmed John.
7b. John thinks that Mary likes John.

8a. «<u>John</u>, <u>John</u>›, Harm›
8b. «<u>John</u>, «Mary, <u>John</u>›, Likes», Belief.›

Although he distinguishes propositions (6a, 6b) from (8a, 8b), Fine would agree that each (a) proposition is trivially inferable from the other, and similarly for the (b) propositions.

The chief attraction of relationism is its simple treatment of some instances of Frege's puzzle. To many, it seems pretheoretically obvious

---

[4] Fine (2007, 39–40, 41, and 122–23). On 39–40, we are told:

> The names 'Cicero' and 'Cicero' in the identity sentence 'Cicero = Cicero' both represent the same object, as do the names 'Cicero' and 'Tully' in the identity 'Cicero = Tully'. But the first pair of names represents the object as the same whereas the second pair does not. . . . An object is represented as the same [by two terms] in a piece of discourse only if no one who understands the discourse can sensibly raise the question of whether it is the same. Suppose that you say "Cicero is an orator" and later say "Cicero was honest," intending to make the very same use of the name 'Cicero'. Then anyone who raises the question of whether the reference was the same would thereby betray his lack of understanding of what you meant.

According to Fine, sentences containing occurrences of terms that represent an object as the same express coordinated propositions. Since it is plausible to take sentences like (4a, 4b) to pass this test, it is plausible to take them to express (8a, 8b). This is confirmed on page 41, where we find the following: "We might also observe that in cases of anaphora (as when I say 'I saw John, he was wearing a bowler hat') we can have two expressions representing an object as the same without the expressions themselves being the same." Pages 120–21 square this analysis of anaphora in terms of coordination with the observation that the pronoun derives its referent from its antecedent.

that one can believe the propositions semantically expressed by 'Hesperus is Hesperus', and 'Hesperus isn't Phosphorus', without believing the propositions semantically expressed by 'Hesperus is Phosphorus' or 'Hesperus isn't Hesperus'. This creates a prima facie difficulty for nonrelational Millianism—to be dealt with by such extrasemantic factors as guises, ways of entertaining a proposition, pragmatic enrichment, the distinction between semantic and assertive content, the multiple assertion theory, and the least common denominator conception of meaning. By contrast, the relationist's distinction between coordinated and uncoordinated propositions accommodates the apparent pretheoretic possibility directly in the semantics. Since this may seem to be an advantage, I ask, *Should Millians become semantic relationists?* One way of taking this question asks whether relationism itself, without auxiliary machinery developed by nonrelational Millians, is sufficient to deal with the full range of attitude puzzles. A more modest way of taking it simply asks whether we should *add* coordinated propositions to the standard Millian tool kit. My remarks will bear on both.

FROM SEMANTIC CONTENT TO ASSERTIVE CONTENT

First, it is necessary to identify cases in which the two approaches have significantly different empirical consequences. Although the two versions of Millianism assign different *semantic contents* to some sentences and discourses, it would be question begging to assume that semantic content is always transparent. In fact, it appears not to be; there are many cases in which competent speakers seem to understand expressions that have same semantic content without realizing that they do, and even thinking they don't.[5] What is required for competence is not the ability to recognize whenever two sentences have the same semantic content, but the ability to recognize most of the information the sentences are used to *assert* or *convey* in various contexts. In this picture, the main role of the theoretical notion *semantic content* is to constrain the information sentences are used to assert or convey. The dispute between relational and nonrelational Millianism is over how this is done. To adjudicate the dispute, we must find cases in which the two accounts lead to different predictions about *assertive* or *conversational* content.

---

[5] See (i) Saul Kripke, the furze/gorse example (1979; p. 134 of the 1988 reprinting); (ii) Salmon's ketchup/catsup example (1989, 216–17; 1990); (iii) Reiber (1992); and (iv) Soames (1986, secs. III, IV, and IX).

INSTANCES OF ASSERTIVE EQUIVALENCE

With this in mind, consider examples (9–12):

9a. Delia Graff is (identical with) Delia Fara.
9b. Delia Fara is (identical with) Delia Fara.
9c. Delia Fara is self-identical.

10a. Delia Fara is a Princeton philosopher and Delia Graff is an MIT PhD.
10b. Delia Fara is a Princeton philosopher and Delia Fara is an MIT PhD.
10c. Delia Fara is both a Princeton philosopher and an MIT PhD.

11a. Mark Twain admired Samuel Clemens.
11b. Mark Twain admired Mark Twain.
11c. *Mark Twain* admired *himself* (i.e., was a self-admirer).

12a. Norma Jeane wanted the public to admire Marilyn.
12b. Marilyn wanted the public to admire Marilyn
12c. *Marilyn* wanted the public to admire *her.*

Relational Millianism takes the propositions *semantically* expressed by the (b) and (c) sentences to be epistemically equivalent; nonrelational Millianism denies this. However, both recognize the sentences to be *assertively equivalent.* Standardly, one who assertively utters (b) asserts the propositions semantically expressed by both (b) and (c). Thus, these examples don't clearly discriminate the two theories.

The Paderewski case is of a similar type, but is, I think, an outlier. Peter, who assertively utters (13a) while wrongly taking the two 'Paderewski' occurrences to be occurrences of referentially distinct, but phonologically identical, names, is, I think, correct in *not* taking himself to assert the absurd proposition (13b).

13a. The composer Paderewski was a brilliant musician, but the statesman Paderewski wasn't.
13b. λz ([the x: Composer x & x = z] (x was a brilliant musician) but [the y: Statesman y & y = z] $\sim$ (y was a brilliant musician)) Paderewski

According to nonrelationism, Peter asserts the proposition semantically expressed by the sentence he utters—which, though necessarily false, is not transparently so. His mistake about the name occurrences, which mediate his relation to the proposition expressed, is responsible for his failure to recognize that it both predicates and denies something of one and the same person. Relationism tells a different story, namely, the semantic content of (13a) is a coordinated proposition that is trivially equivalent to the transparently absurd proposition expressed by (13b). For relationism, Peter's failure to recognize the same name as occurring twice is a failure to understand the sentence he utters, and so to grasp the proposition it expresses.[6] Accordingly, it could be argued, that proposition isn't asserted, and its uncoordinated sibling takes its place.[7] I won't here make anything of the difference between these two stories. Suffice it to say that despite the semantic differences between relationism and nonrelationism, the empirical evidence involving communicative content doesn't clearly discriminate between them in cases like these.

Assertive Utterances of Attitude Ascriptions

To find relevant differences we need to look at assertive utterances of attitude ascriptions in which the content clause contains multiple occurrences of directly referential terms. Of course, not all such examples will do. If Peter assertively utters

14. I believe that the composer Paderewski was a brilliant musician, but the statesman Paderewski wasn't,

he will *not* ascribe to himself belief in the absurd proposition expressed by (13b), or in any epistemically equivalent proposition, for the same reasons as before. By contrast, one who utters (15a), recognizing that

---

[6] As Fine says, "For competence in the use of a name requires that different uses of the same name be coordinated and a proper understanding of the use of a name requires that one understand when its different uses are coordinated" (2007, 105). Since Peter does not understand this, he does not understand his use of (13a).

[7] This isn't the story Fine tells. According to him, Peter has two semantically different uses of the name 'Paderewski', which means that his utterance is not coordinated and so does not semantically express a coordinated proposition. (See chapter 4, especially section E.) This, in my opinion, is a mistake. It confuses semantics, which is about expression types and their occurrences, with pragmatics, which is about instances of language use, such as acts of asserting something by assertively uttering a sentence. The name 'Paderewski' that Peter uses is a name in the common language (which for purposes of the puzzle can be taken to be unambiguous). The sentence, (13a), he utters is also unambiguous, which means that the semantic relationist has no choice but to (implausibly) take its semantic content to be a coordinated proposition. The fact that Peter mistakenly takes two occurrences of an unambiguous name for occurrences of different names (or for occurrences of the same name with different meanings) is a pragmatic fact about him that doesn't magically bring any new semantic content into being for the sentence he utters. From the point of view of relationism, he misunderstands the sentence (despite understanding each of its parts), and for that reason doesn't assert the proposition it semantically expresses when he utters it. Thanks to Alexandru Radulescu for reminding me of the relevant passage in Fine (2007).

the name 'Hesperus' occurs twice, typically asserts and conveys that one believes both the proposition (15b) (semantically expressed by the content clause according to nonrelationism) and the proposition expressed by (15c, 15d)—namely, that Hesperus is a planet that is smaller than Earth.

15a. I believe that Hesperus is a planet and Hesperus is smaller than Earth.
15b. «‹ Venus, *being a planet* ›, ‹ Venus, Earth › *being smaller than* », CONJ ›
15c. Hesperus is a planet that is smaller than Earth.
15d. λx [x is a planet & x is smaller than Earth] Hesperus

Again, the two versions of Millianism produce indiscernible results about assertive content.

What about the sentences in (16)?

16a. Bill believes that Phosphorus is a planet and Hesperus is smaller than Earth.
16b. Bill believes that Hesperus is a planet and Phosphorus is smaller than Earth.
16c. Bill believes that Phosphorus is a planet and Phosphorus is smaller than Earth.
16d. Bill believes that Hesperus is a planet and Hesperus is smaller than Earth.

First consider (a) and (b), which differ only in the order of occurrence of 'Hesperus' and 'Phosphorus'. Since these sentences contain occurrences of different names, relationism and nonrelationism assign them the same semantic content, which represents Bill as believing an uncoordinated proposition in which Venus occurs twice. Since more than this is standardly asserted or conveyed by utterances of the sentences, and since what is asserted or conveyed by an utterance of one often differs from that asserted or conveyed by an utterance of the other, both approaches must appeal to extrasemantic factors to explain this. One such factor is pragmatic enrichment. Since it is widely recognized that 'Phosphorus' names a body seen in the morning, while 'Hesperus' names one seen in the evening, in many contexts (16a)–(16d) would be used to assert or convey the information given by (17a)–(17d).

17a. Bill believes that the body, Phosphorus, seen in the morning, is a planet and the body, Hesperus, seen in the evening, is smaller than Earth.
17b. Bill believes that the body, Hesperus, seen in the evening, is a planet and the body, Phosphorus, seen in the morning, is smaller than Earth.

17c. Bill believes that the body, Phosphorus, seen in the morning, is a planet and the body, Phosphorus, seen in the morning, is smaller than Earth.

17d. Bill believes that the body, Hesperus, seen in the evening, is a planet and the body, Hesperus, seen in the evening, is smaller than Earth.

Distinguishing between the communicative contents of utterances of (16a) and (16b) in this way also distinguishes each from utterances of (16c) and (16d), the communicative contents of which are given by (17c) and (17d). In this way, nonrelational Millianism distinguishes communicative contents of utterances of (18a)–(18d) from one another.

18a. A believes that . . . n . . . m . . . ('n' and 'm' coreferential)
18b. A believes that . . . m . . . n . . .
18c. A believes that . . . n . . . n . . .
18d. A believes that . . . m . . . m . . .

Relationists can do the same, if they are willing to accept, rather than attempt to replace, mechanisms like pragmatic enrichment. Not all are. Fine himself sometimes speaks as if once we have coordinated propositions, we can return to a kind of Fregean transparency about meaning without guises, ways of believing, pragmatic enrichment, and the like (see Fine 2007, 33–35, 40, 46–50, 60–65). The different communicative contents of utterances of (16a, 16b) and of (16c, 16d) constitute a prima facie problem for this ambitious view—to which I will return later.

AN ASSUMPTION ABOUT RELATIONAL QUANTIFICATION

At this point I need an explicit assumption about quantifiers and variables in a relational framework. Informally put, the assumption is that the semantics of formulas containing variables, relative to assignments, parallels that of corresponding sentences containing names. When a and b are different Millian names referring to an object o, the sentence ⌜aRa⌝ semantically expresses a coordinated proposition that arises from the uncoordinated proposition expressed by ⌜aRb⌝ by adding a coordination scheme to the latter that connects the occurrences of o in the proposition corresponding to the two occurrences of a in ⌜aRa⌝. Similarly, when v and v* are distinct variables both of which are assigned the value o by an assignment A, the formula ⌜vRv⌝ semantically expresses a coordinated proposition relative to A that arises from the uncoordinated proposition expressed by ⌜vRv*⌝ relative to A by adding a coordination scheme to the latter that connects the occurrences of o in the proposition corresponding to the two occurrences of v in ⌜vRv⌝. When the existential quantifier is added to ⌜vRv⌝—giving us ⌜∃v (vRv)⌝—the proposition semantically expressed predicates *being sometimes true* of the propositional function that assigns a coordinated proposition epistemically equivalent to the proposition that o self-R's to each object o. Thus, the quantified proposition is epistemically equivalent to the proposition *that something self-R's*. To take a particular case, the quantified sentence 'For some x, x admires x' semantically expresses a proposition p that is epistemically equivalent to the proposition *that someone admires himself* (i.e., is a self-admirer). This proposition, p, follows from the coordinated proposition that Cicero admires Cicero, which is itself epistemically equivalent to the proposition that Cicero admires himself (i.e., is a self-admirer). Similar remarks hold for the universal quantifier. The sentence 'For all x, x admires x' semantically expresses a proposition q that is epistemically equivalent to the proposition *that everyone admires himself* (i.e., is a self-admirer). Proposition q entails the coordinated proposition that Cicero admires Cicero, which is epistemically equivalent to the proposition that Cicero admires himself (i.e., is a self-admirer).

This treatment of quantification fits the guiding ideas of relationism according to which (i) names are Millian, and (ii) differences in logical form are reflected in differences in propositions expressed. Since names are Millian, the semantic content of a name that refers to o is identical with the semantic content of a variable v relative to an assignment of o to v. Since the logical form of ⌜vRv⌝ differs from the logical form of ⌜vRv*⌝ in precisely the same way that the logical form of ⌜aRa⌝ differs from that of ⌜aRb⌝, the treatment of ⌜aRa⌝ as expressing a coordinated proposition dictates that ⌜vRv⌝ does, too. In short, relationism's commitment to (i) and (ii) dictates that the proposition expressed by ⌜vRv⌝ relative to an assignment of the referent of a to v is identical with the coordinated proposition expressed by ⌜aRa⌝.[8]

---

[8] Fine ((2007, 25–32) gives a relational semantics for variables in a first-order language. Since the language is extensional, his semantics assigns only extensions to sentences and other expressions (as opposed to intensions and propositional contents). These limitations mask the significance of his relational semantics, which doesn't fully emerge until hyperintensional considerations are discussed, at which point we get the assignment of propositions to (sequences of) formulas, and the evaluation of hyperintensional constructions. Such constructions aside, coordinated propositions are intensionally equivalent to corresponding uncoordinated propositions. Thus, Fine's semantics for variables verifies the theorems of classical quantificational theory for extensional and intensional languages, but does not do so when hyperintensionality is encountered. (This point is made in endnotes 10 and 11 on p. 139).

Nevertheless, the idea of coordination is central to his semantics at all levels. See, in particular, pp. 30–31, where we are told that it is *coordinated sequences of expressions*

The way this commitment plays out in the analysis of particular cases is illustrated by (19):

19a. Mary doesn't know whether John is F and John is G
19b. John is such that Mary doesn't know whether he is F and he is G
19c. Someone is such that Mary doesn't know whether he is F and he is G

Given that there is someone, John, about whom Mary lacks relevant knowledge, the truth of (19a) should guarantee the truth of (19b, 19c). Since, according to relationism, the proposition semantically expressed by (19a) is epistemically equivalent to the claim that Mary doesn't know whether John is *both F and G*, and since (19c) tells us that what Mary doesn't know about John is something she doesn't know about someone, it should follow that the proposition semantically expressed by (19c) is epistemically equivalent to the claim that someone is such that Mary doesn't know whether he is *both F and G*. This is just what the preceding relational analysis of quantification gives us. If, for whatever reason, the relationist were to deny this account and treat the repetition of variables bound by the same quantifier as being semantically inert, rather than as inducing semantic coordination, he or she would have to characterize (19a) as *true* and (19c) as *false* in a situation in which (i) John is Juan; and (ii) Mary knows that John is F and Juan is G; (iii) there is no one else who either is, or is taken by Mary to be, a relevant candidate for being F, or for being G; and (iv) she fully understands, and is genuinely unsure, whether 'John is both F and G' and 'Juan is both F and G' express truths. Since this disconnect between (19a) and (19c) is counterintuitive, the natural extension of the relational semantics for sentences containing names to formulas with variables—and thereby to the resulting quantificational sentences—is empirically mandated, once relationism about names has been accepted.

(which result from adding coordination schemes to sequences of expressions to mark unbound occurrences of *the same variable* in a manner similar to the way in which different occurrences of the same name are coordinated)—rather than expressions themselves which are the objects of semantic evaluation. This idea is reinforced on pp. 38–39, where the semantic difference between the coordinated 'x = x' and the uncoordinated 'x = y' is used to motivate the semantic difference between the coordinated 'Cicero = Cicero' and the uncoordinated 'Cicero = Tully'. On p. 97 and on pp. 115–17 (which carries note 11 just mentioned). Fine makes explicit his commitment to the propositional semantics given in the preceding text and to the falsity of the usual quantified statement, '$\forall x \forall y (x = y \supset (Fx \leftrightarrow Fy))$', of Leibniz's law (called by him the Substitutivity of Identicals). In this, Fine parts company from Kaplan (see footnote 1), whose treatment of quantification is thoroughly classical.

The same point can be made by the examples in (20).

20a. Each man is such that Mary wonders whether he is F and he is G
20b. Mary wonders, regarding each man, whether he is F and he is G
20c. Mary wonders whether John is F and John is G, whether Bill is F and Bill is G, and whether Bob is F and Bob is G.

We observe that what (20a, 20b) says Mary wonders about each man is what (20c) says she wonders about John, and Bill, and Bob. To deny the relational analysis of quantified cases, while accepting it for names, would require denying this observation and maintaining instead that the truth of (20a)—in a case in which John, Bill, and Bob are in the domain of quantification—does not guarantee the truth of (20c). Since this, too, is counterintuitive, the relationist has strong empirical reasons to extend coordination involving names to coordination involving variables of quantification.

A Semantic Difference That Might Make an Empirical Difference

We are now in a position to consider a difference between the two versions of Millianism that may have significant empirical consequences. We begin by observing that both versions recognize the obvious fact that (21b) follows from (21a) together with the claim *Delia Fara is Delia Graff*.

21a. Don believes that Delia Fara is a Princeton philosopher and Delia Graff is an MIT PhD.
21b. For some individuals x and y, such that x = y, Don believes that x is Princeton philosopher and y is an MIT PhD. (For some pair of individuals, the first of which = the second, Don believes that the former is a Princeton philosopher and the latter is an MIT PhD.)

The two versions of Millianism also agree that (21d) does not follow from (21b).

21c. For some x, Don believes that x is a Princeton philosopher and x is an MIT PhD. (Don believes of someone that she is a Princeton philosopher and she is an MIT PhD.)
21d. For some x, Don believes that λz [z is a Princeton philosopher and z is an MIT PhD] x (Don believes of someone that she is both a Princeton philosopher and an MIT PhD.)

They differ regarding (21c). According to nonrelational Millianism, (21c) is a semantic consequence of (21b), but (21d) is not a consequence of (21c). Conversely, relationism takes (21d) to be a consequence of (21c) while denying that (21c) is a consequence of (21b).

This difference between the two approaches stems from the semantic contents they assign to clauses (22b), (22c), and (22d), relative to an assignment A of the same thing to 'x' and 'y'.

22a. . . . n . . . m . . .
22b. . . . x . . . y . . .
22c. . . . x . . . x . . .
22d. λz [. . . z . . . z . . .] x

According to nonrelationism, (22b) and (22c) express the same proposition, which one can believe without being able to infer proposition (22d). According to relationism, proposition (22d) is epistemically equivalent to proposition (22c), but not to (22b). Just as believing proposition (22b) won't, without further information, put one in position to infer propositions (22c, 22d), so, relationism maintains, believing them won't put one in a position to believe proposition (22b).

How do these semantic claims square with what ordinary speakers would glean from utterances of the sentences in (21)? The points on which the two versions of Millianism agree would, I think, be uncontroversial—namely, that the identification of Delia Fara with Delia Graff plus the truth of what is asserted by an utterance of (21a) *does* license a corresponding utterance of (21b), but would *not* guarantee the truth of an utterance (21d). As for the moves from (b) to (c) and from (c) to (d), I suspect that, taken in isolation, speakers would be inclined to accept each, while being unsure which to reject when the full argument was presented. If so, then both versions of Millianism have little choice but to attribute some common responses to factors other than semantic competence, including, in some cases, speaker error.

Which story is most plausible? Against relationism, its assignment of different truth values to (23b) and (23c) violates a principle—that bindable occurrences of objectual variables must be purely designative—that has been treated axiomatic by Quine and Kaplan, among others (see Kaplan 1986).

23a. Don believes that . . . a . . . b . . .
    b. Don believes that . . . x . . . y . . . (relative to an assignment A of the same value to 'x', 'y')
    c. Don believes that . . . x . . . x . . . (relative to A)
    d. Don believes (or may trivially infer) that λz [. . . z . . . z . . .] x (relative to A)

Consequently, relationism violates the usual formulation (24a) of Leibniz's law while retaining (24b), by denying, contrary to conventional wisdom, that (24a) follows from (24b).[9]

24a. $\forall x \forall y (x = y \supset (Fx \leftrightarrow Fy))$ [where Fx differs from Fy by containing one or more free occurrences of 'x' where Fy contains corresponding occurrences of 'y']

24b. For all x and y, if x is identical with y, then any property of x is a property of y.

Since I am not wedded to (24a), and don't accept the principle that bindable occurrences of objectual variables must—no matter under which constructions they may appear—be purely designative, I don't take this objection to be conclusive.

Against nonrelationism, the move from (23c) to (23d), which nonrelationism claims not to be semantically justified, is indeed hard to resist. But this isn't conclusive either, since the move's attraction can be attributed to a series of steps, one of which is nonsemantic. First, we recognize that if (23c) is true because of what Don believes about some person P, then *P's utterance* of (23-P) would also be true.

23-P. Don believes that . . . I . . . I . . .

Second, we recognize that if this is true, then an utterance, by Don, of (23-Don) using 'you' and addressing P, or using a name 'd' for P, would be true.

23-Don. I believe that . . . you/d . . . you/d . . .

Finally, we recognize that Don's *assertive utterance* of (23-Don) would routinely carry the information (23d+), from which (23d) follows:

23d+. Don believes (or may trivially infer) that λz [. . . z . . . z . . .] you/d

All of this is correct, and within the competence of speakers. But it doesn't show that the proposition *semantically* expressed by (23d) follows from the one expressed by (23c), since, as we saw in our discussion of (15), the move from Don's utterance of (23-Don) to an utterance of (23d+) is *pragmatically* validated, whether or not the proposition semantically expressed by the latter follows from that expressed by the former.

Thus, the sentences in (21) don't provide a decisive advantage for relationism. In fact, the scales seem to tip the other way. It is fairly clear that if (21a) is true, then the proposition expressed by 'Don believes that x is a Princeton philosopher and y is an MIT PhD' is true

---

[9] Kaplan differs from Fine in embracing (24a).

relative to an assignment of Delia to both 'x' and 'y'. But then, the proposition expressed by (21dgf) in a context with Delia as agent, and hence the proposition expressed by (21c), should also be true—even if the propositions expressed by (21d+), and hence (21d), are not.

> 21dgf. Don believes that I am a Princeton philosopher and I am an MIT PhD.
> 21c. For some x, Don believes that x is a Princeton philosopher and x is an MIT PhD. (Don believes of someone that she is a Princeton philosopher and she is an MIT PhD.
> 21d+ Don believes of someone, namely Delia, that she is both a Princeton philosopher and an MIT PhD.

If this is right, then not only have we failed to find decisive evidence in favor of relationism, we have found an objection to it. I will return to this objection after we look at discourses.

THE CONTENTS OF DISCOURSES

Frege's puzzle, which plays an important role in motivating relationism, isn't limited to the cognitive differences between single sentences containing multiple occurrences of the same term and corresponding sentences containing occurrences of distinct coreferential terms. The pairs (25) and (26) are instances of Frege's puzzle every bit as much as (27) and (28) are.

> 25a. Hesperus is a planet.
> 25b. Phosphorus is a planet.

> 26a. Don believes that Hesperus is a planet.
> 26b. Don believes that Phosphorus is a planet.

> 27a. Hesperus is Hesperus.
> 27b. Hesperus is Phosphorus.

> 28a. Don believes that Hesperus is Hesperus.
> 28b. Don believes that Hesperus is Phosphorus.

Although the members of each pair differ in what Frege calls "cognitive value," relationism treats (25) and (26) differently than it does (27) and (28). The (a) and (b) sentences of (25) and (26) are said to semantically express *the same proposition*, and hence to mean the same thing; while the (a) and (b) sentences of (27) and (28) are said to express different epistemically nonequivalent propositions, with those expressed by (28) being truth-conditionally nonequivalent as well. The semantic asymmetry of these claims about meaning is worrisome. To dispel the worry relationism appeals to discourses.

If the parties in a conversation have already used the name 'Phosphorus' in expressing the information that Venus is regularly seen in the morning, while using the name 'Hesperus' in expressing corresponding information about Venus in the evening, then, according to relationism, a subsequent utterance of (25a) will carry different information from a corresponding utterance of (25b)—quite apart from any pragmatic enrichment. Whereas an utterance of (25a) results in the acceptance of the coordinated sequence (29a) of propositions, an utterance of (25b) results in the acceptance of the differently coordinated sequence (29b).

> 29a. ‹ Venus, *being visible in the morning*›, ‹Venus, *being visible in the evening*›, ‹Venus, *being a planet*›
> 29b. ‹ Venus, *being visible in the morning*›, ‹Venus, *being visible in the evening*›, ‹Venus, *being a planet*›

This in turn is supposed to explain why in the former case the information *that something visible in the evening is a planet* is transparent to speakers, while in the latter case the information *that something visible in the morning* is a planet is transparent. In itself, however, this point carries no weight, since, as we have seen, the nonrelationist can explain the same thing on the basis of knowledge of which name has been used twice.

Discourses involving multiple attitude ascriptions are more complicated. This time we imagine a conversation in which it has already been said—*using the name 'Phosphorus'*—that most people, including Don, know that Venus is regularly seen in the morning, and also that a similar remark has been made—*using 'Hesperus'*—about Don's, and others, knowledge of Venus's visibility in the evening. The relationist's account of the difference between uttering (26a) and uttering (26b) in this context is represented by the sequences in (30):

> 30a. «Don, ‹Venus, *being visible in the morning*»›, Belief›, «Don, ‹Venus, *being visible in the evening*»›, Belief›, «Don, ‹Venus, *being a planet*»›, Belief›
> 30b. «Don, ‹Venus, *being visible in the morning*»›, Belief›, ‹Don, ‹Venus, *being visible in the evening*»›, Belief›, «Don, ‹Venus, *being a planet*»›, Belief›

If relationism is to provide a general solution to Frege's puzzle relying on coordinated propositions alone, it must assign different truth conditions to these discourse sequences. One way to do so is to maintain that the conjunction of the three belief attributions is true only if Don believes the coordinated conjunction of the individual propositions he is represented as believing—in the case of (30a), the coordinated proposition (30a-&); in the case of (30b), the coordinated proposition (30b-&).

30a-& «Venus, *being visible in the morning*›, ‹Venus, *being visible in the evening*›, ‹Venus, *being a planet*›, CONJ›
30b-& «Venus, *being visible in the morning*›, ‹Venus, *being visible in the evening*›, ‹Venus, *being a planet*›, CONJ›

Since believing the former is tantamount to believing that a planet is visible in the evening, while believing the latter is tantamount to believing that a planet is visible in the morning, the semantic truth conditions of the two discourses are distinguished in more or less the desired way.

But this can't be right. The principle that one believes P, Q, and R only if one believes their conjunction can't be built into a semantic theory because it is false. Since beliefs have credence thresholds, and since the credence of a conjunction can be far less than the credence of its conjuncts, it is not uncommon for one to believe a sequence of propositions while not believing their conjunction. Clearly, a weaker principle is needed. Here is a thought. The two sequences of belief ascriptions in (30) are, as we may put it, Venus-coordinated. Using this notion of an object-coordinated sequence, the relationist might posit the Belief Coordination Principle.

THE BELIEF COORDINATION PRINCIPLE

A sequence of ascriptions attributing belief in a sequence of o-coordinated propositions to an agent A is true only if A would recognize those propositions as things A believes, while recognizing, or being in position to recognize, that if all the beliefs are true, then the conjunction of properties attributed to o in the sequence is true of a single thing, o.

With this principle, one could assign different truth conditions to (30a) and (30b). However, this principle is almost certainly not quite right, either. As presently stated, it (implicitly) requires any agent capable of believing coordinated propositions—which (one would imagine) ought to include small children and some animals—to have higher-order attitudes about the agent's own mental states, as well as beliefs and other attitudes about sets of propositions, conjunctions of properties, and the relationship between the two when the truth of the former guarantees the latter to be *true of* something. Surely, this is beyond the ken of some possible believers. Nevertheless, I will, in what follows, ignore this difficulty—both to leave open the possibility that the idea behind the Belief Coordination Principle might be restatable in a way that avoids it, and because there is an even more serious difficulty to be faced.

What, given the principle, are we to say about truth values of belief ascriptions in a situation in which the truth conditions for discourse (30a) are satisfied, but those for (30b) aren't? The Belief Coordination Principle is compatible with different options. We could, if we wished, say that the first two ascriptions in (30b) are true, while the third isn't, or we could say of each ascription that it's true while denying that this is sufficient for the sequence of ascriptions as a whole to be true. The difference between these options doesn't matter here. The important point is that in addition to characterizing the sequence of propositions (30a), taken as a whole, as true in the situation, relationism will characterize the sequence (30b)—which is expressed by the discourse (30bw)—as false in the situation.

30bw. Don believes that Phosphorus is seen in the morning. He further believes that Hesperus is seen in the evening. He also believes that Phosphorus is a planet.

Next, consider the discourse (30cw) and the corresponding uncoordinated sequence (30c) of propositions expressed in the discourse.

30cw. Don believes that Phosphorus is seen in the morning. He also believes that Hesperus is seen in the evening. In addition, for some x, Don believes that x is a planet, where x = Phosphorus.

30c. «Don, ‹Venus, *being visible in the morning*»›, Belief›, «Don, ‹Venus, *being visible in the evening*»›, Belief›, «Don, ‹Venus, *being a planet*»›, Belief›

Surely, the sequence (30c) is true. This leads us to the real problems, illustrated by (31).

31a. There is a planet (x) which was such that when the ancients observed it/x in the morning they said and believed that *it/x* was visible only in the morning, but when they saw it/x in the evening, they said and believed that *it/x* was visible only in the evening.

31b. The ancients said and believed, when they saw me in the morning, that *I* was visible only in the morning, but they said and believed, when they saw me in the evening, that *I* was visible only in the evening. (said by Venus)

31c. The ancients said and believed, when they saw you in the morning, that *you* were visible only in the morning, but they

said and believed, when they saw you in the evening, that
you were visible only in the evening. (said by Mars to Venus)
31d. The ancients said and believed, when they saw Venus in the
morning, that *Venus* was visible only in the morning, but
they said and believed, when they saw Venus in the evening, that *Venus* was visible only in the evening, though they
didn't use that name, and were unaware they were observing the same thing, morning and evening.

If semantic coordination were a reality, these examples would correlate with (30bw), and be *false*. The fact that they are *true* is, therefore,
an argument against Millian relationism.

Consider a single example, (31a). Relationism plus the facts about
the ancients entail that (31a) is true only if discourse (32a) is true relative to an assignment of Venus to 'x', which is true only if the coordinated sequence of propositions (32b) is true.

32a. The ancients believed, when they saw x in the morning, that
x was visible only in the morning. They further believed,
when they saw x in the evening, that x was visible only in
the evening.
32b. «Ancients, ‹Venus, *being visible only in the morning*», Belief
(at $t_{morning}$)›, «Ancients, ‹Venus, *being visible only in the eve-*
ning», Belief (at $t_{evening}$)›

However, according to the Belief Coordination Principle, (32b) can't
be true, which means that (32a), and hence (31a), can't be true, either.
Since they are, in fact, true, the Belief Coordination Principle is false,
and the strategy of using discourse correlations to solve instances of
Frege's puzzle involving (26a) and (26b) is in trouble.

Nor will it do to reject the assumption that the relational semantics
of variables relative to assignments parallels that of names. In constructing these examples, I have assumed that when α and β are different Millian names referring to an object o, or different variables both
of which designate o relative to an assignment A, the sentence $\ulcorner\alpha R\alpha\urcorner$
semantically expresses, relative to A, a coordinated proposition that
arises from the uncoordinated proposition expressed by $\ulcorner\alpha R\beta\urcorner$ relative to A by adding a coordination scheme to the latter that connects
the two occurrences of o in that proposition. Although rejecting this
assumption would allow the relationist to acknowledge the truth of
(31a), it would also prevent him or her from correctly characterizing
the relationship between the (a) and (c) sentences in (19) and (20).
Since incurring this empirical cost would leave (31b)–(31d) intact as

counterexamples to the Belief Coordination Principle, nothing would be gained and something further would be lost.[10]

TWO FURTHER DIFFICULTIES

I will mention two further difficulties before ending with more general remarks. First, although Millian relationism sharply distinguishes the propositions semantically expressed by (33a) and (33b), it often trivializes the inference from the former to the latter while wrongly predicting an asymmetry between that and the corresponding move in the opposite direction.

33a. Don believes that Delia Fara bears R to (e.g., paints portraits of) Delia Fara.

« Don, « <u>DGF</u>, <u>DGF</u> ›, R-hood », Belief ›

33b. Don believes that Delia Fara bears R to (e.g., paints portraits of) Delia Graff.

« Don, « DGF, DGF ›, R-hood », Belief ›

According to relationism, (33a) reports belief in a coordinated proposition that is epistemically equivalent to the proposition that Delia self-R's (e.g., paints self-portraits). But if Don can think of Delia once, and ascribe self-Ring to her, he will typically be in a position to think of her twice using two different terms, predicating R of the uncoordinated pair of their referents. Attending one of her lectures, he may say "She [pointing at Delia] is Delia Fara," and from this plus his belief that Delia Fara self-R's conclude "Delia Fara bears R (i.e., paints portraits of) to her"—thereby expressing his belief in the uncoordinated proposition belief in which makes (33b) true. But often, more than this is required to make our acceptance, or assertive utterance, of (33b) correct, on the basis of a similar acceptance, or utterance, of (33a). There is no such shortcut to justify a move in the opposition direction—from (33b) to (33a).

Nonrelational Millianism avoids this asymmetry. Although sentences of the two forms are taken to semantically express the same propositions, nonsemantic factors—guises, ways of believing, pragmatic enrichments, and the like—are used to distinguish the communicative

---

[10] In the appendix I discuss Fine's (2007, 104) claim that 'believe' is semantically ambiguous between a "pure *de re* reading" and a "weak *de dicto*" reading. The argument in this section implicitly presupposes the latter reading. The appendix explains why positing the other "reading" won't save relationism.

and cognitive contents of uses of these sentences in particular contexts. Absent special features of the relation R (such as reflexivity or irreflexivity), the truth of the information carried by a use of (33a)—e.g., that Don believes that the Princeton professor Delia Fara paints portraits of Professor Fara—is no more likely to support the truth of the information carried by a use of (33b)—e.g., that Don believes that the Princeton professor Delia Fara paints portraits of the MIT PhD Delia Graff—than the other way around. This, I believe, is the right result.

One might think that the relationist's problem could be solved by appealing, as the nonrelationist does, to different tacit information associated with the two names. Although this is possible, it risks making the difference between coordinated and uncoordinated propositions irrelevant. To avoid this, the relationist is driven to think of the extra information associated with the names as inducing a larger, partially tacit, discourse represented by a sequence of belief ascriptions in which the content clauses of ascriptions containing the name 'Delia Fara' semantically express propositions coordinated with unexpressed but assumed propositions that represent Don as believing her to be a professor, while the content clauses of the ascriptions containing the name 'Delia Graff' are coordinated with similarly unexpressed but assumed propositions that represent him as believing her to be an MIT PhD. In short, the fix is to solve the problem with the relationist's account of (33) by transferring the explanatory burden to the treatment of discourses counterexemplified by (31). Not very promising, I think.

The final empirical difficulty is illustrated by (34):

34a. *Jim* told Mary that he wasn't *Jim*.
34b. *Each man* told Mary that *he* wasn't *that man*.

Since the two 'Jim' occurrences in (34a) are occurrences of the same name, and since the occurrence of 'he' is anaphoric on the first such occurrence, relationism tells us that entertaining the proposition expressed requires recognizing that the person represented as speaking to Mary is identical both with the person represented as the first argument of the nonidentity relation and with the person represented as the second argument of that relation—from which it follows that grasping the proposition expressed by (34a) guarantees the ability to (trivially) recognize the two arguments of the nonidentity relation to be one and the same. If this means that the complement of 'told' expresses a coordinated proposition, the relationist will get the wrong truth conditions for (34a). If it doesn't mean this, we need to be told what it does mean.

Whatever is proposed must also handle (34b), in which 'he' and 'that man' function as variables bound by 'each man'. This sentence should be true iff for each assignment A of a man to 'x' the proposition expressed by (34c) is true relative to A.

34c. x told Mary that x wasn't x

These truth conditions will be correct only if the proposition expressed by (34c) relative to an assignment of o to 'x' represents Mary as believing the *uncoordinated* proposition that predicates nonidentity of the pair both members of which are o. However, this isn't what relationism tells us; instead, it identifies the remark made to Mary with a coordinated proposition trivially equivalent to the proposition that o is non-self-identical.

I believe this difficulty stems from the wrong way of thinking about anaphora. Consider the contrast between (34) and (35) involving readings of the latter, in which 'his' is anaphoric on 'he', which in turn is anaphoric on the subject of 'told'.

35a. *Jim* told Mary that *he* loved *his* mother.
35b. *Each man* told Mary that *he* loved *his* mother.

36a. λx [x told Mary that λy (y loved y's mother) x] Jim
36b. $\forall$x: Man x [x told Mary that λy (y loved y's mother) x]

In this reading of (35a), the proposition told to Mary predicates *being one who loves one's own mother* of Jim; with (35b) we get such a predication of each man. These readings are possible for (35), but not for (34), because the conditions required for anaphora in the complement clauses are met in (35), but not in (34). To me this suggests that relationism's assimilation of anaphora, which is subject to substantial grammatical restrictions, to cases in which the same name occurs two or more times, which are not, is on the wrong track. Nor, I suspect, will it do to add bells and whistles to a relationist account of anaphora to remedy this defect. Even if the relationist blocks coordination of the pronoun in (34a) with the second occurrence of 'Jim' while insisting on the coordination of each with the first occurrence of 'Jim', it is doubtful that such a maneuver will prevent relationism from assigning incoherent truth conditions to the perfectly coherent dialog (37), spoken in response to an assertive utterance of (34a).[11]

37. What are you saying? That Mary told Jim that he—Jim—wasn't Jim?
Yes, that's exactly what I'm saying.

---

[11] Like the problems posed by (31a)–(31d) those posed by (34a, 34b) and (37) might tempt the relationist to posit "pure *de re*" readings of attitude verbs. This potential defense is explicated and criticized in the appendix, which also revisits the relational treatment of anaphora.

Coordination and the Metaphysics of Propositions

This completes my list of empirical problems for relationism. I close by asking an unabashedly metaphysical question: What are coordinated propositions anyway? Fine takes them to be structured entities, instead of functions from world-states to truth values. This is surely right. Such functions are too coarse-grained to do justice to the attitudes, no matter how fine-grained we make truth-supporting circumstances (Soames 1987, 2008). The unstructured approach also gets the order of explanation wrong, taking truth values and worlds as basic, and using them to explain properties and propositions. This is backward. Instead, give me properties and objects; I will give you propositions. Give me propositions; I will give you truth. Give me truth and propositions; I will give you world-states (see Soames 2010a, 2010b, and chapter 3 of King, Soames, and Speaks, 2014). Finally, the unstructured approach misses the fact that propositions are entities that inherently represent things as being certain ways, and so impose conditions the world must satisfy, if they are to be true. This key fact, which makes them the source of the truth conditions of sentences, is missed by any view that claims that a proposition is merely a set of things (no matter what the things), or merely a function from a set to two distinct primitives that are called "truth values" but which could equally well be the North and South Poles (see chapter 3 of King, Soames, and Speaks, 2014).

It is, of course, also missed by any approach that identifies propositions with n-tuples of objects and properties, or with the nested sets that are familiar stand-ins for such n-tuples. Purely abstract tree structures with objects and properties annotating their nodes are no better, since—in and of themselves, without interpretation by us—they don't represent anything either. Abstract structures of these sorts may serve as models of propositions—so long as we can read off the real propositions, and their genuinely representational structure, from the models. There is, I believe, a plausible way to do this for n-tuples that represent ordinary Russellian propositions.[12] Although that may also be true of Fine's coordinated n-tuples, the challenge is greater.

For me, agents are the source of intentionality. When one thinks that snow is white, one predicates whiteness of snow, and thereby represents it as white. The proposition entertained is a cognitive act in

---

[12] See chapters 3, 6, and 12 of King, Soames, and Speaks (2014) and Soames (2010a, 2010b); see also King (2007) for a different approach to naturalized propositions which rejects the possible-worlds conception of propositions, the traditional views of Frege and Russell, and contemporary variants of the structured proposition approach that ignore the issue of what makes propositions representational.

which an agent predicates whiteness of snow—which is something one does whenever one sees snow as white, imagines that it is white, or judges it to be white. In each case, one entertains p by performing a cognitive act that is p. The simplest propositions are acts in which one merely predicates properties of objects. Complex propositions involve other operations—such as conjoining or disjoining properties, or operating on the two-place relation R to form the one-place relational property *self-Ring*. Complex propositions may also predicate higher-order properties of propositions formed from lower-order predications of simple or complex properties of objects. In this account, the proposition that Cicero is wise is the act of predicating *being wise* of Cicero; the proposition that he is eloquent and wise is the act of first conjoining *being eloquent* and *being wise*, and then predicating the result, *being eloquent and wise*, of Cicero; the proposition Tully shaved Cicero is the act of predicating the shaving relation of the pair each member of which is Cicero; and the proposition that Cicero shaves himself is the act of first operating on the shaving relation to get the relational property of *being one who shaves oneself*, and then predicating it of Cicero.

What, then, is the coordinated proposition that Cicero shaved Cicero, which is supposed to differ from all these? It ought to be the act of predicating the shaving relation of the pair each member of which is Cicero—while judging or assuming the first member of the pair to be the same as its second member. But what does that mean? You might think it means predicating the relation of the pair *while judging or assuming that the individual one's predication represents as the shaver is the same as the individual one's predication represents as being shaved*. But I doubt that. To predicate the relation of the pair, one must think of the relation and of the pair, but one doesn't also have to make a higher-order judgment or assumption about one's act of predication and what it represents. Surely there are actual and possible agents who predicate properties of objects, and thereby have propositional attitudes, without bearing any significant attitude to propositions about their own cognitive activities. Nor can the coordinated proposition be identified with the cognitive act in which one predicates shaving of the pair each member of which is Cicero, while judging or assuming Cicero to be Cicero. This time the problem is to spell out what judging or assuming Cicero to be Cicero is. It can't be bearing the judging or assuming relation to the *uncoordinated* proposition that Cicero is Cicero. Nor can it be bearing that relation to the *coordinated* proposition, since that would involve explaining coordination by taking coordination for granted.

It appears that the only remaining option is to take *judging or assuming the members of a pair to be the same* as primitive—with the stipulation that to predicate shaving of the pair each member of which is

Cicero, while bearing this primitive attitude to the pair, is somehow different from predicating *self-shaving* of Cicero, and also that to predicate *being F* of o, and *being G* of o, while bearing the primitive attitude to them, is somehow different from predicating *being F and G* of o.[13] One may question whether there is such a primitive attitude, but even if there is, this isn't the end of the story. It remains to be shown that this attitude is the kind that is represented in propositional structure— i.e., that plays a role in characterizing *what we think or believe* as opposed to *how we believe it*

In my account, propositions are sequences of cognitive acts. Since the primitive *taking the members of a sequence of objects to be the same* is a cognitive act, it might seem obvious that there are propositions the entertaining of which requires the agent to think of the members of a sequence of objects in this way. However, there are limitations on what cognitive acts can be propositions. Thinking of a certain tune while, or immediately after, predicating redness of an object is a cognitive act, or sequence of cognitive acts, as is predicating a relation of a pair while, or immediately before, feeling affection toward one of its members. However, these cognitive acts, or act sequences, are not propositions because one of their act-type constituents is irrelevant to how the agent represents things to be. This suggests that the question of whether there are Finean coordinated propositions reduces to the question of whether the primitive attitude of *taking objects to be the same* while predicating R of them is representational in the right sort of way.

If there is a primitive attitude of *taking objects to be the same*, it might seem that agents ought to be able to *mistakenly* bear it to nonidentical things. Are we then to suppose that some propositions can be entertained only by one who predicates a relation of nonidentical things while mistakenly *taking them to be the same*? If Fine's coordinated propositions are genuine, one may wonder why these shouldn't also be genuine. However, it's not clear that they are. Suppose an agent mistakenly takes Cicero and his brother (each of whom shaves the other but neither of whom shaves himself) *to be the same* while predicating the shaving relation of them. If this sequence of cognitive acts is encoded by a genuine coordinated proposition, then there must be an answer to the question, *Is it true or not?* Worries arise for either answer. To say that it is true might seem to suggest that the needed primitive attitude is not fully representational, thereby threatening the status of the act as genuinely propositional. To say that it is untrue suggests that in taking a pair of distinct individuals *to be the same* we are, in effect,

---

[13] I now take this primitive to be *recognition of recurrence* in the sense of Salmon (2012).

predicating something untrue of them, violating the core idea that co-ordination doesn't itself involve predication.

The presumption, congenial to relationism, behind this dilemma is that the difference between a coordinated proposition and its corresponding uncoordinated counterpart has nothing to do with truth-conditional, or representational, content but is entirely a matter of what is required to entertain, and to bear other cognitive attitudes, toward it. Fine makes this clear in the following passage:

> But the coordinative aspect of the coordinated content of a sentence, such as 'Cicero wrote Cicero' is entirely lacking in any special descriptive or truth conditional character and relates entirely to how its truth conditions . . . are to be grasped [entertained]. It is a significant feature of the traditional Fregean view that there can be no difference in what it is to grasp [entertain] the sense of an expression without there being a difference in how the sense has application to [or represents] the world. . . . But under the relational view, these two aspects of sense come completely apart. There is no difference in what it takes for the sentences 'Cicero wrote about Cicero' and 'Cicero wrote about Tully' to be true, even though there is a difference in their coordinated content. (Fine 2007, 59)

This suggests the first horn of the preceding dilemma, and with it the worry that the act of predicating a relation of a pair of distinct objects to which it applies while bearing the primitive attitude of *taking the objects to be the same* may involve no *representational* error. One may also ask a related question: Is there, in addition to the primitive attitude of *taking objects to be the same*, also a primitive attitude of taking *objects to be different*? If the positive attitude is genuine, and part of propositional structure, it might seem that the negative attitude should also be.[14] Without a better foundational account of what propositions are, we are not in a position to answer these questions.

---

[14] I now think this contrast is mischaracterized. The crucial distinction is between propositions the entertainment of which requires *recognition of recurrence* and those the entertainment of which requires nonrecognition. In Soames forthcoming, I argue that propositions in which a relation R is predicated of a pair ‹o,o› come in three varieties: those the entertainment of which requires recognition of the recurring argument, those in which it is required that the recurrence not be recognized, and those in which there is no recognition requirement one way or the other. Though one can mistakenly treat a sequence of presentations of distinct objects as a case in which a single object recurs, there is no *recognition of recurrence*, and nothing in the *pseudorecognition* that contributes to the representational content of the act. Hence, the cognitive act involving the mistake is not a genuine proposition. See Soames (forthcoming).

APPENDIX: CAN AMBIGUITY SAVE
SEMANTIC RELATIONISM?

In presenting the argument against the Belief Coordination Principle based on the examples in (31), as well as in discussing the problem raised by (34a, 34b), I tacitly assumed—what I believe to be true— that 'believe' and other attitude verbs are semantically unambiguous as they appear in ascriptions of the form ⌜A attitude verbs that S⌝. In addition, I assumed that the proposition semantically expressed by ⌜A believes that S⌝ is true iff the agent bears the belief relation to the proposition semantically expressed by S. Hence, if there are coordinated propositions, and S expresses such a proposition p, then the ascription is true iff the agent believes p. To this the Belief Coordination Principle adds that when a *sequence of ascriptions* reports belief in a sequence of propositions the members of which are coordinated, *the sequence of ascriptions* as a whole is true only if the agent treats his or her beliefs as so coordinated. Since in (31b)–(31d) the sequences of ascriptions are the conjuncts of a conjunction, this means that the conjunction is true only if that is so—which, as observed, is incorrect. Since, as I showed, similar reasoning applies to (31a), it, too, is wrongly characterized as false.

There is, according to Fine, a reading of 'believe', which he calls "weak *de dicto*," that fits the assumptions in this argument and leads to the conclusion that (31a)–(31d) are false. It is this reading that is tacitly assumed (with no indication that attitude verbs are semantically ambiguous) throughout the first three chapters of *Semantic Relationism* in which belief and other cognitive notions play crucial roles in introducing and explaining coordinated propositions. About halfway through chapter 4, however, Fine mentions another "reading" of the belief predicate, which he calls "the pure *de re*."[15] Unfortunately, he does very little with this reading, and his statement of it (which occurs in a discussion of Kripke's puzzle) is given only in the following oversimplified form, as a preliminary to other "readings" in which he is more interested:

> Suppose we make a composite report of someone's beliefs. We say: he believes S_1, he believes $S_2, \ldots$, he believes S_n. Let us also suppose that the person would express the beliefs we are attempting to describe by means of the sentences, $T_1, T_2, \ldots, T_n$. To avoid needless complications, we may suppose that, except for the choice of names, he would use the very same words in expressing

[15] This reading, which, if genuine, might accommodate the truth of (31a)–(31d), is not to be confused with what Fine calls on p. 96 a "*de re* understanding" of belief reports, which, it is evident, cannot accommodate the truth of (31a)–(31d).

his beliefs as we use in describing them and that the correctness of the report simply turns on there being an appropriate connection between the sequence of names, M_1, M_2, ..., M_k that we use in describing his beliefs and the corresponding sequence of names, N_1, N_2, ..., N_k that he uses in expressing them.

We now ask, Under what conditions might the belief report be considered correct? Three answers suggest themselves.

1. *Pure de re reading*: This is the reading under which all that is required for the correctness of the report is that the corresponding names should be coreferential. Under this reading, of course, Kripke's puzzle will not arise, since it will clearly be correct to report the person as believing both that Paderewski is musical and that Paderewski is not musical. (Fine 2007, 102–3)

This passage is followed by characterizations of two additional readings: the already mentioned "weak *de dicto*," and another, irrelevant for our purposes, called "strict *de dicto*."[16] On page 104, Fine endorses all these readings as genuine semantic ambiguities and focuses his discussion of Kripke's puzzle on the *de dicto* varieties.

This proliferation of semantic ambiguities is, I think, a serious weakness in the theory, and the idea that a "pure *de re* reading" can save it from trouble is an illusion. The thought, of course, is that such a reading would neutralize the difference between coordinated and uncoordinated propositions and so allow the amended theory to accommodate examples like (31) and (34), where the usual appeal to coordination gets things wrong. On this "reading" of 'believe' (and 'say') (31d) could be recognized as true—by virtue of the ancients' (uncoordinated) uses of 'Hesperus' and 'Phosphorus' in expressing their beliefs—despite the fact that the uses of 'Venus' by us are coordinated, as are the members of the sequence of propositions semantically expressed by the pair of complement clauses in our reports. Presumably, the Belief Coordination Principle shouldn't come into play.[17]

The next step would be to extend this result to (31a)–(31c). For this, we need a more general statement of the truth conditions of "pure *de re*" ascriptions than the one Fine provides. There is, however, a difficulty in knowing how to formulate it. The problem in a nutshell is this. In introducing and explaining what a coordinated proposition

---

[16] Fine also mentions what he calls "the regular *de dicto*," p. 138n5.

[17] The simplest way to get this result is to rewrite the principle explicitly indicating that the occurrences of 'believe' and 'belief' that it contains are to be understood as carrying the normal "weak *de dicto*" reading.

is, Fine makes crucial use of a family of cognitive notions expressed by the verbs 'entertain', 'believe', 'know', 'infer', and the like. Indeed, we are told, *the only difference* between a coordinated proposition and its uncoordinated counterpart concerns the extra conditions placed by the former on agents who entertain, believe, know, or infer it (from something else). It is precisely because we understand these attitude verbs without further explanation that we understand what coordinated propositions are supposed to be. This works fine until we run into cases that are problematic for the theory, when we are told that 'believe', and by extension the other attitude verbs, also have "pure *de re* readings" that apply to coordinated propositions in a way that differs from the way we were told they applied when such propositions were introduced. The worry, of course, is that the new reading undermines the previous explanation, or renders it circular. To know what a coordinated proposition is we have to take belief and other cognitive notions for granted, but we can't simply take them for granted because they are, allegedly, ambiguous between readings that differ solely on what it is to bear the relevant attitudes to *coordinated* propositions. *And what are those again?* If all we had been told at the beginning was that the coordinated proposition that Cicero shaves Cicero is a proposition that can be "entertained" ("believed," etc.) *in different ways*—including one in which the agent recognizes that a single individual is both the subject and the object of the shaving relation, and one in which no such recognition is involved—we would have been mystified. Nonrelational Millianism, with its distinction between "ways of entertaining/believing" a proposition, tells us that! However, once relationism has been amended to include Fine's posited ambiguity between the "weak *de dicto*" and the "pure *de re*," we don't have too much more to go on than that. As a result, it is more difficult than might be expected to bring forth examples that definitively refute the predictions of the theory—but only because it is more difficult than expected to definitively identify what it predicts.

Nevertheless, some progress can be made. Since what Fine calls "the weak *de dicto* reading" on page 103 is what he implicitly presupposes, and takes to be normal, in explaining coordinated propositions, we may be able to use it make sense of the alleged "pure *de re* reading." There seem to be two main options for doing so.

Option 1

To believe, in the pure *de re* sense, a proposition p is simply to believe, in the weak *de dicto* sense, the uncoordinated proposition that differs at most from p in containing no coordinated elements. To believe, in the pure *de re* sense, a sequence of propositions

$p_1, \ldots, p_n$ is to believe, in the weak *de dicto* sense, the sequence of propositions $q_1, \ldots, q_n$ that differs at most from the original sequence in containing no coordinated elements.

OPTION 2

To believe, in the pure *de re* sense, a proposition p is to believe, in the weak *de dicto* sense, either p itself, or any of the propositions that differs from p by reducing the instances of coordination. To believe, in the pure *de re* sense, a sequence of propositions $p_1, \ldots,$ p_n is either to believe, in the weak *de dicto* sense (which is governed by the Belief Coordination Principle), either that sequence of propositions itself, or at least one sequence of propositions $q_1, \ldots, q_n$ that differs from the original sequence by reducing the instances of coordination.

For our purposes, we need not choose between these options. There are problems either way.

The first point to notice is this: if we adopt one of Fine's assumptions about when coordination in language and thought occurs, then we can show that neither option gives the relationist what he or she needs. The assumption is that sentences containing pronominal anaphora express coordinated propositions (which may be objects of the attitudes).[18] With this in mind, consider (38).

> 38. The ancients said, and believed, when they saw Venus in the morning, that *Venus* was (exactly) twice the size of *its* nearest heavenly neighbor, but they said and believed, when they saw Venus in the evening, that *Venus* was (exactly) three times the size of *its* nearest heavenly neighbor (though they didn't use name the 'Venus', and were unaware they were observing the same thing, morning and evening).

This example is to be understood as containing two instances of anaphora, one in the content clause of the first ascription—in which an occurrence of the possessive 'its' is anaphoric on an occurrence of 'Venus'—and one in the content clause of the second ascription—in which another occurrence of 'its' is anaphoric on a different occurrence of 'Venus'. So understood, (38) is a variant of (31d). Intuitively, what its truth requires—above and beyond what is required for the truth of (31d)—is a belief held by the ancients, when they observed Venus in the morning, which they expressed by saying "*Phosphorus* (or *It*) is

---

[18] See the passages in Fine indicated in footnote 4 for the justification of this assumption.

twice the size of *its* nearest heavenly neighbor" (taking the possessive pronoun to be anaphoric on the subject), plus a belief they held, when they observed Venus in the evening, which they expressed by saying "*Hesperus* (or *It*) is three times the size of *its* nearest heavenly neighbor" (taking the possessive to be anaphoric, as before).

Though (38), as used by us, bears precisely this reading, it can't be captured either by Fine's imagined pure *de re* reading or by any of his *de dicto* readings. The *de dicto* readings don't work for the same reason they falsify the examples in (31). The pure *de re* reading doesn't work because it doesn't require the ancients to believe of Venus, when observed in the morning, that it has the property *being one that is twice the size of one's nearest heavenly neighbor*, nor does it require them to believe of Venus, when observed in the evening, that it has the property *being one that is three times the size of one's nearest heavenly neighbor*. Since all the examples in (31) could be elaborated in the way that (38) elaborates (31d), positing a pure *de re* reading will not save Fine's semantic relationism from the underlying difficulty illustrated by (31a)–(31d).

This is so, provided one follows Fine in treating anaphora of the sort illustrated in (38) as instances of semantic coordination that result in the expression of coordinated propositions. For him, an important consideration supporting this assumption is that instances of anaphora of this sort appear to pass his informal test for coordination. Applying his test (given on p. 40 of *Semantic Relationism*) to anaphora we get: *Suppose you say ⌜α is F⌝ and later say ⌜β is G⌝ intending β to be understood as anaphoric on α. Then anyone who raises the question of whether the reference (of α and β) was the same would thereby betray his lack of understanding of what you meant.* Fine uses the fact that we can say something similar when α and β are identical names to justify the claim that different occurrences of the name in a discourse are semantically coordinated.[19] Since giving up the assumption that instances of anaphora (of the sort found in (38)) are similarly coordinated casts at least some doubt on this informal test, it complicates the task of showing that names themselves have a relational semantics.

This doesn't, of course, prevent us from imaging a coherent—though perhaps not very well motivated—version of semantic relationism that excludes anaphora from its account of coordination and restricts itself, more or less, to cases involving multiple occurrences of the same term. When anaphora is separated out in this way, relationism takes, e.g., the propositions *that a bears R to a* and *that a is F and a is G* to be coordinated, and to differ from but to be trivially and transparently equivalent (epistemically) to, the uncoordinated propositions *that a*

---

[19] See the passage from Fine quoted in footnote 4.

bears R to itself and *that a is F and G*, respectively, *when the propositions are entertained, believed, or otherwise cognized "in the* de dicto *way"*—i.e., *by one of the* de dicto *attitudes (expressed by the* de dicto *"readings" of* 'entertain', 'believe', *etc.*). However, when these propositions are entertained, believed, or otherwise cognized "in the pure *de re* way"—by a pure *de re* attitude (expressed by the pure *de re* "reading" of the attitude verb)—the propositions *that a bears R to itself* and *that a is F and G* are not apriori inferable from the propositions *that a bears R to a* and *that a is F and a is G*. Why there should be two broad classes of cognitive attitudes that treat these pairs of propositions so differently, and how language users are supposed to catch on to this difference, I leave to proponents (if any) of this possible view.

Though the view is coherent, it faces serious explanatory problems, illustrated by (39–41).

39. The ancients said, and believed, when they saw Venus in the morning, that *Venus* was (exactly) twice the size of the heavenly body nearest to Venus, but they said and believed, when they saw Venus in the evening, that *Venus* was (exactly) three times the size of the heavenly body nearest to Venus (though they didn't use name the 'Venus' and were unaware they were observing the same thing, morning and evening).

40. The ancients said, and believed, when they saw Venus in the morning, that *Venus* was larger than Mars and all the moons of Mars combined, but they said and believed, when they saw Venus in the evening, that *Venus* was smaller than Mars and each of the moons of Mars (though they didn't use name the 'Venus' and were unaware they were observing the same thing, morning and evening).

41. The ancients said, and believed, when they saw Venus in the morning, that *Venus* was a planet and Mars was smaller than Venus, but they said and believed, when they saw Venus in the evening, that *Venus* was a planet and Mars was larger than Venus (though they didn't use name the 'Venus' and were unaware they were observing the same thing, morning and evening).

To get the desired results in these cases, semantic relationism must, of course, treat the attitude verbs occurring in these sentences as carrying their pure *de re* readings. Consequently, the ancients' morning beliefs (and assertions) are not required to be coordinated with their evening beliefs (and assertions), which is all to the good. What is not all to the good is that neither their morning beliefs (and assertions), nor their evening beliefs (and assertions), are required to be internally coordinated (even though the propositions semantically expressed by the content clauses of our attitude reports are, according to the theory, coordinated). This is a problem, since (39a) could be used to assert or convey the information that the ancients' morning thought and talk about Venus represented it as *being twice the size its nearest heavenly neighbor,* while their evening thought and talk represented it as *being three times the size of its nearest heavenly neighbor,* making clear that the ancients were in no position to notice the conflict. Similarly, (40) could be used to assert or convey that the ancients' morning thought and talk about Venus represented it as *being larger than Mars and all its moons combined,* while their evening thought and talk represented Venus as *being smaller than Mars and each of its moons,* and also to explain why the ancients didn't notice the conflict. Finally, (41) could be used to assert or convey that their morning thought and talk about Venus represented it as *being a planet larger than Mars,* while their evening thought and talk represented it as *being a planet smaller than Mars.* Since the propositional content of this asserted or conveyed information is richer than the semantic contents of the "pure *de re* readings" of (39–41) a gap is opened between the meaning of the sentence uttered and the propositional content it is used to assert or convey.

Nothing could be more familiar to the nonrelational Millian, who faces the same problems in these cases that the semantic relationist does. The point is better put the other way around, though. Here, relational Millianism inherits some of the standard problems facing nonrelational Millianism. However, the positions of the two theories are not symmetrical. Whereas nonrelational Millianism has identified and articulated a variety of extrasemantic factors—including guises, ways of entertaining a proposition, pragmatic enrichment, the distinction between semantic and assertive content, the multiple assertion theory, and the least common denominator conception of meaning—to deal with this, and related cases involving the austere semantics and rich pragmatics of sentences containing Millian terms, nonrelational Millianism arises from the, I believe incorrect, conviction that these factors are incapable of solving the problems.[20] This leaves relationists in

---

[20] The problem posed by examples like (39–41) is due to the fact that different contributions can be made, to the assertive or conversational contents of utterances of attitude ascriptions, by occurrences of different but coreferential Millian terms (and in some cases by different occurrences of the same term) in the content clauses of such ascriptions. Depending on the conversational context and the presuppositions of speaker-hearers, some such occurrence contributions may be limited to the referents of the terms, while others may involve a mix of referential and other, in some cases partially descriptive, content. For example, in some contexts that which is asserted or communicated by an utterance of (39) is something along the lines of (i) (plus obvious and relevant consequences of it):

an unenviable position. If, as they maintain, the nonrelational story won't work, then they have no way of dealing with the problems illustrated by (39–41). This is not a minor matter, since *all the problems posed by the attitudes for nonrelational Millianism—including those that motivated relationism in the first place—can be re-created within the relational framework, by examples that force pure* de re *"readings."* So, either nonrelational Millianism is roughly correct (or capable of being made so), in which case relational Millianism—also known as semantic relationism—has not been shown to be needed, or nonrelational Millianism is incorrect (and irredeemable), in which case it is hard to avoid the conclusion that relational Millianism is, too.

References

Fine, K. 2007. *Semantic Relationism*. Oxford: Blackwell.

Kaplan, D. 1986. "Opacity," in L. E. Hahn and P. A. Schilpp, eds., *The Philosophy of W.V. Quine*. Chicago, IL: Open Court.

King, J. 2007. *The Nature and Structure of Content*. Oxford: Oxford University Press.

King, J., S. Soames, and J. Speaks. 2014. *New Thinking about Propositions*. Oxford, Oxford University Press.

Kripke, S. 1979. "A Puzzle about Belief," in A. Margalit, ed., *Meaning and Use*. Dordrecht: Reidel; reprinted in N. Salmon and S. Soames, eds., *Propositions and Attitudes*. Oxford: Oxford University Press, 1988.

Reiber, S. 1992."Understanding Synonyms without Knowing That They Are Synonymous." *Analysis* 52:224–28.

Salmon, N. 1989. "How to Become a Millian Heir." *Nous* 23:211–220.

———. 1990. "A Millian Heir Rejects the Wages of Sinn." in C. A. Anderson and J. Owens, eds., *Propositional Attitudes: The Role of Content in Logic, Language, and Mind*, Stanford, CA: CSLI Publications.

———. 2012. "Recurrence." *Philosophical Studies* 159:407–41.

(i) The ancients said, and believed, when they saw Venus in the morning, that *the body Venus they saw in the morning* was (exactly) twice the size of the heavenly body nearest to *the body Venus they saw in the morning*, but they said and believed, when they saw Venus in the evening, that *the body Venus they saw in the evening* was (exactly) three times the size of the heavenly body nearest to *the body Venus they saw in the evening* (though they didn't use name the 'Venus', and were unaware they were observing the same thing, morning and evening).

Semantic relationism cannot, on its own, get this result because its only means of doing so—by invoking pure *de re* readings of the attitude verbs—has the same effect on coordination involving all terms appearing in the content clauses of those verbs, indiscriminately rendering all such coordination as not required.

Soames, S. 1986. "Substitutivity," in J. J. Thomson, ed., *On Being and Saying: Essays for Richard L. Cartwright*. Cambridge, MA: MIT Press.
———. 1994. "Attitudes and Anaphora." *Philosophical Perspectives* 8:251–72; reprinted in Soames 2009.
———. 2008. "Why Propositions Can't Be Sets of Truth-Supporting Circumstances." *Journal of Philosophical Logic* 37:267–76; reprinted in Soames 2009.
———. 2009. *Philosophical Essays*, vol. 2. Princeton, NJ: Princeton University Press.
———. 2010a. *What Is Meaning?* Princeton, NJ: Princeton University Press.
———. 2010b. *Philosophy of Language*. Princeton, NJ: Princeton University Press.
———. Forthcoming. *Rethinking Language, Mind, and Meaning*. Princeton NJ: Princeton University Press.

12

What Are Natural Kinds?

Though the question is ontological, I will approach it through another, partially linguistic, question. What must natural kinds be
like if the conventional wisdom about natural kind terms is correct?
Although answering this question won't tell us everything we want
to know, it will, I think, be useful in narrowing the range of feasible
ontological alternatives. I will therefore summarize what I take to be
the contemporary linguistic wisdom and then test different proposals
about kinds against it. As we will see, some fare better than others.

Following Kripke, I take natural kind terms to be akin to proper
names.[1] Like names, they are not synonymous with descriptions associated with them by speakers. They are also like names in the way they
are introduced and have their reference fixed. Just as ordinary names
are often introduced by stipulating that they are to refer to certain individuals with which one is already acquainted, so general terms are
often introduced with the intention that they are to designate natural
kinds with which one is acquainted through their instances. For example, we may imagine the terms 'green', 'gold', 'water', and 'tiger' being
introduced by the following stipulations:[2]

> The term 'green' is to designate the color of (nearly) all members
> of a certain class of paradigmatic samples—it is to designate the
> characteristic of object surfaces causally responsible for the fact
> that those samples appear similar to us (and different from para-
> digmatic *non-green*-samples). Hence, the predicate 'is green' will
> apply (at a world-state) to precisely those objects the surfaces of
> which have the characteristic which, at the actual world-state,
> causally explains why the *green*-samples look similar to us.
>
> The term 'gold' is to designate the unique substance of which
> (nearly) all members of the class of its paradigmatic samples are

---

[1] Saul Kripke, *Naming and Necessity* (Cambridge, MA: Harvard University Press, 1980).
[2] These imagined stipulations are slight simplifications. For more detail, see my
"Knowledge of Manifest Kinds," *Facta Philosophica* 6, no. 2 (2004): 159–81.

instances. Substances are physically constitutive kinds—instances of which share the same basic physical constitution. Hence, the predicate 'is gold' will apply (at a world-state) to precisely those objects that share the physical constitution that (nearly) all the *gold*-samples actually have.

The term 'water' is to designate the characteristic shared by (nearly) all members of the class of paradigmatic *water*-samples that explains their most salient features—the fact that they boil and freeze at certain temperatures, that they are clear, potable, and necessary to life, etc. Hence, the predicate 'is water' will apply (at a world-state) to precisely those quantities that have the property that actually explains the salient features of (nearly) all paradigmatic *water*-samples.

The term 'tiger' is to designate the species of animal of which (nearly) all members of the class of its paradigmatic samples are instances. Hence, the predicate 'is a tiger' will apply (at a world-state) to precisely those individuals that are members of the species of which (nearly) all paradigmatic *tiger*-samples are actually members.

These stipulations are, of course, idealized. The terms could have been introduced by them, and behave pretty much as if they had been. However formal stipulations are not required. It is enough if speakers start calling relevant things 'green', 'gold', 'water', and 'tigers', with the intention that they are to apply not only to specimens speakers happen to encounter but to all instances of the kinds to which those specimens belong. Once introduced, natural kind terms are passed from speaker to speaker, just as proper names are.

In addition to being nondescriptive, simple general terms introduced in this way are both rigid and Millian. Since they are rigid, the natural kinds they designate don't change from world-state to world-state. Since they are Millian, there is nothing more to their semantic content, or meaning, than those kinds. The semantic properties of predicates formed using these terms are different from, but determined by, the semantic properties of the terms themselves. For example, whereas the term 'green' rigidly designates the color green—which is both its extension and semantic content—the predicate 'is green' designates the set of individuals to which the color applies, which is its extension. Since the set of green things varies from world-state to world-state, the predicate 'is green' is nonrigid. Similar remarks apply to other natural kind terms and the predicates that contain them. The semantic content of such a predicate consists of the content of its general term plus the content of the copula—roughly, *being an instance of.*[3] For each world-state w, the latter assigns to the argument provided by the content of the general term at w the class of instances of that argument. Since 'green' is Millian (directly referential), its content is the color itself, which is the argument it provides to the copula at every world-state. Thus, the semantic content of 'is green' is the property of *being (an instance of the color) green*, or *being green*, for short.

Next we apply this semantics to theoretical identification sentences. Let T_p be a simple natural kind term—like 'green', 'gold', 'water', or 'tiger'—and let P be the corresponding predicate—e.g., 'is green', 'is (an instance of) gold', 'is (an instance of) water', or 'is a tiger'. Corresponding to T_p, we take T_Q be a term or phrase of the same type—a common noun or noun phrase—and we take Q be the corresponding predicate. We then construct theoretical identification statements.

1a. $\forall x \, (Px \supset Qx)$
1b. (All) tigers are animals.
1c. (Every instance of) lightning is (an instance of) electricity. (i.e., *Lightning is electricity.*)
1d. (Every instance of) ice is (an instance of) H_2O. (*Ice is H_2O.*)

2a. $\forall x \, (Px \equiv Qx)/\forall x,y \, (Px,y \equiv Qx,y)$
2b. Something is (an instance of) water iff it is (an instance of) H_2O. (One reading of *Water is H_2O*)
2c. For all x,y, x is hotter than y iff the mean molecular kinetic energy of x exceeds that of y. (One way of fleshing out *Heat is mean molecular kinetic energy*)
2d. For all objects x, x is green iff x has surface spectral reflectance property SSR_{green}—the property of reflecting substantially more light in the middle wavelength part of the visible spectrum than in the long wavelength part, and approximately the same amount of light in the short wavelength part as in the nonshort part.

3a. $T_p = T_Q$ (if they exist).
3b. Gold is the substance made up of the element with atomic number 79 (if it exists).
3c. Water is H_2O (if it exists).
3d. Green is SSR_{green} (if the color exists).

---

[3] This statement is only a rough approximation. It ignores the subtle difference between the propositions *that o is green* and *that o instantiates (the color) green*. The copula may best be thought of not as contributing *instantiation* as a constituent of a proposition but as signaling the way in which the property expressed by its argument occurs there—e.g., that *green* is being predicated of o.

Since simple natural kind terms, and the predicates containing them, are Millian, these sentences express propositions with kinds as constituents—just as sentences containing simple proper names express singular propositions containing their referents.

Two results ensue. First, our examples are *necessary truths* iff the lambda abstract corresponding to the formula (minus the existence clause) that results from replacing the general term T_p, or predicate P, with a type-appropriate variable, expresses an *essential property* of the kind k designated by T_p. Second, (1–3) are instances of the *necessary aposteriori* iff, in addition, one can know, *de re*, of k that it has this property only by empirical investigation. The necessary aposteriority of these examples is thereby grounded in essentialist claims about kinds which can be known only empirically, just as a similar classification of (4a–4d) is grounded in essentialist claims about individuals and things that can be known only empirically.

4a. David Kaplan ≠ Saul Kripke.
4b. Saul Kripke is a human being (if he exists).
4c. This desk (pointing to the wooden one in my office) was not originally made of metal.
4d. This desk (pointing to one in my office) is made of molecules (if it exists).

These points about the necessary aposteriori can be summarized as follows:

Let p be a true proposition that attributes a property (or relation) F to an actually existing object o/kind k (or series of such), conditional on the object/kind (or series) existing (while not attributing further properties or relations to anything). Then, p will be an instance of the necessary *aposteriori* if (a) it can be known that F is an essential property (relation) of o/k (or the series), if F is a property (relation) of o/k (or the series) at all, (b) knowledge of o/k (or the series) that it has F if it exists can only be had *aposteriori,* and (c) knowing p involves knowing of o/k (or the series) that it has F, if it exists.[4]

Examples like (4b, 4d) are basic cases from which other instances can be derived. For example, since nonidentity essentially relates any pair it actually relates, an argument of this form establishes the necessary

---

[4] To characterize 'Noman is human, if he exists' about a merely possible man as necessary aposteriori, without doing the same for 'Noman is a dog, if he exists', (b) needs to be changed to something like *knowledge of o that it would have F, if it were to exist, can be had, but only aposteriori.* (Thanks to Teresa Robertson.) I will here ignore such cases.

aposteriority of the proposition that David Kaplan ≠ Saul Kripke, if David and Saul exist. Since this proposition is trivially equivalent to proposition (4a), (4a) is also necessary and *aposteriori*. Similar remarks apply to (4c).

The same reasoning applies to certain identities. For example, let 'a' and 'b' name the sperm and egg from which Saul Kripke actually developed. The possibility of identical twins aside, the metaphysical doctrine of the essentiality of origin will then characterize (5a, 5b) as instances of the necessary *aposteriori*.

> 5a. Saul Kripke = the individual who developed from a and b (if Kripke exists).
>
> 5b. λx [$\forall y$ (y developed from a and b $\leftrightarrow$ y = x)] Saul Kripke (if Kripke exists).

The natural kind identities (3b, 3c, 3d) are similar. In these sentences, 'gold', 'water', and 'green' designate natural kinds k_g, k_w, and k_{gn}. The proposition expressed by (3b) is trivially equivalent to the proposition p_g that predicates of k_g the property of being the substance instances of which have a certain atomic structure (if k_g exists), the proposition expressed by (3c) is trivially equivalent to the proposition p_w that predicates of k_w the property of being the substance instances of which are made up of molecules consisting of two hydrogen atoms and one oxygen atom (if k_w exists), and the proposition expressed by (3d) is trivially equivalent to the proposition p_{gn} that characterizes k_{gn} as the surface reflectance property of objects instances of which reflect light in certain proportions. The idea is that we can know, unproblematically, that these properties are essential to the kinds, if the kinds have them at all—even though empirical evidence is needed to justify the claim that they have them. If this is right, then the propositions (3a, 3b, 3c) are necessary *aposteriori*.

How, it might be asked, do we know of the substances *gold* and *water*, and the color *green*, that these properties are essential to them? Given our uncertainty about what kinds are, one might doubt that we have any idea what their essential properties are. However, our epistemic situation is not so dire. Recall the ostensive introduction of the terms 'water' and 'green'. 'Water' was stipulated to designate whatever it is about (nearly) all members of the class of paradigmatic *water*-samples that explains their most salient features—the fact that they boil and freeze at certain temperatures, that they are clear, potable, and necessary to life, and so on. 'Green' was stipulated to be the characteristic of object surfaces causally responsible for the way that paradigmatic *green*-samples appear to us. It follows from these stipulations that *if* the terms have been successfully introduced, then the kind *water* and the color *green* just are the characteristics that causally explain the familiar properties of *water-* and *green-*samples at the actual world-state. Thus, when it is discovered empirically that these characteristics are *being H_2O* and *being SSR_{green}*, we learn empirically that instances of the kinds have these characteristics at every possible world-state in which the kinds exist, in the sense of having instances at all. Variations on this theme explain the necessity of all the truths in (1–3).

In giving these explanations, I haven't said much about what natural kinds are. I have indicated that they exist and have instances at different possible world-states. The color green, though not itself a green object, has green objects as instances. Since different objects are green at different possible world-states, the color remains the same from state to state, even if its instances vary. The same is true of the substances gold and water, and the species tiger.[5] It is natural, in light of this, to take natural kinds to be abstract objects. But abstract objects of what sort? If what I have said about the color *green* and the kind *water* is correct, they would seem to be properties possession of which by their instances explains those instances' possession of other properties. If so, then water is the property of having a certain molecular structure, and green is the property of reflecting light at different wavelengths in the visible spectrum in certain proportions.

What are we saying, when we say that these kinds are properties? Again, it is useful to proceed linguistically. The most basic fact about properties is that they are *true of* things that have them, just as predicates are *true of* things they apply to. As a first pass, then, it is natural to take properties to be the meanings, or semantic contents, of predicates. For example, the meaning of the predicate 'is water' is the property *being made up of molecules consisting of two hydrogen atoms and one oxygen atom*—or, *being H_2O* for short.[6] But now there is a problem. If, in addition to being the meaning of 'is water', *being H_2O* is also the meaning of 'is H_2O', then the two predicates mean the same thing. From this, R1–R3 would seem to follow

---

[5] This similarity doesn't prejudge whether the property of being an instance of the kind is an essential property of things that have it. In the case of the color green it surely isn't, since many things that are green could have existed without being green. In the case of the kinds gold, water, and tiger it is much more plausible to hold that the properties are essential.

[6] Here, and throughout, I use 'H_2O' as short for the description 'the substance (instances of which are) made up of molecules consisting of two hydrogen atoms and one oxygen atom'. Similarly for the predicate 'is H_2O'. I do this solely to simplify the discussion. What it would mean to take 'H_2O' as a genuine name, and why we might want to do this, is explained in Soames, *Rethinking Language, Mind, and Meaning* (forthcoming).

R1 The proposition expressed by 'the stuff in the bathtub is water' is the same as that expressed by 'the stuff in the bathtub is H_2O';

R2 Anyone who believes that the stuff in the bathtub is water thereby believes that the stuff in the bathtub is H_2O; and

R3 The proposition that all and only water is H_2O is knowable apriori, since it is just the proposition that all and only H_2O is H_2O.

But these results seem wrong.

Does this mean that natural kinds like water aren't properties? A parallel problem about propositions suggests that we should be cautious about drawing this conclusion. In addition to being designated by *that*-clauses, propositions can also be named. For example, the proposition that mathematics is reducible to logic may be named 'Logicism'. If Millianism is correct, then, it might seem that this proposition is the meaning, or semantic content, both of the name and of the clause 'that mathematics is reducible to logic'. But then, the same assumptions that led to R1–R3 will lead to R4–R6.

R4 The proposition expressed by 'Russell affirmed Logicism' is the same as the proposition expressed by 'Russell affirmed that mathematics is reducible to logic'.

R5 Anyone who believes that Russell affirmed Logicism thereby believes that Russell affirmed that mathematics is reducible to logic.

R6 The proposition that Logicism = the proposition that mathematics is reducible to logic is knowable apriori, since it is just the proposition that Logicism = Logicism.

Like the earlier results about kinds, these results about propositions seem wrong.

Consider, for example, a student attending her first lecture in the philosophy of mathematics. She is told that Logicism is a proposition about the relationship between logic and mathematics, that Formalism is a doctrine about the interpretation of mathematics, and so on. At this stage, she is unable to distinguish Logicism from other propositions about the relationship between logic and mathematics, or to describe it in any informative way. Nevertheless, she may acquire beliefs about Logicism. She may be told, "Russell affirmed Logicism," and thereby come to believe that Russell affirmed Logicism.[7] Since it doesn't seem

---

[7] See p. 586 of Soames, "Semantics and Semantic Competence," *Philosophical Perspectives* 3 (1989): 575–96.

that she thereby comes to believe that Russell affirmed that mathematics is reducible to logic, there appears to be something wrong with the reasoning leading to R4–R6.

Mark Richard has a diagnosis of what it is.[8] It's not that 'Logicism' and 'that mathematics is reducible to logic' don't directly designate the same proposition. They do. However, the *that*-clause, being syntactically complex, can be understood only by understanding its grammatically significant constituents. To Richard, this suggests that the *that*-clause contributes not only its own content to the proposition expressed by sentences containing it but also the contents of its constituents. Since the name 'Logicism' is syntactically simple, it has no such constituents and thus contributes only its content to propositions expressed by sentences containing it. Of course, the proposition which is designated by both the name and the clause *itself* has constituents. However, when one's epistemic contact with that proposition is mediated by one's competence with the name 'Logicism', one can be aware of the proposition, without being acquainted with, or able to articulate, its constituents. By contrast, when one's epistemic contact with the proposition is mediated by one's understanding of the corresponding *that*-clause, one is acquainted with, and can articulate, the constituents of the proposition— which are just the contents of the grammatically significant constituents of the clause. For Richard, this means that a complex content can occur in a larger proposition in two different ways—one way in which the contents that make it up are themselves constituents of the larger proposition, and one way in which they aren't.

For our purposes, it doesn't matter which of various ways to formally mark this distinction we choose, so long as the distinction is marked.[9] When it is, we can distinguish propositions expressed by sentences containing the name 'Logicism' from those expressed by sentences in which the clause 'that mathematics is reducible to logic' is substituted for it. In this way, we block the problematic R4—without giving up the idea that the name and the *that*-clause are both Millian terms for the same thing. We also block R5. To believe that Russell affirmed Logicism is to *believe of* the proposition that Russell affirmed it—without necessarily knowing how to express that proposition or to articulate its constituents. To believe that Russell affirmed that mathematics is reducible to logic is to believe the same thing of the same proposition

---

[8] Richard, "Articulated Terms," *Philosophical Perspectives* 7 (1993): 207–30.
[9] The best way I know of doing this is given in my *Rethinking Language, Mind, and Meaning*.

while appreciating how it is articulated and broken down into parts.[10] We therefore get the plausible result R7.

> R7   One can know/believe that Russell affirmed Logicism without knowing/ believing that he affirmed that mathematics is reducible to logic, but one cannot know/believe the latter without thereby knowing/believing the former.

Thus, we have a plausible solution to the problem about propositions—which might also be applied to our earlier problem about properties.[11] Just as we can block the unwanted conclusions R4 and R5 (about propositions) while identifying the representational content of a linguistically simple name with the content of a syntactically complex *that*-clause, so we can block the unwanted conclusions R1 and R2 (about properties) while identifying the representational content of the simple predicate 'is water' with that of the syntactically complex predicate 'is made up of molecules containing two hydrogen atoms and one oxygen atom'—or 'is H_2O' for short. As before, we distinguish two ways in which the complex content can occur in a proposition—one way, contributed by 'is H_2O', in which the contents that make up the complex are themselves constituents of the proposition, and one way, contributed by 'is water', in which they aren't. In this way, we distinguish propositions expressed by sentences containing 'is water' from those expressed by sentences in which 'is H_2O' is substituted for it—thereby blocking R1. We also block R2. To believe that the stuff in the tub is water is, in this account, to *believe of* the property of being H_2O that the stuff in the tub is an instance of it—without necessarily knowing how to informatively characterize the property or articulate its constituents. To believe that the stuff in the tub is H_2O is to believe the same thing of the same property while appreciating how the property is articulated and being acquainted with its parts. This leads directly to R8, which parallels R7.

---

[10] Richard acknowledges this point on p. 216, where he says:

> When p is an articulation of q, one who asserts or believes p generally does so, in part, by asserting or believing q. For example, to assert that Russell defended the proposition that mathematics reduces to logic is, *inter alia*, to assert that Russell defended Logicism. . . . If we exclude propositions expressed by sentences in which an articulated term [e.g., a *that*-clause] is within the scope of a modal or temporal operator . . . it seems there are no exceptions to the principle that if one believes or asserts p, and p is an articulation of q, then one has the attitude toward q, too.

[11] Richard does this in "Analysis, Synonymy and Sense," in C. A. Anderson and M. Zeleny, eds., *Logic, Meaning and Computation* (Dordrecht: Kluwer, 2000).

R8 One can know/believe that the stuff in the bathtub is water without knowing/ believing that the stuff in the bathtub is H_2O, but one cannot know/believe the latter without thereby knowing/believing the former.

What is gained from this way of looking at things, and what problems, if any, remain? Can the property *being water* be identified with the property *being H_2O*, while also taking it to be the meaning of both 'is water' and 'is H_2O'? We have seen that there may be a defensible way of doing this that correctly distinguishes the propositions that water is water, that H_2O is H_2O, and that water is H_2O from one another. The account also accommodates the fact that one can believe that water is water without believing that water is H_2O. However, a problem remains. The account predicts that anyone who knows or believes that H_2O is H_2O *knows or believes of* the property water that it is H_2O, and so knows or believes that water is H_2O. This seems wrong. It is possible, we are inclined to think, to learn enough chemistry to have beliefs about hydrogen, oxygen, and H_2O—including the belief that H_2O is H_2O—while still being unaware that water is H_2O.[12] The account also predicts that one can know apriori that water is H_2O, which the conventional wisdom rightly denies.[13]

---

[12] Remember that 'H_2O' is not here used as a name. Rather, it is short for 'the substance instances of which are made up of molecules consisting of two hydrogen atoms and one oxygen atom.' When R8 is understood in this way, it is, I think, plausible that its second half is false. This may lead one to wonder why the second half of R7 isn't also false. There is a reason for this—though as long as R8 is rejected, it doesn't matter for my argument about kinds what we say about R7. Why then, do I find the second half of R7 plausible? It's plausible because it is clear that believing that Russell affirmed that mathematics is reducible to logic involves being *en rapport* with the proposition p named by the 'that'-clause, and believing the bare singular proposition that Russell affirmed p. Since 'Russell affirmed Logicism' expresses the very same bare singular proposition about p, it follows that one who believes that Russell affirmed that mathematics is reducible to logic believes that Russell affirmed Logicism. By contrast, since *the description* 'H_2O' rigidly designates the kind water, *but it does not name it*, 'H_2O is F' and 'Water is F' express different propositions. Moreover, it is not obvious that believing the descriptive proposition expressed by the former requires being *en rapport* with the kind k designated by 'H_2O', and believing the bare singular proposition about k expressed by "Water is F" (any more than believing that 2^{10} is less than 1000 involves being *en rapport* with the number 1024 rigidly designated by '2^{10}', and believing the bare singular proposition that it is less than 1000). Hence one can believe that H_2O is so-and-so without believing that water is so-and-so.

[13] The conventional wisdom is right to deny this, just as it is right to deny that it is knowable apriori that the first person to publish an axiomatic formalization of quantified modal logic is Ruth Marcus. Whether or not it is wrong to deny that it is knowable apriori that *Ruth Barcan is Ruth Marcus*—or, more properly, to deny that the proposition semantically expressed by the italicized sentence is knowable apriori—is another matter. For discussion, see chapters 3 and 8 of my *Beyond Rigidity* (Princeton: Princeton University

These difficulties suggest that the relationship between the simple predicate 'is water' and the grammatically complex predicate 'is H_2O' is *not* analogous to the relationship between the name 'Logicism' and the clause 'that mathematics is reducible to logic'.[14] Whereas Logicism *is* the proposition that mathematics is reducible to logic, which is the representational content of both the name and the clause, the property *being H_2O* can't be the representational content of both 'is water' and 'is H_2O'. Either *being water* isn't *being H_2O*, or one of the two predicates fails to contribute that property to the propositions expressed by sentences containing it.

Perhaps, then, the property *being water* isn't the property *being H_2O*. If it isn't, then the identity statement (6a) in which the general terms 'water' and 'H_2O' flank the identity sign will, of course, be false. However, (6b), understood as having the logical form (6c) or (6d), will still be true.

6a. water $= H_2O$
6b. Water is H_2O.
6c. $\forall x$ [x is (an instance of) water $\supset$ x is (an instance of) H_2O]
6d. $\forall x$ [x is (an instance of) water) $\equiv$ x is (an instance of) H_2O]

Since many theoretical identification statements standardly taken to be instances of the Kripkean necessary aposteriori have logical forms along the lines of (6c, 6d), understanding (6b) in this way presents no special problem. So understood, the proposition expressed by (6b) will be necessary, provided that the properties *being water* and *being H_2O* are necessarily equivalent. This proposition will be knowable only aposteriori provided two natural conditions are met—first, that we can acquire knowledge of the property *being water* by being acquainted with its instances and learning their molecular structure, and second, that having *de re* knowledge either of the property *being water* or of the property *being H_2O* (that instances of it are so-and-so) doesn't guarantee that that one has corresponding knowledge of the other property (that its instances are also so-and-so). And, indeed, why should it? If properties, like propositions, are hyperintensional, then knowledge of a property P, that it is so-and-so, should no more guarantee knowledge of a necessarily equivalent property Q, that it is so and so, than

---

Press, 2002); also "Naming and Asserting," in Szabo (ed.), *Semantics versus Pragmatics* (Oxford: Oxford University Press, 2005). Though the examples there involve singular rather than general terms, the points carry over. Some explicit discussion of examples involving general terms can be found in chapters 10 and 11 of *Beyond Rigidity*.

[14] Note the contrast between R3 and R6. The proposition *that Logicism = the proposition that mathematics is reducible to logic* is apriori, though not for the reason given in R6. (See chap. 2 of my *Rethinking Language, Mind, and Meaning*.) By contrast, the proposition that water is H_2O is not apriori.

knowledge of the truth of one proposition guarantees knowledge of the truth every proposition necessarily equivalent to it.

Put this way, the view seems attractive. However, it can't be correct—if the sketch I have given of natural kind terms is. Recall the idealized stipulation by which I imagined the term 'water' being introduced. 'Water' (I said) was to designate the property shared by (nearly) all members of the class of its paradigmatic samples that explains their most salient features. Since we have learned that these features of *water*-samples are explained by their having the molecular structure H_2O, *being water* must be the property *being H_2O*, which, in turn, must be the meaning of the predicate 'is water' (but not of the predicate 'is H_2O'). Note also that the stipulation introducing 'water' implicitly presupposes that there is only one property that explains the salient features of *water*-samples—since otherwise the stipulation would fail to determine a unique semantic value. So, if the stipulation was successful, no property other than *being H_2O* explains those features. This suggests that properties—*in the sense in which we talk about them in connection with scientific explanation involving natural kinds*—are not hyperintensional.

This result can be seen more easily by looking at a different case. Consider the natural kind term 'green', introduced by the stipulation that it is to designate the property of object surfaces causally responsible for the appearance of paradigmatic *green*-samples. Physicalists about color tell us that this property is a certain surface spectral reflectance property that specifies proportions of light reflected at different wavelengths.[15] Let Q be a complex phrase of English explicitly mentioning those proportions. The color *green* is then the property *being Q*, even though the predicate 'is green' is clearly *not* synonymous with the predicate ⌜is Q⌝. Suppose there is a different complex predicate ⌜is Q*⌝ that specifies the minute physical structure of object surfaces, such that ⌜is Q*⌝ turns out to be necessarily equivalent to ⌜is Q⌝. Since, under this assumption, *being Q** will explain the appearance of paradigmatic *green*-samples just as well as *being Q* does, the conception of properties presupposed by the stipulative introduction of 'green' requires *being Q*, *being Q**, and *being green* to be one and the same property, even though the corresponding predicates clearly differ in meaning.

What then are these properties, and how are they related to the meanings of complex predicates? The argument to this point suggests that natural kinds of the sort we have been discussing are coarse-grained properties that are individuated by their possible instances.

---

[15] See Alex Byrne and David R. Hilbert, "Colors and Reflectances," in *Readings on Color*, vol. 1, *The Philosophy of Color* (Cambridge MA: MIT Press, 1997).

If natural kind properties a and b have precisely the same instances in all (metaphysically) possible world-states, then a is identical with b. Intuitively this seems plausible. It is hard to imagine two distinct species of animal, two distinct substances, or two distinct colors which have precisely the same instances in every possible world-state. In this picture, *being H₂O*—which is identical with the property *being water*—has the same individuation conditions as the intension of 'is H₂O' and 'is water'. Since 'water' is Millian, it has this coarse-grained property as both its meaning and referent, which is the key constituent of the meaning of the predicate 'is water'. By contrast, the meaning of the complex term 'H₂O' can be identified with the structurally complex property of *being the unique substance instances of which are mapped onto truth by the propositional function that assigns to any object o the structured proposition that o is made up of molecules with two hydrogen atoms and one oxygen atom*. Unlike the coarse-grained property *being H₂O*, this complex structural property is fine-grained—having the properties *being hydrogen, being oxygen, being an atom*, the number 2, and the relation *being made up of* as constituents. The term 'H₂O' rigidly designates the coarse-grained property determined by the fine-grained structural property that is its meaning. Since the coarse-grained property is also associated with 'water', each of the statements in (6) is necessary.

The characterization of these truths as aposteriori depends on two assumptions—one extremely plausible, and the other at least defensible. The plausible assumption, which has already been mentioned, is that we can acquire knowledge of the property *being water* by being acquainted with its instances and learning their molecular structure. This ensures that we can come to know that water is H₂O empirically. To seal the deal, we must rule out that the possibility that the same proposition can also be known apriori. There is no problem distinguishing the proposition that water is H₂O (which contains both the coarse-grained property *being water* and the fine-grained structural property involving hydrogen and oxygen) from the proposition that water is water, or the proposition that H₂O is H₂O. There is also no problem recognizing that one can believe that water is water without having any beliefs about hydrogen or oxygen, and hence without believing that water is H₂O. The defensible, but less than fully transparent, further assumption needed to ensure aposteriority is this: *that believing the proposition that H₂O is so-and-so doesn't, in and of itself, guarantee believing (or being in position to come, by further reasoning, to believe) of the coarse-grained property that is the referent (but not meaning) of 'H₂O' that it is so-and-so—any more than believing that the biological father of Saul Kripke is such-and-such guarantees believing (or being in position to come to believe) of Meyer Kripke that he is such-and-such*. Nothing in the account given so far dictates a position on this epistemic assumption. However, the treatment of natural kinds as nonhyperintensional properties—on a par with objects both as constituents of reality and as things we become acquainted with through our causal interaction with the world—makes the assumption a natural one. Since it is also needed to conform to the conventional wisdom about the aposteriority of *that water is H_2O*, it is, I think, reasonable to accept it.

The end result is an account according to which natural kinds are coarse-grained properties, individuated by their possible instances. These properties are both the meanings and referents of simple natural kind terms, as well as being crucial components of the semantic contents of simple natural kind predicates constructed from them. Like individuals, the coarse-grained properties that are the kinds may themselves have properties that are essential to them, even though knowing that they have these properties often requires empirical investigation. Unlike simple natural kind terms, grammatically complex natural kind phrases are not Millian. Although they refer to coarse-grained natural kind properties, their meanings are fine-grained, structurally complex properties. Hence they are not synonymous with simple natural kind terms, and the complex predicates constructed from them are not synonymous with the predicates built from simple natural kind terms. Understood in this way, instances of the necessary aposteriori involving natural kind terms parallel those involving Millian singular terms.[16]

---

[16] The position taken here has important similarities with, and some differences from, that taken by Jeff King in "Structured Propositions and Complex Predicates," *Nous* 29 (1995): 516–35; and "What Is a Philosophical Analysis?" *Philosophical Studies* 90 (1998): 155–79. There, King sketches a unified account of all statements of property identity—called 'analyses'—whether they be philosophical or scientific analyses. Central to his position is the doctrine that the semantic contents of grammatically simple predicates (of all sorts) are properties (whether simple or complex), while the semantic contents of grammatically complex predicates are never properties but, instead, are combinations of the semantic contents of their constituents. Applied to the case of water/H_2O, this means that the property *being H_2O* is the meaning of 'is water', but not the meaning of 'is H_2O'. In this respect, our views are similar. However, we differ on several significant details, including the following: (i) Whereas I take natural kind properties, like *being H_2O* to be intensional, rather than hyperintensional, King apparently takes them to be hyperintensional—since he takes them to be complex entities individuated, in part, by their constituent properties (e.g., the property *being hydrogen* and *being oxygen*). (ii) His reason for denying that the semantic contents of complex predicates are properties (of any sort) is (therefore) different from mine. For him, the meaning of a complex predicate P is a structured complex, the constituents of which are the objects and properties designated by its simple subconstituents—related by a highly complex relation that is parasitic on the abstract linguistic structure of P. Since this relation encodes every aspect of the grammatical structure of the predicate, no matter how trivial, he assigns different meanings even to trivially differing predicates—like 'is an unmarried man' and 'is a man

To appreciate this, it is important not to become confused about the use of the term 'property'. Sometimes in philosophy it is used linguistically, for meanings of predicates whether simple or complex, and sometimes it is used ontologically, as it is in connection with natural kinds and scientific explanation. Although both uses are legitimate, they do not coincide. In one sense of 'property' the property of *being* H_2O is identical with the property *being water*, while in another sense it isn't. If one wants a single, disambiguated terminology, perhaps the appellations 'coarse-grained property', standing for intension-like things, and 'fine-grained property', standing for meanings of structurally complex phrases will do. In either case, we can make sense of what it is for a property to be true of something, either essentially or accidentally. We must simply be careful about their identity conditions.

I close with an observation about the notion *natural* in discussing natural kinds and natural kind terms. Roughly put, I take *natural* kinds to be the things designated by natural kind terms, and natural kind

---

who's not married'. By contrast, he wouldn't deny that the property *being an unmarried man* is the property *being a man who's not married*. Thus, he rejects the claim that properties are meanings of complex predicates. (iii) King's metaphysical account of what meaning is provides him with a further reason for rejecting this claim. In his account, the meanings of grammatically complex expressions are ontologically dependent on the existence of expressions used by agents (whether of a public language or a "language of thought"). This means that if properties were the meanings of complex predicates), then they couldn't exist, or have existed, without speakers. Since he, quite naturally, doesn't want to say this about properties, he concludes that properties are never the meanings of complex predicates. (He does think that these meanings uniquely determine properties, which they are said to *represent*—but he doesn't go into detail about what this relation consists in.) For my part, in addition to finding the ultra-fine-grained view of the meanings of complex predicates in (ii) questionable, I reject the metaphysics of meaning in (iii). If it were true, prior to the use of expressions by agents there could be no propositions and hence no propositional attitudes—beliefs, intentions, etc. However, the existence of these attitudes is surely required for their subsequent "thought," or use of language, to endow anything with meaning. A final point of contention concerns the informativeness of "the analysis" of 'Water is H_2O'. For King this informativeness is to be explained by different competence conditions for the terms 'water' and 'H_2O'—plus the uncontested fact that the proposition expressed by the sentence is different from that expressed by 'H_2O is H_2O'. The key point for King is that competence with 'water' does not require one to know of the complex property associated with the word that it is the property *being made up of molecules with two hydrogen and one oxygen atom*. (See pp. 162–63n16 and 169–71 of "What Is a Philosophical Analysis?") Presumably, however, competence with the complex term 'H_2O' does require this. However, if it does, then being competent with 'H_2O' should involve knowing of the property *being H_2O* that it is the property of *being made up of molecules with two hydrogen and one oxygen atom*. Since, in King's account, to know this is to know that water is the property *being made up of molecules with two hydrogen and one oxygen atom*, it should follow that the nonlinguistic belief that water is H_2O is trivial—even though the metalinguistic belief that 'water is H_2O' expresses a truth is not. This, I think, is questionable.

terms to be those it would make sense to introduce by reference-fixing stipulations like the ones for 'green', 'gold', 'water', and 'tiger'. When does it make sense to introduce general terms in this way? Only, I think, when three prerequisites are satisfied:

P1. The objects to which we wish to apply the term are similar in some respects, which guides our application of it, and allows us, fallibly but reliably, to apply it to new cases.

P2. These similarities have, and are believed by us to have, a single unifying explanation, which, although we typically don't know it, we rightly believe to involve counterfactual-supporting generalizations relating unspecified features of (nearly) all the similar-appearing objects to the respects in which they are similar.

P3. We wish to use the term in law-like generalizations and explanations—and so don't want to identify its semantic content with the cluster of observed similarities.

Satisfaction of P1 is what allows us to consistently and competently use the term prior to discovering the unknown explanatory property that its use is intended to track. Satisfaction of P2 and P3 is what makes the term something more than a tool for noting observed similarities, and what calls for the coarse-grained individuation of the kind designated by the term. Given these prerequisites, one should, I think, expect the ontological and epistemic features of natural kinds, and the linguistic characteristics of natural kind terms, to fall out pretty much as I have outlined.

13

Vagueness and the Law

We all know that much in our thought and language, as well as much in the law, is vague. We are also reasonably good at recognizing cases of vagueness, even though most of us would be hard pressed to say exactly what vagueness is. In recent decades, there has been a flowering of work in the philosophy of logic and language attempting to do just that. Much of this work has focused on what it is for a word or phrase to be vague. The aim of this effort is to clarify what it is for a claim, question, command, or promise expressed using such a term to be vague, as well as how to reason with such terms. Different logico-linguistic theories have different conceptions of the scope of putative laws of classical logic, including bivalence (which states that every declarative sentence or proposition is either true or false) and excluded middle (which asserts all instances of *A or ~A*). Recent decades have also seen a growing interest in vagueness among legal scholars and philosophers of law. Here the focus has been not so much on what legal vagueness is, which is generally assumed to be readily recognizable; rather, the emphasis has been on the extent and sources of vagueness in the law, the implications of vagueness for interpretation and adjudication, the systemic effects of vagueness and the function—i.e., important positive value—of vagueness in certain areas of the law, as opposed to its disutility in others (Endicott 2000, 2005; Soames 2011).

To date, these two investigations of vagueness—in philosophical logic and in the philosophy of law—have been largely independent of each other. This independence has given rise to a natural line of questioning: Can work in one domain contribute to work in the other? Does a commitment to one philosophical theory of what vagueness is carry with it lessons for vagueness in the law? If so, might the need to make good sense of legal vagueness play a role in deciding which philosophical theory of vagueness is correct? Conversely, might one be misled about the pros and cons of vagueness in the law by a faulty conception of what vagueness is? These are the questions to be investigated here, by comparing two leading philosophical accounts of vagueness and exploring their implications for understanding the value of vagueness in the law and the issues at stake in interpreting vague legal texts.

VAGUENESS AND BORDERLINE CASES

In ordinary life, a remark is often considered vague if the information it provides is insufficiently specific to advance the accepted conversational purpose (especially when the speaker is expected to possess that information). Philosophical logicians have focused on one particularly interesting subcase—involving the notion of *a borderline case*—of this more general phenomenon. Vague predicates—like 'old', 'bald', 'rich', and 'red'—are those for which a range of borderline cases separate things to which the predicate clearly applies from those to which it clearly does not apply. These are cases in which there is no clear answer to the question of whether a predicate is, or is not, true of an object o. In such cases, we are pulled in both directions—being inclined to resist definitive verdicts in favor of equivocal remarks like 'It sort of is and sort of isn't'; 'It's not clearly one or the other'; or 'Call it what you like, but neither choice is definitely correct'. In some contexts it may be acceptable to treat the predicate as applying, while in others it may be fine to treat it as not applying. But no investigation into the facts in virtue of which the predicate means what it does could ever identify one of these uses as definitely correct and the other as incorrect. In situations that call for a verdict, this means that a decision is required that is not dictated by knowledge of the nonlinguistic facts under discussion plus the linguistic rules governing vague terms. This is the sense in which "philosophical vagueness" —susceptibility to borderline cases—is an instance of ordinary vagueness: insufficient informativeness (Soames 2011). If a theater director's assistant has been told to cast a bald character, and the chief candidate for the role is a borderline case of baldness, the director's request plus the assistant's knowledge of the candidate are insufficiently informative to determine whether to offer the role. Some further basis for decision is needed.

TWO PHILOSOPHICAL THEORIES OF VAGUENESS

According to one theory, vague predicates are both partially defined and context sensitive. To say that P is partially defined is to say that it is governed by linguistic rules that provide sufficient conditions for P to apply to an object and sufficient conditions for P not to apply, but no conditions that are both individually sufficient and disjunctively necessary for P to apply or not to apply. Because the conditions are mutually exclusive, but not exhaustive, there are objects not covered by the rules for which P is *undefined*. In the case of vagueness, this situation, in turn, gives rise to context sensitivity. Since the rules of the common language, plus all relevant nonlinguistic facts, don't determine P-verdicts for every object, speakers using P in certain contexts have the discretion of extending its range to include some initially undefined cases, depending on their conversational purposes. Often they do so by predicating P of an object o, or denying such a predication. When they do, and other conversational participants accommodate their conversational move, the class of things to which P does, or doesn't, apply is contextually adjusted to include o, plus objects similar to o (in certain respects). In such cases, P is (partly) "precisified" by narrowing the range of items for which P is undefined (Tappendon 1993; Soames 1999, ch. 7; Endicott 2000; Shapiro 2006).

Since what counts as a rule of the language (governing the use of a particular predicate) is also vague, higher-order vagueness arises when one considers the predicate ⌜is determinately P⌝, where for o to be determinately *so-and-so* is for the claim that o is *so-and-so* to be a necessary consequence of the rules of the language governing "*so-and-so*" plus the (relevant) nonlinguistic facts about o. Thus, the range of application for an ordinary vague predicate P can be divided into five regions, as follows:

P	?	Undefined	?	Not P
$R1_{PDP}$	$R2_{PDP}$	$R3_{PDP}$	$R4_{PDP}$	$R5_{PDP}$

Let 'red' be P. Items in $R1_{PDP}$ are determinately red, items in $R3_{PDP}$–$R5_{PDP}$ are not determinately red, and it is unsettled whether items in $R_{PDP}2$ are determinately red or undefined for 'red'. Similar characterizations hold for 'not red', working from $R5_{PDP}$ and moving left. Iterating "determinately" doesn't change things (Soames 2003).

Next, consider the proposition p expressed by 'It's red' relative to an assignment of o as referent of 'it' and a context C including a set of standards governing 'red'. We are *not* here considering the proposition *asserted* by an agent who utters 'It's red' in C, referring to o. The issue is semantic (the proposition semantically expressed relative to a context and an assignment), not pragmatic (the proposition asserted by an utterance). If, given C's standards for 'red', o is in $R1_{PDP}$ ($R5_{PDP}$), then p is true (not true) in C; if o is in $R3_{PDP}$, p is undefined for truth in C. ('False' and 'not true' are interchangeable when applied to propositions.) If o is in $R2_{PDP}$, it is unsettled whether p is true or undefined in C; if o is in

R4$_{PDP}$, it is unsettled whether p is not true or undefined. When a proposition p is not true, it is a mistake to assert p, but it may be correct to deny p—i.e., to assert its negation. However, when p is undefined for truth, it is a mistake to either assert or deny p, because neither p nor its negation can be *known* to be true (Soames 2010). When it is unsettled whether p is true or undefined it is unsettled whether one who accepts it has made a mistake.

Now, consider the related case in which an agent A says "It's red" of o in a context in which the standards governing 'red' *prior* to A's utterance place o in regions 2 or 3, but the audience *accommodates* A by adjusting the contextual standards to render A's remark true. In such a case the proposition q that A uses 'It's red' to assert is different from the proposition p that the sentence semantically expresses, relative to the context (plus an assignment of o as referent of 'it') and prior to accommodation. After accommodation, the partially defined property contributed by 'red' to the asserted proposition has o in its region 1. If o was in region 3 originally, A's remark will be *true by stipulation*, in the sense that it is only because A's sentence has been taken to assert q, rather than p, that A's remark counts as true. By contrast, if o was in region 2 by previous standards, A's remark will again be judged true, but this time it will be unsettled whether it is true *by stipulation*, because it will be unsettled whether the proposition p that A's utterance would have asserted without accommodation is itself true. These instances of smooth accommodation contrast with an attempt to extend the extension of 'red' to an item x in region 4 prior to A's remark. In such a case, A's remark will be problematic and may not be accommodated, since prior to A's utterance it was unsettled whether o was undefined for 'red' (and so open for inclusion under the predicate) or definitely not red (and so outside the range of legitimate speaker discretion).

That, in a nutshell, is one philosophical theory of vagueness. Another important theory is the epistemic theory, according to which vague predicates are always totally defined, with sharp boundaries separating items to which they apply from those to which they don't—-e.g., a single second separating moments when one is young from those when one is not, and a single penny separating one who is rich from one who is not. Borderline cases are those of which we can never *know* the vague predicate P to be true, or to be untrue. So, whereas the previous theory takes borderline cases to be those for which P is undefined, the epistemic theory takes them to be cases for which one can never know how, in fact, P is defined (Williamson 1994). Here I am concerned with the standard version of epistemicism, which does not take vague terms to be context sensitive, as opposed to the version in Fara (2000), which does.

According to this theory, bivalence and the law of the excluded middle hold without exception, even for sentences containing vague language. Sorites paradoxes are blocked by denying the major premise of paradoxical arguments like the following:

> Minor: A newborn baby is young at the moment of birth.
> Major: For every number n, if one who is precisely n seconds old is young, then one who is n + 1 seconds old is also young.
> Conclusion: Everyone is young.

Whereas the previous theory of vagueness rejects the major premise while also rejecting its negation (since both are undefined), epistemicism claims the major premise to be false and its negation to be true, which it asserts:

> ~Major: There is a number of seconds n such that anyone who is precisely n seconds old is young, but anyone who is n + 1 seconds old is not young.

What epistemicism doesn't do is *identify* any number n as the number in question. Unlike still another theory—supervaluationism about vagueness (Fine 1975)—which also preserves the law of the excluded middle, and asserts (~Major), epistemicism acknowledges every instance of the quantified major premise to be either true or false, despite the fact that some of the truths are unknowable.

Higher-order vagueness arises for the epistemicist when one considers the predicates ⌜is an object that can be known to be P⌝ and ⌜is an object that can be known not to be P⌝. When P is vague in the epistemicist's sense, these predicates are also vague. This means that although both predicates are totally defined, and although there are sharp lines separating things to which they apply from things to which they do not, the precise location of these lines is unknowable. Thus, the range of application of P can be divided into four regions as follows:

P and so knowable	P but unknowable	Not P but not so knowable	Not P and so knowable
$R1_E$	$R2_E$	$R3_E$	$R4_E$

Let 'red' be P. Items in $R1_E$ are red and can be known to be so; those in $R2_E$ are also red but cannot be known to be red. Similarly, items in $R4_E$ are not red and can be known not to be, while those in $R3_E$ are not red but cannot be so known. Since the norm of assertion is knowledge (Williamson 1996), this means that to assert of an item x in $R2_E$–$R4_E$

that "It is red," as well as to assert of an item y in R_E1–R_E3 that "It is not red," is to violate the norms governing our linguistic practices, and so to make a kind of mistake. Of course, some of these mistakes are worse than others, since when x is in R_E3–R_E4, and y is in R_{E1}–R_{E2}, what one asserts is also false (in addition to being unknowable). However, all are violations.

This creates a prima facie difficulty. Together, epistemicism plus the view that knowledge is the norm of assertion direct us not to assertively predicate either a vague predicate P, or its negation, of any item in its unknowable range $R2_E$–$R3_E$. In many conversational settings this is unproblematic, since there is often no need to provide definite P-verdicts for particular borderline cases. In some settings, no judgment whatsoever is required, while in others a hedged judgment—e.g., ⌜That may be P⌝, ⌜That is probably P⌝, ⌜That is unlikely to be P⌝—will do. However, if there are situations that do require definite P-verdicts, such hedges will not serve. In these cases, the demand for an unequivocal verdict conflicts with the epistemic theory of vagueness plus the conception of knowledge as the norm of assertion. Since there appear to be legal contexts of this sort, they may provide good test cases for evaluating the dispute between the epistemicism and other theories of vagueness.

Vagueness in the Law

Since vagueness in the law comes in different forms with different consequences, some preliminary distinctions are needed to narrow our focus. Three domains of legal vagueness are particularly important: vagueness in the content of the law, vagueness in the allowable evidence and prescribed procedures used in reaching a legal verdict, and vagueness in the enforcement or effect of the laws. A good example of the latter is the enforcement of the 65-mile-per-hour speed limit on freeways in Southern California. Though the content of the law is precise, the practice of enforcing it includes a range of speeds of roughly 66–70 miles per hour, at which whether one is stopped is (under normal conditions) a matter of substantial discretion on the part of the highway patrol. The effect is to create a range of borderline cases in which it is vague whether, and to what extent, drivers are in legal jeopardy. This sort of vagueness—which has no effect on the content of the law—is valuable and necessary both to allow law-abiding citizens a reasonable margin for error in their attempts to comply with the law, and to allocate the resources of law enforcement and the judiciary reasonably and efficiently.

Vagueness in allowable evidence and prescribed procedures for reaching legally definitive verdicts is different. The standards "preponderance of evidence" and "guilt beyond a reasonable doubt" used in different types of cases are examples of vagueness encoded in legal language that govern the process of reaching a verdict. The exclusionary rule in the United States—which excludes evidence obtained from an illegal arrest, an unreasonable search, or a coercive interrogation (as well as secondary evidence obtained by routes not sufficiently distinguishable from primary evidence so obtained)—is an example of vagueness encoded in authoritative legal texts, including prominent Supreme Court opinions. This type of vagueness can be treated as a subcase of vagueness of content in which the legal provisions are those governing the conduct of trials and other legal proceedings.

I here assume that the content of a law or set of laws is (to a first approximation) that which the appropriate lawmakers assert, stipulate, or prescribe by adopting authoritative legal texts (against the interpretive background provided by already existing laws). I will refer to the contents of these authoritative speech acts as "assertive or stipulative contents," without here going into further detail about the relationship these contents bear to the semantic contents of the sentences used to make the assertions or stipulations (Soames 2009, 2011). Lawmakers are assumed to include legislators enacting statutes, administrative bodies authorized to issue binding rules implementing statutes, ratifiers of constitutions, voters on ballot initiatives, and judges issuing precedent-setting opinions. In the sphere of "private law," lawmakers may also include the parties of a contract, those responsible for legislation regulating the general law of contracts and judges, as well as other judicial bodies adjudicating disputes in this area.

Given this conception of legal content, we can discern two different ways in which vagueness in the content of the law may arise. First, and most obviously, a law may be vague because the authoritative text used by lawmakers to enact it contains vague terms. When this is so, the assertive or stipulative contents of the lawmakers' authoritative speech acts will typically be vague, and so will be ripe for interpretation. The need for such interpretation often arises in legal proceedings in which reaching a verdict requires making an unequivocal decision about the application or nonapplication of a vague predicate P, used to express the relevant law or laws, to a borderline case of P.

The second main way in which vagueness of legal content can arise is through the resolution of contradictions generated by different laws, or provisions of the same law, taken in conjunction with the facts of a particular case (Soames 2011). In these cases, contradictory legal conclusions are derivable from the facts of the case plus different but equally authoritative preexisting legal contents. This glut of legal results is unacceptable and so produces what is in effect a gap in the law that must be filled by modifying the content of the relevant laws. Often, if there is one way of filling this gap, there are many among which the relevant judicial authority must choose. Although the basis for this choice may vary from one legal system to the next, I here confine attention to systems governed by the following norm, RJ (role of the judiciary):

RJ:

Courts are not to legislate but to apply the laws adopted by legislative authorities to the facts of particular cases. When the content of the relevant body of laws plus the facts of a case fail to determine a unique legal outcome in situations in which one is required, the task of the judicial authority is (i) to discern the predominant legislative rationales of the lawmaking bodies in adopting the relevant laws and (ii) to fashion the minimal modification of existing legal content that removes the deficiency and allows a decision to be reached that maximizes the fulfillment of those legislative rationales.

Here, in speaking of the rationale of a law or other legal provision we do *not* mean the mix of causally efficacious factors that motivated lawmakers to adopt it, but the chief reasons publicly offered to justify and explain it (Soames 2011, sec. 7). Though these reasons are often discernible, what counts as "the predominant legislative rationale," "a minimal modification removing the deficiency," and "a modification that maximizes the fulfillment of the discernible legislative rationales" are vague, and so subject to interpretation. Understood in this way, the judicial resolution of legal conflicts can be seen as a subcase of the precisification of vague language, even though the language in question is not limited to that of the authoritative texts, or to legal language in general.

Vagueness in the Law: The Partial-Definition/ Context-Sensitive Model

In the simplest case, vagueness in the content of the law arises when lawmakers employ a vague term in adopting an authoritative legal text. Within the theory of vagueness under consideration, lawmakers may be understood as using the term either with its default content (provided by the rules governing its use in the common language) or with a partially precisified content. In the former case, the application of the law to items for which the term is undefined is left indeterminate, and subject to future precisification by other authorities. In the latter case, lawmakers narrow the range of future interpretation by stipulating in advance how the law is to be applied to certain borderline cases. For example, lawmakers adopting H.L.A. Hart's (1958) ordinance banning "vehicles" from the parks might respond to lobbying on behalf of the disabled by adding a clause "for the purpose of this ordinance, wheelchairs for the disabled, whether motorized or not, shall *not* count as vehicles." In such cases, the extension of ⌜legally P⌝ is a partial precisification of the ordinary extension of P.

What should be done in interpreting a legal text when it emerges that the verdict in a case crucially depends on whether P applies to a given item for which P, as used by the lawmakers, is undefined? In some special cases, it may be possible to send the matter back to them for clarification and precisification. In others, a rule of lenity may dictate favorable verdicts for defendants in situations in which no clear violation is established—where one form of exonerating unclarity involves indeterminacy in the law. But in many cases neither of these exceptions applies, with the result that judges, or other authorities, are expected to fill gaps by precisifying the governing legal provision in a manner not determined, and sometimes not even envisioned, by the lawmaking body. When the relevant judicial decision sets a legal precedent for similar cases, the result is not just an explication, clarification, or application of existing law but an (authorized) modification of the law. Whereas prior to the decision, the law was undefined for, and so silent about, a certain class of cases, it now declares them to have one status or another.

This can be made clearer by considering again the range of a vague predicate P:

P	?	Undefined	?	Not P
$R1_{PDP}$	$R2_{PDP}$	$R3_{PDP}$	$R4_{PDP}$	$R5_{PDP}$

When the item x on which the outcome of the legal case depends is in $R2_{PDP}$ or $R4_{PDP}$, and there are no other complicating factors, it is relatively easy to specify what the outcome should be. If x is in $R2_{PDP}$, and the judge assigns x a certain legal status L+ on the basis of ruling that x counts as an instance of P, it will be unsettled whether x was already in the extension of P or whether the judge has exercised the minimum possible discretion. By contrast, if the judge rules that x does not count as an instance of P, and thereby assigns x legal status L−, it will be unsettled whether the judge has violated the existing law or whether maximal discretion has been exercised. When there are no extraneous issues pulling in either direction, and including x in the extension of P complies with the rationale of the law, such a decision is clearly called for. This will result in the minimum possible change in the law—a class of things for which it had been legally unsettled whether they were L+ or indeterminate in status have now become determinately L+. Analogous results hold when x is in $R4_{PDP}$ and is assigned the legal status L−.

When x is in $R3_{PDP}$ the situation is different. Since P is undefined for x, there is a gap in the content of existing law rendering it silent about the status of x. Since the resolution of the case depends on giving it a status, the judge has no alternative but to make new law. Here, our assumption RJ about the role of the judiciary plays an important role. Returning to Hart's no-vehicles-in-the-park example, we may imagine two scenarios providing the rationale for the city ordinance. In scenario 1, the ordinance was passed to preserve the traditional peace and quiet of the park, which had recently been disturbed by cars, motorcycles, and motor scooters, and also to reduce air pollution in the city, which had grown worse in recent years. In scenario 2, the ordinance was a response to overcrowding in the park resulting in a number of accidents involving cars, motorcycles, and bicycles, all competing for limited space with pedestrians crowding paths, walkways, and roads in the park. Although the content of the law passed in these two scenarios is the same—in both cases simply banning vehicles from the park—the implications for future precisification are different. Against the background of scenario 1, judgments that, for purposes of the ordinance, bicycles, skateboards, rollerblades, tricycles, and little red wagons are not vehicles, are correct. Against the background of scenario 2, at least some of these judgments are not. This difference has nothing to do with which borderline cases of being a vehicle are more like genuine, known vehicles, and which are more like known nonvehicles. Since, according to the view of vagueness under consideration, there simply is no fact of the matter about whether these borderline cases (in $R3_{PDP}$) are, or are not, vehicles, the court's inquiry must be directed toward other matters—which in a legal system featuring RJ is the rationale for the legislation. Once such a precedent-setting judicial decision has been reached, the content of the law will change, bringing its content more fully into line with its original rationale.

It is here that we find the value of vagueness in the contents of laws. In a legal system in which the judiciary operates under a reasonable approximation of RJ, and in which vagueness is understood along the lines of the partial-definition/context-sensitivity model, lawmakers framing legislation with the goal of achieving certain social benefits while avoiding other undesirable results may sometimes rationally prefer a vague law to a more precise one. This will occur when all or most of the following conditions are fulfilled: (i) the vague formulation of the law assigns the clear, nonborderline cases of the term the legal status desired by most lawmakers; (ii) the variety of borderline cases of the term is wide, making them hard to exhaustively anticipate; (iii) the lawmaking body is either divided about the borderline cases or ignorant of the likely consequences of treating some such cases one way rather than another, and so is uncertain about what legal status they should have; and (iv) the lawmakers recognize the value of incremental, case-by-case precisification of the law resulting from adjudication of borderline cases aimed at furthering the law's rationale, in light of the full factual backgrounds uncovered in judicial proceedings. In short, legislation sometimes involves broad agreement about central objectives, combined with disagreement or ignorance at the margins, plus a confidence that those who implement the law and adjudicate disputes arising from it will, through acquaintance with the facts of particular cases and the benefit of an incremental procedure, be in a better position than the lawmakers to further the law's rationale. In such cases, vague language serves the valuable function of delegating rule-making authority to administrative bodies issuing rules implementing the law, to agencies responsible for enforcing the law, and to courts adjudicating disputes arising from it.

Here, it is important to distinguish the value of formulating legal rules with borderline cases—in the sense understood by the present philosophical theory of vagueness—from other values served by the use of words that happen to be vague. It is noteworthy that when vagueness is easily resolvable—e.g., by defining 'adult' and 'child' in terms of precise ages for particular purposes—the law very often does so, with the result that the vague terms one regularly finds in the law—like 'neglect', 'well-being', 'reasonable', 'fair', 'unnecessary', and 'all deliberate speed'—are often what Timothy Endicott calls "extravagantly vague" (Endicott 2005, 6–7). Unfortunately, this is a bit of a misnomer. Although these terms are usefully vague, their exceptional utility in the law comes from the combination of their vagueness with other semantic features related to, but distinct from, vagueness. It is not that the ratios of borderline to nonborderline cases for Endicott's "extravagantly vague" terms are always so much greater than the ratios of such cases for more garden variety cases of vagueness; the crucial fact is that his terms are, for the most part, highly general, multidimensional, and resistant to specific codification—as well as being vague.

Consider, for example, the use of 'neglect' in laws regulating the responsibility of parents and other adults for children in their care. In addition to being quite general, this term is multidimensional in the sense that its application is determined by an open-ended combination of factors that includes providing for the satisfaction of children's nutritional, medical, educational, social, and emotional needs, in addition to their safety. As a result, judgments about whether particular patterns of behavior constitute neglect tend to be holistic, with lows in one dimension capable of being partially offset by highs in others. Consequently, the variation in behavior exhibited by the range of obvious, nonborderline cases of neglect is enormous and incapable of exhaustive legislative enumeration. Even clear (nonborderline) cases of neglect may sometimes bring together surprising clusters of facts which, though unanticipated by legislators, are obvious when brought to light. This situation provides a reason for lawmakers to delegate authority for making judgments about individual behaviors to those best able to gather and evaluate the relevant facts—e.g., social agencies and the courts. This delegation is accomplished by using a general, multidimensional term which, in the nature of things, is also vague. However the value of its vagueness—in the sense of susceptibility to borderline cases—is analytically distinguishable from the value of its generality and multidimensionality.

Vagueness in the Law: The Epistemic Model

Earlier I mentioned a prima facie difficulty for epistemicism, which characterizes assertive predications of a vague predicate P, or its negation, of any item in its unknowable range $R2_E$–$R3_E$ as violations of the norm of assertion:

P and so knowable	P but not knowable	Not P but not so knowable	Not P and so knowable
$R1_E$	$R2_E$	$R3_E$	$R4_E$

Since adjudicating legal disputes sometimes requires authorities to make such predications, one may wonder whether the epistemicist can accommodate the use of vague legal language. The answer, I think, is that the epistemicist can do so, up to a point, but only at the cost of underestimating the value of vagueness in the law.

Although knowledge is the (default) norm of assertion, not all assertions are held to the same standard. We all recognize circumstances—such as planning future actions in light of well-founded assumptions about future contingencies—in which assertions are acceptable even though that which is asserted isn't known. Of course, not anything goes, even in these cases. When definite (nonconditional) plans must be made in the face of uncertainty, the assertions that occur as parts of those plans are still expected to be justified by a preponderance of evidence. This may not be knowledge, but in some cases, it is close enough.

With this in mind, consider a case the outcome of which depends on applying a vague predicate P to an item x in the extension of P that is barely inside its unknowability range (by virtue of differing very little from items known to be in P's extension, while differing much more from those known not to be in it). This is similar to the case for the previous theory of vagueness in which x is in region $R2_{PDP}$, rendering it unsettled whether P determinately applies to, or is undefined for, x. There, the correct decision was to declare that P applies to x, leaving it unsettled whether the court exercised minimal discretion or no discretion at all. According to the theory in question, a precedent-setting decision to this effect changes the content of the law so that a class of things including x comes to have a determinate legal status which, prior to the decision, it would not have been correct to claim it had. For epistemicism, the outcome of the case is the same, though both the justification and the effect of the decision on the content of the law are different.

Here, the epistemicist may make four reasonable assumptions: (i) for many vague predicates P, elements in the unknowability range for P and its negation ($R2_E$–$R3_E$) can be partially ordered along dimensions that determine the applicability of P (e.g., age for 'young'/'not young', income and assets for 'rich'/'not rich'); (ii) knowledge obtained about where such an item x falls within these dimensions can provide evidence for the claim that P applies, or does not apply, to x; (iii) for many such P, evidence that an item x in R2 is closer along these dimensions to things that are known to be in P's extension than to things known not to be in the extension of P provides justification for the claim that x is in the extension of P; and (iv) a corresponding result holds for evidence that such an item is closer to things known not to be in the extension of P than to any item known to be in it. One need not assume that all vague predicates satisfy these conditions to a robust degree, but surely many do.

When this is so, a legal case that turns on whether P applies to an item x in $R2_E$ that is barely inside its unknowability range should ideally be decided by assertively predicating P of x. After all, judicial decisions should be made on the basis of the best available evidence. If conditions (i)–(iv) are satisfied, and the court is in possession of all relevant evidence, the application of P to x in this case will be mandated. Though no decision made by the judge in this case can (according to the epistemicist) be *known to conform*, or *known not to conform*, to the existing law, fidelity to the law requires that x be declared to be in the extension of P, since this decision is supported by a preponderance of evidence. If the decision is precedent setting, *the content of the law*—expressed by ⌈Items that are P have legal status L+, while items that are not P have legal status L−⌉—will not change, even though *the effect of the law* will. Something the legal status of which was before unknown will come, with the precedent, to be known. The vague predicate P at the center of this change will not have changed its extension, even though what counts as sufficient, for legal purposes, for being included in its extension will have changed.

Although the disposition of this case is the same for the epistemicist as it was for the theorist who views vagueness as a matter of partial definition and context sensitivity, the different justifications provided by the two theories generalize differently. The key cases are ones in which the partial-definition theory places the crucial item x in the genuine undefined region $R3_{PDP}$ of the range of P, whereas epistemicism places x well into the unknowable section $R2_E$ of the extension of P (closer to $R3_E$ than to $R1_E$). Recall the two scenarios of this sort extending Hart's no-vehicles-in-the-park example. On the nonepistemicist account of vagueness, two different results were reached for some borderline cases of vehicles (e.g., skateboards), based on different rationales the ordinance was intended to serve in the two scenarios. Since the content of the law (as conceived by the nonepistemicist) makes no claim whatsoever about the legal status of x, fidelity to the law requires that the court make its decision on the basis of the rationale the law was intended to serve. Hence, the different results in the two scenarios.

Such results cannot be reproduced by the epistemicist for those items x in the unknowability range $R2_E$ of P that are more like things *known to be in the extension of P* than they are like things *known not to be in P's extension*, and hence for which there is discernible (though not overwhelming) evidence supporting the claim that x is in P's extension. In these cases, fidelity to the law requires treating x as being in the extension of P (which it in fact is). Except in cases in which such a decision would produce an absurd result that clearly subverts the law's rationale, this decision is mandated by the norm of adjudication RJ. Things may be otherwise in cases in which the evidence is as weak for the claim that x is in the extension of P as it is for the claim that it isn't—as it may be when x is just barely inside the unknowable boundary line separating things in the extension of P from those not in its extension. In such cases, the epistemicist might reasonably argue that fidelity to the law requires a decision based on the law's rationale. However, on the plausible assumption that such cases constitute a proper subset of the cases for which the partial-definition approach mandates decisions based on the rationale, rather than the content, of the law, we have found a significant difference in the jurisprudential consequences generated by the two philosophical theories of vagueness.

This difference has a material effect on the values the two theories accord to vagueness in the law. As we saw earlier, lawmakers who have achieved general agreement on the rationale for a vaguely worded statute, and its treatment of clear, nonborderline cases, may be ignorant of, or unable to achieve consensus on, how best to advance that rationale in many actual and hypothetical borderline cases of the statute's vague terms. If vagueness is understood as partial definition plus context sensitivity, the lawmakers will realize that their vaguely formulated statute is noncommittal about how these items are to be treated. If they are also confident that later administrative or judicial authorities will be guided by fidelity to the law, they will realize that future adjudication of borderline cases will be aimed at how best to advance the rationale that they, the lawmakers, have agreed on. When it is reasonable to expect these authorities to possess important information about how to achieve this goal, which the lawmakers lack, it will be rational for the latter to employ vague language as a way of delegating authority over difficult cases to those in the best epistemic position to advance their goal. Hence, the value of vagueness in the law.

Epistemicism cannot provide a comparable story. The epistemicist will tell you, correctly, that judicial and administrative authorities downstream from the enactment of a statute have no special expertise that the lawmakers lack about where the extension of a (totally defined) vague predicate ends and that of its negation begins. Moreover, since the content of the statute already determines the legal status of every borderline case, the first duty of the downstream authorities is to assign the borderline cases that come before them the legal status those items most probably already have—in situations in which judgments about such relative probabilities can reasonably be made. There may, of course, be items for which such judgments cannot be made, in which case fidelity to the rationale of the statute may then become the basis for adjudication. For this small subset of cases, the two philosophical theories of vagueness can agree on the consequences of legal vagueness, and the basis for adjudicating cases involving it. What the epistemicist cannot do is extend this line of reasoning to the full range of borderline cases for which the proponent of partial definition finds utility in vague legal language. Whereas the latter can properly declare minibikes, skateboards, and children's gravity- or pedal-powered soapbox car racers to be *nonvehicles permitted in the park* in scenario 1 of our extension of Hart's example, while properly declaring them to be *vehicles prohibited from the park* in scenario 2, the epistemicist cannot justify arriving at different verdicts in the two scenarios. More precisely, the epistemicist can't do so on the plausible assumption that he or she can't reasonably deny that some at least of the examples just mentioned are *more probably vehicles than not* (given the epistemicist view that each really is a vehicle, or really isn't). In this way, the epistemicist view of what vagueness really is prevents one from recognizing much of the value that vagueness in the law really has.

IDEALIZATION

So far, I have tried to show two things: First, that if legal actors in an idealized system implicitly knew both that vagueness was what the partial-definition/context-sensitivity model says it is, and that adjudication and implementation of the laws were guided by something like the norm RJ of fidelity to the law, then they would correctly and rationally anticipate jurisprudential consequences of the legal use of vague terms of the sort discussed and rightly assign a high utility to the use of certain vague language in the law. Second, that if they implicitly knew that vagueness was merely epistemic while also knowing that adjudication and implementation were guided by RJ, then they would correctly and rationally anticipate different jurisprudential consequences (discussed in the previous section) and rightly assign a much lower utility to the use of vague language in the law. To these idealized observations I now explicitly add a further, more empirically based suggestion—namely, that the actual jurisprudential consequences of legal vagueness, plus their actual and perceived utility, fit the partial-definition model better than they do the epistemic model.

There are several ways of reacting to these claims. A committed epistemicist could accept all of them, except for the final suggestion about the actual value of legally vague language in systems like ours (as well as the suggestions about which adjudications of certain cases are genuinely mandated). Such a theorist would argue from the presumed correctness of epistemic vagueness to revisionary claims about the function, or lack thereof, of vagueness in the law. The point is not hypothetical; an extreme version of this position is taken in Sorenson (2001). A different sort of legal theorist might agree with me about the value of vagueness in our law while attempting to reconcile epistemicism with this evaluation by challenging the claim that RJ is a governing norm for judicial interpretation. The idea would be to authorize judicial and administrative attempts to further what these authorities take to be the rationale of a law, even in cases in which the weight of evidence indicates that this would result in a revision of its content (which could otherwise be preserved without absurdity). The challenge for this interpretive strategy is to articulate a principled basis for allowing this freedom in cases of vagueness without loosening the constraints on interpretation too far, and so getting undesirable results in cases in which vagueness is not the central issue.

By contrast, one can imagine a committed proponent of partial definition and context sensitivity who agrees with me about the nature of vagueness, but whose legal scholarship leads him or her to suspect (a) that relevant actors in our actual legal system *fail* to implicitly recognize that vagueness is what we both take it to be and (b) that the principles governing adjudication and implementation of the law, as practiced in our legal system, *do not* require very much by way of fidelity to its preexisting content, and are not even approximations of RJ. For this theorist, the job is first to educate our legal actors about what vagueness really is, and then, depending on his or her normative view about the proper relation between legislation and adjudication, to offer a normative argument that fidelity to the law, in the sense of RJ, is what *should* govern adjudication and implementation.

The main lesson I draw from the discussion in the previous sections is different from, and more straightforward than, any of these. It is based on four suppositions: (i) that relevant actors in our legal system should be credited with implicitly knowing, or at least acting as if they know, what vagueness is; (ii) that legal content is, to a first approximation, the assertive or stipulative content of lawmakers' adoption of authoritative legal texts (against the background of already existing law); (iii) that judicial adjudication and administrative implementation of our laws are, and should be, guided by a principle of fidelity to the law that assigns priority to maintaining existing legal content when possible while mandating decisions that further legislative rationale when cases cannot rationally be decided on the basis of existing content alone; and (iv) that vague language in our law really does have, and is implicitly perceived to have, roughly the value assigned to it by the partial-definition/context-sensitive model. Consequently, I conclude that whereas the genuine value of vagueness in the law is naturally explainable on the theory that treats vagueness as a matter of partial definition and context sensitivity, it cannot adequately be accommodated by the epistemic theory of vagueness. If I am right, then the special role played by vague language in the law provides us with an argument for one philosophical theory of what vagueness is, and against another.

REFERENCES

Endicott, T. 2001. *Vagueness in Law.* Oxford: Oxford University Press.
———. 2005. "The Value of Vagueness," in V. K. Bhatia, J. Engberg, M. Gotti, and D. Heller, eds., *Vagueness in Normative Texts*, 27–48. Bern: Peter Lang.

Fara, D. G. 2000. "Shifting Sands: An Interest-Relative Theory of Vagueness." *Philosophical Topics* 28:48–81.

Fine, K. 1975. "Vagueness, Truth, and Logic." *Synthese* 30:265–300.

Hart, H.L.A. 1958. "Positivism and the Separation of Law and Morals." *Harvard Law Review* 71:593–629.

Shapiro, S. 2006. *Vagueness in Context.* Oxford: Oxford University Press.

Soames, S. 1999. *Understanding Truth.* New York: Oxford University Press.

———. 2003. "Higher Order Vagueness for Partially Defined Predicates," in J. C. Beall (ed.), *Liars and Heaps: New Essays on Paradox.* Oxford: Clarendon Press; reprinted in S. Soames, *Philosophical Essays*, vol. 2. Princeton, NJ: Princeton University Press, 2009.

———. 2009. "Interpreting Legal Texts: What Is, and What Is Not, Special about the Law, in S. Soames, *Philosophical Essays*, vol. 1. Princeton, NJ: Princeton University Press.

———. 2010. "The Possibility of Partial Definition," in R. Dietz and S. Moruzzi, eds., *Cuts & Clouds: Vagueness, Its Nature, and Its Logic.* Oxford: Oxford University Press; reprinted in S. Soames, *Philosophical Essays*, vol. 2. Princeton, NJ: Princeton University Press.

———. 2011. "What Vagueness and Inconsistency Tell Us about Interpretation," in A. Marmor and S. Soames (eds.), *The Philosophical Foundations of Language in the Law*, 31–57. Oxford: Oxford University Press.

Sorenson, R. 2001. "Vagueness Has No Function in Law." *Legal Theory* 7:387–416.

Tappendon, J. 1993. "The Liar and Sorites Paradoxes: Toward a Unified Treatment." *Journal of Philosophy* 90:551–77.

Williamson, T. 1994. *Vagueness*, London: Routledge.

———. 1996. "Knowing and Asserting." *Philosophical Review* 105:489–523.

14

Toward a Theory of Legal Interpretation

By "legal interpretation" I mean the legally authoritative resolution of questions about what the content of the law is in its application to particular cases. It is the interpretation of legal texts *by legally authoritative actors*. One aspect of legal interpretation is epistemic, and one is constitutive. The epistemic task is to ascertain the content of laws resulting from previous actions of other legally authoritative sources. The constitutive task is to render an authoritative judgment that itself plays a role in determining what the content of the law is. Sometimes this judgment changes the content of the laws, or legal provisions, that were the focus of the epistemic task.

The content of a law is (to a first approximation) that which the appropriate lawmakers assert, stipulate, or otherwise prescribe by adopting an authoritative text. Just as the assertive content of an ordinary conversation cannot, in general, be identified with the meanings of the sentences used there, or with conversationalists' goals in saying what they do, so the assertive or stipulative content of a legal text cannot, in general, be identified with the ordinary or technical meanings of the sentences in the text, or with the policy goals motivating lawmakers to approve it. Nor can the content of the text be identified with any normative improvement of what they asserted or stipulated, or with any idealization of their speech act, such as what they would have stipulated had they known all relevant facts. The content of a legal text is determined in essentially the same way as are the contents of other texts or linguistic performances, save for complications resulting from the fact that the agent of a legislative speech act is often not a single language user but a group, the purpose of the speech act is not usually to contribute to the cooperative exchange of information but to generate behavior-modifying stipulations, and the resulting stipulated contents are required to fit smoothly into a complex set of preexisting stipulations generated by other actors at other times.

Lawmakers, in my broad sense, are those whose official actions and linguistic performances are constitutive of the contents of the law. They include legislators enacting statutes, administrative bodies issuing rules implementing them, ratifiers of constitutions, voters on ballot initiatives, and judges issuing precedent-setting opinions. In the sphere of "private law," lawmakers include the parties to a contract, those responsible for legislation regulating the law of contracts, and judges, as well as other official bodies adjudicating contractual disputes. Crucially, legally authoritative interpreters of the law are themselves lawmakers, whose actions are in turn subject to further interpretation.

When legal interpretation is understood as the interpretation of legal texts by legally authoritative actors, it naturally follows that such interpretation is itself law governed. The governing legal rules determine the responsibilities of officials who interpret legal texts and make authoritative decisions about them. These rules may or may not be codified in statutes, or expressed in written constitutions. Whether or not they are so codified, they are binding social conventions concerning the duties of specific legal actors. Since the contents of these duties may vary from one legal system to the next, what constitutes *correct* legal interpretation may vary from system to system.

What is the content of the general legal rule governing interpretation and adjudication? Here is my simple take on the content of the legal norm:

RJ:

Courts are not to legislate but are to apply the laws adopted by legislative authorities to the facts of particular cases. When the content of the laws fails to provide reliable guidance in determining a unique acceptable legal outcome—either because it leads to inconsistent outcomes, or because it fails to lead to any outcome, or because it leads to a an outcome that is both patently absurd and unforeseen (in cases in which a single, definite, and otherwise acceptable outcome is needed)—the task of the judicial authority is (i) to discern the predominant legislative rationales of the lawmaking bodies in adopting the laws or legal provisions and (ii) to fashion the minimal modification of existing legal content that removes the deficiency and allows a decision to be reached while maximizing the fulfillment of the discernible legislative rationales of the relevant laws or legal provisions.

Several distinct questions can be asked about this contentious formulation. First:

Q1. Is this, or some such, rule, in fact, part of our legal system (or some other system)?

This is a broadly sociological question, to be discovered by empirical investigation of the accepted governing norms of a given legal culture.

I believe that the rule is a reasonable approximation of the law governing the legal interpretation and adjudication in some courts in the United States. But I don't think I am *obviously* right about this. The situation is muddied by the fact that the norms governing legal interpretation and adjudication continue to be fought over. With regard to the Supreme Court of the United States, as well as those of individual states, there has been, and continues to be, movement toward a more expansive and overtly legislative role for the Court, not unlike that of the British House of Lords of the late nineteenth century.[1] Whether or not I am right that something like the more conservative governing norm is, though under challenge, still more or less in place is not a philosophical or a normative question but an empirical one.

The second question one can ask about the governing norm I have formulated is the following:

> Q2. Should our legal system (or some other designated system) incorporate it?

This is a moral and political question. It shouldn't be worth saying, though I am afraid it is, that for some legal systems and some candidates for governing legal norms, the answer to Q1 may be, yes, it is part of the legal system, even if the answer to Q2 is, no, it shouldn't be. In point of fact, I believe that the rule I have sketched is a reasonably good one that not only does, but should, govern the practice of judicial interpretation in many US courts. That is a matter of political philosophy.

The question I am most interested in today differs from the previous two:

> Q3. What precisely does my purported legal rule RJ require of interpreters, how much latitude does it allow them, and what factors are they to take into account in their interpretations?

To answer this question, one must distinguish it from Q4:

> Q4. What is the morally right thing for judges and other legal interpreters to do in particular cases; what factors is it morally right for them to take into account?

Q4 is a nakedly moral question, whereas Q3 is not. Answers to Q3 specify the *delegated powers and responsibilities* of certain legal actors. Whether these actors should always fulfill those responsibilities, as opposed to violating the legal rules governing them in the name of a higher good, is an independent moral question, which should not

---

[1] Thomas A. Bishop, *The Death and Reincarnation of Plain Meaning in Connecticut: A Case Study*, 41 *Conn. L. Rev.* (2009): 825, 833–42.

be prejudged. Though it may be indelicate to say so, there is nothing but intellectual confusion to be gained by denying the possibility that reaching a morally correct decision may *sometimes* require the members of a court of last resort to overstep not only their *actual* legal authority but also their *legitimate* legal authority in a system in which the legal norms governing their actions are politically and morally optimal.

Finally, I distinguish all the questions so far raised from the "realist" question:

> Q5. What do judges and other legal interpreters actually do? What putative legal norms, if any, do they follow in their interpretations?

For me, the chief interest in answering this question lies in the light that doing so sheds on the other questions—particularly the first, empirical, question about the content of the legal norms governing interpretation. To the extent that judges routinely disregard a legal norm governing their actions, without being rebuked, overturned, disregarded, or ignored by other legal and political actors, their behavior erodes the norm and may lead to its replacement by another norm. This is especially evident for a court of last resort, like the United States Supreme Court. There has been, I think, a trend in the jurisprudence of this court in the past 60 years that has put the norm of legal interpretation I have articulated under stress. For example, it is arguable that much of the jurisprudence involving the Equal Protection Clause of the Fourteenth Amendment to the Constitution,[2] substantive due process,[3] the Civil Rights Act of 1964,[4] and the alleged general right of privacy "emanating" from "penumbras" of limited privacy rights mentioned in different constitutional amendments[5]—does not easily fit into the traditional model of politically impartial interpretation of the laws. If, in the end, it doesn't fit, then we face a difficult dilemma: we must either rethink much of this jurisprudence and replace some of it, or rethink the traditional understanding of the relationship between democratic legislation and judicial interpretation and replace it with a governing norm that elevates the judiciary and legitimizes its expanded political role.

Since resolving such a dilemma is a daunting task, we do well, before undertaking it, to investigate more closely what precisely the traditional norm of legal interpretation demands and allows. With this in mind, I return to Q3, and ask, What factors go into interpretation? and

---

[2] U.S. Const. amend. XIV.

[3] See, e.g., *Beauharnais v. Illinois*, 343 U.S. 250, 277 (1952) (Reed, J., concurring).

[4] Civil Rights Act of 1964, Pub. L. No. 88–352, 78 Stat. 241 (1964).

[5] See *Griswold v. Connecticut*, 381 U.S. 479, 484 (1965).

What latitude do legal interpreters have? As I indicated earlier, interpretation has both an epistemic and a constitutive side. The epistemic task is to determine the content of the existing law bearing on the case at hand. The simple rule for doing this is originalist, even textualist, in nature – but not the form of textualism most commonly espoused. Existing legal content is, I think, neither *original intent* nor *original meaning*; rather, it is the content originally asserted or stipulated by lawmakers in adopting the text. Contemporary philosophy of language and theoretical linguistics distinguish *the meaning of a sentence S* from its *semantic content relative to a context*, both of which are distinguished from (the content of) *what is said, asserted, or stipulated by an utterance of S*. Although in some cases the three types of content coincide, while in still others the final two do, there are many cases in which the third differs from the other two.[6] In every legal case in which there is such a difference, it is the third—asserted or stipulated—content that is required by any defensible form of textualism. Failure to recognize this— owing to confusing the three types of content with one another—has led to errors in the law itself, as well as to theoretical errors about the relation of the law to its authoritative sources.[7]

The tendency to confuse the meaning of a sentence in a text with what the sentence was used to say or stipulate is all too common. The result confuses two different interpretive principles—fidelity to the meaning of the legislature's statutory language versus fidelity to what the legislature asserted or stipulated in using that language. This confusion is evident in Justice Antonin Scalia's otherwise brilliant dissent in *Smith v. United States*, concerning the question whether an attempt to trade a gun for drugs constituted *a use of a firearm in a drug trafficking crime*.[8] Dissenting from the majority ruling that it did, Scalia argues:

> In the search for statutory meaning, we give nontechnical words and phrases their ordinary meaning. . . . To use an instrumentality ordinarily means to use it for its intended purpose. *When someone asks, "Do you use a cane?" he is not inquiring whether you have your grandfather's silver-handled walking stick on display in the hall; he wants to know whether you walk with a cane.* Similarly, to speak of "using a firearm" is to speak of using it for its distinctive

---

[6] See, e.g., Scott Soames, *Philosophy of Language* (Princeton, NJ: Princeton University Press, 2010), 145–73; Scott Soames, *Philosophical Essays*, vol. 1 (Princeton, NJ: Princeton University Press, 2009), 278–97.

[7] See, generally, Stephen Neale, "On Location," in *Situating Semantics: Essays on the Philosophy of John Perry*, ed. Michael O'Rourke and Corey Washington (Cambridge, MA: MIT Press, 2007), 251; Soames, *Philosophical Essays*, *supra* note 6 at 403.

[8] 508 U.S. 223, 241 (1993).

purpose, i.e., as a weapon. To be sure, "one can use a firearm in a number of ways," . . . including as an article of exchange . . . but that is not the *ordinary meaning* of 'using' the one or the other.[9] (my emphasis)

The Court asserts that the "significant flaw" in this argument is that "to say that the ordinary meaning of 'uses a firearm' includes using a firearm as a weapon" is quite different from saying that the ordinary meaning "also excludes any other use." The two are indeed different—but it is precisely the latter that I assert to be true. The ordinary meaning of "uses a firearm" does not include using it as an article of commerce. *I think it perfectly obvious, for example, that the objective falsity requirement for a perjury conviction would not be satisfied if a witness answered "no" to a prosecutor's inquiry whether he had ever "used a firearm," even though he had once sold his grandfather's Enfield rifle to a collector.*[10]

Here, Scalia is strikingly correct both about *what question is asked* by a use of the interrogative sentence "Do you use a cane?" in the situation imagined, and about *what is asserted* when an agent answers "no" to the prosecutor's query "Have you ever used a firearm?" in his second scenario. The proper lesson to be drawn from these scenarios for *Smith v. United States* is that *what the legislature asserted or stipulated* in using the sentence "Whoever . . . uses or carries a firearm [in the course of committing a crime of violence or drug trafficking], shall, in addition to the punishment provided for such [a] crime . . . be sentenced to imprisonment for five years,"[11] was that the *use of a firearm as a weapon* (or carrying it for that purpose) is subject to additional punishment. This is what Scalia would have concluded, had not he, and the rest of the Court, confused the meaning of that sentence with what it was used to assert.

Unfortunately, owing to this confusion, he formulated his conclusion differently, maintaining that the *ordinary meaning* of "anyone who uses a firearm" pertains only to the uses of a firearm as a weapon.[12] This is not so, as the majority correctly points out:

When a word is not defined by statute, we normally construe it in accord with *its ordinary or natural meaning.* . . . Surely petitioner's treatment of his [gun] *can be described* as "use" [of the firearm] *within the everyday meaning of that term.* Petitioner "used"

[9] *Id.* at 242.
[10] *Id.* at 242 n.1, my emphasis.
[11] 18 U.S.C. § 924(c)(1) (2006).
[12] 508 U.S. at 242 n.1.

his [gun] in an attempt to obtain drugs by offering to trade it for cocaine."[13] (my emphasis)

Of course, Smith's action *can be described* that way, and, of course, the statute employs the phrase 'uses a firearm' with its ordinary literal meaning. The reason the action *can be so described* is that the ordinary meaning of 'uses an N' is *silent* about how the thing in question is used. Consequently, when the phrase occurs in a sentence, the resulting assertion must be *completed*, either by the content provided by an explicit qualifying phrase—such as 'as a weapon' or 'as an item of barter'—or (when no such qualifying phrase is present) by content that is presupposed by those using the sentence to assert or stipulate something. Since the latter option was employed by Congress, the job of the Court was to infer *what Congress asserted* from the incomplete semantic content provided by the statutory language. What textualists should be seeking is fidelity to what the legislature asserts or stipulates, not what the sentences used to do so mean.

The focus on meaning rather than assertion or stipulation has also led textualists to wrongly dismiss the role of legislative intent in legal interpretation. Taking the contents of legal texts to be "their ordinary meanings," Scalia concludes that inquiries into legislative history to discover the *intent* of the lawmakers are irrelevant. Worse, he worries that formidable epistemic problems often make it impossible to identify true legislative intent, leaving jurists free to read their own policy preferences into texts under the pretext of reading the legislative mind. Note how Scalia leans on the contrast between *what is said* versus *what one means or intends to say* to support this extreme view about irrelevance of legislative intent in these two passages from *A Matter of Interpretation*.

> You will find it frequently said ... that the judge's objective in interpreting a statute is to give effect to "the intent of the legislature." Unfortunately, it [this principle] does not square with some of the (few) generally accepted concrete rules of statutory construction. One is the rule that when the text of the statute is clear, that is the end of the matter. Why should that be so, if what the legislature *intended*, rather than what it *said*, is the object of our inquiry. . . . [14]

> When you are told to decide, not on the basis of what the legislature said, but on the basis of what it *meant* ... your best shot

---

[13] *Id.* at 228.

[14] Antonin Scalia, *A Matter of Interpretation: Federal Courts and the Law*, ed. Amy Gutmann (Princeton, NJ: Princeton University Press, 1998), 16.

at figuring out what the legislature meant is to ask yourself what a wise and intelligent person *should* have meant; and that will surely bring you to the conclusion that the law means what you think it *ought* to mean. . . . [15]

While Scalia is right to give primacy to *what was said* in adopting a given legal text over what *further* legislative goals were intended by legislators, this quite defensible priority must not be confused with giving the *linguistic meanings* of the sentences they used priority over *all* their intentions, and it cannot be used to justify the claim that when *linguistic meaning* is clear, all appeal to intentions is to be ruled out.

If Scalia weren't so prone to confusing what is said with the meanings of the sentences used to say it, he would see this. Since what language users *intend* to say, assert, or stipulate is a crucial factor, along with the linguistic meanings of the words they use, in constituting what they *do* say, assert, or stipulate, the intentions of lawmakers are directly relevant to the contents of the laws they enact. In many cases, these constitutive intentions are completely clear, as are the relevant assertive or stipulative contents. When this is so, Scalia is right in maintaining that no further appeal to intent is needed—provided that what is said is not crucially vague, that what is said together with the facts of the case is not inconsistent with other equally authoritative laws or legal provisions, and that applying the asserted or stipulative content of the text enacted does not lead to transparently absurd and unforeseen results that fail to advance, or even subvert, the lawmakers' legislative rationale. Subject to these provisos, what is said is primary, even though certain intentions are constitutive of it, and even though other intentions may be brought into play by different sorts of conflict.

For these reasons, we cannot accept Scalia's dismissal of intentions at face value. Nevertheless, his worries have a point. They are, I believe, grounded in a proper understanding of the rule that courts are to apply the law enacted by legislative authorities to the facts of particular cases, avoiding constitutive changes in the content of the law except in special, designated circumstances. Although he mischaracterizes the rule in certain ways, he is right both in judging that some such rule is operative in our legal system and in taking it to be normatively desirable. This makes it all the more important to correct his errors, in order to elucidate more clearly what is really going on. Since legislative intent of two different sorts play at least two distinguishable roles in legal interpretation, it is worthwhile to begin with a fundamental distinction.

[15] *Id.* at 18.

The most basic distinction between different types of legally relevant intentions is between *illocutionary* intentions—to say, assert, or
stipulate that P, by enabling one's audience to recognize one's intention to do so—and broader *perlocutionary* intentions—to cause or bring
about something as a result of one's having said, asserted, or stipulated
that P.[16] For example, members of a legislative town council might intend to reduce the risk of sexual assault against the town's school children by enacting a law prohibiting strangers, defined as anyone other
than family members or trusted friends of the family, from picking up
children in automobiles after school. They enact the law by adopting a
text with the illocutionary intention that their linguistic performance
be recognized as asserting or stipulating that, henceforth, any stranger
providing such a ride shall be a misdemeanor. Since it is this intention
that gives the law its content, no theory of legal content, or of legal
interpretation, can afford to dismiss it.

The role of *illocutionary* intentions in determining what is asserted
or stipulated in adopting a legal text makes identifying them a central
component of the first, epistemic, part of the interpretative task. Although this part of the task is often routine, there are cases in which it
is not, including those involving uses of vague language,[17] referential
uses of expressions to make assertions about things to which those expressions do not semantically apply,[18] and uses of grammatically complete but semantically underspecified sentences, the contents of which
must be contextually filled out for an asserted or stipulated content to
be reached.[19]

Once the epistemic task of identifying the asserted or stipulated contents is complete, legal interpreters may ignore the lawmakers' *perlocutionary* intentions unless one of three situations holds.[20] The first occurs
when the asserted or stipulative content is vague, and facts crucial to
the resolution of the case fall within the range of this vagueness. In
these cases, the facts plus the preexisting legal content do not result
in a definite verdict. In many cases of this sort, the court's duty is to

---

[16] See J. L. Austin, *How to Do Things with Words*, ed. J. O. Urmson (Oxford: Clarendon
Press, 1962), 109–19 (distinguishing between illocutionary and perlocutionary acts).

[17] See Scott Soames, "Vagueness in the Law," in *The Routledge Companion to the Philosophy of Law*, ed. Andrei Marmor (New York: Routledge, 2012). See also Soames, *Philosophical Essays, supra* note 6 at 418–21.

[18] See Soames, *Philosophical Essays, supra* note 6 at 407–10.

[19] *Id.* at 412–15.

[20] The three types of situations summarized below are discussed in greater detail in
Scott Soames, "What Vagueness and Inconsistency Tell Us about Interpretation," in *The
Philosophical Foundations of Language in the Law*, ed. Andrei Marmor and Scott Soames
(Oxford: Oxford University Press, 2011), 31, 43–51.

modify the vague content by partially precisifying it so as to reach the result that most closely conforms to the legislators' rationale for adopting the law or legal provision.[21] The rationale of a law is, to a first approximation, what the legislators intended to accomplish by adopting it. To discover this, interpreters need to identify certain of the lawmakers' perlocutionary intentions, which often requires an inquiry into legislative history of precisely the sort disparaged by Justice Scalia.

The second kind of interpretive situation in which lawmakers' perlocutionary intentions are relevant to legal interpretation is one in which several equally authoritative laws bear on a case in opposite ways, so that the contents of the laws plus the particular facts of the case entail inconsistent verdicts. When this occurs, the legal interpreter may be required to fashion the minimal modification of existing legal content that removes the inconsistency and allows a unique verdict to be reached while maximizing the fulfillment of the discernible legislative rationales of the laws in question. Again, this appeal to legislative rationale is an appeal to certain *nonillocutionary* intentions of lawmakers.

The final interpretive situation in which perlocutionary intentions are relevant is one in which the facts of a particular case generate an inconsistency not between the contents of different statutes but between the content of a single law and the transparent purposes for which it, or related laws, were adopted. In these cases, the law as it exists, plus the facts of the case, entail an unforeseen result that does nothing to further the purposes for which it was passed while violating either its rationale or the rationales of other legal provisions. In such cases, the legal interpreter may, again, be required to minimally modify the content of an existing law while maximizing the fulfillment of discernible legislative purposes.

Lest this discussion seem too abstract, consider again the imaginary ordinance—"It shall be a misdemeanor in the Township of Plainsboro for anyone other than close family members or trusted family friends to provide any child with transportation by automobile from school to that child's home or elsewhere"— enacted for the purpose of stopping a rash of sexual assaults by men from out of town picking up high school girls after school. Imagine that months after the wave of crimes has abated, Susan, a high school senior late for her afterschool job at the Mini Mart, accepts a ride from an obviously sweet, distinctly not dangerous, older woman, the widow Gasperetti, who works at the school cafeteria and lives next to the Mini Mart, but is only a passing

---

[21] Different accounts of what vagueness is sometimes lead to different legal results in cases like this, and to different elucidations of the function of vagueness in law and interpretation. See Soames, "Vagueness in the Law," *supra* note.

acquaintance of Susan's, and is unknown to the rest of the family. Since in this circumstance a literal application of the law would harm Mrs. Gasperetti, without serving the purpose for which the ordinance was clearly intended, the local magistrate might defensibly rule in her favor in a way that narrows the legal effect of the ordinance. Surely, this exercise of judicial discretion is justified.

It might even be expected. Why, after all, might the town council have formulated the law as it did? Perhaps they considered various formulations explicitly referencing the danger they were concerned to minimize, e.g., "It shall be a misdemeanor in the Township of Plainsboro for those who might reasonably be thought to be a potential danger to school children to provide said children with automobile transportation after school." Such formulations might well have been rejected on the sensible grounds that asking people to make judgments about who might be dangerous and who was certainly not could be counterproductive, and also that including such a contentious term in the statute might easily cause uncertainty in enforcement and difficulty in prosecution. Better, the council members may have reasoned, to leave the language unadorned and let the judge be guided by their evident intention—to reduce unnecessary risk of assault to the town's school children—when sorting out cases in which the ordinance should apply from those in which it shouldn't.

To adopt this policy is to put anyone outside the family or its close circle of friends who offers a ride to a child on notice that he or she may be subject to criminal penalties. The council members may plausibly have taken it to be predictable that innocent exceptions would come to be recognized and, eventually, would lead to the carving out of special cases that would narrow the effective legal content of the ordinance. However, they may also have regarded the precise identity of such carve-outs to be unforeseeable in advance, and best arrived at piecemeal. In any case, the result was to leave the boundaries between them and cases in which one's behavior in offering a ride might make one vulnerable to legal penalty vague and usefully unpredictable. Seen in this light, passing the ordinance establishes a strong, but rebuttable, presumption against the behavior to be discouraged. Expressing the presumption in a broad and open-ended way provides motivation to avoid any behavior that might fall into that category. Recognizing that presumption to be judicially rebuttable reduces the disadvantages of the (overly) universal description of that behavior in the ordinance itself. All in all, the council members may reasonably have thought, a good bargain.

A similar dynamic is at work between original enactment and discretionary interpretation in constitutional law—which is often framed in sweeping and easily understood language that requires considerable adjustment over time. Consider the portion of the First Amendment to the United States Constitution guaranteeing freedom of speech:

Congress shall make *no law* respecting an establishment of religion, or prohibiting the free exercise thereof; or *abridging the freedom of speech, or of the press*; or the right of the people peaceably to assemble, and to petition the Government for a redress of grievances.[22]

Despite the broad, unqualified language of the amendment, the Supreme Court has acknowledged that there may be forms of speech that are sometimes validly restricted by law, including defamatory and libelous speech,[23] commercial speech,[24] publication of state secrets injurious to national security,[25] and incitements to violence (including the use of "fighting words").[26] Today there are even legal restrictions on political speech, in the form of campaign contribution restrictions.[27] Although the correctness of some of these exceptions is contentious, and the scope of any of them could be challenged, there is, I think, no serious argument supporting the conclusion that what the First Amendment requires is precisely what its words seem, literally, to mean—namely, that there shall be no law whatsoever restricting *in any way* what one may choose to say, or what the press may choose to publish.

---

[22] U.S. Const. amend. I, my emphasis.

[23] See, e.g., *New York Times Co. v. Sullivan*, 376 U.S. 254, 279–80 (1964) (acknowledging that false and defamatory statements may be unprotected if made with "actual malice").

[24] See, e.g., *Central Hudson Gas & Elec. Corp. v. Public Serv. Comm'n of New York*, 447 U.S. 557, 566 (1980) (noting that commercial speech may be restricted if it concerns illegal activity, is misleading, or if the government's interest is substantial, the restrictions directly advance the government's asserted interest, and the restrictions are no more extensive than necessary to serve that interest).

[25] See *Snepp v. United States*, 444 U.S. 507, 509 n.3 (1980) (implying that the "compelling interest" of national security could justify the government's imposing some restrictions on the activity of its employees that would otherwise be protected by the First Amendment).

[26] See *Chaplinsky v. New Hampshire*, 315 U.S. 568, 572 (1942) (stating that " 'fighting' words—those which by their very utterance inflict injury or tend to incite an immediate breach of the peace"—are a limited exception to the right of free speech); see also *Brandenburg v. Ohio* 395 U.S. 444, 447 (1969) (implying that free speech guarantees may not prohibit the State from proscribing advocacy directed at inciting imminent lawless action and likely to incite such action).

[27] *Citizens United v. Fed. Election Comm'n*, 130 S. Ct. 876, 898 (2010) (allowing that a law may burden political speech if the restriction furthers a compelling interest and is narrowly tailored to achieve that interest).

To understand this gap between the meaning of the English sentence "Congress shall make no law abridging the freedom of speech, or of the press," and the content of the (relevant part of) the First Amendment as we accept it today, it is important first to recognize the gap between the meaning of that sentence and that which the framers and ratifiers asserted in adopting it. Surely, it is safe to assume, they did not take themselves to be endorsing a complete ban on all conceivable laws governing all conceivable speech—i.e., they were not asserting what the sentence they used literally meant. There are, it is natural to think, two significant contributors to this gap between meaning and assertion.

First, it may plausibly be argued that 'freedom of speech', as used by the framers and ratifiers of the First Amendment, was already a legal term of art, the meaning of which was narrower than the literal (compositionally determined) meaning of the phrase in English—which is roughly, "the freedom to speak (without restriction)." Rather, the argument goes, it was understood along the lines "the freedom to speak *in ways long recognized as protected and legitimate.*" Though these ways were, to be sure, vague and open-ended, it would be foolish to suppose that they didn't provide an important starting point for future discussions of the distinction between protected and unprotected speech. However, it would also be foolish to suppose that they rigidly established all relevant parameters for establishing the contours of this distinction as we recognize today.

This brings us to the second contributor to the gap between the meaning of the framers' sentence and the assertion they used it to make. Since the range of quantified expressions of the sort *"no law . . ."* on a given occasion of use is determined by the illocutionary intentions reasonably attributed to users of the phrase, there is room to view the asserted or stipulated content enacted by the framers of the First Amendment to be something other than either a complete ban on all conceivable laws limiting the freedom to speak in ways then long recognized as protected and legitimate in common law, or a blank check allowing the government to impose restrictions on new types of speech not previously contemplated (and thus not so recognized). If this view is correct, then the original assertive content enacted with the ratification of the First Amendment must be seen as considerably more nuanced than the literal meaning of the sentence used to express it. Even so, however, the amendment's original assertive content surely did not encompass all the exceptions (and expansions) that have now come to be recognized as legitimate. Rather, these accretions are the result of (mostly) legitimate legal interpretation and adjudication.

This interpretation and adjudication is a vastly more important and complicated version of the same template on which the simple story about the magistrate's interpretation of the ordinance passed by the Plainsboro Town Council was based. The key point was the Town Council's goal of reducing sexual assault, their adoption of a broadly formulated legislative stipulation as a means to that end, and their anticipation that future adjudication would lead to piecemeal refinements by carving out innocent but unanticipated exceptions preserving their original rationale. A similar, though admittedly hypothetical, story can be told about a line of reasoning open to the framers and ratifiers of the First Amendment. What was wanted, we may imagine, was a strong, but rebuttable, legal presumption against the passage of laws by Congress regulating the freedom of speech, or of the press.[28] The sweeping, open-ended content of the language used was, we may suppose, reasonably intended to put present and future members of Congress on notice that any law restricting freedom of speech, or of the press, risked being judged unconstitutional (and so invalid).[29] We may further suppose that it was anticipated, at least by some, that, over time, reasonable exceptions to the prohibition would come to be recognized, with a consequent narrowing of the legal content of the amendment's guarantee. This is not to say that the precise scope and contents of these exceptions could be foreseen. What could be foreseen was that the process by which the exceptions would come to be recognized would be piecemeal, and that the boundaries between them and the laws to which the prohibition would continue to apply would remain vague and usefully unpredictable. In short, the First Amendment provision on freedom of speech, and of the press, would amount to a strong, but rebuttable, legal presumption discouraging the sort of legislation the framers and the ratifiers wished to limit.[30] Not perfect perhaps, but, again, not a bad bargain—and well within the range of acceptable interpretation provided by the traditional conception of the norm governing legal interpretation formulated previously (RJ). If this is what it takes to have a "living Constitution,"[31] then, long live the Constitution!

What I have said up to now about the traditional model of legal interpretation rests on the assumption that legal interpreters often are

[28] In the interest of simplicity, I here put aside the other freedoms covered by the amendment.

[29] The far-reaching implications or practical feasibility of such a judgment—particularly because judicial review did not exist at the time of the ratification of the First Amendment—are complicated and outside the scope of this analysis.

[30] In this instance and in other references, I use "legal presumption" and "presumption" in their ordinary connotation, as opposed to their technical legal designations as terms related to burdens of proof or persuasion. In the context of my argument, a legal presumption is simply a *policy* that relevant legal actors must follow.

[31] Scalia, *supra* note 14 at 38.

able to discern the purposes of a piece of legislation. The identification of such purposes typically occurs in the second, constitutive, stage of interpretation—which calls for interpreters to make normative judgments about what modifications of existing legal content *best* advance the lawmakers' legislative rationale. Identifying these purposes is primarily a descriptive task that needn't involve subscribing to them. However, it does require clarity about the kinds of purposes one is seeking.

The search for legislative rationale is *not* a search for causally efficacious factors that motivated the required number of lawmakers to enact the law or legal provision. In addition to being private, and often difficult to discern, these motivating factors may be as individual and various as the legislators themselves. An individual lawmaker may be motivated by personal or political self-interest, a desire to advance the economic interests of friends or former associates, devotion to the political fortunes of a particular faction or party, or identification with a privately held, or publically expressed, ideology. Any attempt to aggregate these and to identify the dominant motivators of the relevant group or majority, will, typically, face severe epistemic obstacles. Whether or not these obstacles can ever be overcome in interesting cases, the attempt to do so in the service of legal interpretation is fundamentally mistaken. The purposes of a law or other legal provision, sought in the adjudication of hard cases for which a constitutive judicial decision is needed, are *not* the causally efficacious motivators that produced the law or provision but the chief *reasons* publically offered to *justify* its adoption.

In the simple case alluded to earlier of a Town Council adopting an ordinance prohibiting strangers from picking up children after school, the purpose was to reduce the risk of sexual assault. This, we may imagine, is what the local newspaper agitated for and how the council members explained and defended their action. Whatever private personal or political motives they may have harbored are irrelevant. The same is true of complicated real-life cases, like the Affordable Care Act that passed the United States Congress in March 2010.[32] Among the motivators of individual lawmakers were political payoffs in the form of special benefits for their states or districts; political contributions from groups favoring, and companies profiting from, the legislation; fear of retaliation from the administration and its allies; a desire to advance the fortunes of their party and the agenda of their new president; as well as an ideological commitment to expanding government control over the economy and ushering in a more socialistic system of

---

[32] Patient Protection and Affordable Care Act, Pub. L. No. 111-148, 124 Stat. 119 (2010) (to be codified in scattered sections of 42 U.S.C.).

medicine and political economy. However, none of these were among the purposes of the legislation, in the sense relevant to subsequent legal interpretation. Rather, its chief purposes were (i) expansion of health insurance among the previously uninsured; (ii) reduction of the total amount spent on health care without jeopardizing quality; (iii) reduction of its cost to most citizens, including the poor, who would be more heavily subsidized; (iv) equalizing access to health care and health insurance; and (v) making both more reliably available by severing their connection to employment.[33]

Since these were central elements of the public rationale offered for the Affordable Care Act, the bill's purposes are easily discernible, and recognizing them does not presuppose endorsing them. In this case, knowledge of legislative purposes is relatively unproblematic and does not involve substituting the normative judgments of legal interpreters for those of legislators. Genuine normative issues can be expected to arise when details of implementation collide with presently unappreciated facts in ways that bring either the chief purposes of the bills, or the more specific, subsidiary purposes behind particular sections or clauses, into conflict with the contents of the bill's many provisions. At that point normative decisions will be required in implementation and administration, as well as in likely judicial challenges. However, the normativity involved is defensible and, I believe, easily conforms to the limitations recognized by the essentially conservative conception of the role of the courts, and other legal interpreters of complex legislation, encapsulated in the rule RJ .

Although this discussion barely scratches the surface, its analytical framework applies to many instances of legal interpretation, of which constitutional interpretation is a particularly good example. Often, constitutional provisions are stated in language the broad purpose of which is plain, even though the assertive content of that language is, by design, overly general. The intent is to articulate a clear, enduring normative goal, the advancement of which, over time, will involve concrete implementations that cannot be foreseen. The overly general content of the provision keeps the normative goal in mind while signaling that although care must be taken to adhere to it, the actions counted as doing so may not always strictly conform to the literal content of the provision but rather are, to some extent, up for negotiation. The foundational feature of the law exploited in this process is the necessary role of interpretation in resolving conflicts that arise when

---

[33] See U.S. Dep't of Health & Human Servs., In Focus: Health Disparities and the Affordable Care Act, http://www.healthcare.gov/news/factsheets/2010/07/health-disparities.html (last visited Sept. 22, 2011).

the purposes a law is designed to serve clash with literal applications of its existing content in new cases.

Though the legislative function inherent in this procedure is unavoidable, it must also be limited, lest the Supreme Court's traditional deference to constitutional and other democratic authority be undermined, and the legal rule governing its position in our system of government be subverted. The Court is no House of Lords, with the authority to veto or amend any legislation with which it has policy disagreements. Its proper role is to legislate only when it must, (i) to fit vague laws to borderline cases in ways that advance the lawmakers' legislative rationale, (ii) to resolve conflicts between different legal provisions jointly inconsistent with relevant and established facts in a way that minimizes changes in legal content while maximizing the realization of the legislative rationales, and (iii) to reconcile clear discrepancies between the literal content of a statute or constitutional provision and the evident rationale that the statute or provision was intended by its framers or ratifiers to advance. The most important element in all these cases is the identification of the relevant legislative rationale. If judicial legislation is to be contained, and abuses minimized, there must be strong constraints on what counts as a proper identification of this sort.

The point is illustrated by a slight extension of the earlier example of the Plainsboro Town Council. The purpose of the ordinance it passed was to reduce the danger of sexual assaults against the town's children. Since such assaults on children constitute a form of harm to the town's residents, the ordinance may also be said to be aimed at reducing the danger of harm to residents. However, it is only the more specific and complete of these two designations of purpose (rather than the more general designation, which provides a merely partial specification of the aim of the legislation) that is relevant to future judicial interpretation. For example, even if the Mini Mart, where Susan worked, were in a dangerous part of town, and so a likely target for armed robbery, no one could reasonably argue that Mrs. Gasperetti should be held guilty of violating the ordinance for offering Susan a ride to work—even though the motorist was both not dangerous and someone with whom Susan had a nodding acquaintance—on the grounds that ruling against her would further its purpose of reducing the danger of harm to residents. On the contrary, since the purpose of the ordinance, in the sense relevant to deciding the case, is its complete purpose (given by the more specific designation), a ruling in her favor would be correct.

Though the case is artificial, the point it illustrates is essentially the same as the one standardly made against the landmark decisions reached in *Griswold v. Connecticut*[34] (concerning laws restricting the sale of contraceptives) and *Roe v. Wade*[35] (concerning laws restricting abortion). According to Justice William O. Douglas, writing for the majority in Griswold:

> [The guarantees in] the Bill of Rights have penumbras, formed by emanations from those guarantees that help give them life and substance.... Various guarantees create *zones of privacy*. The right of association contained in the penumbra of the First Amendment is one, as we have seen. The Third Amendment in its prohibition against the quartering of soldiers "in any house" in time of peace without the consent of the owner is another facet of that *privacy*. The Fourth Amendment explicitly affirms the "right of the people to be secure in their persons, houses, papers, and effects, against unreasonable searches and seizures." The Fifth Amendment in its Self-Incrimination Clause enables the citizen to create *a zone of privacy* which government may not force him to surrender to his detriment.[36] (my emphasis)

The standard criticism of this decision is that whereas it is true that several constitutional amendments were adopted to establish particular privacy rights, no general right of privacy covering contraception (or abortion) was established. Using the analytical framework outlined here, we acknowledge that the provisions mentioned by Douglas were adopted for the purpose of establishing strong, but rebuttable, presumptions against the passage of laws infringing the particular privacy rights specified. We further acknowledge that the original assertive or stipulative contents of the relevant constitutional clauses were not intended to settle, for all time, precisely which prospective laws would be constitutionally prohibited. The earlier discussion of the First Amendment emphasized legitimate future narrowings of the original guarantee applying to speech. A similar allowance can be made for a limited expansion to some forms of expression which, though not strictly speech, share with speech the primary function of communicating ideas. Even recognizing all this, under our framework Douglas's decision cannot be reached. Although the contents of the constitutional guarantees he mentions may evolve over time to better serve their motivating purposes, and although each may correctly be said to have been aimed at securing privacy (of a certain sort), such a characterization of purpose is incomplete and insufficiently specific. Once

---

[34] 381 U.S. 479 (1965).
[35] 410 U.S. 113 (1973).
[36] *Griswold*, 381 U.S. at 484.

this defect is eliminated, and the purposes governing the constitutional provisions are fully and specifically stated, the resulting set of privacy rights does not encompass any general right to privacy that prohibits laws against contraception or abortion.

Similar points can be made about other landmark decisions interpreting the Fourteenth Amendment. Here is the relevant section, the most salient part of which is italicized:

> All persons born or naturalized in the United States, and subject to the jurisdiction thereof, are citizens of the United States and of the state wherein they reside. *No state shall make or enforce any law which shall abridge the privileges or immunities of citizens of the United States; nor shall any state deprive any person of life, liberty, or property, without due process of law; nor deny to any person within its jurisdiction the equal protection of the laws.*[37]

The primary rationale for the amendment, adopted in 1868, was to guarantee the full rights of citizenship to the newly freed African Americans and their descendants after the Civil War.[38] More broadly, that rationale may legitimately be described as preventing the states from denying the normal rights of citizenship on the basis of race.[39] Since the extent of those rights in 1868 was not the same as what it is now (regarding voting, participation in public life, and public education for example), the proper scope of the guarantee is not limited to the particular rights that the framers of the amendment had in mind. Rather, the assertive content of the amendment indicates that the rights guaranteed are those of *citizens*, whatever those rights may be at any given time. As for the language specifying the right of *persons* to due process of law and equal protection of the laws, both the specific rights guaranteed and the class of individuals to which the guarantees apply are less clear—though it is certainly not unreasonable to think, as the Supreme Court has held, that some rights, such as the right to trial by jury, and closely related rights of this sort, apply to many noncitizens, as well as to citizens.[40]

The importance of the rights guaranteed by the Fourteenth Amendment became particularly prominent in modern jurisprudence in the 1954 case *Brown v. Board of Education*,[41] which struck down legally

[37] U.S. Const. amend XXIV, § 1, my emphasis.
[38] See, e.g., Slaughterhouse Cases, 83 U.S. 36, 37 (1872).
[39] See *Loving v. Virginia*, 388 U.S. 1, 10 (1967).
[40] See *Wong Wing v. United States*, 163 U.S. 228, 238 (1896) ("The fourteenth amendment of the Constitution is not confined to the protection of citizens." [quoting *Yick Wo v. Hopkins*, 118 U.S. 356, 369 (1886)]).
[41] 347 U.S. 483 (1954).

mandated segregation by race in public education. Though the assertive content of the vague and abstract phrase "equal protection of the
laws," as understood in 1868, is unclear and imprecise, the centrality
of race to the rationale of the amendment, and the clear intention of
its framers to bestow full citizenship on former slaves and their descendants, lend a high degree of credence to the idea the rights of
the African American plaintiffs in 1954 fell within the purview of the
amendment. Since the state of public education in America in 1868
was very uneven, and far from universally available, there was then little thought about what, if anything, the Fourteenth Amendment would
mean to access to public schools, even for full-fledged citizens. By
1954, however, the ubiquity and importance of systems of public education made it prima facie plausible that citizens of a state have a right
to the public education provided by the state. It was also plausible that
the so-called separate but equal system to which African Americans
were in some places then confined[42] was, in fact, inherently unequal to
the system reserved for the majority, and hence that some individuals,
including descendants of those the plight of whom the amendment was
originally intended to address, were being denied the rights of citizens
because of their race.

Though this core aspect of the reasoning in *Brown* is justifiable
within the traditional conception of legal interpretation I have defended here, it is not clear that the same can be said for later appeals
to the Fourteenth Amendment in general, and the Equal Protection and
the Due Process Clauses in particular. In the decades following *Brown*,
the section of the amendment quoted, including the concepts of equal
protection and due process, have repeatedly been put to use in all manner of cases, including those involving welfare benefits,[43] exclusionary zoning,[44] the apportionment of seats in state legislatures,[45] sexual
discrimination,[46] morals legislation,[47] the rights of aliens,[48] abortion,[49]
and access to the courts.[50] Though the use, or misuse, of the Fourteenth
Amendment in these cases deserves extensive investigation in each of
these areas, there is a general worry uniting them. If one starts by
considering the content asserted by the framers of the amendment,

[42] *Id.* at 488.
[43] See, e.g., *Shapiro v. Thompson*, 394 U.S. 618 (1969).
[44] See, e.g., *Moore v. City of East Cleveland*, 431 U.S. 494 (1977).
[45] See, e.g., *Reynolds v. Sims*, 377 U.S. 533 (1964).
[46] See, e.g., *United States v. Virginia*, 518 U.S. 515 (1996).
[47] See, e.g., *Lawrence v. Texas*, 539 U.S. 558, 577–78 (2003).
[48] See, e.g., *Plyler v. Doe*, 457 U.S. 202 (1982).
[49] See, e.g., *Roe v. Wade*, 410 U.S. 113 (1973).
[50] See, e.g., *Boddie, v. Connecticut*, 401 U.S. 371 (1971).

constituted in part by their illocutionary intentions, and one continues by supplementing this content with the perlocutionary intentions that provided their rationale for adopting the amendment, one will *not*, I suggest, reach the broad content read into it by the Supreme Court in a string of related decisions in the last fifty years. Nor, I think, can the cumulative increments of constitutional substance arising from these decisions be fully explained as the result of (i) justified judicial precisification of vague language required in cases for which no legal result would otherwise have been forthcoming, (ii) justifiable judicial rewritings of the Equal Protection Clause required by the joint inconsistency of the facts of specific cases together with either (a) other equally authoritative constitutional provisions or (b) the clearly discernible rationale of the framers in adopting the amendment.

Whether I am right about this is a large and contentious question. If I am, then an important strain in authoritative constitutional interpretation in the past half century is not in accord with the rule, RJ, that I have put forward as a social convention that is normatively justified and empirically embedded in our legal system with the force of law. Since I take this rule to be both normatively justified and legally authoritative, I am inclined to view some portion of one substantial body of court-made law of the last fifty years as problematic, and to think that, henceforth, it should be construed as having only limited precedential weight. Those who think otherwise are invited either to show that this body of court-made law is, in fact, consistent with something like my traditional conception of the norm governing legal interpretation and judicial responsibility, or to articulate an alternative governing norm with which this body of law is consistent. Those opting for the latter task must show either (i) that a strong empirical case can be made that the alternative norm is the one that is actually operative in our legal system or (ii) that a strong moral or political argument can be given that shows it to be normatively preferable to the conception I have outlined, or both. In my mind, the chief challenge to doing this is to justify the idea that, for example, justices of the Supreme Court, who hold lifetime positions designed to be insulated from democratic politics, possess either the political wisdom or the moral authority to exercise what might fairly be described as an absolute and largely unconstrained legislative veto over all other representative bodies and offices in a democratic republic.[51]

[51] Thanks to Bill Rosen of the NYU School of Law for his research and editorial assistance.

15

Deferentialism

A POST-ORIGINALIST THEORY
OF LEGAL INTERPRETATION

In this paper I present a new conception, *deferentialism*, of legal interpretation, which has close affinities with originalism while shedding much of its accumulated baggage. The new conception includes two dimensions of deference to original sources: one to a species of original meaning; the other to a species of original intent. The dimensions are ordered. The first task is to identify the relevant original meaning; intent becomes a constitutive, as opposed to merely evidential, only after that meaning has been identified.[1]

The first question in interpretation is, *What does the law say, assert, or stipulate?* Saying, asserting, and stipulating are *speech acts*—or, in more technical philosophical terminology, *illocutionary acts*—as are *confirming, denying, ordering,* and *promising* Each of these involves taking a certain stance toward the content of the act. To *say* or *assert that so-and-so* is to commit oneself to its being true that so-and-so, as is to *confirm that-so-and-so* in the special case in which whether *so-and-so* has been the subject of previous interest or inquiry. To *deny that so-and-so* is to commit oneself to its being false that so-and-so. To *order someone to do such-and-such* is to direct that person to make it true *that he or she does such-and-such, while to promise to such-and-such* is to commit oneself, often by asserting that one promises, to *making it true* that one does such-and-such. Stipulation is similar. For a proper authority to *stipulate*

[1] Deferentialism applies equally to statutory and constitutional interpretation. Unlike Scalia's originalism, which holds that what he calls lawmakers' "intent" is relevant for constitutional, but not statutory, interpretation, what I mean by 'intent' (to be explained) is relevant to both. Elsewhere I explain why and how intent in my sense often plays a larger role in constitutional interpretation than it does in statutory interpretation. But the theoretical framework governing interpretation is the same in the two cases. See pp. 244–59 of "Toward a Theory of Legal Interpretation," *New York University Journal of Law and Liberty* 6 (2011): 231–59.

that, say, the speed limit on certain roads in New Jersey is 60 miles per hour is for the authority *to assert that the speed limit is 60 miles per hour* and for *that very assertive act to be a, or the, crucial component in making what is asserted true.*

To discover *what the law asserts or stipulates* is, in the first instance, to discover what the lawmakers asserted or stipulated in adopting an authoritative text. As with ordinary speech, this is usually *not* a function of the linguistic meaning alone; it *is* a function of meaning plus background beliefs and presuppositions of participants. In general, *what a speaker uses a sentence S to assert or stipulate* in a given context is, to a fair approximation, *what a reasonable hearer or reader who knows the linguistic meaning of S, and is aware of all relevant intersubjectively available features of the context of utterance, would rationally take the speaker's use of S to be intended to convey and commit the speaker to.* In most standard linguistic communications all parties know, and know they all know, the linguistic meanings of the words and sentences used, plus the general purpose of the communication and all relevant facts about what previously has been asserted or agreed upon. Consequently, what is asserted or stipulated can usually be identified with what *the speaker means and the hearers take the speaker to mean* by the words used on that occasion. Applying this lesson to legal interpretation, the deferentialist looks for *what the lawmakers meant and what any reasonable person who understood the linguistic meanings of their words, the publically available facts, the recent history in the lawmaking context, and the background of existing law into which the new provision is expected to fit, would take them to have meant.* This—not the original linguistic meaning of the words they used—is the content of the law as enacted.

The point is illustrated by two well-known examples from Antonin Scalia's dissent in *Smith v. United States.*[2] The relevant legal text in the case is the following sentence in an act of Congress:

> Whoever . . . uses or carries a firearm [in the course of committing a crime of violence or drug trafficking], shall, in addition to the punishment provided for such [a] crime . . . be sentenced to imprisonment for five years.[3]

The key fact in the case was that Smith traded a gun for illegal drugs, thereby committing a crime of drug trafficking. The crucial question was whether this constituted *using a firearm* in the commission of such a crime in the sense of the statute.[4] After a lower court found that it

---

[2] 508 U.S. 223, 241, 1993.

[3] 18 U. S. C. § 924(c)(1) (2006).

[4] Oddly, the issue of *carrying a firearm* did not play a major role in the case.

did, Smith, wishing to avoid the extra five years in prison, appealed to the Supreme Court. The Court majority upheld the lower court, finding that the ordinary meaning of the phrase 'uses a firearm' covers uses of any sort, including trading a firearm for drugs.

Justice Scalia's dissent, though wrongly formulated in terms of a restrictive and inaccurate thesis about *the ordinary meaning of the words in the statute*, nevertheless tracked what should have been the real issue—namely, what the lawmakers *asserted* in adopting the text. Two of his examples forcefully drive the point home. The first concerns the content of the question an interrogative sentence is used to ask:

> When someone asks, "Do you use a cane?" he is not inquiring whether you have your grandfather's silver-handled walking stick on display in the hall; he wants to know whether you walk with a cane.[5]

The second concerns the content of an assertion made in response to a question in a hypothetical legal proceeding:

> I think it perfectly obvious, for example, that the objective falsity requirement for a perjury conviction would not be satisfied if a witness answered "no" to a prosecutor's inquiry whether he had ever "used a firearm," even though he had once sold his grandfather's Enfield rifle to a collector.[6]

In both cases, Scalia is right about the content of the speech act performed by speakers using the words in the situations imagined. The *question that would standardly be asked* by a use of the sentence 'Do you use a cane?' in an ordinary context (without special stage-setting) is, *Do you use a cane to walk?*; the proposition asserted by saying "No, I have never used a firearm," in response to the prosecutor's inquiry is *that one has never used a firearm as a weapon*.

But these correct observations about the contents of the agents' illocutionary acts of questioning and asserting in ordinary situations *do not* translate into similarly correct observations about the linguistic meanings of the sentences they used. The sentences 'Do you use a cane?' and 'I have never used a firearm' *do not* have the same meanings in the English language as the sentences 'Do you use a cane *for walking*?' and 'I have never used a firearm *as a weapon*'. To be sure, the former pair of sentences can, and in many contexts naturally would, be used *to ask the same question or make the same statement as* corresponding uses of the latter pair. But in other contexts, in which the background

[5] *Id.* at 242.
[6] *Id.* at 242, n.1.

circumstances and presuppositions are different, the sentence 'Do you use a cane?' can be used to ask whether you use a cane to prop open a window, or to protect yourself from wild dogs, while the sentence 'I have never used a firearm' can be used to assert that one has never used a firearm in one's comedy skit, or that one has never used a firearm for any purpose at all.

Since a sentence with the phrase 'use a firearm' in it can be employed to assert widely different contents in different contexts, *its linguistic meaning cannot plausibly be identified with any of those contents*. Rather, its meaning is a kind of schema that provides a common element to be filled out in different ways on different occasions. Since the content of a law enacted by adopting a text containing such a sentence must be a completed truth evaluable content, there is no real alternative in the Smith case to identifying the legal content with *what Congress actually asserted* (as opposed to what it could have asserted using the same words had the arguments, debates, and legislative history been different). Had Scalia been a deferentialist rather than an originalist, his central thesis would have been that in adopting the text

> Whoever . . . uses or carries a firearm [in the course of committing a crime of violence or drug trafficking], shall, in addition to the punishment provided for such [a] crime . . . be sentenced to imprisonment for five years.

Congress stipulated that the *use of a firearm as a weapon* (or carrying it for that purpose) is subject to additional punishment. This, I believe, is what both he and the Court would have concluded, had not he, and they, confused *the meaning of that sentence with what it was used to assert or stipulate.*[7]

My next illustration of the first task of deferentialist interpretation—discovering original asserted or stipulated content—is the Due Process Clause of the Fifth Amendment to the US Constitution (1791), copied and applied to the states in the Fourteenth Amendment (1868):

> [No] person shall . . . be deprived of life, liberty, or property, without due process of law.

The clause presents an interpretive problem. One can understand English perfectly well without knowing its content, and hence without knowing what rights it guarantees. This is *not* because the words 'life',

---

[7] See the discussion in Stephen Neale, "On Location," in *Situating Semantics: Essays on the Philosophy of John Perry*, ed. Michael O'Rourke and Corey Washington (Cambridge, MA: MIT Press, 2007), 251–393; also Soames, "Toward a Theory of Legal Interpretation, *NYU Journal of Law and Liberty* 6 (2011): 231–59."

'liberty', or 'property' have undergone substantial changes in ordinary meaning. They haven't. The main source of interpretive unclarity is the phrase 'due process of law'. Even here, no individual word is unclear. Moreover, the phrase has a literal meaning—roughly *without the process to which, by law, one is due*. But one can't rely on this meaning alone without rendering the guarantee vacuous, which neither it nor the rest of the Bill or Rights was. On the contrary, the Due Process Clause made an important contribution to the guarantees demanded by the people of thirteen newly independent states, who were nothing if not jealous of their rights and suspicious of any central authority that might transgress them. The interpretive task is to discover the presupposed understanding of the process to which one was widely believed to be entitled that the language of the Fifth Amendment was used to express.

To discover the substance of this presupposed understanding of the framers and ratifiers of the Fifth Amendment, and later of the Fourteenth, requires historical research. Much of this has been done by Nathan Chapman and Michael McConnell of the Stanford University Law School in their recent paper "Due Process as Separation of Powers."[8] The short version of their story begins in 1215 with a provision in chapter 29 of the Magna Carta stating, in effect, that the king may not deprive a subject of his rights under existing law without adjudication by an independent judicial body. By 1354 this idea was expressed in a statute in which the application of existing law by a judicial body was summed up in the phrase "due process of law." In 1628, Parliament passed the Petition of Right, which stated that subjects could be deprived of rights only according to what is described variously as "the Law of the Land," "due processe of Lawe," or "by the lawful Judgment of his Peers." Chapman and McConnell sum up the lesson as follows:

> Each of these phrases was a way of expressing the same two institutional checks on the King's power to deprive persons of rights: only pursuant to positive law (common law or parliamentary statute) and only after judgment by a common law court. The "substantive" side of due process was positive standing law; the procedural side was adjudication by a court. . . . When [Sir John Selden] Coke stated in a later commentary that Chapter 29's "law of the land" was equivalent to the phrase "due process of law"— the commentary relied on by early Americans to equate the two constitutional guarantees—he was summarizing these two aspects of the rule of the common law.[9]

---

[8] Nathan S. Chapman and Michael W. McConnell, "Due Process as Separation of Powers," *Yale Law Journal* 116 (2012): 1672–1807.

[9] Ibid., 1688.

From the end of the English Civil War through the late eighteenth century, Parliament gained power as the supreme arbiter of the law of the land. By the 1770s, Parliament was not itself seen, except by a small number of Whig members of Parliament and their American supporters, to be lacking in power to deprive subjects of rights as it saw fit, without submitting to common-law procedures. However, there was a movement to restrict the procedures it employed when acting judicially. This effort was taken further in the American colonies, where it was increasingly argued, including by the First Continental Congress, that Parliament itself had violated the law of the land—due process—in passing the Boston Port Act, the Massachusetts Act, and the Coercive Acts in 1774, which deprived colonists of jury trials in certain cases, and revoked other rights originally granted in the charter of the colony.

In the 1780s, the constitutions of American states had established separation of executive, legislative, and judicial powers, and courts were declining to enforce legislative acts deemed to operate retrospectively, or to decide essentially judicial matters without benefit of trial. Alexander Hamilton argued that ex post facto laws against Loyalists violated "due process of law" in his 1787 "Remarks on an Act for Regulating Elections" made to New York State's General Assembly. His rebuke was not that the legislation violated fundamental rights but that it usurped a properly judicial function, and so deprived persons of procedural rights that a judicial process guarantees.

This was the understanding of "due process of law" shared by the framers of the US Constitution and Bill of Rights. To be guaranteed not to be deprived of certain rights without due process was to be guaranteed that one would not be stripped of them without being charged with violating a constitutionally legitimate law in an independent judicial proceeding, with all the safeguards inherent in such a process. The rights protected were not unrestricted, unenumerated rights but specific rights having to do with life, liberty, and property. The idea is illustrated by liberty, which was taken to be a natural right to act as one chooses *so long as it is not contrary to established law*. The Constitution and Bill of Rights, along with many state constitutions, restricted such law by putting certain activities, including exercise of freedom of speech, press, and religion, beyond its reach. It was also understood that to pass muster legislation must be general, rather than specific, in application, and prospective rather than retrospective. Other unmentioned aspects of natural liberty—to travel, to work, to contract for goods and labor, to raise a family, etc.—were taken for granted as instances of liberty that could not be deprived *without a proper judicial procedure*. However, no restrictions were placed on the degree to which these natural rights could be regulated by legislation. What the Fifth

Amendment guaranteed was that one would not be deprived of any of these rights without a judicial proceeding pursuant to positive law.

There was no significant change in this understanding when the Due Process Clause was included in the Fourteenth Amendment. As Chapman and McConnell argue, antebellum state courts had used due process concerns, though not of course the Fifth Amendment, against legislative acts that abrogated procedural protections of common law, or deprived persons of liberty or vested property rights; but the grounds for these decisions were that legislatures had performed essentially "judicial acts" that usurped the role of the courts, thereby violating separation of powers and due process. The Supreme Court's first major Due Process Clause decision came in 1855 in *Murray's Lessee v. Hoboken Land and Improvement Co.*[10] At issue was a law passed by Congress authorizing executive branch officers in the Treasury Department to seize private property (seeking to recover money owed)—in this case they placed a lien on the property—without judicial warrant or jury trial. The Court ruled, in accordance with the by then traditional understanding of the separation of governmental powers, that due process required the use of either traditional common-law judicial procedures or an alternative procedure providing the defendant with equivalent procedural guarantees. In so ruling, the Court stated that the Due Process Clause restricted Congress's ability *"to make any process 'due process of law' by its mere will,"* and identified the processes to be observed as those required by other constitutional provisions and by the *"settled usages and modes of proceeding existing in the common and statu[t]e law of England before the emigration of our ancestors"*—in effect, by the traditional procedures of common law.[11]

The history I have cited is merely a sample of the richer and more detailed account provided by Chapman and McConnell, who maintain that the original understanding of the Due Process clause didn't change when it was included in the Fourteenth Amendment and applied to the states. Until the late nineteenth century it was taken to state (i) that no rights involving life, liberty, and property may be deprived without protection of a judicial process conforming to the separation of powers doctrine or to the traditional procedures of common law; (ii) that among those rights are those explicitly noted in the Constitution, which can't be abrogated by the legislature; and (iii) that while other traditional rights can be modified by legislative acts, such acts must be distinguished from judicial acts in being general rather than specific in application, and forward looking rather than retrospective.

[10] 59 U.S. (18 How.) 272 (1855).
[11] See Chapman and McConnell (2012, 1774–75).

This discussion illustrates the first dimension of deferentialism—*identification* of legal content—by showing how it applies to an important and disputed constitutional provision. It also provides background for the second dimension of deferentialism—*rectification*—which specifies the rationale for when and how judicial resolution of a case may, correctly, *change the content of the law or laws being applied*. Rectification begins where identification leaves off. According to deferentialism, the content of a legal provision can no more be identified with the meanings of the sentences in the text, or with the lawmakers' policy goals in adopting it, than the contents we assert in ordinary life can be identified with the linguistic meanings of the sentences we use, or with our conversational goals in using them. The contents of laws also can't be identified with normative idealizations of what the lawmakers said or stipulated—including what they would have stipulated had they known relevant facts. Legal content is determined in essentially the same way that the asserted or stipulated contents of ordinary texts are—though it is important to note that (i) since the paradigm aim of legal speech is authoritative stipulation, its natural counterparts include ordinary commands, firm requests, or action-guiding directions, rather than cooperative exchanges of information; and (ii) legal stipulations must be understood in the context of complex systems of previous stipulations.

This naturalistic, nonnormative conception of the contents of legal texts and performances leads, inevitably, to a second interpretive dimension that any originalist theory must address. If the existing laws are what various legally authoritative actors have said or stipulated, then legal contents resulting from those assertions and stipulations can be as vague and indeterminate, as conflicting and contradictory, and as ill-suited to furthering the goals for which the assertions or stipulations were made as the contents of ordinary texts and other linguistic performances can be. When ordinary speakers leave crucial contingencies unaddressed, when they unwittingly undertake inconsistent commitments, and when what they advocate transparently defeats the goals of their advocacy, we don't pretend that Beneficent Providence has filled every gap, removed every contradiction, and rationalized every linguistic performance.

The same is true in the law. When the assertive or stipulated contents adopted by legal actors are indeterminate, when they are contradictory or inconsistent with other legal provisions, or when they are self-defeating in particular applications, we should not pretend that Beneficent Providence has rescued the legislation by transubstantiating the lawmakers' flawed performance into a determinate, consistent, rationalized, and morally acceptable product. There is no such transcendental legal product. In such cases existing legal contents are either indeterminate, and so provide no answers in cases that require one, or they are inconsistent, and so provide conflicting answers, or they are self-defeating, and so provide only answers that subvert the publically expressed rationales offered in their support and for which they were adopted. In these circumstances, the task of the judicial interpreter is *not* to discover an idealized law that is already there; *it is to make new law.* The challenge to deferentialism is to articulate what form of deference to original, or at any rate antecedent, sources should guide this process.

The first type of rectification is *precisification.* This is what is needed when the asserted or stipulative content of the legal provision is vague, and facts crucial to the resolution of the case fall within the range of this vagueness. In these circumstances, no determinate verdict is entailed by the facts plus the preexisting legal content. Deferentialism maintains that in such cases, the court's duty is to adopt the minimum principled precisification of the indeterminate existing content that allows a definite verdict to be reached that most closely conforms to the original lawmakers' rationale for adopting the legal provision.[12] By 'rationale', I do not, of course, mean the causally efficacious motives that led them to act, which are often epistemically inscrutable and constitutively irrelevant. In addition to being private and difficult to discern, motives are as individual and various as the actors themselves. Attempts to aggregate them and identify the dominant motivators are at best speculative and at worst invitations to disguised judicial policy making. A law's rationale consists not in the causally efficacious motivators of lawmakers but in the chief reasons publicly offered to justify and explain the law's adoption. This is what is worthy of deference, as well as being epistemically discernible in most cases.[13]

This is not to say that a law's rationale might not itself be vague. It often is. But this won't affect its utility in resolving a case the factual background of which places the case in the indeterminate range of the content of the law as enacted, unless those facts also happen to fall in the indeterminate range of the publically stated reasons for it. Often, this will not be so. And when it is, what then? Here the legally

---

[12] See my "Vagueness in the Law," in *The Routledge Companion to the Philosophy of Law,* ed. Andrei Marmor (New York: Routledge, 2012), 95–108; and "What Vagueness and Inconsistency Tell Us about Legal Interpretation," in *Philosophical Foundations of Language in the Law,* ed. Andrei Marmor and Scott Soames (Oxford: Oxford University Press, 2011), 31–57.

[13] This point is illustrated at p. 251 of "Toward a Theory of Legal Interpretation," where it is applied to the Patient Protection and Affordable Care Act, Pub. L. No. 111-148, 124 Stat. 119 (2010) (codified in scattered sections of 42 U.S.C.).

authorized interpreter, often a court, must look at the contents of, and rationales for, the body of surrounding laws into which the original law fits. As before, the aim is to craft the minimum principled precisification of the indeterminate content of the original law that allows a definite verdict to be reached. What is new is that the precisification sought is the one that most closely conforms to a composite of the original rationales of potentially several laws, in additional to the one explicitly at issue in the case. Since the process is not algorithmic, it requires judgment, and so is open to abuse. But the point of a deferentialist conception of judicial action and authority is not to *prevent* abuse, which no reasonable conception can do. The point is to lay down justifiable principles for guiding and evaluating the inevitable exercise of judicial judgment.

The lawmakers' rationale for adopting a legal provision is also crucial for another kind *of* judicial *rectification* in which correct adjudication changes the law being applied. This sort of rectification *involves harmonizing* several equally authoritative laws that bear on the facts of the case in opposite ways, with the result that inconsistent verdicts are entailed by the contents of the laws plus the relevant facts. When this happens, the judge is required to fashion the minimal modification of existing laws that removes the inconsistency and allows a unique verdict to be reached while maximizing the fulfillment of the discernible legislative rationales of the laws in question. Again, deferentialism demands deference both to the original rationale of the legislation and to its original, though problematic, legal content—which is to be preserved to the maximum extent possible, consistent with eliminating inconsistency.

Harmonization also occurs when the facts of a particular case generate an inconsistency not between the contents of different statutes but between the content of a single law and the transparent rationale for which it, or related laws, were adopted. In these cases, the law as it exists plus unanticipated facts of the case entail an unforeseen result that fails to conform to, and may even subvert, the purposes for which it was approved. In such cases, the deferentialist is again required to minimally modify the content of existing law while maximizing the fulfillment of the discernible legislative rationale.[14]

Since judicial rectification legitimately makes law in all three of these types of situations, judges are themselves lawmakers. Thus, their assertive stipulations constitute new legal contents to be discerned by

[14] At pp. 244–59 of "Toward a Theory of Legal Interpretation," I argue that this third kind of legislation by interpretation plays a special role in much constitutional interpretation.

other judges in future cases. In addition, the stated rationales for their decisions provide grist for further processes of *rectification* when initial judicial stipulations are vague, when they conflict with other authoritative legal contents, or when literally applying them to subsequent, unanticipated facts subverts their original rationales.

With this in mind, I turn to some well-known "substantive due process" decisions that appear to be at variance with the original legal content of the clause they interpret. The questions at issue are (i) whether the changes in the understanding of due process in these cases are justified by a deferentialist understanding of how correct interpretation can change legal content and (ii) whether, if they are not so justified, this casts doubts on the decisions, or on deferentialism itself.

Pride of place in the string of well-known post–Fourteenth Amendment cases that changed the law of due process goes to *Lochner v. New York* in 1905.[15] In this case, the Supreme Court struck down a statute limiting the hours per day and days per week worked by bakers on the grounds that it deprived them and their employers of liberty without due process of law. The liberty in question was freedom of contract. According to the Court, "the general right to make a contract in relation to his business is part of the liberty of the individual protected by the Fourteenth Amendment."[16] Although the Court recognized that states have the right to prohibit certain kinds of contracts in the name of safety, health, morals, and general welfare, such prohibitions must pass certain tests. Which tests those were depended on which justice one read —ranging from the *necessity* of the prohibition to attain the desired end, or its *reasonableness*, to whether the contract right interfered with was what a "rational and fair man" would regard as a "fundamental right."[17]

The reasoning behind, and substance of, this application of the Due Process Clause were new, and with the coming of the New Deal, were short-lived. How did *Lochner* square with a deferentialist understanding of the clause? The fact that the decision changed the content of the law does not itself condemn it, provided the change was a proper instance of rectification, which it wasn't. Although the deferentialist understanding of Due Process does restrict constitutionally permissible legislation, it does so in a manner different from the enumeration of substantive rights—e.g., freedom of speech, of the press, of association, and of religion—provided by other parts of the Bill of Rights. By contrast, the Due Process Clause together with the general constitutional scheme defining the separation of powers requires that any legislation

[15] 198 U.S. 45 (1905).
[16] *Lochner*, 198 U.S. at 53.
[17] Id. at 58, 68, 76.

limiting unenumerated traditional rights must be distinguished from judicial acts in being general rather than specific, and forward looking rather than retrospective, in application. Since the freedom of contract required by *Lochner* is not enumerated in the Constitution, while the legislation struck down was, by its generality and prospectiveness, clearly *not* judicial in nature, the decision was clearly invalid by deferentialist standards—no matter what one may think of its other merits or demerits.[18]

Although *Lochner* is not popular today, it is possible to defend it using a kind of reasoning which though significantly aprioristic does have some contemporary currency. One begins by observing that the specific rights explicitly mentioned in the Constitution and Bill of Rights are fundamental rights. Next, one reasons that, surely, they are not the only fundamental rights. Since it is not plausible to suppose that the founders thought otherwise, one continues by imagining that they wished—or supposing that they *should rationally have wished*—that these other rights would also be constitutionally protected while realizing that they themselves could not be expected to enumerate them all. Having gotten this far, one asks, How might a rational framer of the Constitution accomplish this?—to which one answers, By inserting a vague, catchall clause in the Bill of Rights to cover the multiplicity of fundamental rights that future interpreters may discover. This, the story goes, is the role played by the right to liberty—in the trio "life, liberty, and property" of the Due Process Clause.

Of course, it is understood—and this part of the reasoning is historically accurate—that in saying that rights may not be deprived *without due process of law*, the framers were saying *both* that to deprive persons of their liberty (or other rights), those persons must be afforded the protections of a judicial proceeding in which the deprivation is judged to be in accordance with positive law, and that the law itself is legitimate. The innovation, in this *Lochnerian* defense, is the claim it makes about what is required for a law to be legitimate; it is *not* sufficient that the law not infringe any of the rights explicitly guaranteed in the Constitution and Bill of Rights, as well as being general rather than specific, and prospective rather than retrospective, in application. In addition, the law must not infringe any unenumerated fundamental right that the justices "discover."

To turn this into a defense of *Lochner* one would, of course, have to claim that a virtually unfettered right of contract is a fundamental right, which few today are willing to do. But *Lochner* and the right of

---

[18] For an interesting and well-reasoned defense of the Court in *Lochner* against various nondeferentialist charges see David E. Bernstein, *Rehabilitating Lochner* (Chicago: University of Chicago Press, 2011).

contract aside, *this form of constitutional reasoning,* in which the Due Process Clause serves as an all-purpose catchall for unenumerated rights, is quite general—as I will illustrate by discussing a lengthening line of more recent cases that exemplify it. The point to be made here is that this form of reasoning is *not* deferentialist. To take it to be so, one would have to argue that the framers and ratifiers of the Fifth and Fourteenth Amendments *understood and announced* in the public rationale offered on behalf of the amendments that the Due Process Clause was an intentionally vague *tabula rasa* on which future interpreters could write what they wished. Obviously, the framers and ratifiers did no such thing.

Nor would it have made sense for them to do so. The key to the Due Process Clause is *not* the enumeration of rights the deprivation of which require *due process of law* but the specification of those processes of law that are sufficient to deprive persons of the rights in question. *Other provisions* of the Bill of Rights enumerate rights which are not to be deprived or diminished by any legislative or executive action. The function of the Due Process Clause is to provide judicial protection for deprivations of rights that *are* constitutionally proper subjects of legislative and executive action.

The modern cases to be examined for their departure from deferentialism are *Griswold v. Connecticut,*[19] *Roe v. Wade,*[20] *Planned Parenthood v. Casey,*[21] and *Lawrence v. Texas.*[22] These cases mark the return of unenumerated fundamental rights. This time the rights in question are not public economic rights, which have long been politically subordinated to the vastly expanded power of federal and state governments. Instead, they are private rights having to do with personal sexual morality, the traditional restrictions on which, though not without expression in law, had their sources in religious and other private cultural institutions, rather than in the economy or the state. This difference, which is by no means accidental, is interesting. Why should it matter in the search for unenumerated fundamental rights whether the rights concern public and economic behavior versus matters of private, personal morality? Since deferentialism recognizes no such significant difference, while the modern cases insist on one, it is clear that these cases are not guided by any version of deferentialism. It is, therefore, left to nondeferentialist defenders of these cases to explain why new, judicially "discovered," fundamental rights should occur in one narrow

[19] 381 U.S. 479 (1965).
[20] 410 U.S. 113 (1973).
[21] 505 U.S. 833 (1992).
[22] 539 U.S. 558 (2003)

range of human activity, but not in others. Here, I will concentrate less on which "rights" have found favor and more on the argumentative structure of the revival of *Lochner*-style constitutional reasoning.

Griswold was a vital precursor of the other cases both in opening up a trove of supposedly fundamental rights not explicitly mentioned in the Constitution and in taking economic rights off the table by declaring—with dubious relevance—that the Court would not "sit as a super-legislature to determine the wisdom, need, and propriety of laws *that touch economic problems, business affairs, or social conditions.*"[23] In this way, the Court endorsed the New Deal repudiation of *Lochner* while simultaneously reviving *Lochner*-style constitutional reasoning in a domain of human life in which it felt confident about the moral and political correctness of its superlegislative judgments.

The lynchpin of the case was the supposed discovery of a general right of privacy discernible from "penumbras, formed by emanations" of the First Amendment right of association, the Third Amendment right not to have soldiers quartered in one's home, the Fourth Amendment right against unreasonable searches and seizures, and the Fifth Amendment right against self-incrimination.[24] The problem, of course, is that although these rights are genuinely guaranteed, there is no epistemically legitimate inference by which a general right to privacy encompassing matters of sexual morality such as contraception (which was at issue in *Griswold*) can be derived from them. On the contrary, Justice Douglas's "penumbras" and "emanations" were simply camouflage for a nondeferentialist doctrine that, in 1965, dare not speak its name.[25]

Roe v Wade,[26] which followed *Griswold* in 1973, was braver than *Griswold*. As in the earlier case, the Court in *Roe* relied on a protected right of privacy. However, unlike in *Griswold*, it did not seek to derive the right of privacy from "penumbras formed from emanations," or in any other way including by any appeal to long-standing tradition, as attempted in the Harlan concurrence in *Griswold* (which couldn't possibly have worked in *Roe*). Rather, it simply invoked *stare decisis* on

---

[23] 381 U.S. 479 at 482 (my emphasis).

[24] *Id.* at 484.

[25] As Chapman and McConnell note (p. 1796), Justice Harlan's concurrence (381 U.S. at 499) offered a different rationale. Instead of attempting to derive a general right of privacy from Douglas's enumerated rights, he judged the then-moribund Connecticut statute prohibiting the sale of contraceptives to a married couple to violate a liberty (covered by the due process clause of the Fourteenth Amendment) *traditionally* afforded to married couples. Though this justification is certainly superior to Douglas's, it still fails to pass deferentialist muster, since traditional common-law liberty does not trump legislative enactments in a deferentialist understanding of due process.

[26] 410 U.S. 113 (1973).

the basis of the eight-year-old decision that had struck down a law in one state that wasn't then being enforced anyway.[27] This "settled law" was the ground for vastly extending the right of privacy invented in *Griswold* to a much more problematic domain, thereby striking down the laws—some quite recent and many allowing abortion in certain circumstances—of all fifty states. In sum, the decision was reached by *Lochner*-style reasoning from the premise of *Griswold* privacy.

This time the Court did not suggest, by irrelevant declaration, that it was not acting as a "super-legislature." This new reticence was a step forward, since the tautological claim that in ruling on a noneconomic case the Court was not acting (improperly) as a "super-legislature" on economic matters did nothing to show that it was not, in fact, acting (improperly) as a "super-legislature" on other matters. If the Court had essentially nothing new to say about why its Lochnerian reasoning was acceptable, but the reasoning in *Lochner* wasn't, silence—throughout a great many pages—may have been the best policy. The effect of *Roe* was to deliver the nakedly nondeferentialist punch thrown by the nakedly nondeferentialist *Griswold*.

The question in the next case, *Planned Parenthood of Southeastern Pennsylvania v. Casey*,[28] was whether the state can, without violating a woman's right to an abortion under *Roe*, require her (in nonemergency cases) to (among other things) give her informed consent to the procedure, to wait twenty-four hours, and, if a minor, to obtain the consent of a parent (with the possibility of a judicial bypass). The Court ruled 5-4 upholding *Roe*, but accepting those of the state's restrictions that, neither in their purpose nor in their effect, placed an "undue burden" on or a "substantial obstacle" to a woman seeking an abortion (which the Court ruled most, but not all, of the state's restrictions did not do). Having put itself at the center of what, prior to *Roe*, had always been a legislative matter in the several states, there was no way, short of repudiating *Roe*, of freeing the Court from having to make further legislative decisions about which details of new state legislation represented wise, or at least reasonable, trade-offs—here expressed in terms of the hopelessly vague distinction between burdens that are "undue" versus those that are not, and obstacles that are "substantial" versus those that are not. Despite this vagueness, the message both to voters and to the states was clear: *Nothing having to do with abortion is up to you anymore;*

---

[27] While *Roe* cites new cases as sources of particularized privacy rights, *Griswold* is the key to the Court's justification because it asserts a general right of privacy. The Court implicitly invokes *stare decisis* by accepting that this line of cases, with *Griswold* at its center, establishes a right a privacy before determining that "it is broad enough to encompass a woman's decision whether or not to terminate her pregnancy." *Roe*, 410 U.S. at 152–53.

[28] 505 U.S. 833 (1992).

you may do only what we in the future decide you may do. With messages like these to a population raised to revere self-government, it is not hard to understand why the politics of abortion in the United States became so poisonous.

Beyond reaffirming *Roe*, the notably new element was the way in which the Court attempted to justify the decisions in this line of cases as legitimate *substantive* interpretations of the Due Process Clause of the Fourteenth Amendment. Without repudiating the generalized right to privacy asserted in *Griswold* and *Roe*, the Court took "the controlling word in the cases before us" to be "liberty," thereby bringing the Due Process Clause directly into play.[29] Privacy was, in effect, subsumed under liberty as a special case, with the Court asserting that its "obligation is to define the liberty of all."[30] As for definition, the nearest we get is Justice Kennedy's astounding assertion that "the heart of liberty is the right to define one's own concept of existence, of meaning, of the universe, and of the mystery of human life."[31] This is classic *Lochner*-style reasoning dressed up in contemporary pseudophilosophical form—with an utterly vague, subjective, and general conception of liberty serving as a placeholder into which the justices may insert whatever new fundamental rights they take themselves to discern, whether or not the supposed rights are derivable from explicit constitutional texts, embedded in tradition, or even enjoy a current national consensus. In this way, the Due Process Clause is made into one of the Court's leading legislative enablers.

Anticipating objections to this judicial blank check, the Court in *Casey* concedes that "a literal reading" of the Due Process Clause might suggest that "it governs only the procedures by which a State may deprive persons of liberty."[32] But it quickly adds that this can't be so because "for at least 105 years . . . the Clause has been understood to contain a substantive component as well."[33] Really? What do we find 105 years prior to *Casey*? The case cited by the Court is *Mugler v. Kansas*[34] which initiated the economic-substantive–due process line leading to *Lochner*. So what begins with *Griswold's* enthusiastic endorsement of the long-standing *repudiation* of economic due process cases like *Lochner*— and the Court's pious, but unsupported, suggestion that *Griswold* is to be sharply distinguished from them—is first extended in *Roe*, and later ratified and cast in due process terms in *Casey*, where substantive due

---

[29] 505 U.S. at 846.
[30] *Id.* at 850.
[31] *Id.* at 851.
[32] *Id.* 846.
[33] *Id.*
[34] 123 U.S. 623 (1887).

process is articulated, given full expression, and *defended* by appealing to the supposedly *105-year-old validity* of the long-repudiated *Lochner* line. Whatever else this may be, it is not a coherent defense of the Court's nondeferentialist practice.

The final case in this line that I will mention is *Lawrence v Texas*,[35] in which the Court invalidated a Texas statute against consensual homosexual sex. The case is significant mainly as further entrenchment of the evolving substantive due process doctrine arising from *Griswold, Roe*, and *Casey*. As in *Roe* and *Casey*, the Court simply asserts its undefined and seemingly unlimited power to "define for all" the fundamental rights it wishes to put beyond the reach of democratic politics at any level of government. If one thinks that the Supreme Court is, or should be, a super-legislature with the power to invalidate legislation in any manner it wishes, then one may plausibly defend its application in *Lawrence* on the grounds that the result reached is not only good but would probably be supported by most citizens. However, if one thinks that the Court in our system of government is not, and should not be, a super-legislature, then one must judge its essentially legislative actions in *Griswold Roe, Casey*, and *Lawrence* to have exceeded its legal authority, even though the policy results achieved are sometimes good. My own conclusions are that (i) *Lochner, Griswold, Roe, Casey*, and *Lawrence* cannot be given deferentialist justifications and (ii) the Supreme Court has produced no other coherent justifications for them.

What kind of justification should we be looking for, not just for individual decisions, but for deferentialism itself? The justification I am most concerned with is *descriptive*. When legal interpretation is understood as the application of law to the facts of particular cases by authorized legal actors, one expects the task to be governed by legal rules that determine the responsibilities of those charged with it. Although legal rules are normative, the claim that a particular set of such norms is taken by citizens and holders of public offices to be legally authoritative is descriptive. It is just such deeply and commonly accepted norms that constitute the distinctive authority of any system of laws. The descriptive questions to which I seek answers are (i) *What are the legal obligations of judges, justices, and others charged with applying the law to particular cases in the United States?* (ii) *Does the deferentialist conception properly characterize them?* and (iii) *How do other conceptions of the legal obligations of those applying the law to particular cases compare with it?*

My schematic answer to the first question is that courts are not to legislate but are to apply laws adopted by the legislature to facts of particular cases. To do so they must determine what the lawmakers

---

[35] 539 U.S. 558 (2003).

stipulated in adopting the relevant texts and apply that content to the facts of the case. When this fails to determine a unique, acceptable legal outcome—either because the legal content leads to inconsistent outcomes, or because it fails to lead to any outcome, or because it leads to an unforeseen outcome that subverts the predominant legislative rationale of the lawmakers in adopting the relevant laws— the task of the judge is to fashion the minimal modification of existing legal content that removes the deficiency and allows a decision to be reached while maximizing the fulfillment of that rationale. If this is roughly correct, then so is deferentialist legal interpretation. Is it correct? Surely, something approximating it has been the dominant understanding of the educated portion of the populace throughout most of the history of the United States. Though that consensus has diminished among the political elites in the last half century, adherence to this conception is, I think, still widespread.

There is, to be sure, a decades-old strain of nondeferentialist interpretation in courts at all levels. This could not be so were there not substantial opposition to deferentialism among legal professionals, legal theorists, journalists, and politicians. But it isn't obvious to what extent support for these decisions is results oriented, and to what extent it reflects genuine opposition to a deferentialist conception of the proper role of the judiciary. Consider a common form of argument: It begins with the claim that it is vitally urgent that the country address some issue. It is then claimed that political institutions have proven unable to accomplish what needs to be done because they are deadlocked. So, it is argued, courts must do the job, by ruling *such-and-such*, even though there is no deferentialist justification for so ruling.

It is important to notice that, in itself, this is *not* an argument against the descriptive claim that the legal responsibilities of judges are as deferentialism defines them. They may be so defined, even if *sometimes* it is *morally better* for judges to do what they are not *legally* authorized to do. Although this may sound unfamiliar, it shouldn't be shocking. It's not shocking because virtually any position, short of that of absolute ruler, carries with it limitations on one's authority. As a result, circumstances can arise in which the morally best thing to do exceeds one's authority. This can happen with judges as much as with those in other positions. But if it does happen, a judge cannot very well admit it, since quite apart from the penalties the judge would face, a public admission of what amounts to illegally achieving a desired legal result would, in many cases, invalidate, or at least undermine, that very result. Consequently, one cannot expect judges inclined to violate their authority to achieve "a higher good," or commentators who wish to aid them, to speak forthrightly about what they are doing. This explains the unfamiliarity of what would otherwise be an obvious point. The mere fact that some morally or politically good results can't be, or couldn't have been, achieved by deferentialist justices doesn't demonstrate that deferentialism is an incorrect account of the legal responsibilities of those now, or in the past, charged with applying the law to the facts of particular cases.

The activist argument is not even a *normative* argument against deferentialism—unless one can show that a *better* workable system is possible in which no constraints on what judges are *legally authorized* to do could ever prevent them from reaching a morally optimal result in a particular case. Absent such an unlikely showing, the argument that *sometimes* judges *should* arrive at nondeferentialist results fails to demonstrate that the deferentialist conception of the role of the judiciary isn't *normatively* optimal, let alone that it isn't descriptively correct.

To argue against deferentialism, one needs to specify a competing conception of judicial responsibility. One such *antideferentialist* conception might naturally begin by admitting that lower courts—as well as the executive and the legislature—are legally required to follow higher court rulings in an essentially deferentialist manner. Of course, the Supreme Court would not be so restricted. Like the former British House of Lords, it might be granted the power to void any legislation bearing on cases brought before it.[36] Moreover, it might be maintained that when considering the law in a case, the Court is free to alter its content for whatever moral or political reasons it finds compelling, taking account of the need to maintain stability and consistency in the laws, and to render their application reasonably predictable.

The chief difference between this antideferentialist conception of the role of the judiciary and the deferentialist conception is that the former grants vast legislative authority to the Supreme Court, which the latter denies. Thus, I believe, the deferentialist conception more closely approximates descriptive adequacy concerning accepted legal norms in the United States than does the alternative. My reasons are as follows:

(i) Deferentialism better reflects the fundamental importance of the separation of powers in the history of the United States than antideferentialism does.

(ii) Although there have been many nondeferentialist decisions, they have not generally been accompanied by articulations of an antideferentialist conception of the role of the judiciary. Why, if the governing conception of that role is really antideferentialist, haven't courts been forthright in stating

---

[36] See G. Slapper and D. Kelly, *The English Legal System*, 9th ed. (2009), pp. 71–72.

their rationales? Judges and justices almost never say they are legislating their own political or moral views but, rather, claim to derive their antideferentialist results from old, accepted, and authoritative principles.[37] In so doing, they implicitly acknowledge that the deferentialist conception they seek to undermine is the governing conception from which their authority derives.

(iii) The very incoherence of the changing and conflicting justifications given by the Supreme Court in *Griswold, Roe,* and *Casey* is itself a reflection of justices who know their authority derives from a deferentialist ideal which they, as a body, do not share. That they don't share it *is* a blow to the authority of deferentialism. But they don't, as a body, share any articulated competing view either. The authority of deferentialism can't be replaced until a compelling alternative is articulated and embraced by the most widely known and respected legal and political figures. This hasn't happened.

(iv) The appointment of judges, their tenure, and their code of conduct reflect the nonpolitical nature of legal responsibilities of deferentialist judging rather than the political character of antideferentialist "interpretation." Federal judges are appointed, not elected; during their appointment hearings they are excused from answering questions on issues that might come before them in order to preserve their neutrality;[38] their code of conduct restricts political activities and requires recusal in various circumstances.[39] All this makes sense in a deferentialist conception of their judicial responsibilities; it does not make sense in an overtly political conception of them.

For these reasons, I take the deferentialist conception of the legal responsibilities governing judicial application of the law to particular cases to be more descriptively accurate than the antideferentialist conception. Given the problematic nakedness of the legislative authority granted to the Supreme Court by the antideferentialist view, I suspect a hybrid view that is partially deferentialist/ partially nondeferentialist would be a stronger competitor.

With the foregoing in mind, consider an alternative conception in which the Court can exercise its authority to alter the content of the

[37] See, e.g., *Griswold v. Connecticut,* 381 U.S. 479, 484 (1965).

[38] See, e.g., *The Nomination of Judge Sandra Day O'Connor of Arizona to serve as Associate Justice of the Supreme Court of the United States: Hearings before the Senate Committee on the Judiciary,* 97th Congress 57–58 (1981).

[39] *The Code of Conduct for United States Judges,* U.S. CT.

law *only* in cases in which deferentialism allows it to do so—when (i) the antecedent legal content is vague concerning aspects of the case needed to reach a result, or (ii) that content plus the facts of the case inconsistently leads to contradictory results, or (iii) the literal application of that content would produce a result that subverts the original rationale for its adoption. However, when one of these conditions is met the Court is *not*, according to the hybrid conception, restricted to making the minimum change to existing law that reaches a result that maximizes the fulfillment of the original rationale for the law in question. Rather, it can substitute its own moral and political judgment for those of the original lawmakers to produce a change in the law, provided it articulates a reasoned argument that the change is an improvement that preserves aspects of the previous legal content not directly relevant to the case.

The deferentialist aspects of the view are its conception of legal content and its restrictions on when the Court is justified in rectifying that content (by modifying or replacing it). The nondeferentialist aspect of the view lies in the expanded legislative authority granted the Court to change the law in the rectification process, with less respect paid to the content being replaced and minimal concern for the original legislative rationale for that content. As before, one can judge this conception of judicial responsibility either normatively or descriptively. The most obvious normative worry about the hybrid conception is that it gives unelected political actors with unlimited tenure too much authority to place matters beyond the reach of democratically elected representatives. In so doing, it also puts the genuinely judicial function of the Court at risk. By investing so much authority to *change the law* in the group that also decides *what the content of existing law is*, the hybrid risks losing the integrity needed to perform the latter, indispensible task. The knowledge, abilities, and motivating interests needed to correctly discern existing legal content in difficult cases are very different from those needed to promulgate wise and politically effective new laws. To authorize justices to perform both tasks is to risk having them performed by individuals who are not good at either and who are perhaps not much interested in the genuinely judicial task.

Since, I suspect, these normative worries would be widely shared, I believe that the hybrid conception of judicial responsibility is *not* an accurate *description* of what the educated populace plus the army of legal actors and public officials in the United States now take to be the authorized powers and responsibilities of the judiciary. Nor would those who like the results of *Griswold*, *Roe*, *Casey*, and *Lawrence* find the hybrid position normatively acceptable, *since it, too, would prevent those results from being reached by any of the means the Court actually employed.* The problem for nondeferentialists of this stripe is that further departures from deferentialism needed to vindicate those results would likely invite further defections from any suitably articulated principle of interpretation designed to reach them. So, although deferentialism is threatened and the legal norms governing the judicial application of the law to particular cases in the United States are in flux, the challenge of replacing deferentialism remains unmet.

That said, deferentialism faces a challenge of its own. Because of the many anti- or nondeferentialist decisions in past decades, any effective renewal of deferentialism must include a strategy for dealing with the body of existing law created by those decisions. Since neither wholesale revocation nor wholesale preservation of previous nondeferentialist decisions in their current form is compatible with a lasting deferentialist judiciary, finding a workable middle way is the most daunting task of rectification that confronts deferentialism. The way to think of this task is, I suggest, to treat it as a subcase of *harmonization of conflicts in law,* where (at least) one of the laws in conflict is judgemade. When the Supreme Court finds that the facts of a new case create a conflict between some valid legal provision and the law produced by a previous decision that the Court now finds unjustified, the task of the Court is to remove the conflict by making the minimal changes needed to the conflicting laws while furthering, to the extent possible, the rationales for both. How this would, or should, work in particular cases is, of course, a large, open-ended question. But the principle of respecting both laws, despite their provenance, and aiming for limited adjustments—which may, over time, become cumulative—is, I think, the best general procedure.[40]

---

[40] Thanks to Andrei Marmor and David Manley for their helpful comments.

Index